BRIGHT BOULEVARDS, BOLD DREAMS

"*Bright Boulevards, Bold Dreams* brims with . . . personal accounts of black Hollywood in the making, from its beginnings in the early 1900s to the civil rights era of the 1960s. . . . [It] is a valuable historical document, entertaining and educational, uplifting and sad."

—*Los Angeles Times Book Review*

"Nobody tells the story of Black Tinseltown like Donald Bogle."

—*Essence*

"It's the story behind the camera, the tales of nightclubs, agents, and the social scene, that makes [*Bright Boulevards, Bold Dreams*] stand out. . . . Highly recommended."

—*Library Journal*

"Shameful, funny, enlightening, and sobering, this tale of movieland's dark side is a must-read for any student of film history."

—*Entertainment Weekly* (Editor's Choice)

"Bogle's book soars. . . . His tales . . . are captivating."

—*Contra Costa Times*

"*Bright Boulevards, Bold Dreams* is a fascinating, anecdote-filled history of black Hollywood in the segregation era . . . and a delicious compendium of tasty tidbits regarding interracial affairs, mixed-race social events, extravagant lifestyles and careers gone awry."

—*The Philadelphia Inquirer*

BRIGHT BOULEVARDS, BOLD DREAMS

BRIGHT BOULEVARDS, BOLD DREAMS

The Story of Black Hollywood

DONALD BOGLE

ONE WORLD
BALLANTINE BOOKS · NEW YORK

2006 One World Books Trade Paperback Edition

Published in the United States by One World Books, an imprint of The Random
House Publishing Group, a division of Random House, Inc., New York.

ONE WORLD is a registered trademark and the One World colophon is
a trademark of Random House, Inc.

Originally published in hardcover in the United States by One World Books,
an imprint of The Random House Publishing Group,
a division of Random House, Inc., in 2005.

Library of Congress Cataloging-in-Publication Data

Bogle, Donald.
Bright boulevards, bold dreams : the story of Black Hollywood / Donald Bogle
p. cm.
Includes bibliographical references.
ISBN 0-345-45419-7
1. African American motion picture actors and actresses—Biography.
2. African Americans in motion pictures.   I. Title.

PN1995.9.N4B59 2005
791.4302′8′092396073—dc22
[B]   2004054781

Printed in the United States of America

www.oneworldbooks.net

2 4 6 8 9 7 5 3

Text design by Deborah Kerner/Dancing Bears Design

CONTENTS

INTRODUCTION

ong ago—when I was just beginning to research the work of African American performers in Hollywood—I made a trip to Stamford, Connecticut, to interview actress Fredi Washington. She had been retired from show business for decades. But in 1934, Fredi Washington had gone to Hollywood to appear in *Imitation of Life* and afterward became one of the most talked about black actresses working in the movies. For black America, she was the "black girl who looked white" or "the girl with the boy's name." Her movie career, however, had been something of a dead end because Hollywood didn't have a place for her. By this time in her life, Washington wasn't exactly a recluse. But she didn't see many people, other than old friends, and she clearly didn't need any kind of spotlight to go about the business of her life. Nor was she an actress consumed with the past. Yet, through Bobby Short, she had said she was interested in meeting me. I wasn't sure what to expect. Would she be bitter about Hollywood? Would she be unwilling to delve deeply into that period of her life?

That afternoon, I found Fredi Washington living simply and *very* comfortably in a well-furnished apartment with a bit of show business memorabilia around but not much. Slender and casually dressed—with piercing blue-green eyes that could look right through you—she still possessed the elegant good looks and stylish sophistication that had made her so distinct in the past, and her mind was as sharp and quick as ever. By then, I had already interviewed a number of entertainers, but I don't think I had ever met any as intelligent as Washington. Or as fascinating.

As she talked about her career, an array of images floated by: the days of the Harlem Renaissance and New York theater from the 1920s into the 1950s. She had rich, evocative memories of a gallery of African American stars of an earlier time: Paul Robeson, Ethel Waters, Duke Ellington, Josephine Baker, Alberta Hunter, and her own sister, actress Isabel Washington Powell. The New York entertainment scene on which she commented was not unfamiliar to me. But when she discussed her time in

Hollywood, something else came to light that I had not really expected. Like everyone else, I had always thought of classic Hollywood in terms of those golden age icons: stars such as Garbo, Gable, Harlow, Tracy, and later Monroe, Taylor, Brando, and Dean. There had been restaurants such as The Brown Derby and Romanoff's, nightclubs such as the Mocambo and Ciro's, hotels such as The Ambassador and The Beverly Hills, a famous street, Sunset Boulevard, and an even more famous intersection, Hollywood and Vine.

But Washington spoke of another Hollywood, which most people probably didn't even know existed: of a part of Los Angeles where many African Americans had once resided, first the Eastside, later the Westside. Her eyes lit up when she mentioned the grand thoroughfare Central Avenue, where black nightclubs flourished and where the Dunbar Hotel, home to the black elite, stood like a mighty fortress. There had been glittering and unpredictable personalities, such as Bill "Bojangles" Robinson, Hattie McDaniel, Louise Beavers, Stepin Fetchit, and Nina Mae McKinney. Slowly coming into view was a vision of the old Black Hollywood, which was both a distant place and a distant frame of mind. During the several hours I spent with her, Washington transported me to another age.

She brought into sharper focus a world of which I had caught a glimpse earlier when I had interviewed Vivian Dandridge, the older sister of Dorothy, who then lived on Manhattan's Upper West Side. Having spent most of her childhood and her young adulthood in the movie capital, Vivian had experienced the giddy heights of success and the devastating, heartbreaking effects of failure. She spoke as if she had left Los Angeles on the run—for her sanity and her life. Yet, oddly, she had vivid, sweet memories of Black Hollywood. Both Dandridge and Washington offered me a bird's-eye view of the black movie colony's way of life during the first half of the twentieth century—and the glamour ideal that the town and much of the entertainment industry in general valued. Each understood the relentless drive and energy it took to work and ultimately survive in the town. Each was shrewdly aware of movieland culture: the unwritten values and rules that governed the lives of so many. And though each had left, both understood the strangely magical magnetic force that drew so many entertainers to Hollywood.

During the years that followed, I grew even more curious about how African Americans worked, played, and socialized in Hollywood. Everyone to whom I talked—from Mantan Moreland, Clarence Muse, and director King Vidor to Herb Jeffries, Bobby Short, Phil Moore, Olga James, and Ivan Dixon—had something surprising to say. Yet Black Hollywood didn't fully take shape for me until I met Geri Branton. Branton had been the first wife of Fayard Nicholas, of the great Nicholas Brothers, and the closest friend of Dorothy Dandridge. Highly intelligent and knowledgeable without a shred of pretense or any fears of being *too* honest, she had known the major stars of the 1940s and 1950s, and she had been a part of the social and political shifts in the community. Talking to her, I realized that the old Black Hollywood had died in the post–World War II era as America saw the rise of the civil rights movement and as Hollywood became more integrated.

Finally, I decided the time had come to write about Hollywood's black film community in the first half of the twentieth century. In my earlier books, I had sometimes written about the private lives and personal tensions of black film stars, but I had concentrated primarily on screen images: what the camera had recorded, what encoded messages the performers were sometimes able to communicate even while playing the most stereotyped roles.

But now I wanted to look at what happened just before the cameras rolled—or once the performers left the studio to go home. I wanted to examine the beginnings of Black Hollywood, the lives and careers of early performers in town at a time when the movies themselves were new to America. I wanted to trace how such performers were able to find movie work. And I wanted to explore the way in which others found positions in the industry, sometimes as servants or assistants to the powerful, and later as composers, choreographers, agents, and even spouses, all of which really helped to open the movie industry up and make the presence of African Americans a fact of being. I also wanted to show the way in which movie mania affected the black community in Los Angeles as much as it did the white population.

But mainly, I wanted to see how people lived and socialized. Some, such as Stepin Fetchit, had an offscreen life that appeared to be all show, all ostentatious high style. Others, such as the actresses Hattie McDaniel and Louise Beavers, had a surprisingly grand black bourgeois matronly sophistication, the very antithesis of their screen personas as jolly, overweight, desexualized mammies. Still others, such as Lena Horne and Dorothy Dandridge, in part because of their looks, had a glamour that was very close to that of mainstream Hollywood. Yet it was also an internal glamour that came from the way the women expressed themselves, regardless of makeup, hairstyles, or fashion.

Of course, *Glamour* is one of the two big-G words in Hollywood. The other is *Gossip*. In Hollywood, what people were said to be doing could be far more telling than what had actually transpired. Some personalities, especially the early African American servants to the powerful, knew how to use gossip. Others—such as Dandridge, Horne, Sammy Davis Jr., and James Edwards—realized how detrimental gossip could be when talk spread about their interracial affairs. And so it would be important to record the stories and tales of the day.

All African Americans in Hollywood in the first half of the twentieth century also lived with an acute awareness of the racial lines within the movie industry and throughout Los Angeles. Not a single performer was blind to the town's racism. Yet with the odds stacked so heavily against them, African Americans kept coming west to pound the bright boulevards in pursuit of their bold movie dreams. What did they believe Hollywood could offer them? Ultimately, their very presence in the studios was sometimes a challenge to the system. And as in other parts of America, out of their separate existence—their separate parts of town, their separate ways of entertaining themselves, their camaraderie—there grew a cohesive community with a common sense of purpose and drive as well as a distinct cultural identity. No matter what happened at the studios, most African American performers became respected, integral parts of the larger black community in Los Angeles.

In writing this book, I often thought of a comment Geri Branton had made about the old Black Hollywood: "In those days, we only had each other." She remembered a communal cohesiveness that she felt had died. That became a goal: to celebrate that cohesiveness and to show the various social shifts in American culture that led to the collapse of the old Black Hollywood and the birth of the new.

BRIGHT BOULEVARDS, BOLD DREAMS

The Teens

IN THE BEGINNING

Among the old-timers, the story went like this: *A woman known to everyone as Madame came to California from Kentucky with her children and her husband. But once they were in the Gold Rush State, her husband left her. Desperate to find work, she introduced herself to a movie director named D. W. Griffith. He not only cast her in his movie, but the two became friends for life. And with this woman, called Madame Sul-Te-Wan, Black Hollywood began.*

Of course, there was more to it than that, but Hollywood always liked a good story, and the tale of Madame Sul-Te-Wan was a good enough place to start. So, too, was the early romance of Los Angeles for all those who journeyed westward.

Even before the movies, Los Angeles held the promise of a world of endless sunshine and unlimited possibilities. Here was a city with warm days and cool nights, with winding canyons, steep hills, and stately mountains looming large and mysterious on the horizon—and not far from a breathtaking view of an ocean that was clear and blue, cool and inviting. Those early pioneers of color who ventured west were as entranced as everyone else. When Los Angeles was founded in 1781—as a city of angels—by a group of eleven families, it seemed to throw out a welcome mat to people of color. After all, of that founding group—forty-four men, women, and children—twenty-six were of African descent, black or "black Spaniards," as they were sometimes called. In those very early years—before California joined the Union in 1850—Los Angeles must have seemed like a dazzling confluence of races and cultures, religions and creeds, a heady brew of ambitions and aspirations, of unexpected energies and colorful personalities, a city cut off from the rest of the country and its rules. Here in the wild and woolly West, no one appeared to think much about the races mixing. Interracial marriage was sanctified by the church and the authorities—and was commonly practiced.

Race did not seem to hinder prosperity either. Black Americans were long a part of city legend and lore. That was certainly true of the early landowner and "black Spaniard" Francisco Reyes, who owned all of the vast San Fernando Valley and in 1793 became the *alcalde* or mayor of Los Angeles. And of Maria Rita Valdez de Villa, the adventurous granddaughter of two of the black founders of the city, who married a Spanish colonial soldier, Vicente Fernando Villa. After her husband's death in 1841, Maria received the title to his lush, green 4,449-acre ranch known as Rancho Rodeo de las Aguas. In 1854, in the midst of mounting financial pressures, Maria was forced to sell her land—and to part with her adobe situated near what later became Alpine Drive and Sunset Boulevard. In time, the stunning Rancho Rodeo de las Aguas that she had loved so intensely became a prime piece of Los Angeles real estate known today as Beverly Hills.

But of those early pre–movie era pioneers, none was better known than a tough-minded former slave girl named Bridget "Biddy" Mason. Born in 1818, Biddy had been the "property" of a Mississippi plantation owner—and a Mormon convert—named Robert Marion Smith, who migrated with his family first to the Utah Territory in 1847 and later to San Bernardino, California. During the two thousand–mile trek across country, Biddy's job was to keep the cattle herded together behind the long line of wagon trains, some three hundred by one account. By then, Biddy was married with three daughters, who were said to have been fathered by the noble Mormon Robert Marion Smith.

In California, Biddy quickly adjusted to her new life *and* a new sense of identity. Then, one day, Smith informed Biddy and his other slaves that he had decided to return to Mississippi and that they should all prepare for the journey back. Smith may not have realized that California had been admitted to the Union as a free state. But Biddy knew. She went to the local sheriff, made her plea, and petitioned the court to let her remain in California. In 1856, Biddy Mason won freedom not only for herself and her children but also for another slave family. Afterward, she moved to Los Angeles, and the city had its first great black heroine.

Biddy shrewdly understood that her day-to-day work as a nurse and midwife would not guarantee a secure future for her family and herself. In the West, nothing was more important than land. And in Los Angeles, there was still much of it—acres upon acres—to be had. Saving her money, she slowly purchased property—the first on Spring Street for $250. Before anyone realized it, Biddy Mason had become a woman of means and one of L.A.'s first black female landowners. In 1872, she joined twelve other charter members in establishing a place of worship for colored Angelenos, the First African Methodist Episcopal Church of Los Angeles. She donated money to schools and nursing homes, provided aid for flood victims, and carried food to local jails. By the time of her death in 1891, Biddy Mason had a personal fortune of almost $300,000, and her vast real estate holdings constituted what later became downtown Los Angeles.

In a town where larger-than-life personalities and drive and discipline would be treasured, those early black pioneers, like great movieland production designers, dressed the set for those who followed. Most others would not have such huge holdings. But they'd come with vast dreams and visions and a view of themselves just as grand and as audacious. They'd also believe that in Los Angeles, any minute you could turn a corner, and something extraordinary might happen. And that always this sunlit city with swaying palm trees and fragrant eucalyptus offered a chance not just for self-advancement but for self-reinvention. What fueled that kind of dream in the early years of the twentieth century was the new medium that startled and delighted almost everyone in the nation: the movies.

THE MOVING PICTURES ARRIVE

The movies, of course, transformed Los Angeles from a sleepy western kind of country town into a sprawling metropolis. Eventually enveloped by Hollywood, Los Angeles became a company town that exuded glamour—along with extravagance and excess—and in time represented the *ultimate* kind of American success: a place where everybody, in some way or another, felt connected to those magical moving pictures that gleamed and glittered on screens in darkened theaters. And the concept of

Hollywood would encompass other areas where movie people lived and worked: Beverly Hills, Bel Air, Burbank, Culver City, Universal City, Westwood, Santa Monica, the San Fernando Valley—and for black Angelenos, parts of the city's Eastside and later Westside, in and around a bustling thoroughfare named Central Avenue.

Originally, movie production had been in the East, with New York at the center. That changed, however, when the Motion Picture Patents Company—the huge trust in the East that controlled the patent claims of major companies like Edison, Biograph, Lubin, Pathé Exchange, and Vitagraph—insisted that no company be permitted to produce, distribute, or exhibit films without its licensing. Huge fees for the use of cameras and other motion-picture equipment covered by their patents forced many independent producers out of the movie business. Other filmmakers moved West, as far away as possible from the reach of the Patents Company. With its citrus groves and its avocados and especially its acres of unspoiled land and its perpetual sunshine, California proved appealing. Here, production could continue outside year-round.

Among the early filmmakers from the East were Cecil B. DeMille, who arrived in 1913 to shoot *The Squaw Man,* and director David Wark Griffith, who brought his stock company of New York actors to California—during the winter months—to shoot scenes for his films as early as 1910. When he began production on his ambitious Civil War epic, originally called *The Clansman* and later retitled *The Birth of a Nation,* Griffith knew that California was where his mighty battle scenes had to be filmed and where he could re-create the city of Piedmont, South Carolina, the central setting of his epic.

By then, Griffith had already established himself as an important director. Born in 1875 in La Grange, Kentucky, and reared in Louisville, David (Lewelyn) Wark grew up hearing stories of the Old South's power and grandeur. From 1908 to 1913, Griffith made 450 films at the Biograph Studios on East Fourteenth Street in New York City. Many had been short one-reelers. But with the four-reel *Judith of Bethulia,* he began making longer, more ambitious films. Developing an arsenal of techniques that included crosscutting, intercutting, expressive lighting, camera movement, and the close-up, Griffith helped create a syntax for the language of motion pictures. In the fall of 1913, Griffith left Biograph to join Reliance-Majestic. A year later, working on what would be his mighty, racist masterpiece *The Birth of a Nation,* D. W. Griffith arrived on the West Coast.

CALL HER MADAME

So did an ambitious young African American woman, who had been born Nellie Wan in Louisville, Kentucky, in 1873. Her mother, Cleo de Londa, had been a singer; her father, a traveling preacher named Silas Crawford Wan, whom she once said was Hindu. Whether that was true or not was anybody's guess. Later, the story went over well in Hollywood, which loved those people who created their own colorful biographies. "My father didn't mount to nothing," she once said. "He had the Bible in one hand and all the women he could get in the other." When Silas deserted the family, Nellie's mother was left to fend for herself, working as a laundress for actresses in Louisville. Young Nellie often delivered the laundry. Silently, she studied the entertainers: their dance steps, vocal mannerisms, and routines. Infatuated with the world of make-believe, little Nellie—at age eight—tried to run away to join a circus. Seeing that she was a born cutup, the white actresses Mary Anderson and Fanny Davenport both urged the mayor of Louisville, James Whaler, to let young Nellie audition for a special event: a contest among twenty-five buck-and-wing dancers at the city's Buckingham Theater. Nellie won first place.

At the time, colored entertainers were just starting to come into their own. Only after the Civil War did they have real opportunities to work professionally, usually in traveling minstrel or medicine shows, sometimes in circuses and carnivals, and eventually in black vaudeville. But always, it was a rough, demanding life, a mad scramble to find jobs and to stretch earnings.

Taking the dare, Nellie moved to Cincinnati, joined a company called Three Black Cloaks, and billed herself as Creole Nell. She also formed her own theatrical companies and toured the East Coast. She was developing into a striking-looking young woman, not pretty by the standards of her time but charismatic and assured: she knew that she was *somebody*. Perhaps she had also mastered by then what was to be one of her trademarks in films: that steely eyed, tough, *evil* stare that let people know that she was sizing them up—and that they couldn't trifle with her.

Her life changed when she married Robert Reed Conley. Around 1910, with her husband and her two young sons, she moved to Arcadia, California, near Pasadena. Certainly, Nellie, like other colored Americans of the time, envisioned Southern California as a land of opportunities. Property was cheap, which meant that in time, homes could be bought. Work was plentiful, too, especially on the railroads. Around the country, the Negro press and Negro organizations soon encouraged black Americans to go west. During the first decade of this new twentieth century, the city's population grew to some 320,000 citizens, of which some 7,600 were African Americans.

For Nellie Conley, a new life meant a new identity. She henceforth called herself Madame Sul-Te-Wan—and insisted that everyone else do the same. "We never did discover the origin of her name," actress Lillian Gish once said. No one was bold enough to ask. Madame may have had any number of reasons for her new name. In the South, many colored citizens were addressed by their first names by whites. Or as Aunt or Uncle. Rarely were they referred to as Miss or Mr. or Mrs. But now if anyone called her by her first name, then they would be addressing her as Madame. If anyone wanted to say Aunt Madame, then that was his or her business. Either way, she would never be spoken to in familiar terms by anyone. And her very name evoked the budding grandeur and glamour for which the movie colony would be known.

But the new life that looked so promising for Madame Sul-Te-Wan quickly turned sour. Her husband walked out on her and their three sons. Her youngest was only three weeks old. She was also ten months behind on her rent. Hers became a hand-to-mouth existence, day by day worrying where her next meal was coming from. When she learned of a colored group called the Forum that put on shows with black entertainers to help them earn money for food and lodging, she went to the organization with her children by her side. As she explained her plight, she broke into tears. Her oldest son, not yet seven, looked up at her and said, "Mother, you are not begging. We are going to sing and earn what they give you." The children then performed. Later, she enlisted the help of a group called the Associated Charities of Los Angeles to move her children and herself into a place in the city. But a long dry period followed. To make matters worse, the local booking companies refused to handle colored performers. Madame Sul-Te-Wan knew she might end up working as a maid.

Then she heard talk of a film being shot by a director from her hometown in Kentucky. She had heard of the director D. W. Griffith from a man named Dad Ready, whom she met while working in a circus. Ready had told her of Griffith's plans to film *The Clansman* and wrote her a letter of introduction. "Madame, if you ever go to California and hear anything at all about D. W. Griffith," Ready told her, "get in touch with him because if D. W. Griffith ever sees you, you're made." She still had Ready's letter, and she decided to see if it could get her some work.

MEETING GRIFFITH

Moviemaking was still rather casual, and for most newcomers, living in Los Angeles demanded a period of adjustment. "California left much to be desired—the land where the flowers had no perfume and the women no virtue," recalled D. W. Griffith's master cinematographer Billy Bitzer. "The Los Angeles River was a thin trickle of water, reminding us all that this had once been desert. The sewage was bad and when it rained the whole area of Los Angeles would be flooded. The tap water was full of alkali, and you drank only the water sold in large tanks and delivered to your door." Then, too, the weather was always the same, "except after sundown, when the cold winds came from the mountains and a sweater or a coat was needed."

In this atmosphere, everything was a little makeshift. Studio life itself was not yet highly structured. "*The Birth of a Nation* was made practically in the back yard of the Reliance-Majestic studio," which, Bitzer recalled, "consisted of a few bungalows amid a tract of fig trees at Sunset Boulevard and Gower. One bungalow for the office, another for my cameras, and one in which the Thorn family, who owned the property, lived. A large barn sufficed for dressing rooms and indoor stage. A platform was being set up in the yard for an outdoor stage."

In these days when there were no studio gates and no security guards to check passes and identification, Madame thought she might have a chance. "So one day I came out to see Mr. Griffith and a bunch of colored people had come over. At that time you could see pictures made, but you couldn't go under the rope. They had the great big rope around them in the street and you just stood around and saw moving pictures being taken." Sul-Te-Wan caught sight of actor Henry B. Walthall. Cast as the Southerner Ben Cameron, Walthall was seated in a carriage, dressed in his costume. "I looked bad that day," Madame said. "I had a little ole' funny black dress on." She reluctantly approached him.

"Pardon me, gentleman, but can you tell me who D. W. Griffith is?" she asked. "I'd like to see him." Walthall simply stared at her "because I looked so funny I guess to be asking for a man like Mr. Griffith. He kind of had a little twist of the mouth like he wanted to laugh."

"Well," he said, "I don't know whether you can see him or not, but that's him way up on the hill there with a megaphone in his hand."

The tall, lanky Griffith was dressed in a short gray suit, "and his coat was hitting him way up his back," said Sul-Te-Wan. He also wore a straw hat with holes in it. "I was very ignorant in them days," she later recalled, "and I don't know if I got so much sense now, but I was looking for this great man to be dressed beautifully, I guess he was up there in his old work clothes and I didn't believe Henry Walthall and I thought he was just telling me that because I'm a colored woman.

"I moved on up a little further and the place was packed with people up against the rope," she recalled. "I kept watching and looking back and inching up the side of the rope and finally I noticed nobody wasn't looking at me and I started to run and they hollered at me and up that hill I flew."

She made her way to the man in the straw hat, who was standing with the white actor George Siegmann, cast in the film as the mulatto Silas Lynch. Startled and annoyed to see her, the man in the straw hat told her she had no business there, then started to walk away. "Pardon me, gentlemen," Madame said politely, "but have I the honor of meeting D. W. Griffith?" Only then did the man pause and smile, apparently charmed. "I don't know about the honor," he told her, "but this is Griffith."

She quickly made her case. "I'm out here on the West Coast with three little children and I'm a victim of circumstance," she said. "Unfortunately, I'm an actress." She then pulled out Dad Ready's letter and handed it to Griffith. He "commenced to reading and everybody has said from that time there never was a scene like that on that hill with D. W. Griffith, myself, and George Siegmann." Griffith realized she was desperate. "He held my hands and shook with emotion," Madame recalled, "and tears come to Griffith's eyes and I cried." Telling her not to cry, he said, "You'll be all right." Then he told her, "I'm going to let you do all the dirty work on *The Clansman* for me."

"I don't care how much dirty work it is," Sul-Te-Wan said. "I have three little children and unfortunately I can't do nothing but act."

Madame was put on the payroll. Tough and shrewd—keys to her survival in the industry and the town—she knew when to flatter, when to charm, when to make fun of herself, when to play up to someone, when to act dumb, when to get *attitude*. Madame Sul-Te-Wan rarely seems to have been relaxed. She never let herself be caught off guard. Like many who would follow her to the movie capital, she was able to enter a room, survey it, and quickly *read* everyone there, to determine immediately who had influence and who had power. Yet there was also a streak of sentiment that ran deep and hard. She never forgot those who had helped her along the way—nor those who had hindered her. Always, though, Madame Sul-Te-

Wan was on the lookout for an opportunity that might land her in front of the camera.

"There were practically no Negro actors in California then and, as far as we knew, only a few in the East," recalled Griffith's leading lady Lillian Gish. "Even in minstrel shows, the parts were usually played by whites in blackface." Gish remembered that a big scene "in which actual Negroes appear in *The Birth* is the one in which the Stoneman boys, visiting the southern Camerons, are taken out to the plantation to see Negroes working in the cotton fields. When the scene was filmed in Death Valley, where the Negroes worked, they danced and played their banjos for the visiting actors."

"To economize, Mr. Griffith used many of the actors in more than one role," said Gish. "Bobby Harron, for instance, might play my brother in the morning, and in the afternoon put on blackface and play a Negro." All the major black characters were played by white performers. "But one young Negro woman did play in the film—Madame Sul-Te-Wan," recalled Gish. "She was first employed to help us keep our dressing rooms clean at the studio." Then Griffith—in need of actors for his minor black characters—decided to put Madame on-screen. "Madame Sul-Te-Wan played many small parts," said Gish, "with the help of various costumes."

Sometimes, Madame's inexperience showed. During one mob sequence, she carried a fan given to her as a girl by the actress Mary Anderson. As the camera rolled, she suddenly realized she had lost the fan, and in a panic, she started to look for it. Filming immediately stopped. In the distance—through his megaphone—Griffith asked what was wrong. When she mentioned the fan, Griffith shouted, "Go on. I will buy you another fan. Your acting is good. Go on."

Always, though, she was determined to make an impression on-screen. One small role had some bite, that of "the first colored woman that ever come into riches and had property, jewelry and clothes and things like that," Sul-Te-Wan said. Griffith took her aside and coached her.

For her role as a rich colored woman, he explained, "You have to be dressed gorgeous and you're going to walk down the street and they're going to call you a nigger and you'll resent that and then you go to the fence and spit on them and that's your part." But Sul-Te-Wan was concerned about her costume. During these years when there were no studio wardrobe departments, performers were sometimes expected to furnish their own clothes. "I didn't have the fine clothes," she said. "I only had one dress that I used to do the cakewalk in way back in my young days when I used to cakewalk on the boats from Cincinnati, Ohio to Louisville, Kentucky."

Madame's big moment occurred in a scene on the street when, dressed in her best, she was to greet the white Southern matriarch Mrs. Cameron, played by white actress Josephine Crowell. When Crowell's Cameron snubbed this nouveau riche colored woman, Madame's character spat in her face. "After the picture was made," reported Delilah Beasley, the historian who documented black life in early California, "the censors cut the part."

Once *The Clansman* was completed, Sul-Te-Wan went to see Griffith in hopes of getting the money that he had promised to pay for her fan. Said Beasley, "Mr. Griffith gave her a check for twenty-five dollars and placed her on the pay-roll at five dollars per day, work or play." "Later, when Madame was having financial difficulties," Lillian Gish recalled, "he sent her money to help herself and her small sons."

D.W. AND MADAME

Sul-Te-Wan's relationship with Griffith endured during the heated controversy that followed *The Birth of a Nation*'s premiere at Los Angeles's Clune Auditorium on February 8, 1915. Praised for its technical innovations, its epic sweep, and imagination, the film drew huge crowds around the country, becoming Hollywood's first true blockbuster, leading to the further rise of Hollywood itself. *The Birth of a Nation* even drew a presidential endorsement when at a special White House screening, President Woodrow Wilson proclaimed, "It is like writing history in Lightning. And my only regret is that it is all so terribly true."

But *The Birth of a Nation* was also denounced as racist by leaders in the African American community as well as by white liberals, who were outraged by its idyllic portraits of the Old South where masters were kind and the darkies were content and were shocked by its images of the Reconstruction in which oversexed black renegades were depicted as lusting after power and worse, white women. The film climaxed with a restoration of order in the South, thanks to a cadre of stalwart white men dressed in sheets and hoods, thus celebrating the birth of the Ku Klux Klan.

Throughout the nation, protests against the film flared up. In Los Angeles, before the film's official opening, the local NAACP charged in court that *The Birth of a Nation* was a threat to public safety. Other branches of the civil rights organization followed suit as the film opened in other major cities. In Los Angeles, the Negro newspaper *The California Eagle* chronicled the protests of "our civic organizations and others who stand for common decency." "They first protested to the board of censors but the protest fell on deaf ears." Ultimately, the paper denounced the city's mayor Henry Rose for taking no action against the film. "Our people have had such little comfort from his administration that they have long since passed up the mayor as an arch enemy," wrote *The California Eagle*. "Colored voters lined up for him to a man, because it was thought he stood for a square deal for all; they found out their mistake, but, alas! too late."

The film "misquotes the history of those periods, and belittles the morals of Afro-Americans," *The Eagle* later commented, adding "that as long as the Afro-Americans of this country sit supinely by and raise no voice against the injustice heaped upon them, conditions for them in this country will gradually grow worse."

Even at this early time in motion-picture history, African Americans saw the power of film as propaganda and also the frightening way in which African American experiences could be distorted and caricatured in a piece of work considered both great entertainment and an artistic triumph. More than any other early film, *The Birth of a Nation* gave birth to the shocking and degrading stereotypes that were to plague African American movie images throughout the twentieth century. The outcries against the film helped galvanize the political forces within Los Angeles's black community as well as in the rest of the nation.

Sul-Te-Wan was stunned by the protests. She was also out of work. When she picked up her envelope with her week's pay at Reliance-Majestic, she received a notice informing her, "You are no longer needed." Because Griffith was then in New York, she couldn't appeal to him. A production manager at the studio explained that a white actress had accused Madame of stealing a book. Finally, he told her—or so Madame was to say—that she was considered responsible for all the criticism within the colored community against *The Birth of a Nation*.

"Madame Sul-Te-Wan was very angry," said Beasley, "and replied that her struggle for bread for her three children had prevented her from coming in contact with the educated members of the race who had time to read and study as to whether the film was detrimental to the race." Madame contacted the prominent attorney Edward Burton Ceruti, who sent letters on her behalf to both the production manager in Hollywood and Griffith in New York. She was put back on the payroll, and Griffith cast her in his next spectacle, *Intolerance*, in 1916.

For the rest of Griffith's life, they remained friends. Theirs was an odd alliance: the colored woman struggling to keep her family afloat and to make a career for herself, and the director considered by many to be racist. Yet with all the outrage and controversy, Madame Sul-Te-Wan remained his steadfast defender. "She was devoted to Mr. Griffith," said Lillian Gish, "and he in turn loved her."

"Why you know I love that man, oh my God yes," Sul-Te-Wan said. "If my father was living and was going to be drowned and Mr. Griffith was going to be drowned, and they say now Madame there's two men out there in the water and it's possible you could save one of them, but you can't save but one, I'd step on my dad's back to get solid foundation to drag D. W. Griffith out."

For years, Griffith rode a high wave of success. But eventually, the man who had invented Hollywood found himself rejected by the town as a new generation of filmmakers emerged and especially once the talkie era began in the late 1920s. Madame, however, remained close to him. She never hesitated to make light of herself if she thought that was to her advantage. When Griffith and his second wife, Evelyn, divorced in 1947, Lillian Gish recalled that Madame "offered to take their three cats, adding wryly that, as the animals resembled her more than anyone else in the family, she wanted to take them."

When Griffith suffered a cerebral hemorrhage in Los Angeles in July 1948 and was rushed to Temple Hospital, Madame was seen "waiting outside the hospital room when he died," said Gish. "She was one of the few friends near him." Of those who attended Griffith's funeral at Masonic Hall, few could forget Sul-Te-Wan's appearance there. "Outside the Hall, the bobbysoxers, autograph seekers, and amateur photographers swarmed, treating the sad moment as if it were a premiere," said Gish. "Inside, producers, actors, and actresses filed past David's coffin with solemn faces. Toward the end of the line came Madame Sul-Te-Wan." When she reached the coffin, "she burst into tears."

Years later, when asked if Griffith left her something, she replied, "Yeah, he left me something. He left me with love in my heart for him."

During the teens and 1920s, knowledge of the Griffith/Sul-Te-Wan friendship sparked stories and rumors within the industry. And in all likelihood, Madame shrewdly used the knowledge of that friendship to

Madame Sul-Te-Wan (right)—the woman at the center of old Black Hollywood—in The Maid of Salem.

advance herself whenever possible. At her urging, Griffith instructed Frank Woods, who had cowritten the script of *The Birth of a Nation,* to write a letter of recommendation that read:

To Whom It May Concern:
This is to certify that the bearer, Madam [*sic*] Sul-Te-Wan, is a colored actress of exceptional ability and has been a member of our stock company for the past three years. She has played a number of very good parts in our pictures and gave very good satisfaction.

Yours very truly
MAJESTIC MOTION PICTURE COMPANY
By Frank E. Woods

Griffith introduced Sul-Te-Wan "to some of the leading motion picture film producers on the Pacific Coast," said Delilah Beasley, as well as some of the great stars including Theda Bara, Mary Pickford, Lillian Gish, Cecil B. DeMille, Douglas Fairbanks, and Charlie Chaplin. Through Griffith,

Madame's son John also appeared in Theda Bara's *Madame DuBarry*. Erich von Stroheim and Raoul Walsh also later used Madame in their films.

She kept working. Sometimes in bits. Sometimes in supporting roles. In the teens and 1920s, she appeared in *Hoodoo Ann, Stage Struck, The Narrow Street*, and *Uncle Tom's Cabin* as well as in the then shocking brothel sequence in von Stroheim's *Queen Kelly*.

Sul-Te-Wan proved that there could be a place for African Americans in Hollywood cinema, in the emerging studio system itself. Her relationship with Griffith was the first black/white alliance in the film colony. Away from mainstream Hollywood, she also created her own black social circles. The idea of a Black Hollywood—a segment of L.A.'s colored community that worked in films and lived by a code of glamour and allure—took root. For a time, Madame was the budding Black Hollywood's most important performer, known by the aspiring black entertainers who soon knocked on Hollywood's door.

THE TOWN

Los Angeles itself seemed to be changing daily as more and more colored Americans came west.

L.A. could still boast of decent race relations. The new black immigrants were able to live wherever they wanted without great restrictions—*at first*. Yet there were areas where black Angelenos knew they were not welcome. From the late 1800s into the early years of the twentieth century, many African Americans lived in rooming houses on First and Second streets in the city's downtown area. Whites also resided in the area. By 1906, a black community emerged that was bordered "on the South by Ninth Street, on the North by 4th, and on the West by Maple Avenue." Then, from 1910 into the teens, black residents occupied an area in south central Los Angeles known as the Furlong Tract.

A few years earlier, a wealthy landowner named James Furlong had begun selling property to blacks in the southeast corner of the intersecting area of Vernon and Central avenues. The Furlong Tract, bordered on the west by Long Beach Boulevard and on the east by Alameda, spanned several city blocks from Fiftieth Street to Fifty-fifth. Eventually, it became a busy center with stores, offices, and restaurants that catered to black residents. For years, black Angelenos lived mostly here in what was known as L.A.'s Eastside—and gradually moved farther and farther west to what was known as the Westside. The main thoroughfare was Central Avenue, which ran north to south—and which became black L.A.'s most famous street. In time, the area around it also had "stately homes representing the cream of Black society, rentals and apartments that housed the new southern migrants, and the business and professional offices of the Black middle class. In essence, poverty and prosperity existed side by side on Central Avenue."

Early on, the black parts of town became lively social centers, especially as Los Angeles grew to be a haven for black musicians. Creole bands came to the city as early as 1908. In time, piano teachers, dance teachers, violinists, and choral directors all flourished there as well. By 1915, a city newcomer named Lillian Jeter Davis took out an ad in *The California Eagle,* announcing herself ready to prepare students in drama, tragedy, comedy, pathos. So black L.A. soon had its acting teachers, too. For a time in the teens, the hot spot, to see and be seen, was the Golden West Hotel. Located near Third Street and Stephenson Avenue and trumpeted by *The California Eagle* as "the largest Negro hotel west of Chicago," the Golden West was celebrated for being *the* place "for all who desire good service, food and entertainment." By 1911, the Clark Hotel, located on Central Avenue and Washington Boulevard, was also in business. Then came the Lynons Hotel at Eleventh Street and Central Avenue and The Lincoln at 549 Ceres Avenue. Restaurants like the Louisiana Café and clubs like The Alhambra opened on Central Avenue. To service all the railway companies—the Union Pacific, Southern Pacific, and Santa Fe railroads—making stops in the city, Union Station opened on Los Angeles and Alameda streets in 1939. But earlier, a major terminal was erected at Fifth and Central. So traffic was always heavy, especially with the crew of Pullman porters in town and in search of a place to stay between stops. Ninth and Central—and later Twelfth and Central—became the epicenter of what would be a glittering avenue of social and commercial activities for decades to come.

Those whites still in the area began moving out from this part of town that was becoming *too* colored. Civic concerns grew—about the quality of life in black Los Angeles. In 1913, one of L.A.'s prominent black citizens, the dentist Dr. John Somerville, established the local branch of the NAACP to ensure and fight for the rights of these new citizens of the West.

Reporting on black life in the city were the black newspapers *The Liberator* and *The Owl.* Originally, *The Owl* was published by a Texan named John Neimore. But that changed not long after a young woman named

Charlotta Spears came to Los Angeles from Rhode Island in 1910. In poor health, she hoped the warmer climate might help her improve. She found herself in need of money and took a job at *The Owl*. Two years later, when Neimore died, Captain G. W. Hawkins bought the publication and put it in Spears's hands. Beneath her thick-rimmed eyeglasses and rather sweet country-girl smile was a serious-minded, highly intelligent crusader who had toughened the editorial quality of the newspaper, now called *The California Eagle*. In 1914, Charlotta Spears married another immigrant to the city, Joseph Blackburn Bass, who had founded the *Topeka Plain Dealer*. Together, they bought and operated *The California Eagle*. Mr. Bass managed all business details. Mrs. Bass was in charge of the editorial department. With their high goals and ideals, especially with Charlotta Bass's social activism, the Basses became a well-known couple, important to the ever-growing city and the emerging Black Hollywood.

With *The California Eagle*, black L.A. had a newspaper that would record the social, political, and cultural issues of the African American community for decades—providing everything from front-page coverage of a speech by Booker T. Washington in Long Beach in 1914 and then front-page coverage a year later on his death; to the five-year jail sentence given to Marcus Garvey in 1923; to a visit to the city by millionairess A'Lelia Walker, daughter of Madame C. J. Walker, under a headline that read "Los Angeles Welcomes Race's Wealthiest Woman"; to a scholarship fund for a Harvard-bound graduate of the University of Southern California named Ralph Bunche. *The California Eagle* also covered the comings and goings of a rich entertainment scene: from protest over *The Birth of a Nation*, to the highjinks of newcomer Stepin Fetchit.

FINDING L.A., FINDING HIMSELF

Also arriving in Los Angeles during these early years was a strapping, good-looking hunk of an aspiring actor named Noble Johnson. Like Madame Sul-Te-Wan, he had his eyes set on working in pictures. Light-skinned, broad-shouldered, and athletic, Johnson had traveled widely and had done a little of any number of things.

He had been born in Marshall, Missouri, in 1881, the son of a black father, Perry Johnson, and, so he said, a white mother, Georgia Reed. The couple had four children: Virgel, Noble Mark, Iris, and George. Two days after George's birth, in 1885, in Colorado Springs, twenty-four-year-old Georgia Reed Johnson died from complications related to the birth. The oldest son, Virgel, was put in charge of caring for Noble—then four years old—and Iris. Baby George was sent to live with a colored servant who worked nearby in the home of a wealthy white couple.

At the public schools in Colorado Springs, Virgel and Noble struck up a friendship with a scruffy, rugged white kid with whom Noble often went riding. Years later, that kid, Lon Chaney, would become one of Hollywood's biggest silent-screen stars.

Restless and adventurous, the teenage Noble dropped out of school and wandered from one job to another, from one part of the country to another. At first, he spent two summers working the racing circuits with his father, who taught the boy everything about the training, handling, breeding, and racing of horses. Noble loved the animals. He loved the outdoors, too. And he loved the seemingly carefree lives of the older cattlemen whom he observed. He decided he wanted to be a cowboy himself, but his father would not hear of it.

The next summer, Noble and another young man headed for cattle territory. He found a job with the Sanborn and Kaiser Company of Jefferson, Colorado, one of the country's largest cattle ranchers. That winter, he returned to Colorado Springs. During his free hours, he boxed, wrestled, and performed athletic stunts with other boys. By now, he had grown taller—he would stand six feet two inches—and more muscular. Again, he left for cattle country, working at ranches from Colorado to Wyoming, enjoying the rough-and-tumble camaraderie of this man's world. Yet the teenager also prided himself on his own self-sufficiency and valued solitude. In the winter of 1903, he spent four months camping out in the mountains where the temperature dropped to fifty-five degrees below zero and the snow was sometimes five feet deep.

By 1905, his wanderlust had led him to New York City, where he trained horses for the wealthy at their estates in Westchester County and on Long Island. He was also employed as a private coachman in New York City. During his off-hours, he performed punching-bag exhibitions and four-round boxing contests at "smokers" at the private clubs of wealthy New Yorkers. He set out to become a professional boxer but was forced to give up the ring following a boxing injury—a broken hand.

Still, Noble Johnson seemed unable to stop moving. In 1910, he went to Los Angeles, where a newfound interest in motor cars helped land him a job at White's Garage, the largest motor club in the city. Johnson then traveled by steamship to Portland, Oregon, and Grays Harbor and North Yakima in Washington State. On a nearby Yakima reservation, he ran footraces, played baseball, and raced horses. In 1913, he was back at White's Garage in Los Angeles, where he became foreman.

The next year, in Colorado Springs, his life took a dramatic turn. In June 1914, all that folks in the area could talk about was the Lubin Manufacturing Company of Philadelphia, which had come to Colorado to shoot scenes for an eight-reel motion picture called *Eagle's Nest*. When the company desperately needed to replace an actor injured in a horse stunt, Noble's reputation for handling animals brought him to the attention of the director, who hired him to play an Indian. In Philadelphia, the management at Lubin, impressed with the footage of him on horseback, contacted Johnson and asked him to come to Philadelphia and sign as a Lubin player. He seemed a natural for the movies. Good looks. Tall and robust. Athletic. And light-skinned enough that most people probably wouldn't even know he was a colored man. Johnson's roustabout days ended.

He appeared in short films for Lubin, playing nonblack characters. Then, in 1915, movie work took him back to Los Angeles, where moviemaking was becoming big business. Adolph Zukor and Jesse L. Lasky joined forces to form Famous Players–Lasky, which later became Paramount Pictures. Carl Laemmle built Universal City for his Universal Studios. Other companies came, such as the Fox Film Corporation as well as the Metro Pictures Corporation and the Goldwyn Picture Corporation. The comedy film companies of Mack Sennett and Hal Roach were also in California. The star system was emerging. Fans were excited by Charlie Chaplin, Mary Pickford, Douglas Fairbanks, Gloria Swanson, and Harold Lloyd. Extras were needed to appear in crowd scenes. Stuntmen were required to perform demanding and sometimes dangerous physical exploits. The country—and the city—were becoming hooked on the movies.

A DIFFERENT KIND OF MOVIEMAKING: THE LINCOLN MOTION PICTURE COMPANY

With his ability to perform any number of stunts, Johnson found steady work at Universal in serials and films like *A Western Governor's Humanity,* in 1915, and *Kinkaid, Gambler,* in 1916. He also appeared briefly in *Intolerance*. Immediately noticed by the black press, he was called "the race's daredevil movie star" as well as "America's premier Afro-American screen star." After all those years of wandering, Noble Johnson suddenly saw *possibilities*. He became fascinated by moviemaking and

Noble Johnson, born to be a leading man but relegated to bits and small roles until he helped found the Lincoln Motion Picture Company.

quickly grasped the mechanics of popular films: how they were written, cast, shot, financed, and distributed. On Central Avenue, he also observed colored audiences. Movie houses in the black neighborhoods were pulling in patrons with crudely made short films that sometimes featured bug-eyed, grinning stereotypical black characters. Yet nowhere in that big-screen Olympian splendor that so entranced audiences were there heroic or dashing or romantic Negro characters. Clearly, movies were not being made for colored moviegoers. Johnson also understood something else: he himself was leading-man material. But the Hollywood studios would never give him a chance to prove that.

At Universal, he shared his observations with a friend, Harry Gant, a white cameraman—as well as with his younger brother George, then working in a post office in Omaha, Nebraska. Los Angeles already had black actors like Clarence Brooks, Beulah Hall, George Reed, and Lottie Boles. So there was plenty of talent around. And some money to be found, too. Prominent local businessmen, both black and white, might be tapped for investment capital. Johnson went to work on getting seed money. With $75,000 raised, he joined forces with several other African Americans in Los Angeles to form the Lincoln Motion Picture Company to make Negro films—sometimes called race movies—for the Negro market. Johnson became the company's president. The well-to-do black druggist Dr. J. Thomas Smith became vice president; actor Clarence Brooks, secretary; and Dudley Brooks, assistant secretary. Cameraman Harry Gant was the company's only white member. Now Los Angeles had its first black movie studio. Within three years, the company released three films, all tales of black progress, endurance, and drive and all starring Noble and shot by cameraman Gant: *The Realization of a Negro's Ambition,* for which Johnson also wrote the screenplay; *The Trooper of Company K,* in 1916; and *The Law of Nature,* in 1917.

At the colored theaters in Los Angeles and other cities, Lincoln's films fared well enough. Four prints of its first film, *The Realization of a Negro's Ambition,* were sent into circulation through the East and the South. Certainly, that might have been small potatoes for a big, established movie company. But for a fledgling organization, it was healthy business. For a time, Johnson was a dashing leading man with a charisma and rugged appeal that shone through even in stills. But Lincoln struggled with financing, distribution, and promotion. Every day was an effort to stay afloat. Johnson couldn't even be paid a salary. A setback occurred shortly before the scheduled opening of Lincoln's second film, *Trooper of Company K,* in 1916, when a fire broke out at the laboratory where the film was being developed and printed. Most of the film was salvaged. But some key scenes were destroyed and had to be reshot. The film finally opened, however, with fanfare. An advertisement in *The California Eagle* proclaimed:

THE LINCOLN MOTION PICTURE CO.
PRESENTS THEIR SECOND PRODUCTION
"*THE TROOPER OF CO. K*"
A THRILLING, INTERESTING, AND PATRIOTIC THREE-REEL
MOTION PICTURE DRAMA FEATURING
NOBLE M. JOHNSON
SUPPORTED BY MISS BEULAH HALL AND JIMMIE SMITH
Over 300 people used in making this production, consisting of
ex-9th and 10th Cavalrymen, Mexicans, Cowboys and horses.
Colored Persons Shown True to Life On the Screen at the
NEW ANGELUS THEATER

The California Eagle wrote a glowing review, calling the production "an exceptional picture if only for its historical value."

But the delayed opening as well as the day-to-day expenditures of maintaining the company were costly. After the third Lincoln production, Johnson arrived at a board meeting with devastating news. Lincoln was in no position to mount a new production, he explained. Nor was he in a position to continue working without pay as he had done with the first three productions. He asked that the company no longer use his name, presumably in seeking financing for future projects, and resigned from the company.

Johnson's resignation puzzled some. Various explanations were given. Outside Negro movie houses, posters of Johnson had been prominently displayed. Often enough, his Lincoln films played at theaters next to those where Universal Studios productions were shown. Often enough, too, in these black neighborhoods, Johnson's Lincoln films outgrossed Universal's. Rumors circulated that Universal Studios had given the actor an ultimatum: either leave Lincoln or leave Universal.

Lincoln was shaken by Johnson's departure. His brother George, still working in Omaha, was asked to be the company's general booking manager. George had already created the first weekly colored newspaper in Tulsa, Oklahoma, and later, he would establish the Pacific Coast News Bureau, a news-gathering organization for colored newspapers around the country. At the Lincoln Motion Picture Company, his duties entailed setting up branch offices to handle promotion and advertising for the company's films in cities such as Philadelphia, Washington, D.C., Atlanta, and New Orleans. In smaller towns, he also created a booking system whereby theaters could exhibit Lincoln films. On his way to establishing a national Negro booking organization, George P. Johnson eventually moved to Los Angeles. Caught up in the moviemaking fervor, he wrote the script for Lincoln's feature *By Right of Birth.*

What the company now needed was a new star to headline its productions. For its next films—*A Man's Duty,* in 1919, and *By Right of Birth,* in 1921—that new star was Clarence Brooks. Like Noble Johnson, he was light-skinned with the type of keen features believed to attract black patrons. Likable and serious, Brooks, however, did not have Johnson's larger-than-life virile glamour. Still, Lincoln announced ambitious plans for another film, *The Heart of the Negro,* to star Brooks with Edna Morton and Lawrence Chenault, but its finances remained wobbly, and the proposed film was never made. The Lincoln Motion Picture Company folded.

Clarence Brooks would continue to work in other race movies, such as *Am I Guilty?*, *Dark Manhattan*, and *Harlem Rides the Range*, and would also give an impressive performance as a doctor in the West Indies in the 1931 Hollywood adaptation of Sinclair Lewis's novel *Arrowsmith*. But other key players in the company saw their careers end.

Noble returned to Universal. Unlike the few other early black actors now in Hollywood, he would not be cast as bumbling, stumbling, eye-popping characters. Still relegated to supporting or bit roles, he nonetheless portrayed various ethnic types in some of the biggest silent spectacles of the 1920s: Cecil B. DeMille's films *The Ten Commandments* and *The King of Kings;* *The Four Horsemen of the Apocalypse*, starring Rudolph Valentino; *The Thief of Bagdad*, starring Douglas Fairbanks; Buster Keaton's *The Navigator;* and MGM's blockbuster *Ben-Hur.*

Noble met an old friend while working on *West of Zanzibar* at MGM in 1928. Its star was none other than that kid from Colorado, Lon Chaney. One day, George Johnson—compiling items for his Pacific Coast News Bureau—visited Noble on the set. During a break in filming, he eased up next to Chaney and nudged him. Never having forgotten the Johnson kids, Chaney reminisced with George about old times in Colorado Springs.

Noble Johnson managed to make the leap to sound films in the 1930s. In *Moby Dick*, he played Queequeg to John Barrymore's Captain Ahab. In *The Mummy*, starring Boris Karloff, he played the Nubian servant. In *Safe in Hell*, he was a good-looking military man on a Caribbean island. In *King Kong*, he played the native chief. And in *The Ghost Breakers*, he was cast as a zombie who terrified Bob Hope and black actor Willie Best. For years, he would be the busiest black actor working in the movies. But he may well have been the most complicated and most remote. He kept to himself, lived quietly, held under wraps whatever torments or frustrations he experienced, and managed, for a man as handsome and appealing as he was in a town that would thrive on gossip, to have a fairly unknown love life. He married at least twice: first to an early sweetheart, Ruth Thornton, in Denver in 1912 and, some years later, to Gladys Blackwell. But most in Black Hollywood felt that Noble was a loner.

Other black newcomers arriving in Los Angeles in the teens found employment, if not in the movies then with movie people. Black servants—cooks, maids, butlers—began working for industry people and at the studios, too. Possibly the earliest African American at a studio was a hairdresser and all-around aide-de-camp known simply as Hattie, who was employed by Cecil B. DeMille at Famous Players–Lasky. Silent-screen star Gloria Swanson remembered that on her first day at the studio, one of DeMille's assistants "led me to the hairdressing department and turned me over to Hattie, a tiny Black woman who was standing at an old-fashioned ironing board ironing a long switch of dark-brown hair. She was wearing a narrow-brimmed black straw hat, beneath which she seemed to have very little hair of her own, and she kept a watchful eye on the ten or fifteen girls who worked under her. 'This is your hair I'm ironing,' she said with an enormous smile. 'Over there are the sketches. See if you like it.' "

Hattie also explained the ways of the world in Hollywood. "While she worked, I did my make-up and we talked," recalled Swanson. "She told me Mr. DeMille was the most remarkable man she had ever met—a real per-fectionist." And later, when one of Swanson's films hit it big, Hattie was the first person to give her the news. "One morning all the girls who worked under Hattie were twittering like birds, so I asked what was going on. 'Haven't you heard?' Hattie exclaimed. 'Your picture has been held over for a second week. They got word from New York this morning.' " Still later, when Swanson became upset about unfounded rumors of a romance between DeMille and herself, Hattie assured her that was just something that happened to famous people. "Don't feel bad about being famous," Hattie told Swanson. "That's what everyone out here wants to be. Why, I'm famous myself on Central Avenue now, just because I work with you."

"Many of our women make good wages serving motion picture ac-tresses," wrote that early historian of African Americans in California, Delilah Beasley, in 1919. Arriving in L.A. that very year was Virginia-born Lillian Moseley, who worked as a maid for actress May Allison. "Ever since my early childhood, I've wanted to work for show people," Moseley once recalled. "My aunt took me to Philadelphia after my parents died and at the age of 11 years, I had to look to myself for support.

"Then in 1918 I went to New York City for the first time, and walked along the Broadway theater district, trying all the stage doors, asking if anyone wanted a personal maid. That's how I found my job with [actress] Ina Claire and then, a few months later, I met May Allison and came to California with her," Moseley recalled. "Hollywood was just a few streets and orange groves and a desert stretched from downtown Los Angeles to the movie studios." There was a street car line "but it seemed the cars never ran. But the studios were exciting."

Within the next two decades, servants would become important to big stars—in unexpected ways—and especially important within Los Angeles's black community. Some would use domestic work as a springboard to film roles, if not for themselves then for their families. That was certainly true of a chef named Ernest Morrison Sr., who moved from New Orleans to work for the wealthy tycoon E. L. Doheny in Beverly Hills in 1917. Doheny had discovered oil in the city in 1892, leading the way for Los Angeles's first oil boom. Doheny and his partner had first dug for a well with shovels near Glendale Boulevard and Second Street. Afterward, oil derricks shot up. The Dohenys—along with the Chandlers and the Mulhollands—became one of the city's "old" families.

Morrison may have spent most of his day in the kitchen of Doheny's palatial dwelling, but now, like just about everyone else in the town, he kept his ears open for casting news. When a guest at the home—John Osbourne—spotted Morrison's energetic little son Ernie Jr., he thought the boy might be just right for a part in the short films in which his daughter, Baby Marie Osbourne, was then starring at Pathé. Morrison Sr. agreed. So did the producers at Pathé, who fell in love with the five-year-old kid with the large eyes, a sweet smile, and an engaging personality. The public would come to love him, too. And so began what, especially in the 1920s, would be a remarkable career for a black child. From 1917 to 1919, little Ernie Morrison worked in fourteen of Baby Marie's movies as well as appearing in other films, including *The Sheriff*, starring Fatty Arbuckle.

The big change in Morrison's career came about through Margaret Roach, the wife of movie producer Hal Roach. She had worked with Morrison on the Osbourne comedies and recommended that her husband take a close look at the child. In 1919, Morrison signed a two-year contract with Roach, the first such contract for any black performer then working in Hollywood. The young actor was kept busy at the Roach studios, appearing in comedy shorts with Charley Chase and Snub Pollard. Eventually, audiences black and white came to know him as a playful kid called Sunshine Sammy, America's first black child star. Other Morrison family members got into the movie business. Ernest Jr.'s sister Florence worked with him in *Penrod*. His other sister, Vera, also won roles, as did his father.

n the late teens, Los Angeles continued to grow and prosper with an influx of new settlers. A cluster of sporty nightclubs sprouted up along Central Avenue, and black Angelenos flocked there for fun and relaxation

The little boy with the big contract: Ernest Morrison inks his deal with producer Hal Roach while his father looks on.

in the evenings and especially on the weekends. The Clark Hotel opened the doors of its Clark Annex to cater to the new crowd's hunger for entertainment. The New Angelus Theatre became the movie house where black Angelenos could see the latest moving pictures. Jazz, a new kind of music, came to town and caused some frowns among black businessmen and a budding black middle class. But jazz would invigorate the nightlife in the city. Jelly Roll Morton was said to have first set foot in L.A. as early as 1907 and then became a regular between 1917 and 1922, performing at the sexy, swanky Cadillac Club as well as at other niteries along Central Avenue. Also on the L.A. scene was the young singer Ada Smith, who performed—along with Jelly Roll—at the black club Murray's. Later, when she ran off to Paris, she emerged as the darling of the international set and became known as Bricktop.

By the late teens, everybody in the city seemed to have a touch of movie fever. Even when movies still were silent, the black band Wood Wilson's Syncopators got itself hired to appear as musicians in the short *Penny Dance*, in 1916. Other musicians, such as Kid Ory, who worked at the

Cadillac Club, headed out to the studios to perform mood music for the actors while silent scenes were being shot.

By the end of the teens, no real black film community yet existed. But Noble Johnson, Madame Sul-Te-Wan, and little Ernest Morrison had become African American pioneers. They would work in pictures for decades to come, but they could never have envisioned exactly how much the industry would change. Nor could they have predicted the way in which sound in the 1920s would transform everything in Hollywood—and, in turn, lead to the new growth and glamour of a distinct black film colony.

2
The Twenties

I n the 1920s, Hollywood—fast becoming the nation's dream factory—
was a boomtown. More studios opened; the star system became firmly
locked in place; a new group of directors, producers, and personalities
rose up the ranks. Columbia Pictures was incorporated in 1924. So, too,
was MGM, the consolidation of the Metro, Goldwyn, and Louis B.
Mayer picture companies, soon to be the mightiest of studios. Warner
Bros., incorporated in 1923, took over First National Pictures and Vitagraph in 1925 and a year later created Vitaphone to develop a sound-
on-disc technology that would, by decade's end, revolutionize the
motion-picture industry. Erich von Stroheim, King Vidor, Frank Borzage,
F. W. Murnau, and Cecil B. DeMille directed some of the new era's most
talked-about films. Fan magazines like *Motion Picture* and *Photoplay*—
answering the need of a public now fascinated by moving-picture people—
reported on life in the movie colony: the beautiful homes, the clubs and
restaurants, the retinues of assistants, secretaries, and servants; the fabulous wardrobes, jewels, and cars; and the offscreen exploits of the stars
themselves. Chaplin, Pickford, Fairbanks, Valentino, Swanson, Pola Negri,
Harold Lloyd, Ramon Novarro, Clara Bow, John Gilbert, and Garbo—all
these magical beings basked in the light of their own glamour. Hollywood
seemed like an enchanted kingdom.

During this era, more African Americans turned up on the doorsteps of
the studios. Performers such as Mildred Washington, Carolynne Snow-

den, George Reed, Gertrude Howard, Charles Moore, Mattie Peters, Edgar Washington, Oscar Smith, Zack Williams, and Roberta Hyson found roles, if not consistently then at least sporadically enough to draw some attention within the black community itself. Noble Johnson continued working, while child star Sunshine Sammy signed a new major studio contract. And crafty, resourceful Madame Sul-Te-Wan would utilize the black press to help create something of a legend for herself.

By decade's end, two major studios would produce two all-talking, all-singing colored features. Performers such as Ethel Waters, Nina Mae McKinney, and a lanky bag of bones named Lincoln Perry, known as Stepin Fetchit, would all be considered stars *of sorts* by the industry—even if they were the type of stars no one in Hollywood knew quite what to do with.

During the great migration of African Americans from the South to the North—in search of a better life with more opportunities and a chance at better living conditions—many African Americans also flooded into Los Angeles. By 1920, some 15,579 African Americans resided in the city. Yet by then, the once open city had started to become segregated. When there had not been much of a black population, white residents appeared not to have great concerns about racial matters, especially pertaining to where African Americans lived and socialized. But those same residents soon felt threatened by the new immigrants. The idea of residential race mixing soon became an issue. Not only had there been white flight from the Central Avenue area as blacks moved in, but fears of African Americans moving into other neighborhoods led white citizens and city officials to establish restrictive housing covenants, whereby certain parts of the city became legally off-limits to black residents. For those white homeowners living in areas near predominantly black neighborhoods, there were contracts within the title deeds to their property that prohibited them from selling or leasing their homes to people of color: Negroes, Mexicans, Japanese, Chinese, and American Indians. Protests shot up against such covenants. But in 1919, the California Supreme Court ruled that such restrictive covenants were legal.

By 1920, African Americans lived in four distinct areas. Foremost was still the Furlong Tract. Another district—the Westside on Jefferson Boulevard between Normandie and Western—became home to the new black middle class. African Americans also found a haven in East Los Angeles in Boyle Heights and what was known as the Temple Street area northwest of the downtown section between Alvarado and Hoover. About 40 percent of the city's black residents lived in a district of thirty blocks of Central Avenue. With African Americans confined to these areas, Los Angeles was emerging all the more as a city with not only separate housing but also very separate cultural identities.

Slowly, a black film colony was taking shape. In some way or another, everyone was affected by the glitter and glamour. To be so close to the enchanted kingdom was to want, all the more, to be a part of it.

THE LITTLE BLACK PRINCE OF MOVING PICTURES

In the early 1920s, the kingpin—the most famous black actor in Hollywood—was still little Ernest Morrison, known as Sunshine Sammy. By now, he had become the one black movie performer who could be identified by his face, if not yet his name, by the industry and audiences alike. Shrewdly and perceptively, his father, Ernest (sometimes called Joseph) Morrison, understood that as the movies were becoming even bigger business, there might be a chance for his son to become *really* famous.

In this new era, Sammy's big break came when he appeared with Harold Lloyd—who, by the early 1920s, was already challenging Charlie Chaplin as the screen's most popular comedian—in the films *Get Out and Get Under, Haunted Spooks,* and *Number, Please?* Sometimes, Sammy's appearances could be surprisingly nonstereotypical. In *Get Out and Get Under,* his first film with Lloyd, he was just a curious but pesky little boy who shows up while the hero is trying to get a stalled car running again. Fascinated by the man at work, the kid proves to be a delightful, funny hindrance to Lloyd's progress. Audiences may have waited for the kind of racial gag that usually occurred when black performers then appeared in films, but nothing happened here, marking a kind of triumph in films of the period. Chaplin had child star Jackie Coogan. Lloyd had Sunshine Sammy.

Producer Hal Roach was impressed with Sammy—for a number of reasons. Sammy had the discipline and the focus and energy needed for life at the studio. He had the right kind of family, too. They kept the boy on a tight schedule. Another child star, Eugene Jackson, recalled that while Sammy's father ensured that the boy's career stayed on track, negotiating contracts and arranging tours, his mother, Louise, was in charge of the house. The couple also had four daughters: Florence, Vera, Dorothy, and Ethel. Mrs. Morrison oversaw what all her children did: what they ate, how they dressed, when they studied, when and where they played, and with whom they associated. But special attention had to be lavished on Sammy. Both Louise and Ernest Morrison understood it was essential that every evening Sammy be prepared for the next day's work. His parents rehearsed and drilled him, put him to bed early in the evening, woke him at the crack of dawn, and drove him to the Roach Studios in Culver City.

Once there, Sammy quickly learned to adjust to a new set of rules. At his home not far from Central Avenue, Sammy lived in an all-colored world. But at the studio, the world was now almost all-white, populated with people who might speak differently, move differently, even think differently. Already, movie sets were lively and uninhibited, all the more so when the cameras were not rolling. But they could also be coarse and vulgar places with all types of sexual or racial jokes. Children, however much their parents might try to shield them, heard and saw much that they had to act as if they hadn't heard or seen. The word *nigger* was commonplace at the studios. That was the term used to describe a certain device that film technicians used for darker shading, or dimming. *The nigger light.* Even at this young age, Sammy had to simply swallow hard and shrug off any questions he might have.

Moviemaking could be long and tedious. As he worked more on films, Sammy was assigned a tutor to keep him up on his studies. But psychologically, he had to be able to shift gears—to drop his books, go onto the set to perform. He also learned to keep his energy level high—to be able to do one take after another if necessary. Here perhaps was the most difficult aspect of moviemaking for Sammy—as it was for other child stars and adult stars, too: being clearheaded about the line separating movieland fantasy from the reality of life away from the Hal Roach Studios. Morrison always appeared to be a sensitive, sweet-tempered boy, and in the years to come, studio life took its toll on him.

Excited by Sammy's potential, Hal Roach set out in 1921 to create a series to star the child, certainly a bold move for the time. Once the first short in the proposed series appeared, *The Pickaninny,* Roach's distributor, Pathé, launched a publicity campaign. One trade advertisement featured a photo of a smiling Sammy, under which the copy read:

HAL ROACH

presents

SUNSHINE SAMMY

in

THE PICKANINNY

"Hot Dang! I'se Heah, Gemmens!"

Who doesn't know "Sunshine Sammy," the funny little darkie of the Hal Roach Comedies?

Millions have laughed at him, exhibitors have commented upon his popularity with their audiences, though he wasn't starred,—just a wide-grinning, little coon, loose jointed, full of pep, a "pip" of a "feeder" to the comedy stars he supported.

Now he is starred in one two-reel comedy, made the way Hal Roach knows how to make 'em.

Hot Dog! This one isn't a gamble, it's just sure to please.

Though the studio prided itself on promoting its little colored star, nobody appeared to even consider the racial attitudes, to put it mildly, that were built into the promotion campaign. Still, exhibitors, who were well aware of *their* racial attitudes, objected: Roach was informed that mainstream theaters would not show shorts featuring a colored star. Roach then set out to do a series of short films about kids: their pranks, their attitudes, their games, their shenanigans, and their relationships. Roach scoured high and low to find the right performers. "About 40,000 children were interviewed," recalled former child star Eugene Jackson. "Only 41 were placed under contract, with salaries ranging from $37.50 to $75.00 a week." Finally, in 1922, Roach launched the series of his dreams, Our Gang—with Sunshine Sammy, Jackie Condon, and Peggy Cartwright as the original stars.

In black L.A., young Sammy was the star of the day. *The California Eagle* fed the growing curiosity about him, reporting in 1922 that Sammy had "just signed a 5 year contract with a local motion picture corporation calling for a yearly salary of $10,000," which was "indeed pleasing to the thousands of admirers of the 7-year old Race lad who is now the highest salaried member of the Race in movies today." Other black newspapers around the country also wrote about this child-star phenomenon. Along Central Avenue and throughout the Furlong Tract, Sunshine Sammy's career was a dream come true.

Ernest Morrison—known as Sunshine Sammy—dressed for
success as America's most famous black child star of the early 1920s.

Black Hollywood pinned its hopes on this little Black Prince of Moving Pictures. Gossiped about, fawned over, adulated, Sammy became a national celebrity who appeared to enjoy the perks and privileges of stardom *and* making big enough bucks to be livin' large. When he appeared in town, Sammy was always well dressed, well groomed, and well behaved. No child-star tantrums for him. When he went on a tour arranged by his father, the whole community was abuzz for days. "Sammy was such a big shot," remembered Eugene Jackson, who lived right around the corner from Sammy. "He was an established star. When he arrived home, the entire neighborhood would come out to see him. He had a great big limousine a mile long." A black child star of a later era—Fayard Nicholas—also recalled his excitement and glee as a kid whenever he saw Sunshine Sammy on-screen, or heard some tidbit about the way Sammy lived.

Morrison worked in the Our Gang series for two years, appearing in twenty-eight episodes. Sometimes, his character was called Booker T. Bacon; at other times, Sorghum. But moviegoers still knew him as Sunshine Sammy. His fame rubbed off on his father, who—billed as Ernest Morrison Sr.—also worked in such Our Gang episodes as *Saturday Morning, A Pleasant Journey, Lodge Night,* and *A Quiet Street* (playing Sammy's father). Roach also hired Morrison Sr. in 1923 as the assistant director on the Our Gang short *Dogs of War.*

But in 1924, the bottom fell out of Sunshine Sammy's world. Morrison Sr. took the child out of the series. Or so Morrison Sr. liked to say. *The California Eagle* reported that Sammy had "completed his contract with Hal Roach last March," but the "elder Morrison failed to renew the contract." Plans were announced to star the young actor in comedies at Finer Arts Studio. But the truth was that Sunshine Sammy, now eleven, was an oldster by the standards of Our Gang. Throughout the long run of the series into the talkie era, as the children, black and white, grew older, Roach would periodically replace the older children, eventually bringing in such other black child stars as Eugene "Pineapple" Jackson, Billie "Buckwheat" Thomas, and Stymie Beard. Sammy had even worked with the little actor who would be his replacement, Allen Clayton Hoskins, known as Farina.

Sammy's departure did not go unnoticed. "The kid situation seems to be worrying the powers that be at the Hal Roach Studio," reported *The California Eagle.* "They are trying to get along without Ernest Morrison (Sunshine Sammy) but the big question is will the exhibitors accept *Our Gang* comedies without Sammy or a Race star other than Farina. It is rumored that two of the *Our Gang* Series that were made without Ernest were returned from the Eastern exchange marked N. G. [no good]."

Sunshine Sammy became one of Hollywood's first child stars to fall victim to the fickleness and the ruthlessness of the industry. By the time he reached puberty, he was a Hollywood has-been. Problems and discord also flared up in the Morrison household. In 1928, Louise Morrison sued for divorce and was awarded custody of her four daughters as well as alimony that was considered "the largest ever granted a colored woman in California." Through a division of community property, she ended up with property in Los Angeles and Watts. Morrison Sr., however, landed on his feet. He opened a grocery-store chain and a confectionary business.

During the next sixteen years, Sammy appeared in only one other film, a 1929 short called *Stepping Along.* But performing was all he knew; so afterward, he spent years in vaudeville, at one point commanding a reputed income of $25,000 a year. For a time, he lived in New York, appearing in an act with such partners as Napoleon Whiting and Sleepy Williams. On-stage, he tap-danced, sang, and at one time headed his own band, Sun-shine Sammy and His Hollywood Syncopators.

Returning to Hollywood in 1940 to appear in *Fugitive from a Prison Camp,* he landed work in another series: The East Side Kids comedies, produced by Monogram Pictures, starring such teen favorites of the day as Leo Gorcey, Huntz Hall, and Bobby Jordan. East Side Kids was, in a sense, an adolescent version of Our Gang: a tale of the comic mishaps and obsessions of slum teenagers in the gritty, rough-and-tumble environment of New York City. Morrison's character—the only black who appeared regularly in the series—was called Scruno: sort of an endearing, goofy, dim-witted fellow whose eyes might bug if he thought he saw a ghost coming and who sometimes was on the receiving end of racial jokes. The titles of some of the eleven East Side Kid comedies in which he appeared during a three-year run—*Spooks Run Wild, Smart Alecks, Ghosts on the Loose,* and *The Ghost Creeps*—give a sense of his roles.

Then came the Second World War. Serving as a USO performer in the army, Morrison was injured in an automobile accident in Hawaii. After-ward, he had a permanent limp.

Leaving show business, he worked for years as a factory inspector at an aerospace firm in Compton, California. In later years, he looked a little lost, as if struggling to find his bearings. He occasionally appeared in small roles on such television series as *The Jeffersons* and *Good Times* as well as in a documentary on Harold Lloyd and at an Our Gang reunion in Palm Springs. The veteran of 145 motion pictures, he died in 1989 at the age of seventy-six, forgotten by the industry and audiences as well.

O ther black children joined the Our Gang cast. According to studio publicity, Allen Clayton Hoskins—the next important child star, who played Farina—was reportedly discovered when he was a one-year-old who happened to follow Sunshine Sammy into the studio. Roach took one look at the infant and knew he was star material. Moviegoers were in-trigued by the new kid on the block—"the chocolate-coated fun of Hal Roach's Rascals"—all the more so because they couldn't figure out if this cute little urchin, with the full head of hair and the cherubic face, was a boy or a girl. The studio decided to try to keep Farina's gender something of a mystery, thinking this would help the child's career. *The California Eagle* soon reported on him, informing its readers that Baby Farina had "a home

Sammy (upper right) with Baby Farina (lower right) and other friends in the Our Gang series.

of his own and a car of his own." Hoskins lived with his mother, aunt, and sister Jannie on East Thirty-third Street, not far from Sammy's home.

Like most families of the kids in Our Gang, the Hoskins clan had been relatively ordinary folks, arriving in L.A. in search of a better life, away from the grime and congestion of the ghettos of the East. L.A. may also have had its ghettos, but they were flooded with sunshine and open spaces and lined with palm trees. The Hoskins family became just as infected with movie mania as almost everybody else in Los Angeles. Mrs. Hoskins got her daughter Mango in such movies as *Big Business, Monkey Business, Bring Home the Turkey,* and *Lazy Days.* Making movies was now a family affair.

The same was true of the family of Eugene Jackson, who also joined the Our Gang series. Born in Texas in 1916, little Eugene probably would have remained there had not his mother, Lillie Foster Jackson Baker, decided to make a fresh start in the wake of two failed marriages. Lillie had relatives in Los Angeles. Eventually, she loaded her son Eugene, his younger half brother Freddie Baker, and her father onto a Southern Pacific

Off screen, Allen Hoskins—Our Gang's Farina—
sits with his mother.

train that carried them to the train terminal—sometimes called Central Station—on Fifth Street and Central Avenue. Waiting to meet them was a relative who piled the whole family—and their luggage—into his Model T Ford. As the car cruised along Central Avenue, little Eugene remembered—for years to come—the splendors of that busy street, teeming with people and shops: the offices of *The California Eagle,* the "YMCA, Second Baptist Church and the oldest and second oldest black fire stations. This was the 'Black Belt' of Los Angeles," Jackson said. "It was a Broadway. I had never seen so many colored people in my life. I was like a windmill, turning my head and twirling my body so as not to miss a scene."

Rooming houses then still offered the best deals for city newcomers. Lifelong resident Johnetta Jones remembered a friend of her family's "who made a nice living with a room and board. She did not work. And she did the cooking herself, and she took care of the house. She always had a full house." Lillie Jackson Baker moved her family into such a rooming house on Twelfth Street. Then she hit the pavement and found work as a maid in various apartments in Hollywood and some private homes. Not yet a city where the automobile was king, L.A. had a fairly decent trolley-car system. That was how family members first got around the city. The trolley lines ran out to different studios: to Culver City, where MGM, the Hal Roach Studios, and the Thomas Ince Studios were located; to Warner Bros., out in Burbank.

Jackson and the rest of his family were all entranced by the movies. His grandfather would take him to the "colored" theater, the Rosebud, on Twelfth and Central. There, little Eugene sat spellbound by those Olympian gods and goddesses on that huge, mysterious screen. "Saturday matinees would star such screen giants as Tom Mix, Hoot Gibson, and Harry and William Desmond," Jackson recalled. Other times he would watch other great stars, everyone from Clara Bow to Norma Shearer, Buster Keaton, Harold Lloyd—and on rare occasions, a black star like Charles Gilpin.

When he heard that the Rosebud Theatre held amateur-night contests, Eugene entered, sang and danced the shimmy, and walked away with first prize—a large box of groceries, which he knew his mother could use. He went back and won so often that he was called the "Shimmy King." The manager of the theater told Jackson's mother that he believed her son had enough talent to be in movies. "So when I was seven, Mama and I boarded the W Yellow Street Car for Thomas Ince Studios, on Washington Boulevard in Culver City, for a part in *Her Reputation,* a [1923] silent movie starring May McAvoy," Jackson recalled. "A little boy was needed to fall in a fish pond." Though Eugene was nervous, he proved himself a pro. "The pay was five dollars, but I did such an excellent job of showing fear with my big eyes that I was paid $7.50."

Now hooked on a show-business career, Jackson felt he had to learn more to succeed. Acting would never be enough. Hopping from one dance school to another, Eugene studied with the dance instructor Alma Hightower as well as with the Covans, who later appeared in movies and also taught dance numbers to white stars at the studios. He also got into the classes of the well-known Lauretta Butler, who ran a dance studio primarily for girls out of her home.

For black Angelenos of the time, Butler was top-of-the-line. "Mrs. Butler had about fifty children," recalled actress Avanelle Harris, who studied with Butler. "And different classes. The very young. And the middle size. And then she had a group she called 'the big girls.' . . . We went there practically every afternoon but always on Saturdays." "We would see her on weekends," recalled another student, Etta Jones, who studied at the studio in the early 1930s, along with Vivian Dandridge and the little girl who would later be Butler's most famous student, Dorothy Dandridge. "There were two girls, Nettie and Helen Mitchell, and their father was an entertainer: Strut Mitchell," said Jones. "They taught us to dance. And Lauretta played the piano. She could whale on that piano. And she gave me piano lessons."

"This woman was miraculous," said Avanelle Harris. "She had a great big house—a huge living room, great hardwood floors—and her living room, dining room, and music room were all part of her studio more or less. And she played piano and sang along. . . . Mrs. Butler was smart. After she taught you a little and you knew something, she would ask you to go help the younger children."

Butler herself was a "very, very commanding presence. She was a big, tall woman," said Harris. "Very strict and disciplined. Everything she taught you had to do with the discipline of the theater. And she knew how to make the connections." Every year, Butler put on a recital with her Kiddie Minstrel Show. "Very professional. She taught you about your lighting. She taught you how to come into the auditorium with your music and present it to the orchestra leader. She just gave you the whole rundown on the whole entire picture of what this business was."

While Eugene Jackson studied dance, he also worked as a page at the Criterion Theater, sold *Collier's* magazine at the studios, and won roles in the movies *Penrod and Sam* and *Boy of Mine.* Then the director of *Her Reputation* informed Jackson's mother of Hal Roach's search for a new black child actor. "I met with Mr. Roach," recalled Jackson, "and he liked my natural acting ability. I did some impromptu acting, and he said I had an open freshness with a million dollar smile." Jackson signed a three-year contract; he was called "Pineapple" and cast as Farina's older brother. He was assigned a dressing room at the studio. A tutor was also on the set for him. At Thanksgiving and Christmas, he, along with the other children in the series, was given "new suits, toys and trains from the major department stores such as May Company and Broadway." "Whatever one child received the other children received," said Jackson. The kids were also made even more famous by the Our Gang merchandising. Their faces "appeared on balloons, coloring books, lunch boxes, packs of gum, skates, shoes, and clothes."

Jackson left Our Gang before his three-year contract ended. Other opportunities had come up: roles in the Buster Brown and Mary Jane series and in shorts for Century Comedies. And then came appearances with the era's most famous stars—with Douglas Fairbanks in *The Thief of Bagdad* and with Mary Pickford in *Little Annie Rooney*. "I was hot as a firecracker, popping from one studio to the next and working two or three studios a day. I would be picked up by a limousine at one studio and be dashed to the next." Fairbanks took a special liking to him and also for a nearly seven-foot-tall black actor named Sam Baker. When his friends, such as Rudolph Valentino or Ramon Novarro, Harold Lloyd or Chaplin, visited the set, Fairbanks would ask Jackson and Baker to perform for them. "I would do my shimmy dance with my fancy steps," said Jackson, "and Sam would do his imitation of a roaring lion." No one would know how Sam—the friendly gentle giant—felt about performing in this way, as a deluxe form of comic relief for great stars in the middle of a workday. But black actors were sometimes expected to remain "in character" and perform on the set, if called upon, whether or not the cameras were rolling.

Working in the movies made Jackson, like Sammy and Farina, known throughout black show-business circles. He earned enough money to buy a car and to move his family to a house—their first—at 1429 East Fifteenth Street. Passersby pointed to the modest house, the place where little Pineapple lived. Jackson later appeared in such major sound films as *Hearts in Dixie* and *Cimarron* and remained an entertainer all his life, even turning up in episodes of the TV series *Julia*.

SERVING STARS, KEEPING SECRETS

The black children in Our Gang were successful, but these stars, after all, were children. In the mid-1920s, no adult black performer had attained this kind of prominence in Hollywood.

Instead, the greatest inroads in the growing Hollywood infrastructure still seemed to be by way of a back door—or the servants' entrance. Beginning in the 1920s, Hollywood could boast of perhaps the largest servant class in America. With so much money floating around (stars didn't yet pay income taxes—and some, such as Pickford and Fairbanks, earned in the millions), and with stars expected to fulfill endless social commitments—parties, luncheons, receptions, dinners, press interviews—a fleet of servants, including maids, butlers, chauffeurs, and gardeners, not only added to the glamorous, extravagant setting but was practical and necessary.

Occupying an important place in the social scheme of Black Hollywood from the early 1920s to the 1940s were the black servants. Some used their domestic service to carve out a niche for themselves within the industry—or as springboards to actual acting careers. Others found themselves close to the epicenter of Hollywood's demimonde and some of movieland's big scandals. Almost all the servants were privy to Hollywood's secrets, aware of the town's bordellos and gambling hideaways, its speakeasies, gin joints, and opium dens, aware, too, of the secret assignations, the extramarital affairs, the taboo liaisons, the backstabbings, and the deal making. The clever, resourceful servants became part of the emerging mythos of Hollywood stardom itself.

For the image-conscious movie elite—who thrived on a philosophy of conspicuous consumption, flaunting their wealth whenever they could—servants were a mark of status and success. An ordinary plain-Jane maid or a dull-as-a-doornail butler might be fine in Topeka, Kansas. But in dreamland, stars and executives liked being waited on by the *right* kind of help. Having a black maid, chauffeur, dresser, or bootblack *or* a Filipino houseboy *or* a Japanese gardener was soon fashionable among Hollywood's upper echelons. On the MGM lot, the studio's powerful production chief Irving Thalberg enjoyed impressing guests in his office by having his very proper Negro butler arrive with a tray in hand to serve afternoon tea and highballs. Friends of sleek and elegant actress Leatrice Joy—who popularized the short "bobbed" hairdo that became the rage of the era and who married John Gilbert in 1922—were no doubt equally impressed by her dutiful black maid Julia Hudlin.

SERVANTS MAKING THE ROUNDS

Sometimes, servants made the rounds, going from one palatial residence to another, climbing the social ladder as much as their status-conscious employers. Julia Hudlin eventually left Leatrice Joy and later worked for the even more glamorous actress Dolores Del Rio. Over the years, the shrewd Blanche Williams worked for such actresses as Rosalind Russell, Hedy Lamarr, and Zsa Zsa Gabor. But Williams's most famous employer was Hollywood's first blonde bombshell, Jean Harlow.

The servants proved themselves indispensable. "In the old days, before the union brought in wardrobe mistresses," actress Rosalind Russell recalled, "a star's maid handled her wardrobe, ran back and forth between set and dressing room, fetching hats and gloves and furs, not to mention

ABOVE: *Cary Grant and Randolph Scott in their bachelor pad with their trusty butler Jim.*
AT LEFT: *Service with a smile: Lauren Bacall with actor/ servant Freddie Clarke.*

cooking the star's breakfast and lunch and bringing her glasses of water and ashtrays." Russell developed friendships in the 1930s and 1940s with her maids Blanche Williams and Hazel Washington. Often, servants became an integral part of a star or filmmaker's life.

Many stars of the silent era, having come from working-class backgrounds without formal educations, were insecure in social situations and uneasy about handling their stardom, their money, and their fame. Some felt more at home with the domestic help, people with whom they didn't have to pretend. Word spread that Garbo, shy and nervous about speaking English, tried learning the language from her black maid. The Swedish star, who at times felt culturally adrift and isolated, may have learned a few other things from her servant. In the 1930s, when Ethel Waters popularized Irving Berlin's "Harlem on My Mind," a tale of longing for a familiar place and time, in the Broadway show *As Thousands Cheer*, Garbo apparently couldn't get enough of the song. Gossip columnist Sheila Graham reported that when Garbo went to nightclubs in London, that was the song she always requested. Garbo's domestics knew her eccentricities. When her chauffeur-driven car would depart from MGM, Garbo, fearful of being recognized by passersby, would hide on the floor of the vehicle— and make her maid, Hazel Washington, do the same, knocking Hazel "clean off the seat." "Pow!" Washington recalled, "I was down there wrestling on the floor, and I didn't know what hit me." When Garbo wasn't working on a film, she also didn't see much point in continuing to employ her servants. "Because I was willing to pay Hazel fifty-two weeks a year," said actress Rosalind Russell, "she came to work for me."

SERVANT BLUES

Occasionally, employers became embroiled in a crisis confronting one of their servants. At his home in Hollywood, Paramount executive B. P. Schulberg and his highly cultivated wife Ad, who later became one of Hollywood's major agents, had their meals prepared by their Negro maid/cook, Lucille, and were driven around town by their black chauffeur, Lloyd. The couple had brought their light-skinned colored governess, Wilma, with them from New York to care for their children. But away from family and friends Wilma struggled to adjust to her new life.

Then she met a white studio electrician named George who worked on an apartment that was set up for her above the Schulbergs' garage. When

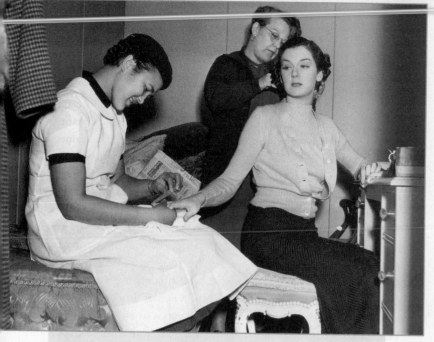

Striking a pose: Hazel Washington, giving a publicity-style manicure to Rosalind Russell, her employer and future business partner.

a romance blossomed, Wilma discussed the situation with her parents back East. But in the Hollywood—indeed, in the America—of the time, there was little hope for the two to marry. One afternoon, Ad Schulberg sat her governess down for a frank talk. "Even if you tell him you're"—there was a discreet pause—"what your background is, and he says it doesn't matter, believe me in time it will. Especially if you have children. And they turn out to be—well, the color of your sister. Or your father. It might not matter to people of intelligence and education. But is it fair to the children themselves? They could go through hell, raised out here in a white neighborhood. And sooner or later, it's bound to affect your relationship with George." That afternoon, Wilma cried. Then she broke off the romance.

Afterward, Budd Schulberg would see her sitting on the balcony above the garage, "nodding at me with a smile of gentle resignation." When the two would talk, Schulberg felt "as if the light was slowly flickering out of her." In time Wilma grew ill and left sunny Los Angeles to return to New York.

SERVANTS GETTING THAT BIG BREAK

Any number of servants yearned for careers themselves, and they understood that servanting was something akin to acting, a form of show business itself. On cue, you had to smile, nod, agree, acquiesce, soothe, reassure, comfort, and charm—often when you didn't want to. You also had to please people you frequently couldn't stand. Hollywood's colored domestics were like servants everywhere in the country, except that their role playing was far more intense, matching the dramatics of their employers. Servanting was also a way to get a foot in Hollywood's door.

Madame Sul-Te-Wan again proved a pioneering spirit here, having first cleaned out dressing rooms for the cast of Griffith's *Birth of a Nation*—while at the same time forging a close relationship with the filmmaker. Louise Beavers—another of Leatrice Joy's maids—also always aimed to please. Chunky, round-faced, with large, expressive eyes and a cheery, relaxed disposition, Beavers was a model domestic. But the first chance she got, she dropped her real apron and put on a movie-made one. Her on-screen roles were perhaps no different from those she had originally *played* while in Leatrice Joy's employ. The same was true of Fred Clarke, who worked for Humphrey Bogart but slipped out of his butler's uniform whenever possible to appear in such movies as *Blossoms on Broadway* and *The Kid from Kokomo*.

Sometimes, when a Hollywood servant got a break, he or she could be just as high-strung as the employer. When Mae West's maid Libby Taylor first arrived in L.A. from New York, she, like Beavers, appeared devoted to her employer, eager to prove she was all things to Mae: "watchdog, dresser, personal maid and guardian angel." But once acting roles came Taylor's way, she had little time for Mae. "When she began wanting me to wake her up in the morning," West once quipped, "I told her she'd better stop being a maid and give all her time to the public." As it turned out, Taylor played West's maid in *Belle of the Nineties* in 1934.

OSCAR THE BOOTBLACK

Oscar Smith was also shrewd; he first worked as a valet for Paramount Pictures star Wallace Reid. When the handsome all-American Reid died at age thirty-two while in a sanitarium where he had been treated for an addiction to morphine, Smith apparently kept quiet about whatever he knew of the actor's drug usage. He stayed on at Paramount, where he operated a shoeshine stand. "Oscar the Bootblack, as he was known to thousands of white employees on the Paramount lot, had his stand just outside the main studio gate," recalled Budd Schulberg, whose father was a vice president at Paramount. There, Smith learned to give Hollywood what he knew it enjoyed, its version of an acceptable, sometimes laughable image of an African American man. "Part of his job was shining shoes and part was serving as a squealing, supposedly good-natured target for the passersby who would sneak up behind him and goose him outrageously," said Schulberg. "He knew the names of everybody on the lot and he'd chuckle, 'Now, Mr. Sutherland' [Eddie, the comedy director]—or 'Mr. Holt' [Jack, one of the stars]—'You stay 'way from me, heah? You stay 'way from me!' Sometimes they'd flip him a quarter or half a dollar just to hear his exaggerated squeals. Oscar probably earned more money every day than the average extra. And he presided over his stand rain or shine. I thought he was happy, when I was twelve."

More ambitious than he appeared, Smith emerged as one of the early African Americans considered by the black community to have something of a position at a studio. Eventually, Smith persuaded Paramount executive Jesse Lasky that he could add something to Paramount's movies. Lasky "has made a huge success out of one of our boys in the person of MR. OSCAR SMITH," reported *The California Eagle*. "Being in close proximity to the people who work and make pictures, he studied them and their ways carefully. Recently, he has had the opportunity to work in small scenes, almost immediately, the directors saw in him qualities that would fit him for more important roles. . . . Motion picture magazines have been loud in their acclaim of him. Better watch this fellow Smith, gang. He's a real rising star." From the 1920s to the mid-1940s, Smith played porters, valets, and chauffeurs in such films as *The Freshman, Midnight Madness, The Canary Murder Case, The Fleet's In,* and *Henry Aldrich Plays Cupid.*

Later, when a teenage Schulberg, enrolled at Deerfield Academy, began researching the history of lynching in America, his thoughts turned to Paramount's bootblack. "The closest I had ever been to a lynching was the playful if sometimes spiteful goosing of Oscar the Bootblack at Paramount Studio," recalled Schulberg.

SLICKEM

But best known among the early studio workers was Harold Garrison, who also ran a shoeshine stand—at MGM. Nicknamed "Slickem"

Paramount Pictures' bootblack turned actor, Oscar Smith.

(sometimes, "Slickum") because of the spit shine he could put on a pair of shoes, Garrison was known for doing a little song-and-dance routine as he used his shoeshine brush. Sometimes requested by MGM to chauffeur Irving Thalberg and other executives, he also had a reputation for being a confidant of various stars and studio people. Like Oscar Smith, Slickem may have been—in the eyes of the folks at MGM—simply a shoeshine boy, but *he* never saw his role as so limited. Through his shoeshine stand, he channeled his energies and ambitions, in a sense to build some kind of lopsided power base. Slickem always kept his eyes and ears open—not only for job opportunities but also for personal information. When MGM produced movies such as *Hallelujah* and *Operator 13*, which employed large numbers of black actors and extras, Slickem was hired to work behind the scenes, to help manage the crowds.

Both Smith and Slickem were servant icons at their studios. If you did not know them, you were not an insider in the industry or certainly not part of the life at Paramount and MGM. As boys, Budd Schulberg and his friend Maurice Rapf, whose father, Harry, was an executive at MGM, would compare the movies, directors, and star discoveries of their fathers' respective studios. "We even compared bootblacks—the only Blacks I remember on the lot," said Schulberg. "I had Oscar and he had Kid Slickum."

KEEPING THE STUDIO IN ORDER

Other industrious newcomers also scrambled to find work at the studios—from the wardrobe departments to the janitorial services. Lula Evans, a former schoolteacher from Little Rock, Arkansas, had moved to Los Angeles in 1918 with her husband. To qualify as a teacher in California, she needed three more years of education. But when her husband suddenly died, she had to find immediate employment to support her two children, Lois and Will. Desperate to keep herself financially afloat, she took a job as a maid to actress Norma Shearer. Evans and Shearer got along well. When she left the actress's employ, Evans was put on the payroll at MGM, where, in 1923, she became the head matron in charge of stars' dressing rooms, a position she held for more than twenty-five years.

Each morning, the seemingly quiet Evans arrived at the studio and promptly opened the building at 5:15 A.M. It was said that she kept the keys to the studio. The stars would arrive about 6:00. Lula helped many of them dress, and like others in the services, she witnessed their good days and their bad, their sensitivities or their biases. When she had to deal with a British star who "didn't want a brown-skinned woman to attend her," Lula simply quietly went about her work. But in the 1930s, Jean Harlow—"A Honey. Very democratic"—invited her to lunch. She also tried to reassure a very nervous Garbo. "Very hard to know," said Evans. "Timid—shy about her English. I even had to answer her telephone for her." Of all the MGM stars in the years to come, she once said she found Katharine Hepburn "the most democratic in her general attitude towards everyone—not only to Negroes, but to anyone downtrodden and oppressed."

The last thing Evans wanted was for her sixteen-year-old daughter, Lois, to have to go into domestic service. She yearned to see young Lois become a doctor. Knowing that a medical doctorate was an expensive degree to acquire, Lois instead decided on a career in chiropody. For four years, Lula saved every dime she could to earn money for Lois's tuition and board at San Francisco's College of Chiropody. During her summers off, Lois worked as a maid. Shortly before Lois's graduation, Lula went to her old employer Norma Shearer, now the wife of MGM's production head Irving Thalberg. The two launched a campaign for Lois to become the studio's official podiatrist. Lula recalled that Shearer had to "fight right to the top." But once the young Dr. Evans was put on the MGM payroll, she was ensconced in an office in MGM's screenwriters' building and became known as the Foot Doctor to the Stars; her patients included MGM's top performers and executives: everyone from Myrna Loy, Judy Garland, Greer Garson, Ann Miller, Jeanette MacDonald, Irene Selznick, and hairstylist Sydney Guilaroff to Louis B. Mayer himself.

Lois Evans discovered that her patients had a great deal of curiosity about Negroes, and she once said she had to indulge in "a lot of race talk." "I treat some patients who ask right away how I happened to become a doctor. What they mean is how did a colored girl rise so high. Some say, 'When I talk to you, Dr. Evans, I never think of you as being colored!' Or they express surprise when I say I'm a Methodist Episcopalian. But I guess they don't realize they're being insulting." For Lois, life at the studio was never "a bed of roses." "Some people tried to get me out of Metro-Goldwyn-Mayer right after I went there. But a woman doctor is regarded as kind of an oddity—people sort of think I'm better than I really am. That's made it easier." Lois also opened an office for private practice away from the studio. She and her mother were so well known within black L.A. that eventually they ended up on the cover of *Ebony*.

Lillian Moseley spent years climbing her way up the ladder in Hollywood, going from one servant job to another. After working for actress May Allison, she took a job with actress Leatrice Joy. (Joy employed some of the most colorful and resourceful maids in the business.) Joy wanted her studio to pay Moseley's salary. But Paramount balked and agreed to pay her twenty-five dollars a week only after Moseley qualified as a makeup woman to Joy. Later, Moseley worked for the wife of filmmaker Frank Borzage, director of such 1920s films as *Humoresque, Seventh Heaven,* and *Street Angel.* She had no qualms about domestic duties—actually, she saw herself as an assistant—and always believed her employment with people in pictures enabled her to live without the usual daily discrimination that most African Americans experienced. "In my work with the stars, I've traveled many miles and in foreign countries, too," she once said, and "not as a maid, but as a personal companion." She recalled that on trains she had her own drawing rooms and that when she "traveled to Honolulu with the Frank Borzages, local citizens would invite the producer to dinner.

Upon inquiry as to the number of guests in his party, he would reply, 'We are four, my wife, her companion, my brother-in-law, and myself.' "

On those occasions when Moseley did have problems, she spoke out. At a hotel in New York, she was told by an elevator man not to take the front elevator, instead to go to the back entrance. But she wouldn't hear of it. "I wasn't a servant," said Moseley. "I was a guest in his hotel and I told him so." She immediately contacted Mrs. Borzage, who called the man on the phone. When he told her that it hadn't been him but someone else who had spoken to Moseley, Moseley said, "That isn't true. You were the boy who told me to use the freight elevator. You and nobody else." Director Borzage's wife said "that if I couldn't go up on the front elevator, we would check out of the hotel immediately. I didn't have any trouble after that." With the Borzages, Moseley traveled extensively to countries as distant as China. Moseley eventually returned to Los Angeles and worked for actress Ann Sothern.

Working for a major star in one capacity or another gave you status within the industry. When a black extra—or even an actor or actress—showed up on the set or at the front gate of a studio in the mid-1920s, he or she was, in status-conscious dreamland, really *nothing*. But when a star's personal domestic arrived, generally heels clicked and he or she was accorded a degree of respect.

In the 1930s, Moseley became a matron at Columbia Pictures. There, she was well known both to Columbia's contract players and to stars on loan from other studios. Like many studio employees, Moseley no doubt lived vicariously through the magnetic figures whom she served. She relished the afternoon that she ran into MGM star Clark Gable so many times that he told her, "This must be our lucky day, Lillian." Developing friendships with performers like Joan Blondell and Lucille Ball, she also comforted the sweet, vulnerable Rita Hayworth through the actress's marriages to Orson Welles and Aly Kahn.

Moseley was keenly aware that she was probably underpaid by the studio. "One never could get rich on wages alone," Moseley once said. "A matron's pay averages from $1.25 and $1.50 an hour." But she knew how to pull in an extra dollar or two or more by doing favors for the stars. What certain stars, such as Rita Hayworth, might value most was an ear—to listen to their troubles—and of course, discretion. "She doesn't care for small talk and nothing infuriates her as much as a petty gossip," Moseley once said of Hayworth. "She wants her curtains drawn together to keep out the sun and she wants soft music on the radio—a twilight atmosphere for her mornings." Early on, Hayworth confided her attraction to international playboy Aly Kahn and later invited Moseley to her wedding. Moseley knew, however, that unlike Hayworth, other stars loved gossip—as long as it wasn't about them—and in some cases, they knew they could rely on their servants to get some juicy tidbit from another performer's domestic help.

Sometimes, stars knew the names of servants of other big stars—who would serve them at lunches, dinners, or parties and whom they might corner in the kitchen for an extra slice of cake *or* a little dirt on what was happening with the other guests that evening. Servants or studio employees like Moseley understood that in Hollywood, information of almost *any* kind—and again, discretion—were forms of power or a way to maintain one's position in a star's home or within the studio system. Moseley appeared to know when to play her hand and when not to. On Christmas mornings, she would usually receive "three bottles of champagne—each with a check wrapped around the bottle—from Melvyn Douglas, Ralph Bellamy, and Cary Grant," she said. "But I never did favors for stars as much for money than as for the joy of giving."

SERVING IN THE MIDST OF STAR SCANDALS

Never was the importance of some black domestics more apparent in the 1920s and the years to come than in those cases in which a star might be at the center of a scandal. When Jean Harlow's sexually tormented husband Paul Bern, an executive at MGM, was found nude, lying in a pool of blood, dead from a self-inflicted gunshot wound in Harlow's home in 1932, the blonde star's maid Blanche Williams as well as MGM's bootblack Slickem were grilled at the L.A. coroner's inquest about Bern's activities on the night before his death. While on various chauffeuring missions, Garrison, of course, became familiar with the haunts and forbidden pleasures of any number of MGM employees. Slickem informed the police that he had driven Bern to The Ambassador Hotel, that the dead man had always carried a gun, and that Bern had spoken of suicide. Williams testified that she believed Bern had committed suicide.

During the following years, Williams was witness to Harlow's drunken outbursts as well as her affection. Blanche was one of the few "people who never get on my nerves," said Harlow. Finally, Williams saw Harlow suffer a painful death from acute nephritis at age twenty-six. As might be ex-

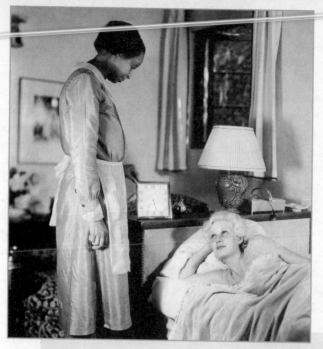

*Seeing a star through scandal and death: Blanche Williams
with her employer, Jean Harlow.*

pected, throughout Harlow's ordeals, Williams and Slickem were models
of discretion. But the idea was that if anyone wanted the real scoop—the
real dirt—then they had to talk to the help.

One of the early domestics who found himself embroiled in the seedier
side of Hollywood life as well as a player in a headline story was Henry
Peavey, manservant to the filmmaker William Desmond Taylor. An important director at Famous Players–Lasky, later Paramount Pictures, Taylor was considered a ladies' man and had well-known relationships with
movie comedienne Mabel Normand and ingenue Mary Miles Minter.
Dapper and sophisticated with a rather mysterious background, he lived in
one of the fashionable bungalows in a courtyard on Alvarado Street in the
Westlake district.

There, Taylor was attended by Henry Peavey. On the gossip mill, everyone seemed to take for granted that the high-pitch-voiced, rather prissy
Peavey—once described by Kenneth Anger, in his sensationalistic book
Hollywood Babylon, as a man who "liked to crochet doilies and scarves"—
was homosexual. In Hollywood, follies and foibles, eccentricities and sex-

ual peccadilloes were grist for the gossip mill, but no one put heavy moral tags on unconventional behavior. Anything out of the ordinary would be tolerated as long as such behavior never surfaced to affect public perceptions about the morality of the movie colony, which consequently might affect the box office. Also, the last thing anyone wanted was for some self-appointed guardians of morality—the church and civic leaders around the country and opportunistic politicians—to dig up some dirt and then come crawling all over the industry. Although the engagements, marriages, separations, divorces, and conventional affairs of stars might be frowned on by the morality watchers, such goings-on were becoming commonplace and accepted (as well as enjoyed) by much of the public. But public revelations about anything out of the norm could be trouble. So *unusual dalliances* could never be brought to light. That was a code by which the film colony was already living in the mid-1920s.

That code, however, was violated on the morning of February 2, 1922, when Peavey arrived at the bungalow on Alvarado Street and found William Desmond Taylor faceup on the floor of his study, dead from a bullet pumped into his back. Stunned and then hysterical, Peavey ran into the courtyard, where he screamed at the top of his lungs that Taylor had been killed. "Henry Peavey, the soprano manservant," wrote Kenneth Anger, "traipsed up and down sedate Alvarado Street like a demented thing, incessantly screaming, 'Dey've kilt Massa! Dey've kilt Massa!' until much later, some neighbor phoned the cops to 'come collect the crazy coon.'"

Slowly, details were leaked to the press that made the William Desmond Taylor murder one of Hollywood's great juicy, sexy scandals, all the more sensational because crucial evidence appeared to have been destroyed. By the time the police showed up at the bungalow on Alvarado, Paramount executives were already on the scene. In an attempt to dispose of any incriminating items, the men started burning papers in the fireplace. In this age of Prohibition, Taylor's illegal liquor was disposed of. Evidence of any sexual indiscretions was also destroyed. Also present was Mabel Normand, along with actress Edna Purviance—a costar and one-time lover of Charlie Chaplin—who lived in the bungalow court. Purviance had telephoned Normand as soon as she heard of Taylor's death. Now she stood watching as Normand searched for her love letters to Taylor. The police found Peavey in the kitchen washing dishes. "During all of this commotion," commented historian Sidney D. Kirkpatrick, "on the floor of the study, William Desmond Taylor, one of the most important directors in Hollywood, lay dead."

Soon, there was a lineup of suspects. The main focus was on Mabel Normand and Mary Miles Minter, both of whom had visited Taylor the night before he was killed. When it was learned that Minter's mother, Mrs. Charlotte Shelby, appeared to have an interest in Taylor, she, too, became a suspect. Much discussed was Taylor's closeness to Peavey and the fact that the director had paid the rent on a nearby room where Peavey sometimes stayed. A week earlier, Peavey had been arrested in nearby Westlake Park for soliciting young boys. On the day of the murder, Taylor had been scheduled to be in court to vouch for Peavey's character.

When Taylor's background was investigated, nothing was as it at first seemed. This dashing bachelor had actually been the once very married William Deane Tanner, who had left a wife and daughter in New York. Women's lingerie was found in Taylor's closet. And it looked as if this rather polished, elegant man-about-town had been carrying on affairs with all three of the female suspects. But that wasn't all. Reporters uncovered information about Taylor's frequenting "queer meeting places" where "strange effeminate men and peculiarly masculine women dressed in kimonos sat in circles, where guests were served marijuana, opium and morphine, the drugs wheeled in on tea carts." Speculation about Taylor's relationship with Peavey continued to grow. Obviously, the employer and employee were friends. Were they also more than that?

The story stayed in the headlines, and public outcries were heard about the depravity of the movie industry. The fact that Normand had been involved in this tawdry tale marked the beginning of the public's disenchantment with her. The virginal Mary Miles Minter also saw her movie career end. Peavey discovered that there was no place for him in Hollywood either, not even as a domestic. His last statement to the press came in 1930, when he said that "Taylor had been killed by a famous actress and her mother" and that he "had been silenced by authorities and told to 'get out of town.' "

For decades, the identity of the murderer remained one of Hollywood's great unsolved mysteries. Fascinated by the case, Taylor's contemporary, director King Vidor, investigated the killing on his own in the 1960s and 1970s. What he uncovered was a scenario even Hollywood could not have imagined. Vidor discovered that the actual murderer was the jealous mother of Mary Miles Minter, Charlotte Shelby. And the supposed ladies' man Taylor actually had an interest in young men. Peavey apparently had procured boys for Taylor and was probably on such an assignment when he had been arrested in Westlake Park. Vidor believed that Taylor paid for

Peavey's room so he could use it as a secret hideaway, a place of assignation with the young men Peavey had picked up for him.

The Peavey story pointed up what everyone knew: that in Hollywood, it never hurt if you had someone to procure for you, no matter what your tastes. And servants, especially those working for unmarried stars and personalities, could be very useful. But the Peavey story was also a cautionary tale: if you do procure, don't get caught. Peavey moved to Sacramento, where he spent his last years in poverty. He died in 1937.

Another servant entangled in a headline scandal—albeit on the sidelines—was the woman identified simply as Sally, black maid to a sexy, up-and-coming, young white star named Helen Lee Worthing. The demure Helen Lee Worthing was a Ziegfeld girl, one of the captivating beauties who paraded in the Broadway *Ziegfeld's Follies*. With dark, expressive eyes and delicate features, Worthing was named one of the five most beautiful women in the world. Pursued by men, young and old, she once said, she had her pick. But love seemed to elude her.

By the mid-1920s, Worthing was appearing in such movies as *Janice Meredith*, with Marion Davies; *The Swan*, with Adolphe Menjou; and *Don Juan*, with John Barrymore. Of her appearance in *The Swan*, *The New York Times* critic wrote: "Miss Worthing is capital in this part, very pretty and carefully gowned." Clearly headed for stardom and enjoying Hollywood's fast-paced social life, Worthing had a wide circle of friends, many of whom were ambitious and en route to the big time. But Worthing's life and career took an unexpected, disastrous turn following a chance meeting with a physician.

One evening after leaving the studio while working on *The Swan*, Worthing attended a party in Beverly Hills. She returned home feeling ill. Due on the set early the next morning, she asked her maid, Sally, if she knew a good physician who could be called immediately.

"That I do, Miss Helen," Sally told her. "I know the best doctor in town. A colored doctor."

"I don't care if he is green," Worthing said. "Get him."

When Dr. Eugene Nelson walked into her bedroom that night, "something happened to my heart," Worthing recalled. Struck by his looks, she found him "quite handsome," she said, "with dark, rather sad eyes, crisp, black hair and skin smooth tanned to a light bronze." Cordial, helpful, and professional, Nelson examined Worthing, left medication for her, then politely said good night.

But the next morning, she heard Sally answer the door and then saw her carrying a box filled with dozens of roses. "To the loveliest lady in all the world. From her adoring doctor," read the card, which was signed by Eugene Nelson. Later, when he called to invite her to dinner, Worthing was in a romantic swoon as she confided in Sally, who helped her prepare for the date. Only Sally was aware of Worthing's attraction to this Negro doctor.

"Well, that night marked the beginning of the happiest days of my life," said Worthing. Afterward there were dinners in Chinatown and the San Fernando Valley—as well as outings to clubs for dancing and romantic drives along the coast and to Palm Springs.

Then one evening, within a month after they had met, the two drove "high up in the Hollywood hills to watch the sunset," Worthing recalled. "As I rested my head contentedly on his shoulder, I felt his arm go protectingly around me." Nelson then asked her to marry him. Worthing barely had time to answer him. "As we drove back to Hollywood, we were seized with a sort of recklessness. Life was suddenly wonderful, intoxicating and we were together. We decided to drive on down the coast to Tijuana and get married. The night was perfect—and as Gene's sleek, new Cadillac sped down the Coast highway, the waves danced like handfuls of shimmering diamonds from an almost full moon overhead. . . . The wedding ceremony was brief and—we were husband and wife." The couple had motored to Tijuana because interracial marriages were now illegal in California.

They checked into a hotel in La Jolla—"the jewel of the West Coast." "Our luxurious hotel suite looked out over the ocean and during the night I could hear the surf breaking on the rocks below," said Worthing. "Once I remember thinking, dreamily—the restless waves are like my soul—yearning and seeking for peace. And now at last I have found it."

But of course, this romantic evening was the quiet before the nasty storm. The next morning, Worthing returned to her apartment. Sally had the day off. Alone, Worthing picked up the morning paper and glanced at the front page. "What I saw stopped me dead in my tracks. My picture was staring at me from the paper and above it the headline: 'FILM COLONY SHOCKED AS HELEN LEE WORTHING MARRIES COLORED PHYSICIAN!' " Stunned that news of her marriage somehow had been leaked to the press,

Worthing collapsed onto her bed. For the first time, she thought of the consequences her interracial marriage might have on her career. Yet Worthing was determined to remain Nelson's wife, even later that evening when he appeared willing to dissolve the union if that was what she wanted.

The two moved into a luxurious home on Wilshire Boulevard. "I took Sally with me," said Worthing, still trusting her servant more than others in her life. Convinced that she could save her career and that her friends would accept Eugene once they had a chance to know him, the couple attended the Los Angeles opening of a Broadway play at the Biltmore Theater. She arrived wearing a mink and a corsage of orchids. By her side was Nelson in a tailored tuxedo. They were a striking couple.

But once they stepped out of their limousine at the theater, where crowds of fans and onlookers stood, Worthing saw another side of Hollywood of which she had naïvely been unaware. At first, she heard fans remarking on how lovely she looked. Then there were comments about her Negro doctor husband. Then a man in the crowd made a loud coarse remark that had the fans laughing. Worthing and Nelson rushed into the theater.

During intermission, she saw yet another reaction from friends and acquaintances. There were whispers, and when she approached an old friend from the *Ziegfeld's Follies,* Worthing was stunned when the woman "turned and looked at me, but there was no recognition or friendliness in her eyes. I might have been an utter stranger to her." Worthing never forgot "the ordeal of that night! No one spoke to me. Not one person and there were many there whom I knew well and some I had considered good friends. But many stared, women tittered and men's lips curled disdainfully. Backs were turned when I approached. But I stuck it out—a frozen smile on my lips, and unbearable pain in my heart."

Later that evening at a speakeasy, Worthing drank heavily, more than she had ever done in the past. She also looked intensely at her husband, "aware of all the pain that lay behind his eyes and the lines of anguish that life had etched in his face. Suddenly I felt a great rush of sympathy and understanding for the colored race who had fought so valiantly for their rightful place in this great American democracy. I forgot my own hurt in the realization that nothing is ever gained without some pain."

In the months—and years—that followed, Worthing endured other snubs and whispers whenever she and her husband were seen together.

Though she appeared in such other films as *Night Life of New York, Flower of the Night, Vanity,* and *Thumbs Down,* the movie offers soon dwindled. By 1927, at age twenty-two, she was already finished in pictures and out of money. "White Film Star Who Married Physician Is Gone Bankrupt," read the headline in the September 2, 1927, edition of *The California Eagle.* Worthing had listed liabilities of $1,986.62 with assets of $680.00, "of which she claimed exemption on $500." Slowly, she drifted into alcoholism and drug addiction. The marriage suffered and was later annulled. In 1948, Worthing, alone and broke, died from an overdose of sleeping pills.

Worthing's decline and her banishment from Hollywood served as a warning for many other stars who followed. Interracial relationships were clearly taboo, *perhaps* occasionally tolerated within the industry but only if carried on clandestinely, but even then, there could be problems and repercussions. An interracial marriage would spell the death of a white star's career.

POST–WORLD WAR I OPTIMISM: ALL AROUND TOWN

During the years following World War I, Los Angeles, like New York, enjoyed a rich outpouring of creative activities—in music and dance, in theater, in the world of nightclubs, in architecture. In this age when black and white soldiers were returning home after having witnessed unspeakable horrors on the battlefields of Europe, many Americans lived with a heightened awareness of the fragility of human life. A disillusionment had set in that in some respects also proved liberating. The old rules no longer applied. In the big cities, in particular, there was a desire to break free of past restrictions and hang-ups, to live each day more intensely, and to push beyond the old boundaries. These were the years of giddy flappers and fun-loving playboys, hard-drinking writers and adventurous artists, secretaries and regular Joes flocking to nightclubs and the movies in search of the latest thrill, the boldest and most daring new sensations. In urban areas, audiences also appeared receptive to new experiments in theater and art, which opened doors for African American creative talents, who, during the flowering of the Harlem Renaissance, were able to make new inroads in music as well in fiction, poetry, and drama. The promise of new opportunities also swept through Los Angeles like a wildfire, sparking a newfound optimism and confidence. Something seemed to be happening everywhere, all of which helped create a stronger sense of community in black Hollywood.

FAMILIAR FACES

During these years, Madame Sul-Te-Wan and Noble Johnson found new work and now had solid reputations within Los Angeles's black community, thanks partly to the black press. As aggressive as ever, Madame frequently turned up in the pages of *The California Eagle*, which ran a four-part series on her—"How She Arose from Obscurity to Stardom"—in the summer of 1926. A year later, the paper visited her on the set of the movie *Uncle Tom's Cabin*. Also visiting her at the studio that day, *The Eagle* reported, were Dr. John Somerville and his wife, Dr. Vada Somerville. The Somervilles were a well-educated, well-regarded black couple who took their social roles as community leaders very seriously. Yet they were as captivated by the spectacle of moviemaking as everyone else. By now, Madame herself was recognized on the black bourgeoisie's social circuit. Never would she truly be a member of such social circles. She was too much a character for that—and of course, lacked the background and education on which the black bourgeoisie prided itself. But her movie work was considered an achievement not to be ignored. She also understood the importance of an offscreen image. Never would she earn the big bucks, and she herself would comment that many a month, she wondered where her rent money was coming from. But she pinched her pennies, dressed fashionably and colorfully, and was able to draw attention to herself. She even managed to move onto the exclusive Beverly Boulevard, where "she is the only one of her type." All of this went over well in Hollywood.

The coverage indicated the hunger of the community and the press for a black presence in the movies. Yet while publicizing Madame's talents and accomplishments, the politically conscious *Eagle*, under the watchful eye of Charlotta Bass, was always quick to point out how Madame's career had been stunted by the movie industry's racial biases. "Madame is a real actress and we hope that some day she will really get something worth while to do. On any set you find her there is always someone to say that she is a D. W. Griffith find," the paper reported. "Sul-Te-Wan had the misfortune, in the eyes of the white man, to be born black. Else today her name might be spoken with reverence and her picture adorn the hall of famous celebrities."

Still the handsome outsider, the brooding Noble Johnson remained reticent. Though he worked far more than Sul-Te-Wan in feature after feature in the 1920s, he drew less press coverage. By the mid-1920s, other African American actors, such as Zack Williams, Floyd Shackelford, Charles Moore, and Edgar Washington, were also working in silent films, but none had anything approaching the status of Madame and Noble.

EXTRA, EXTRA

For many black performers, a big goal was often to find work as extras: those nameless, sometimes faceless, background performers. By the early 1920s, Los Angeles was overrun with thousands of hopefuls, mostly white, flocking to the film capital to find such work. Whites *and* blacks boarded streetcars every morning and headed out to the studios. "There were dozens of applicants for every job," wrote the historians Christopher Finch and Linda Rosenkrantz of early Hollywood. "And work was often assigned on the basis of favoritism, bribery, and sexual services rendered." These were the years when many young women—and some young men— were introduced to the casting couch. For most, a walk-on or bit part might materialize, but little more. Finally, the industry—in an attempt to avoid scandal—decided something had to be done to clean up a situation that was fast becoming wholly corrupt. In 1926, the major studios teamed with some of the smaller independents to create the Central Casting Corporation—a talent pool and clearinghouse for those seeking work as extras.

The Central Casting Corporation benefited the performers *and* the studios. If Cecil B. DeMille needed thousands of extras for a spectacle like *The King of Kings,* his studio casting directors simply contacted Central Casting. And now rather than hopping from one studio to another, an aspiring actor or actress checked with Central Casting for work. The bureau listed performers in various categories. Among them were the dress extras (who wore formal clothes), young extras, Oriental extras, and Negro extras. For the latter category, casting directors had been known to hunt up and down Central Avenue in search of colored performers. Typical of Hollywood procedures—for years to come, even—was an incident that musician Buck Clayton recalled during the time that the 1933 *King Kong* was being cast. "The casting people came down to Central Avenue to hire all of the Black people they could to use as natives in the movie" and hired "everybody they could find" for seven dollars a day. The next day, a studio bus picked them up on Central Avenue.

But once at the studio, Clayton had to pass still another test. "The casting people asked us to all line up. We got in line and they began selecting people from the line. It seemed to me that they were taking everybody until they got to me." He was rejected because they "just didn't want any light complected, gray-eyed natives running around in the *King Kong* movie, so I was probably the only person on Central Avenue that didn't get a job in the picture. That really hurt me. Too light to be black and too black to be white." Hollywood wanted its Negroes to look like its idea of what all Negroes were supposed to look like. Child star Eugene Jackson also recalled that the studios preferred black kids "with a dark complexion, big lips, and kinky hair." Light-skinned Noble Johnson, who appeared in the movie, was heavily made up for his role as the village chief. But otherwise, lighter performers need not apply. Only when spotlighting certain glamorous, sexy African American female stars would the movie companies seek lighter performers.

Already, there were black casting directors. "A casting office for colored people, run by Jimmy Smith and Charles Butler, was located on Twelfth and Central," recalled Eugene Jackson. Later, Jasper Weldon supplied extras.

Butler was considered the top casting director for African Americans. When he was hired by Central Casting in 1927 to find black performers for big pictures, he had a newfound status. "Mr. Butler is responsible for the collecting, classifying, and distributing of the Negro 'extras,' " reported Floyd Covington for the Urban League publication *Opportunity*. Etta Jones remembered that as a little girl, she and Vivian and Dorothy Dandridge were taken to Butler's office. "You would have to go through him," said Jones. "If he liked you, he would have you go out and audition at the studios." Butler was assisted by his wife, Sarah, who was also a minister. The choir at Sarah Butler's church was considered a good screening ground for her husband to locate talented performers to sing spirituals in talking movies. Some in Black Hollywood griped that Butler had too much power, but he remained a vital force for the next two decades.

During the 1920s, additional opportunities for black extras sprang up when Hollywood became infatuated with plantation dramas and "jungle pictures" set in "darkest Africa." Paramount hired about six hundred black performers to go to Palm Springs for two weeks of shooting on the Merian C. Cooper / Ernest B. Schoedsack production *Four Feathers*. Such Lon Chaney movies as *West of Zanzibar, The Road to Mandalay,* and *Where East Is East* employed so many black extras to play everything from Eskimos to Asians to Africans that within Black Hollywood, this former childhood friend of Noble Johnson was referred to as "the revered Lon Chaney." "Negroes are natural actors," Chaney's assistant told the Negro press. "You can pull any one of them out of the mob and they can act. It is only a matter of makeup and costume to create anything from a Chinaman to an Eskimo."

Aside from the movies, black L.A. also had a variety of theater productions that, though not on the scale of New York's, provided dramas, comedies, and musicals. Black vaudeville also flourished in the city. Angelenos were also always excited by the West Coast appearances of prominent black stars from the East, such as Ethel Waters, Bill "Bojangles" Robinson, and Duke Ellington. And the performances of the touring New York theater group the Lafayette Players drew crowds and headline coverage in *The California Eagle.*

With so much interest in the movies as well as theater, organizations for writers and performers sprang up. A group of actors formed the Erosion Club and elected Oscar Smith president. Spotting all the creative talent in Los Angeles, the visiting writer, sociologist, and social activist Charles S. Johnson—a prime mover in the Harlem Renaissance as well as the editor of the Urban League's new monthly publication *Opportunity,* and the man who Langston Hughes said "did more to encourage and develop Negro writers during the 1920s than anyone else in America"— formed the Ink Slingers, an organization for California's black writers, in 1926. Among the Ink Slingers members was Fay N. Jackson, who became an important writer covering black L.A.'s entertainment scene, with articles appearing in *The California Eagle* and *The Pittsburgh Courier.* In the 1920s, *The Pittsburgh Courier* was also reporting on the entertainment scene and, in years to come, would provide excellent coverage of black activities in Hollywood. Writer Wallace Thurman, an alumnus of the University of Southern California and later a resident of Harlem, where he wrote the play *Harlem,* launched the publication *The Outlet,* an L.A.-based journal on the West Coast arts scene.

PAUL WILLIAMS: NEW STYLE ARCHITECT

Perhaps the most unexpected arrival on the scene was architect Paul Williams. Just as unexpected was his impact on Hollywood. Before Williams, few envisioned that an African American could make a place for himself in this ever-growing city's hotly competitive, exclusive white men's club of architecture. A Los Angeles native, born in 1894, Paul Revere Williams was the younger son of Chester and Lila Williams, who had moved from Memphis, Tennessee, where Chester had worked as a waiter at that city's fashionable Peabody Hotel. In California, he opened a fruit stand at the city's old town Plaza.

Before Paul turned five, both his parents died. He and his older brother were sent to separate foster homes. He grew up in a kind of lonely isolation. At the Sentous Avenue Grammar School, he was the only black in his class. Early on, he started drawing pictures of buildings, fascinated by their shapes, sizes, contours, and interiors. A local businessman saw the drawings and encouraged the boy to think of a future in architecture. But when young Williams spoke of his dreams for such a career, his adviser at Polytechnic High dismissed the idea. "He stared at me with as much astonishment as he would have had I proposed a rocket flight to the moon," Williams recalled. "Whoever heard of a Negro being an architect?" the man told him.

Undeterred, Williams graduated from Polytechnic in 1912 and then studied for three years at the Los Angeles School of Art and the Beaux-Arts Institute of Design. To find a job, he looked up the names and addresses of the city's architectural firms. He ended up taking a nonpaying position at a firm where he believed he could learn more. But by the end of the first week, the company was impressed enough to put him on a salary of three dollars a week. In 1914, he won the first prize of two hundred dollars for the design of a civic center in Pasadena. A year later, he earned his certification as an architect. The next year, he began studying— as one of eight students—architectural engineering at the University of Southern California.

Williams made a point of learning different aspects of design: landscaping at the firm of landscape architect Wilbur D. Cook Jr.; and at the firm of Reginald D. Johnson, residential design, especially of homes in the then popular Hispanic-Mediterranean and Spanish colonial revival styles. Later, in the offices of John C. Austin, "Williams had his first opportunity to design buildings other than houses: office buildings, hotels, industrial structures, multiple housing, and public buildings," said architectural critic David Gebhard. "Williams not only experienced architectural practice on a large scale, but was also exposed to an even broader stylistic range, from beaux-arts classicism to the Hispanic and the Moorish." There, he assisted in the drawings for the city's famous Shrine Auditorium and the First Methodist Church. In 1920, he was appointed to the first Los Angeles City Planning Commission, where, Williams later recalled, "I looked forward to shaping our growing city."

Acquiring his architectural license in 1921, he was approached by a former classmate, Louis Cass, to design a ninety-thousand-dollar home in a new development known as Flintridge, named after "the same Senator Frank Flint to whom [as a boy] I sold newspapers," said Williams. "When Senator Flint asked me to design a number of homes in his new development, he was shocked to find out I was that same little newspaper boy." For Louis Cass, Williams created a dazzling English Tudor residence.

With the commission money, he opened his own firm, Paul Williams and Associates—with offices at the Stock Exchange Building and later on Wilshire Boulevard. A bold move. Running the risk of being rejected by real estate agents in an area where African Americans were hardly welcomed, Williams knew that because his clients would be among Los Angeles's upper crust, he had to locate outside the environs of Central Avenue. Williams was breaking down barriers for future generations in a city that still lived by its restrictive covenants. In 1923, he became the first African American member of the American Institute of Architects.

Soon came commissions from the rich and socially prominent. Lon Chaney hired Williams to design a home for him in the Hollywood Hills and afterward a weekend retreat known as "the rockhouse." Thirty years later, the home would be featured in the movie biography of Chaney, *Man of a Thousand Faces*. Still another home in the Hollywood Hills was designed by Williams for Victor Rossetti, the president of Farmers & Merchants Bank. The next year—1929—racehorse owner Jack Atkin asked him to create a home in Pasadena that recalled "memories of his childhood in England." Nothing captured his imagination, Williams said, as much as the creation of this spacious half-million-dollar English Tudor for Atkin. The residence was later used for the 1937 movie *Topper*. All these luxurious, stately homes reflected the success of their owners—and Williams's impeccable taste and masterful eye for detail, harmony, and a sweeping romantic grandeur.

Most likely, what aided Williams in his steady professional climb were his looks and demeanor and his own keen awareness of race in America. Solidly built with broad shoulders, light-skinned with dark, intense eyes, dark hair, and a well-groomed mustache—and probably often mistaken for being Hispanic—he looked like a courtly gentleman from another time and place. Perceptive, intelligent, and in many respects, conservative, Williams never overstepped his bounds with clients. Aware that some whites might not like an African American man leaning over their shoulders to show them a design, he learned to write upside down so that he could face clients while drawing a sketch they could see right before them.

He also knew that he was designing spaces in areas to which he himself would often be denied entry. So Williams did his job and went his way. Though working more and more for wealthy whites, he rarely socialized with them, preferring instead to relax with other young African Americans considered prime movers on the Los Angeles scene, those ambitious, race-conscious members of Du Bois's "talented tenth" who staunchly believed in doing something "to elevate the race." When he married a young beauty, Della Mae Givens, whom he met at the First A.M.E. Church, they were considered—even at this early phase of their life together—a dazzling young presence on the African American social scene.

Though Williams designed the Hollywood YMCA, more memorable for him was his design for the Twenty-eighth Street YMCA, the first for "colored boys and young men." "I had grown up going to the Ninth Street YMCA—twenty blocks away—and knew how badly we needed one in our community," he once said. "I also knew how important it was for young people to have role models, so I incorporated likenesses of the abolitionist Frederick Douglass and educator Booker T. Washington into the ornate design on the facade of the building."

Before the end of the decade, Williams foresaw great opportunities for the future—for himself and the city. "Los Angeles grew as many people, particularly in the entertainment industry, moved West," he recalled. "Coming from crowded New York City, these new Angelenos found the open fields of Beverly Hills an invitation to build new homes. And guess who wanted to be their architect?" Within a few years, Paul Williams would become one of Hollywood's foremost architects, considered the designer for the stars—making greater inroads in the industry than those black actors and actresses.

NIGHTS OUT ON THE TOWN

Along Central Avenue, new establishments sprang to life during the post–World War I era. Now black moviegoers could go to movie houses like the Rosebud and the Globe, later renamed the Florence Mills. The theaters also had special-event evenings, either amateur nights or appearances by stars. Some had Midnight Frolics: live minstrel-style revues with plenty of high-stepping dancers, singers, and comedy acts—and with plenty of audience participation.

Most spectacular was the Lincoln Theatre. Located at Twenty-third and Central, the theater opened in 1927—with a performance by L.A.'s Curtis Mosby with his Dixieland Blue Blowers. At a reported cost of half a million dollars, the Lincoln was considered by *The California Eagle* "the finest and most beautiful theater in the country built exclusively for race patronage." Everyone marveled at its spacious outdoor promenade, its grand lobby on the ground floor, and its swanky mezzanine above. Patrons could sink into deep-cushioned seats. Or between shows, they could lounge on luxurious divans and large sofas that were positioned throughout the theater. The Lincoln also had a $35,000 Wurlitzer organ and "the latest ventilation system," which ensured comfort in warm or cool weather. Backstage were fourteen elaborate dressing rooms and showers for performers. "Judging from the class of theater the Lincoln is to be and the class of entertainment that is to be given the public," *The California Eagle* urged Los Angeles's black community's support. "It has so often been said that all we want is an equal break with the other fellow and we would support it. Now is our chance to prove that theory because the Lincoln Theatre is as good as any theater in Los Angeles."

The Lincoln became best known and celebrated for its elaborate stage shows, its knockout chorus girls, and in the decades to come, its famous headliners, such as Bill "Bojangles" Robinson, Duke Ellington, and Count Basie. The big names were not only onstage. The theater's most successful early event was a special memorial benefit in honor of singer Florence Mills, shortly after her death in New York in 1927. Huge crowds gathered, and a line stretched from Twenty-third to Twenty-fifth streets. Inside, Bill "Bojangles" Robinson hosted the evening's festivities. That night, as on so many others, everything about the Lincoln exuded glamour, and well-dressed patrons clamored to get in. The word was that you had to look good even to work at the Lincoln. "On top of that, they had probably twelve of the most beautiful black girls in town as usherettes at the theater," musician Marshall Royal remembered. "A lot of the men around the neighborhood just came to look at the usherettes."

New nightclubs flourished too. In 1919, the Eighteenth Amendment had forbidden "the manufacture, sale, or transportation of intoxicating liquors." But at the clubs and speakeasies, you would never have known. There, the atmosphere was all the more heated and exciting because of the availability of illicit booze and dope.

Regardless of the financial burden of keeping a nitery going, the clubs just kept coming. The splashy opening in 1924 of Central Avenue's well-touted Humming Bird Cafe was front-page news in *The California Eagle*. Two years later, under different management, the Humming Bird was re-named the Legion Club. The Blue Bird Inn, known as a place for the rich of the community, showcased Paul Howard's Quality Serenaders. That group, of which a young Lionel Hampton was a member, also appeared at the Quality Café. For a time, the Kentucky Club was another place to hang. In 1927, Frank Sebastian opened a West Coast version of the Cotton Club in Culver City. Like its New York counterpart, the white-owned club catered primarily to white patrons but featured African American en-tertainers. A huge nitery, the West Coast Cotton Club had three separate dance floors and could accommodate twelve hundred patrons.

Frequently turning up at the clubs, especially the more exclusive ones, was L.A.'s select group of black doctors, lawyers, schoolteachers, and other professionals. Regular everyday folks would also save for a big night out. During these times when people still *dressed* to go out, no matter what their day jobs, no one dared show up at a club looking, as the popular say-ing went, like a field hand. Patrons paraded about in the latest glitzy high fashion: women in satin and silk gowns with jewels, men in well-tailored suits and ties. Also arriving in style were the servants to the influential or powerful in the town. Lionel Hampton recalled a performance "at the an-nual ball of the Antique Art Club, one of the biggest black clubs in Los Angeles. A lot of the members were maids and butlers to the rich white Hollywood folks, or porters and attendants in 'comfort rooms' of the big stores on Rodeo Drive, and in those days if you worked for the high and mighty, you were pretty high and mighty yourself. The chauffeurs were the hottest things out there, with those slick outfits on—the chicks went for that."

But *the* hot spot was the Apex, which opened on Thanksgiving evening 1928. Showcasing West Coast talents, the Apex was owned by popular bandleader Curtis Mosby. The last or perhaps the only stop on an evening of high spirits, the Apex could boast of having all the amenities of a white nitery like the Cocoanut Grove, such as valet parking and a head waiter who knew whom to seat where and whom to ignore. Musician Marshall Royal recalled that people from Hollywood and Beverly Hills "came to go slumming. It was a Black-owned place that would have 90 per cent white audiences. The Blacks didn't have the money to spend. That was during Prohibition, and you had to hide your bottle underneath the table. The Apex would sell food and setups. Periodically, the federals would come in, raid the whole joint, and take everybody to the hoosegow."

Big movie stars like Fatty Arbuckle, the Talmadge sisters—Norma, Natalie, Constance—and cowboy hero Hoot Gibson showed up. Scouts for the studios and sometimes the more daring executives also sat in the audience bowled over by the kind of high-energy and provocative entertainment that couldn't be found in the white nightclubs. The studios may not have known what to do with certain talents, but they could spot talent. And the Apex and other clubs on Central Avenue were the places to find it.

At the Apex, a newcomer like singer Ivie (sometimes spelled "Ivy") Anderson—brown-skinned, slim, sleek, and elegant with a mellow, polished, sometimes melancholic style—became a great crowd pleaser and was dubbed L.A.'s Ethel Waters. Also performing were the Anderson brothers, the most talented of whom was Eddie, who danced as well as performed comedy routines. Other popular L.A. comedians known as Bilo (of the act Bilo and Ashes) and Rooster had patrons in stitches. Perhaps considered too ethnic or colored to make it in movies, Bilo—with his masterful double takes and impeccable timing—specialized in the kind of raunchy blue humor that Redd Foxx would popularize years later. Some black performers in the clubs did get their breaks. Ivie Anderson later was signed to be the girl singer for Duke Ellington's band; she became Duke's favorite female vocalist. Eddie Anderson would become famous and hugely popular as the manservant Rochester on Jack Benny's radio show in the next decade.

Studio scouts noticed Carolynne Snowden, who appeared at other niteries like Frank Sebastian's Cotton Club. But then how could they not? Tall, curvy, and brown-skinned with dark, curly hair and as dramatic as they come, Snowden was considered a performer to the nth degree, a woman ready to devote every minute of her day to making it. "I'd rather work than eat," she once told the press, "and it's to the worker that the

"SEBASTIAN'S COTTON CLUB"

Frank Sebastian's Cotton Club on the West Coast where its chorus girls were every bit as "tall, tan, and terrific" as their counterparts in New York.

plums fall." Born Carolyn Artiemissia Snowden in Oakland, California, she was making her way in the world at fifteen, soon after her mother's death. Discovered on a high-school stage in San Francisco by the producing team Fanchon and Marco, she seemed a natural. "I never had a lesson until Fanchon spotted me," she once said. "But all my life from the time I was a child, I practiced dance steps before a mirror, posing as youngsters will, the most graceful attitudes that I could." At a club in San Francisco, she became the first black performer to appear in a white show. A prized role followed in the popular 1923 West Coast black musical *Struttin' Along,* which starred blues singer Mamie Smith.

Fiercely ambitious, Snowden wanted to call the shots. She billed herself as Creole Carolynne and hired her own group of chorus girls and began directing, choreographing, and producing her revues. "Creole Carolynne Snowden with Her Dark-Town Tantalizers and Dancing Creoles" was how she was publicized when she presented her revue *Narcisse Noir.* At Frank Sebastian's Cotton Club, she was "The Queen of Jazz," when she appeared in a cast of forty dancers, singers, and other entertainers.

Carolynne Snowden, the perennial hopeful who was hired to teach Joan Crawford the Charleston.

In this age of the flapper when Clara Bow and Joan Crawford were heating up the screen, Snowden believed she, too, had the goods to make it in the movies. As much as her white counterparts, the haughty Snowden personified the hell-bent-on-breaking-the-rules modern young woman—not bound by the old prewar rules and restrictions that men had created. And perhaps from her point of view, she was just as startling a creation as that other ebony stallion who was knockin' 'em dead in Europe, Josephine Baker. She even told the press that the Folies Bergère had sought her as a replacement for La Baker.

Finally, the studios hired Snowden—not as an actress but to teach jazz dancing to such white stars as Constance Talmadge and Bessie Love and the Charleston to Joan Crawford. Some on-screen work came her way, too. She danced in von Stroheim's *The Merry Widow* and played small roles in *The Gilded Butterfly, Orchids and Ermine,* and Lois Weber's *The Marriage Clause.* Maintaining a backbreaking schedule, she performed in the clubs, often two or maybe three shows a night. Then she went to her home on East Fifty-fifth Street for a few hours of sleep, usually no more than four. By 8:00 A.M., she was at one studio or another. Snowden seemed determined to be the first black woman to make it in Hollywood. Not as a character actress, but as a sexy goddess.

Shrewdly making her way around town, she did all she could to get her name in the papers. One night, she took her entire company to the Legion Club for some fun and fast times—making sure the black press knew she was there. After she completed a sixty-eight-week run at L.A.'s Cotton Club, Snowden decided to take a vacation—for two weeks in New York. It was about time those easterners got to know something about her.

"Carolynne Snowden, Hollywood Movie Star, Dazzles New York When She 'Steps Out,' " proclaimed a headline in *The Pittsburgh Courier*. The black press was told of her every move and the details of her wardrobe: fifty dresses with shoes, hat, and gloves to match. "She has twenty ensemble suits and a cocoa brown ermine coat trimmed in fox," reported Floyd J. Calvin. "When she gets all decked out for the evening she is the cynosure of all eyes. Add to that her vivacious and charming personality and you have a complete picture of what an approved star from Hollywood is like." The paper also reported that Snowden had her own personal dressmaker/designer, identified as La Melle. And Snowden let it be known that at age twenty-three, she had a maid, jewels and furs, a chauffeured Locomobile, and a six-thousand-dollar roadster.

The publicity paid off. Snowden was offered engagements at New York's Roxy and Paramount theaters. But she turned them down to head back to L.A.

CURTIS MOSBY: MAN ABOUT TOWN

At the center of black club life was Curtis Mosby, who was not only the proprietor of the Apex but also one of early L.A.'s best-known bandleaders. His Dixieland Blue Blowers was for a time the house band at the Lincoln and then at the Apex. Light-skinned with wavy hair and a broad, beaming smile, Mosby often had a cigar stuck in his mouth as he energetically promoted himself and his club. He almost looked like a caricature of the crusty, aggressive, self-promoting, backslapping club entrepreneur that he was. Among members of bands around the city, Mosby was considered only an average musician, who played the drums—or *tried* to play, so the joke went. But no one joked about his adroit and sometimes unscrupulous skills as a businessman. At various times, Mosby was brought before the musicians union for not paying his performers. Despite such hassles, Mosby was popular. He made important contacts at the studios and secured movie employment not only for other musicians but for himself, too. With his orchestra, he appeared in movies at Paramount, MGM, and Al Christie's studio.

Mosby and the young beauty Mildred Washington produced elaborate revues at the Apex—with sensuous, long-legged chorus girls every bit as "tall, tan, and terrific" as those in New York clubs. One of their most spectacular ventures, *A Night at the Orient,* used a Far East theme to spotlight its high-yaller chorus girls. Their *Spanish Revue* presented a portrait of Old World Spain with Ivie Anderson doing specialty numbers. Wednesday at the Apex was known as the night when other entertainers might show up. If someone like Carolynne Snowden was sitting in the audience, she would be asked to get up and perform. These could be fiercely competitive evenings, and entertainers had to be in top form to please their peers. In San Francisco, Mosby opened another Apex Club. In time, he also became the self-appointed mayor of Central Avenue. Annually, onlookers lined Central Avenue to see the parade led by Mayor Mosby, seated in a convertible and waving to the crowd.

To survive, Mosby understood when to play up to whites with power or influence, but he didn't kowtow. In 1929, when the Apex was going strong, the cops raided his club, and the police commission sought to close the place down. Mosby suspected, as did many others, that race lay at the heart of the police commission's complaints. Wisely, he informed *The California Eagle* of his troubles. Never one to back away from a battle, Charlotta Bass put the support of her paper behind Mosby. No one now wanted to see a top black-run establishment go under. Nor did anyone want to see the Apex's 150 employees out on the streets. Mosby's case became a cause célèbre.

"Police on with Their Program of Prejudice and Hate," read the headline in *The California Eagle*. "Let us hope it is a new day to Municipal policies and a new era is upon us and that we have a Police Commission which will act upon merit and not upon the cut and dried methods of gone by days," the paper reported. "Our good white folk should be as proud of Curtis Mosby and his musical genius as we are ourselves. It has advertised Los Angeles and pleased hundreds of thousands of our visitors with melody and harmony." The real issue here was that Mosby, a colored man, "was in somebody's way or somebody wanted him out of the way."

Throughout L.A.'s black community, the fate of the Apex Club was topic number one. A young white woman came to Mosby's general defense with a statement to the DA's office that she'd been asked by another white woman to lure Mosby into a compromising sexual situation—whereupon he'd be promptly arrested. If Mosby could be framed, the first woman would receive five thousand dollars, and the second, five hundred dollars. On the case's first day of hearings, the courtroom was packed with supporters for the Apex. The case didn't last long. The panel of "fair-minded and just Police Commissioners saw the situation and boldly without fear or favor said—AWAY WITH THIS and to Curtis Mosby said—GO YOUR WAY." The headline in *The California Eagle* proclaimed: "APEX NIGHT CLUB WINS SMASHING VICTORY AS POLICE COMMISSION DISMISS [*sic*] CHARGES FILED BY POLICE TO REVOKE PERMIT."

But Mosby still had to defend himself against charges that he had liquor on the premises of the Apex. For a time, he weathered the storms and kept his club going. Eventually, he lost the Apex and served a brief prison term. But he remained on the L.A. scene for years to come.

ALL ALONG THE AVENUE

Along with the new nightclubs, Central Avenue glimmered with the bright lights of stores, cafés, and restaurants. Hot nights were made cooler by the opening, in 1927, of the ice-cream parlor called The Vogue. Showbiz folks also gathered at Adams Sweet Shop to snack and swap stories. Musicians could buy records and sheet music, or just hang out, at the music store at Twelfth and Central run by the Spikes brothers, Benjamin and Johnny. Showbiz figures themselves, the brothers wrote the lyrics for the musical *Steppin' High* and were instrumental in helping musicians get work at the studios. Curtis Mosby also opened a music store on Central Avenue. In time, all along the boulevard there were barber shops, beauty parlors, doctors' and dentists' offices, cleaners, insurance companies, and churches. Also on the block, according to lifelong Los Angeles resident Willard Brown, was "a house of prostitution next to where I lived on Ninety-seventh and Central." Stories spread that many a Hollywood star paid a visit to the establishment. "My mother worked there as a cook," said Brown. "And I can remember my mother coming home and telling my sister, 'Guess who came in today?'"

CENTRAL AVENUE'S JEWEL IN THE CROWN:
THE SOMERVILLE

But the jewel in Central Avenue's crown was the hotel that opened on June 23, 1928. Named after its original owner, Dr. John Somerville, the Hotel Somerville became Black Hollywood's premier establishment. Born in Jamaica, known for his taste and intelligence and strong social consciousness, Somerville had migrated to San Francisco at age twenty, then moved to Los Angeles, where for two years he worked in a bowling alley, saved two hundred and fifty dollars, and enrolled in the University of Southern California's dental school. His white classmates threatened to leave. But Somerville would not back off and became the first African American graduate of the university's dental school in 1907—*and* first in his class. When he took the state dental board exam, he scored the highest marks of the time. Later his wife, Vada, became the second black graduate of USC's dental school—and the first black woman certified to practice dentistry in California. Somerville became a United States citizen and the first black member of Los Angeles's chamber of commerce. He also became something of a legendary figure in the black community. Determined to help meet the housing needs of the influx of African Americans into the city, he built a twenty-six-unit apartment building in 1926, which was called La Vada. The Somervilles might sometimes seem pompous, but no one ever questioned their social convictions and accomplishments. For years, along with Charlotta and Joseph Bass, they fought tooth and nail for a free and open Los Angeles and an improved quality of life for black Angelenos.

As the community continued to grow, Somerville realized that black businesspeople and big-name entertainers came to town with few choices in accommodations. Comfortable rooming houses abounded, but none had the amenities of a first-class hotel. John Somerville envisioned a grand hotel for colored people: black L.A.'s answer to the posh Ambassador and Beverly Hills hotels at a time when African Americans were still not accepted at such tony establishments. Ads were taken out in *The California Eagle* inviting individuals to invest in the new hotel. Once ground was broken and construction began, the community anticipated its opening with bated breath.

An estimated two thousand onlookers lined the avenue the day the Somerville opened its doors. The hotel proved to be a dream come true. Patrons could sit in the beautifully furnished lobby with its colorful murals

Dr. John Somerville: the man who built
black L.A.'s first grand hotel, the Somerville.

and lavish tapestries. Or they might dine in the elegant dining room, which could accommodate one hundred. Above the dining area was a balcony where an orchestra would quietly perform. Guests could also be seated at the splashy outdoor patio with its fountain and potted palms. Throughout, impeccably groomed uniformed waitresses served meals from eleven in the morning to ten at night. The special price at the time of the hotel's opening? One dollar a plate.

Guests staying in the one hundred rooms enjoyed all the modern conveniences. Male guests could get haircuts at the barbershop on the ground floor. Female guests could get the latest in hairstyles—or a manicure—at the Unique Beauty Shoppe. Prescriptions could be filled and a variety of personal items could be purchased at the pharmacy. A dapper gentleman could breeze into the hotel's flower shop to buy a bouquet of roses or an orchid corsage for a lady friend. Banquet rooms were available for special occasions. Live entertainment was not provided at the hotel. But within a few months of the hotel's opening, Curtis Mosby opened his Apex Club and later there was a cocktail lounge called the Turban Room, both adjacent to the hotel. When the NAACP held its nineteenth annual national conference in Los Angeles that June, the opening session was held at Philharmonic Hall while early civil rights leaders gathered at the Somerville. W.E.B. Du Bois and James Weldon Johnson were guests along with Lincoln Steffens, Arthur B. Spingarn, William Pickens, and Mary White Overton.

Du Bois himself commented, "It was a hotel—a jewel done with loving hands. . . . It was full of sunshine and low voices and the sound of human laughter and running water. The hotel Somerville was an extraordinary surprise to people fed on ugliness—ugly schools, ugly churches, ugly streets, ugly insults. We were prepared for—well, something that didn't leak, that was hastily clean and too new for vermin. And we entered a beautiful new inn with a soul. . . . Funny that a hotel so impressed—it was so unexpected, so startling, so beautiful."

But Somerville's timing was off. After the stock market crashed in 1929, he lost the hotel. Then, Lucius Lomax entered the picture.

OLD MAN LOMAX COMES TO TOWN

For members of Los Angeles's black community, Lucius Lomax and Dr. John Somerville were polar opposites, representing the conflicting future drives and attitudes within Black Hollywood. Whereas Somerville and his wife, Vada, prided themselves on being educated, cultivated, upright emblems of a new day in Negro life, Lomax was a gritty, tough-minded, sometimes ruthless buccaneer from the other side of the tracks. Lomax emerged as one of Black Hollywood's most colorful characters—and an unexpectedly important figure in L.A. entertainment history.

Known in later years as Old Man Lomax, to set him apart from his son Lucius Lomax Jr., he was born in southeast Texas, the son of former slaves. With little education but vast reserves of ambition, he served in the United States military in the Spanish-American War and—for money rather than any political ideology—rode with Pancho Villa during the Mexican Revolution. Upon his return to Texas, he lived in high style—albeit through various shady endeavors. But trouble struck during a heated argument over a white woman. The story went that Lomax had killed a Texas Ranger, then had to get out of town. Whether true or not, he "climbed into his Stutz-Bearcat and drove to the West Coast," said his grandson. There, he boarded a ship that took him to Japan for two years. When he returned to the States, he lived in Seattle, where his granddaughter Melanie Lomax said, "He established a series of bootleg operations and whorehouses up and down the West Coast, starting in Yakima, Washington. His operations were gambling, whorehouses, and bootleg liquor, which he ran with his sister." "He was a thief and a killer," said his grandson Lucius Lomax. "He was not a drug trafficker [but] only because at the time he was 'in business' drug use was not widespread enough to be profitable. But he was involved in every other kind of illegal activity." Later he brought his network of illegal operations to Los Angeles. "Grandfather was a practical businessman who saw crime as the most profitable market for his talents."

A crusty man who could never be messed with, he always carried a gun. In time, he became the man whom anyone with a problem came to see: a kind of godfather for the African American community. Musician Phil Moore recalled that when he first relocated from Seattle, where his father, also a gambler, had known Lomax, he was told to speak to Old Man Lomax about getting situated in town. "He was the boss in the colored area and owned and ran most of the front and back room enterprises along Central Avenue." "Mr. Lomax was *the* businessman of this town," said Melanie Lomax. "When you wanted something, you went to Mr. Lomax. If you wanted a ticket fixed, if you wanted anything, you'd go to my grandfather."

Phil Moore remembered that he was "rather tall and bronze with straight dark brown hair and high cheek bones." He looked part black, part Native American, recalled his granddaughter. And he was "extremely handsome. Just startlingly so. And he just had incredible bearing."

"He did not marry," said grandson Lucius. "For his only mate, he had chosen a bourgeois schoolteacher from light-skinned, Black Philadelphia social circles." Her name was Minnie. The couple had one son, Lucius.

As his West Coast empire grew, Lomax eventually moved into a huge plantation-style home with a palm-lined paved driveway. Two cars were usually sitting in the drive: a Lincoln and a Studebaker, "always parked, forever immobile," said grandson Lucius. "There was one uncommon feature about his house. . . . Everywhere, in each room, under a cushion or under a pillow, on top of cabinets, in drawers and even in the refrigerator, there was a loaded pistol."

Once established in Los Angeles, however, Lomax sought respectability. "He now was a landed gentleman who loved to play golf," said Phil Moore, "and was a very good oil painter." His son graduated from Northwestern University and married an ambitious, bright young woman named Almena. Lomax Jr. was known as smart, hardworking, and trustworthy. Some found it hard to reconcile that Lomax Sr. and Lomax Jr. were indeed father and son. "He was determined he would have a child who was educated," said Melanie Lomax. "My grandfather was trying to legitimize the next generation." Still, the real route to legitimacy and respectability for Old Man Lomax ultimately became the hotel that John Somerville lost. Boldly, Lomax bought the hotel. The details of the acquisition would always be murky—but what a coup, to possess one of black L.A.'s classiest establishments. "It didn't go over well with Somerville," said Melanie Lomax. "Nor did it go over well with him that its [name] was changed." The Hotel Somerville was renamed the Dunbar, after African American poet Paul Laurence Dunbar.

Perhaps to the dismay of John and Vada Somerville, the hotel, as the Dunbar, saw its giddy glory days, becoming *the* place where the famous and the infamous, the glamorous and the socially ambitious, gathered to see and be seen. Over the years, when the African American community's most prominent personalities and leaders hit town, they headed straight to the Dunbar. A gallery of famous entertainers might be spotted sitting in its lounge. Bill "Bojangles" Robinson. Duke Ellington. Louis Armstrong. Thurgood Marshall. Langston Hughes. Count Basie. Lena Horne. Dorothy Dandridge. Billie Holiday and Nina Mae McKinney—those troubled, doomed divas, lost and emotionally adrift—found sanctuary in rooms at the hotel where a young social gadfly, actor Joel Fluellen, helped nurse their psychic wounds. Lomax himself occupied the penthouse suite. A special suite was also kept for Ellington. Lomax installed his son as the operator of the Dunbar Hotel's cocktail lounge. In time, Hollywood stars such as Cary Grant, Gary Cooper, James Cagney, and Randolph Scott popped into the cocktail lounge, where the drinks were good and the atmosphere festive. For years, the Dunbar stood as a symbol of all that was glamorous and exciting on Central Avenue—and in Black Hollywood.

Lomax remained a powerful figure for decades, yet he never quite acquired the respectability he sought. He remained in control of himself, however, to the bitter end. After he was diagnosed with cancer, he spent his last days in pain, confined to his large home, cared for by his son and a servant. One day when Lomax Jr. was not in the home, the elder Lomax asked his servant to cover his bed with a rubber sheet. Then, Lomax gave him the rest of the day off. "The Old Man laid down," recalled his grandson. "He reached under his pillow and pulled out a .44 revolver. He raised the barrel above his ears and shot himself." The rubber sheet was there to catch the blood.

The clubs, the theaters, the movie houses, the shops, the music and dance studios, even some of the African American churches, and the Dunbar were all becoming meeting places and stomping grounds that further contributed to this sense of an African American entertainment community. Hardly as hip as the Somerville/Dunbar, the Clark remained a lively establishment where some entertainers resided; where others stayed—mainly, if the Dunbar was booked up; and where Pullman porters would stop over between trips. The clientele tended to include African American social figures, too, solid members of the black bourgeoisie. Though black L.A. was far more spread out than Harlem, black show-business folks nonetheless got together regularly. They traded stories, talked about movie gigs at studios, dished dirt, consoled one another over missed opportunities or the lack of opportunities in the business. Feuds and rivalries developed. So did close friendships and professional partnerships. Just as with the larger Hollywood community, an entertainer understood the importance of being seen around town, of being considered a presence.

For those who preferred privacy, the entertainment industry would take its toll. In the larger community, where a star like Garbo would agonize over the necessity of public appearances, her studio, MGM, ultimately would create a mythic persona for her built around her need to be left alone. Black actresses such as Fredi Washington, Lena Horne, and the young Dorothy Dandridge would not have studios to shield them. Their private/professional lives would be held in a delicate balance.

Still, as the Black Hollywood community grew, the question uppermost in everyone's mind was whether big roles or big pictures for African Americans would ever materialize. A film that roused black L.A. was MGM's horse-racing drama *In Old Kentucky*, directed by John Stahl, which featured that perennial hopeful Carolynne Snowden as the servant girl Lily May. When the director signed her to a five-year contract with John Stahl Productions, all eyes in Black Hollywood briefly turned her way. "To a race that has produced such outstanding figures as Booker T. Washington, Roland Hayes and Paul Robeson another interesting name must be added—Carolynne Snowden, the only Negro girl who is today taking important parts in leading film productions," wrote Joseph Polonsky in *The Pittsburgh Courier*. But despite the fanfare, most of the attention in the 1927 *In Old Kentucky* went to a newcomer named Lincoln Perry, who became famous using another name, Stepin Fetchit.

Leading parts for colored performers now turned up. *Uncle Tom's Cabin* had been filmed before. But Harry Pollard's 1927 version at Universal was a full-scale, big-time feature that employed a large cast of black actors, including Madame Sul-Te-Wan, Louise Beavers, and Eugene Jackson. Universal immediately set out to cast Charles Gilpin in the title role. The most celebrated and admired Negro dramatic actor of his time, Gilpin had risen to remarkable heights in the theater. He grew up in Richmond, Virginia, the son of a nurse and a steel-mill worker, and had worked as a printer's assistant before traveling on the road with various minstrel companies. Between jobs throughout his career, he rolled up his shirtsleeves and worked again as a printer's assistant as well as a porter, an elevator operator, and a prizefight trainer. In 1915, he appeared in New York with the Anita Bush Players at the Lincoln Theater. Four years later, he made his Broadway debut in John Drinkwater's drama *Abraham Lincoln*, which convinced Eugene O'Neill that Gilpin was just the actor to play the title role in his play *The Emperor Jones*. Gilpin triumphed in the part. Afterward, the NAACP awarded him its prestigious Spingarn Medal in 1921. The Drama League voted him one of the ten people who had contributed the most to the theater that year. Some members balked at his selection and threatened not to show up at the league's awards dinner. But that night, Gilpin received a rousing reception. President Warren G. Harding also received him at the White House.

Yet Gilpin knew the prospects for a dramatic acting career were dim. In the theater, producers and directors still preferred the black buffoons and dense servants. Gilpin was defiantly proud, and his professional frustrations made him quarrelsome and easily riled. While performing in *The Emperor Jones* in New York, he changed the dialogue, refusing to say the word *nigger*, using instead *Negro* or *colored man*. The change infuriated O'Neill, who threatened to fire him. "I am a race man—a Negro and proud of being one," said Gilpin, "proud of the progress Negroes have made in the time and with the opportunity they have had. And I don't want the public to think anything different." Some nights, Gilpin drank during his performances. Other nights, waiting in the wings to go on, he would ask the stage manager, "What's the scene, what's the scene?"

Still, many hoped that Gilpin, who appeared in L.A. in a 1923 production of *The Emperor Jones* and also in the independently produced film *Ten Nights in a Barroom* in 1926, might become a movie star. Much talk circulated about Cecil B. DeMille's plans to do an all-colored picture—based on *Porgy,* the novel by DuBose Heywood and a stage success—with Charles Gilpin in the title role and Paul Robeson as the villain, Crown, but the project never materialized. Little seemed to go right for Gilpin on the West Coast. Tormented and restless, Gilpin was an odd man out, in all likelihood baffled by this town where everything was based on success and money. He reportedly clashed with Universal and walked off the set of *Uncle Tom's Cabin,* to be replaced by James B. Lowe, a good-looking stage actor hungry for a meaty role.

THEY SING, THEY DANCE, THEY TALK: SOUND!

Then came sound—and finally, the big pictures—which changed the color of the silver screen and led to an even more cohesive, vital, and *employed* Black Hollywood. In 1927, Al Jolson smeared burnt cork onto his face and sang his heart out to the tune of "Mammy" in Warner Bros.' *The Jazz Singer.* The talkie revolution had begun. Huge new sound stages were built. Vocal coaches were imported from the East to train the silent stars in *elocution.* Theater actors were in demand. And movie houses everywhere began wiring for sound.

Black Hollywood was suddenly abuzz with the news of the talking picture. The Harlem Renaissance had already made the Negro entertainer acceptable in theaters and clubs frequented by whites. Soaring sales of race records—those recordings by black artists for black listeners—had made music companies realize that record buyers couldn't get enough of artists like Bessie Smith, Duke Ellington, Louis Armstrong, and the champ of all crossover vocalists, Ethel Waters. Already, Noble Sissle and Eubie Blake—composers of the hit black musical *Shuffle Along*—had been seen and heard in an experimental DeForest Phonofilm short in 1923. Now the movies wanted the sound of Negro voices, and rumors sprang up that the Negro voice recorded better than a white one. In New York, Bessie Smith was tapped to make her only movie appearance in the 1929 short *St. Louis Blues.* That same year, Ellington—with the girl of his dreams by his side, the iridescent, melancholic Fredi Washington—was recruited to portray a suave and sophisticated hero, basically be himself, in the short *Black and Tan.* "The question has been continually raised whether there has been or will be a Negro star in Hollywood," wrote Floyd Covington in *Opportunity*. "With the introduction and improvement of talking pictures, comes perhaps the Negro's real opportunity to produce stars in his own right."

ZANUCK CALLING: GET ME ETHEL WATERS

The powerful Hollywood studios now hauled out the mikes to capture black sound. As Warner Bros. was about to go into production on its melodrama *On with the Show*, the studio decided to pull out all the stops. Not only would this be an all-talking picture with the stars Betty Compson, Louise Fazenda, and Joe E. Brown and with dancing by the Four Covans, but the studio also planned to shoot the picture in the then two-color Technicolor process. Then Warners learned that Harlem's Ethel Waters was appearing in Los Angeles on the high-powered Orpheum vaudeville circuit. For Black Hollywood, Waters was an almighty queenly figure from the East: celebrated, discussed, acclaimed. For the larger Hollywood community, she was a black star it couldn't ignore.

Everybody already knew something about her life and music. Born out of wedlock in 1896 outside of Philadelphia, Waters had grown up in a red-light district, where she ran errands for prostitutes, served as a lookout for pimps, and married at thirteen and divorced at fifteen. She then worked as a chambermaid in a Philadelphia hotel. Once she hit the road as a singer, she performed raunchy blues songs while doing bumps and grinds on stage, known as Sweet Mama Stringbean. Once she settled in New York in the early 1920s, Waters had "refined" her hot/cool style to become one of the first African American entertainers whom whites rushed uptown to see. Eventually, her hit records like "St. Louis Blues" and "Dinah" sold to record buyers, white and black, making her even more famous.

Life in and out of show business had not only brought Waters fame but had also toughened her. Stories flew all over New York and L.A.—then and in the years to come—about her stormy relationships with men *and* women. Her marriages to Eddie Mallory and Clyde Edward Mathews failed. So did her long-term affair with black impresario Earl Dancer. Seeming to thrive on the *drama* of romance, and spending money as fast as she got her hands on it, Waters once said she wanted to buy the current man in her life an automobile that stretched from one end of the block to the next. She likewise lavished gifts on her women. And she unleashed her fury on just about anybody who crossed her, raising holy Cain with night-club owners and managers she claimed had cheated her—and outcursing and outshouting those fellow performers she thought were trying to up-stage her. Her rivalry with Josephine Baker was legendary. She couldn't abide Lena Horne, who in the 1940s had the audacity to do a new version of "Stormy Weather," which Waters had recorded in 1933—and which had always been associated with her.

During much of her life, Waters remained scarred by her troubled childhood and the racism she experienced. Having been made to use back doors and side entrances for years, she had become embittered and, in the words of actress Fredi Washington, "suspicious of almost everyone." She never forgot the cruelty she had been forced to endure. "Only those who are being burned," she once said, "know what fire is like." Becoming in-creasingly difficult and easily agitated by the late 1920s, Waters didn't let anyone trample on her toes—or even look as if they would. Regardless of her reputation, Warner Bros. production chief Darryl F. Zanuck wanted Waters for *On with the Show.*

Composer Harry Akst, who was writing the score for the movie, saw Waters's performance at the Orpheum and afterward visited her back-stage. He discussed the proposed film, the studio, and his music. He showed her a tune on which he was working. The song was "Am I Blue?" Later, Akst and Waters spent time working together to get the song in shape for the studio to hear. Then he took her out to the Warners studio in Burbank. Tall, brown-skinned, big-boned, and shapely, with intelligent, perceptive eyes, and that quick temper, Waters carried herself in a stately manner. To any observer on the Warners lot, it must have been clear that this East Coast star had brought her hauteur to Hollywood. Introduced to production chief Darryl F. Zanuck in his office, Waters—who knew when to turn it on and off—was all creamy charm. She appeared to like the young studio executive, who treated her respectfully. "Mr. Zanuck listened to my interpretation of 'Am I Blue?' said 'This is it,' and asked what would I nick him for two weeks' work on his spacious and sunny movie lot."

Waters knew how to play her hand. "Well, Mr. Zanuck," she told him, "I have commitments on the Orpheum time, but I will see if I can post-pone them."

"How much do you get?" Zanuck asked.

Waters told him $1,250 a week. But she informed him that she'd have to readjust her tour schedule with the Orpheum people. "I will probably lose more than two weeks of my valuable time. So if agreeable to you, Mr. Zanuck, I would like to have a four-week guarantee at $1,250 a week, which will come to a nicely rounded five thousand dollars."

On with the Show: Ethel Waters, appearing in her first Hollywood movie on her terms.

"You drive a pretty good bargain for yourself, Miss Waters," he told her with a friendly smile. He agreed, and Waters became the first African American woman to deal with Hollywood on her *own* terms.

Perhaps what bolstered Waters's confidence was the simple fact that she didn't take Hollywood very seriously. She thought of herself as a New York club and recording star, and though she hadn't yet triumphed on Broadway, she had hopes of doing so. She didn't need movies. With only two numbers to perform in *On with the Show,* Waters knew her performances were considered by the studio to be a *specialty act,* which soon became the way most studios usually handled big-name Negro performers. Rather than cast the black stars as characters integral to a film's story line, they simply filmed their musical numbers.

On the Warners soundstage, Waters performed sensational renditions of "Am I Blue?" and "Birmingham Bertha." Composer Askt believed that the latter song would score higher on the music charts. But the mellow, sweetly melancholic "Am I Blue?" became an extraordinary national hit for

Waters, a classic that would be heard for decades to come. The studio offered Waters an extra thousand dollars if she'd dub the voice of white star
Betty Compson singing. But Waters refused: no way was her voice going
to be heard coming out of someone else's body. Completing her work in
On with the Show, Ethel Waters packed her bags, got out of town, and resumed her tour on the Orpheum circuit. But in subsequent years, Hollywood would bring her back.

Waters's work in pictures was a bright sign for everyone. Warners ended
up using black singer Lorainne Winston to dub Compson. "Lorainne was
out of camera sight on a balcony," reported *The California Eagle*. At Paramount, Josef von Sternberg cast a stunner named Theresa Harris—glamorously dressed as she sang—in a suggestive black nightclub sequence in
Thunderbolt. Also featured was Curtis Mosby with his band, along with
numerous black extras. The town was alive now with *possibilities*.

SPENCER WILLIAMS

Over at Christie Studios, black writer Spencer Williams got a chance
to do something most African Americans had not yet envisioned as
possible: to actually write screenplays for a Hollywood film company.
Round-faced with a husky voice, a stocky build, and a seemingly easygoing manner that masked his burning ambitiousness, Williams—born in
Vidalia, Louisiana, in 1893—had arrived in Hollywood, like so many others, with a colorful, checkered past. Having attended Wars Academy in
Natchez, Mississippi, he studied at the University of Minnesota for two
years, then joined the army, where, among other things, he was a bugler
under the command of General Pershing in Mexico. Traveling to places as
diverse as Honolulu, Corregidor, Japan, Russia, and San Francisco,
Williams, had been stationed in France as "an intelligence sergeant" during World War I, so he liked to say and so the studio publicity handouts
announced.

Once discharged from the army in 1923, he eventually made his way to
Los Angeles. In a short period of time, he became known to the locals as
well as key studio people. When Erich von Stroheim was set to direct *The
Swamp* (later retitled *Queen Kelly*), starring Gloria Swanson, for her production company, then headed by Joseph Kennedy (father of the future
president), Williams was hired to cast the colored players needed for a sequence set in Africa.

But Williams's real coup was persuading Christie Studios to hire him. Christie was low-ranked among studios, but it was a Hollywood company nonetheless. On Christie's sets where he worked as a sound technician, Williams keenly eyed everything—the way scripts were written, the way cameramen shot sequences, the way directors directed, the way actors and actresses used tricks to steal scenes or pull at the emotions. Christie set out to film a series of low-budget short black movies—crude and rigidly stereotyped—based on Octavus Roy Cohen's stories published in *The Saturday Evening Post*. The studio enlisted Williams to work on the films.

Though Williams received no credits, he wrote continuity and dialogue for the films *The Framing of the Shrew, The Lady Fare, Melancholy Dame*, and *Oft in the Silly Night* as well as *Music Hath Harms*, on which he also served as assistant director. Williams also appeared in most of the films and, in all likelihood, helped cast them with performers whom he had seen in the clubs or theaters or met at the watering holes along Central Avenue, including such prominent stage performers as Evelyn Preer, Edward Thompson, and Lawrence Criner, along with Roberta Hyson.

Williams also produced the silent *Hot Biscuits* in 1929. "I didn't make any money on it because everybody wanted to see talkies," he said. In the 1930s—when Christie went out of business and Williams knew there wasn't much chance the major companies would hire him—he gave up on the Hollywood studio system to write, direct, and act in independent race movies for almost two decades. After World War II, he left L.A. to live in Tulsa, Oklahoma—only to return in the early 1950s to play Andy Brown on the *Amos 'n' Andy* TV show, filmed at CBS, which stood on the very site at Sunset Boulevard and Gower Gulch where the old Christie Studios had once been located.

BIG PICTURES, BIG STUDIOS, NEW STARS

But the ambitious big pictures came from the big studios: Paul Sloane's black-cast *Hearts in Dixie* at Fox and King Vidor's all-colored *Hallelujah* at MGM. Both became landmark productions in Hollywood history.

The California Eagle eagerly reported on *Hearts in Dixie*, every aspect from its cast to its story line. Fox combed the chorus lines at the clubs to find young women to dance in the film, which was originally conceived as a collection of musical sequences with something of a story wrapped around the music. Signed for a role was chorine Mildred Washington. But because Washington was thought to be too light-skinned, *The Eagle* reported, the makeup department darkened her. Also in the cast were a teenage Eugene Jackson, handsome young Clifford Ingram, and such other performers as Gertrude Howard, Zack Williams, Dorothy Morrison (Sunshine Sammy's sister), A. C. Brillbrew, the dancing Covans, Vivian Smith—and a newcomer about whom everyone was talking, Stepin Fetchit. Much of the cast was transported to Bakersfield, California, where key sequences set in the South were actually shot.

Charles Gilpin was set to star in the role of the elderly grandfather Nappus. But once again, the troubled Gilpin had a falling-out with the studio. "Charles Gilpin Is Ousted" read the headline of the December 14, 1928, edition of *The Eagle*. "He came here with a reputation for his dramatic speech not enjoyed by many. His acting ability was unquestioned. Yet he is out. How come?" commented *The Eagle*. "What could have happened? Was it money matters? He was reported to have signed a contract for $1200.00 a week. Was that too much? He was also reported to be a heavy drinker. Was drink the reason for his let-out?" According to Eugene Jackson, the answer was emphatically *yes*. Gilpin "drank himself out of this part," said the actor, and "held up production for two weeks." By now, many feared that Gilpin's professional disappointments—a great actor without great roles—had turned him desperate and self-destructive, a man who in the end had become his own worst enemy.

To have lost two major roles at a time when the whole town was scrambling even for bits—this was something Black Hollywood was saddened by yet couldn't really understand or sympathize with. Playwright/director Moss Hart, who had worked with Gilpin in New York, once said that Gilpin had "a timeless resignation and disenchantment about everything he did or said." Yet as an actor, Gilpin's "effect was shattering. He had an inner violence and a maniacal power that engulfed the spectator. . . . Had he not been a Negro . . . he would have been one of the great actors of his time." For some black actors, Hollywood would prove a brutal place where, at every turn, the men felt their fundamental masculinity, much of their sense of identity, being challenged. Like Gilpin, others would also lose themselves in drink and despair. Two years after losing the *Hearts in Dixie* role, Charles Gilpin, living in near poverty in New Jersey, would be dead at the age of fifty-two.

Fox sought to replace Gilpin with the respected stage actor George Reed. But Reed, too, ended up *out* of the picture. James B. Lowe lost the part too—and ended up disappearing from show business altogether. Still, such news about the behind-the-scenes machinations of *Hearts in Dixie*—the very idea that a studio now was concerned and fretting about the Negro actor to be the lead in a movie—was unprecedented and, in an ironic twist, another optimistic sign.

Finally, Fox signed Clarence Muse, the kind of African American actor that Hollywood heretofore hadn't seen. Born in Baltimore in 1889 and known for his stentorian tones and rather serious, some might say pompous and pretentious, demeanor, Muse informed all who would listen that he had studied international law at Dickinson College in Pennsylvania, appeared with the Lincoln Players in New York, and cofounded New York's famed Lafayette Players. Considered an erudite man of the theater, Muse surprisingly adjusted quickly to life in Southern California *and* the politics of Hollywood moviemaking. Shrewd, observant, confident, and calculating, he made himself an important part of the *Hearts in Dixie* production. He advised director Paul Sloane on directing the colored actors in key sequences and sought to infuse the film with some signs of African American cultural authenticity.

Within Black Hollywood, Muse would become respected. He was one of the few actors in *Hearts in Dixie* who afterward worked nonstop in movies, making a real career out of his studio jobs. In the next decade, newcomers would seek his advice on getting work and establishing careers. The story he relished telling years later was of the time a woman who had recently arrived in Los Angeles showed up at his door with her tiny daughters. Could he help her get the girls into the movies, she wanted to know. The woman was Ruby Dandridge. The girls were Vivian and Dorothy. Muse loved saying he foresaw Dorothy's stardom. But the part of the story that he often neglected to mention was that he had told Ruby Dandridge to forget Hollywood and take her girls back to Cleveland where they had come from: they were too light-skinned for the movies.

He could also be brutally competitive. Eugene Jackson recalled that during the filming of *Hearts in Dixie,* Muse had landed a radio show. "Family and friends could not understand why I was not invited to appear on this show since I was the child star," said Jackson. "One day I was told point blank Clarence did not like that."

Not standing very tall—he was probably about five feet seven inches with strong features—Muse carried himself like a star in waiting. At first glance, some might have thought he suffered from a Napoleonic complex, so cocky and sure of himself—and so sure of knowing what was best for everyone else, too. At second glance, others probably *still* thought he suffered from a Napoleonic complex. Though sometimes insufferable, Muse was endowed with a fundamental integrity, playing his characters with his idea of dignity and fighting against caricatured roles—at a time when images of blacks in Hollywood were not yet widely discussed, much less even thought about.

Like Spencer Williams, Muse was a new-style power player. He may have shined shoes on-screen, but never would he have done so off. Muse was never afraid to show his intelligence or how articulate he was. Oscar Smith and Slickem may shrewdly have played dumb to make inroads at the studios. But Muse never let himself appear dumb.

He spoke out early against the use of the word *nigger* on movie sets to describe a device used to dim lights. Eugene Jackson recalled the day at Fox Studios when Muse heard a technician say, "Bring that nigger over here." Both shocked and angered, the actor immediately spoke to the director, who explained what the term meant. But that didn't satisfy Muse. Finally, according to Jackson, production that day was closed down. "Clarence, being a man of high principles and standards, would not back down," said Jackson. "He stuck to his guns, his beliefs, until a change was made. I was merely a youth, but I was taught something that day that has stayed with me all of my life: if you know and believe in your heart that something must be changed, act on it."

Despite all the buzz and gossip, *Hearts in Dixie* didn't seem to have the glamorous glow of the year's other black production, King Vidor's *Hallelujah.* A major American filmmaker, King Vidor had directed such lauded and successful films as *The Big Parade, The Crowd, The Patsy,* and *Show People* and worked with some of the biggest stars of the silent era, such as John Gilbert and Marion Davies. As a child growing up in Galveston, Texas, he had been fascinated by the African American life and culture he saw all around him. "For several years, I had nurtured a secret hope. I wanted to make a film about Negroes, using only Negroes in the cast. The sincerity and fervor of their religious expression intrigued me, as did the honest simplicity of their sexual drives," Vidor said. When he informed MGM of his desire to direct a sound picture about Negro life in the South, the studio balked at the idea. Only after he put up his salary— "I said I would invest my guaranteed salary, dollar for dollar, with the investment of the company"—was he able to persuade Irving Thalberg, Louis B. Mayer, and mainly Nicholas Schenck, who was chairman of the board of Loew's, owner of MGM, to let him do it. Schenck told him, "If that's the way you feel about it, I'll let you make a picture about whores."

For his cast, Vidor brought west such performers as Daniel Haynes and blues singer Victoria Spivey. Originally, he wanted Ethel Waters for the female lead. Finally, the coveted part of Chick—a high-stepping bad girl who tries to go good—went to a striking young New York showgirl named Nina Mae McKinney.

As *Hallelujah* was about to roll into production, editors at *The California Eagle* urged the studio to employ African Americans behind the cameras. MGM ended up enlisting the services of Harold "Slickem" Garrison, to whom the black press referred as the assistant director on the film. At Central Casting, Charles Butler was responsible for finding extras. For one camp-meeting sequence that was to be shot on a Sunday morning, he had to locate 340 extras. And all had to be able to sing. That Sunday morning, black church choir benches in the city were said to be practically empty.

Aiming for realism, Vidor shot parts of the film on location in Tennessee and Arkansas. There, he enlisted the help of local black residents and ministers for technical advice on everything from river baptismal services to revival meetings. Black choral director Eva Jessye—director of the original Dixie Jubilee Singers and the Eva Jessye Choir—supervised key choral sequences. Curtis Mosby and his Dixieland Blue Blowers performed in the "Suwannee Shuffle" and "Blue Blowers Blues" numbers. Though *Hallelujah* had a familiar story line—good religious man, corrupted by a seductive good-time gal, abandons his family and the church, only to return repentant later—and though sequences of black crapshooters and rowdy cabaret folks were familiar images, nonetheless the film sometimes attained a highly moving cultural authenticity.

At MGM, studio workers had never seen anything like it: large numbers of black actors and actresses showing up at the gates *with passes*. The same was true at Fox when *Hearts in Dixie* was in production. Hair and makeup departments were not sure what to do. Poor Victoria Spivey looked as if she tended to her hair herself.

During production, the entire community was dazzled by Nina Mae McKinney. Possessing the kind of look the industry then valued in black women who played leads, she was dubbed the "dusky Clara Bow"—with light skin; a pouty mouth; large eyes; keen features; dark, straight hair; and energy to burn. Born in 1913 in Lancaster, South Carolina, McKinney at thirteen went to live with her mother in New York City. A few years later, she won a spot in the chorus line of Lew Leslie's stage hit *Blackbirds of*

Nina Mae McKinney.

1928. Sitting in the audience one night was director Vidor, who decided then and there that McKinney would play Chick. He always remembered that she was "the third from the right" in that chorus line. When McKinney arrived in L.A., she was sixteen years old.

Right away, much of Hollywood, black and white, had its eye on McKinney. Silent-screen star Louise Brooks never forgot her—nor an incident involving Nina Mae and Brooks's free-spirited friend Pepi Lederer, the niece of actress Marion Davies, the mistress of media magnate William Randolph Hearst. When Brooks ran into Pepi in New York in the late 1920s, her friend told her she was there doing "self-inflicted penance for having upset Marion and Mr. Hearst in Hollywood." It had come about following "a most original weekend party" that Pepi had given at the family home in Beverly Hills while Marion's sisters Rose and Ethel were away. Earlier, Pepi had visited the set of *Hallelujah* on its last day of production. Struck by McKinney, Pepi invited "the vivacious" Nina Mae and other cast members out to the house in Beverly Hills. One thing led to another, and there they all partied for some three days—and might have done so longer. But "a neighbor, shocked by the sight of black people running in and out of the mansion, telephoned Marion, who sent Ethel to end the party." Brooks recalled Pepi's delight in telling the story. Laughing and "dropping any show of remorse," Pepi ended by informing Brooks, "And I shall never forget the expression on Ethel's face when she opened my door and saw me in bed with Nina May [*sic*]."

Such stories about McKinney ran rampant up and down Central Avenue—and perhaps up and down some of the plush boulevards in Beverly Hills. In a town that prized excess, she was known to spend wildly: on clothes, on jewelry, on friends, on nights on the town, eventually, on drugs. When McKinney later took up with a maharaja, she was behaving in the glamorous larger-than-life fashion expected of a movie goddess, black or white. As Floyd Covington's comments in the Urban League's *Opportunity* had suggested, Black Hollywood wanted, and understood it *needed,* a fabulous, high-flung star—and Nina Mae looked like the one. When *Hallelujah* was released, McKinney received rave reviews—and a five-year contract at MGM. Production chief Irving Thalberg told Vidor that she had everything it took to be a star. Said Vidor, "She was beautiful and talented and glowing with personality." But McKinney discovered that Hollywood had next to nothing for her. In 1931, she appeared in *Safe in Hell* at Warners and also performed in MGM's *Reckless* in 1935, but her scenes in this latter film were left on the cutting-room floor. For a time, she performed with Curtis Mosby's band at the clubs in L.A. There, patrons were willing to fall under her sexy spell. But there still were no substantial movie offers. What does a woman who is considered a glamorous ideal in Black Hollywood do when she finds herself unemployed? Could she return east after having been exposed to all this heady buildup? She tried. In New York, she appeared in two shorts with the young Nicholas Brothers: *Pie, Pie Blackbird,* in 1932, and *Black Network,* in 1936.

In the mid-1930s, McKinney ended up going to Europe, performing in cafés in Paris, Dublin, and Budapest, where she was sometimes billed as the Black Garbo. In England, she won a plum role opposite Paul Robeson in *Sanders of the River.* But that was about it. Once the war started, she returned to the States, where she married Jimmy Monroe (a onetime husband of Billie Holiday), with whom she put together a band and toured.

TOP: *Nina Mae McKinney: the sexy glamour goddess all those movie executives could fantasize about as she performed in nightclubs.*
BELOW: *McKinney in the race movie* Gun Moll.

Back in Hollywood, she found work in clubs and as the star of such race movies as *Gang Smashers* and *The Devil's Daughter*. But now the most talked-about woman on Central Avenue was rumored to be strung out on dope and booze. By the late 1940s, the race-movie star roles had come and gone, and McKinney, sometimes working unbilled, was reduced to playing maids in such B pictures as *Together Again*, *The Power of the Whistle*, and *Night Train to Memphis*. Her last big appearance was in *Pinky*. Restless and searching, she later lived in Athens, then returned to the States. But there was no hope of movies now. Her Kewpie-doll looks were gone. So were her sexy curves. Years later, a technician from *Hallelujah* recalled attending a dinner party in New York where he was served by an obese and blowzy maid who looked familiar to him. He was shocked to realize it was Nina Mae McKinney. True or not, the story became a part of McKinney's legend.

THE UNEXPECTED STAR: STEPIN FETCHIT

Despite McKinney's glamour, it was *Hearts in Dixie* rather than *Hallelujah* that gave birth to a seemingly more durable—albeit controversial—black star. A comedian walked away with the picture: Stepin Fetchit. The arrival of Fetchit, more than any other personality, really led to the growth of Black Hollywood, the idea that a colored actor could have a highfalutin career in the movies—and could be every bit as flamboyant, as reckless, as talked-about, even as rich as his white counterparts. As the silent era came to an end and the age of the talkie began, Fetchit, in many respects, fully embodied values shared by both the larger film colony and Black Hollywood.

He had been born Lincoln Theodore Monroe Andrew Perry in Key West, Florida, in 1892—although the studio publicity releases were to say the year was 1902. Told by his father—a cigar maker—that he had been named after four presidents, Fetchit once said, "I can't see how in the world he named me after Theodore Roosevelt. He wasn't even president yet!" After the death of his mother, Fetchit was adopted by a wealthy white couple, so he *and* studio publicity handouts claimed. But now, black stars, like white ones, rewrote their personal histories, constructing stories, anecdotes, and incidents that gave their lives ironic turns and made them appear destined for their stardom. It was hard to know where biographical truth ended and where self-invention began. Sent to study at St. Joseph's College in Montgomery, Alabama, Fetchit left after his third year to join

Stepin Fetchit: in character, *posing for a publicity still in a chauffeur's uniform.*

a plantation show; later teamed up with a partner, Ed Lee; and appeared in a steady round of other plantation shows, medicine shows, and carnivals.

His stage/screen name came from a lucky racehorse on which he had bet—and about which he wrote a dance song. But he didn't use the name until an appearance in Oklahoma. Then billed with his partner, Ed Lee, as Skeeter and Rastus—The Two Dancing Crows from Dixie—the pair was booked into a white theater in Tulsa. "In place of putting our names Skeeter and Rastus," said Fetchit, "he put Step and Fetchit and he made that our names." But Lee didn't show up that night. "No, it's not two of us, it's just one of us," Fetchit told the manager. "I was the Stepin Fetchit." Onstage that evening, patrons saw the emergence of Stepin Fetchit's distinct comic persona: a slow-moving, slow-talking, slow-thinking, befuddled, and seemingly dim-witted fellow who was often ducking work. "I got the lazy idea from my partner," he said. "He was so lazy, he used to call a cab to get across the street."

By the time Fetchit made his way to Los Angeles, he was earning $300 a week in vaudeville. But the work was infrequent. Then, a talent booker informed him of a movie, *In Old Kentucky*, about to go into production at MGM with a role for a colored actor. "Go out and see what's going on," he said. At the studio, where he learned what the role called for, Fetchit believed it "was the exact part I used to do in the plantation shows." He won the part. And critical raves. "Much mush stuff, but the MGM finish to the film, and a colored comedian hold up the picture," wrote the critic for *Variety*. "He's just a lazy, no good roustabout, wheedling money out of the colored help but he's no mean pantomimist." Afterward, Fetchit appeared in *The Ghost Talks*.

Because the idea of a movie career didn't seem credible to him, Fetchit continued to work in vaudeville. Touting him as "truly one of the greatest colored actors ever to appear on the silver screen," *The Eagle* was quick to inform its readers that he "was one of the few people of our race enjoying a movietone [*sic*] contract." Fox had signed him to a long-term deal. In a very short period, both Fox *and* Fetchit realized he was a star—and Fetchit started to enjoy himself. Director John Ford took an interest in his career and cast him in the Naval Academy drama *Salute*. When Ford took the cast of *Salute* to the U.S. Naval Academy in Annapolis to shoot some scenes, the director was invited to stay at the commandant's house. "He had me stay in the guest house," said Fetchit. "At *Annapolis*!" Assigned as a prop man on the film was a former college football star originally named Marion Morrison whom Ford thought might make it in the movies. The athlete also assisted Fetchit. Later, Morrison indeed did become a star after having changed his name. Fetchit, in turn, forever delighted in saying, "And on that picture, John Wayne was my dresser!"

Fetchit rapidly became the movies' most famous black actor. "I was an artist, a technician. I went in and competed among the greatest artists in the country," he said. "When I was about to make a movie with Will Rogers, Lionel Barrymore went to him and said, 'This Stepin Fetchit will steal every scene from you. He'll steal a scene from anything—animal, bird, or human being.' That was Lionel *Barrymore* of the *Barrymore* family!" Even Clarence Muse praised him as "the fastest comical dancer you ever saw" and, in short, "the greatest artist in the world."

As dazzled as everyone else by his fame, Fetchit began to act and live in a manner befitting a star. For the residents of Central Avenue and beyond, stories circulated of his opulence and his extravagant spending sprees. As fascinated by automobiles as the rest of the Hollywood community—the Pierce-Arrows, the Duesenbergs, the Locomobiles—he bought one car after another until he had a fleet, often as many as twelve, one of which was a pink Rolls-Royce with his name lit up in neon lights on the side. Yet for a long time, Fetchit didn't even know how to drive. "I always said when you owned an automobile, you should have a chauffeur," he told the press. That changed one rainy morning when Fetchit, a devout Catholic, wanted to go to mass but couldn't find his driver. He slid into the passenger seat of one of his cars and instructed his valet to take him to Washington Boulevard. Finally, Fetchit just took over the wheel—much to the surprise of the valet—and taught himself to drive. "When I would go places I would just have them follow me in a different car," he said. On such occasions, Fetchit might have three or four cars to escort him.

But the extravagance didn't stop there. When he bought a home that had been owned by silent-screen matinee idol Ramon Novarro in the Westlake area, he moved beyond the property boundaries set for black Angelenos. The house had a swimming pool and a chapel where Fetchit had mass. He bought other homes, which he staffed with at least fourteen Chinese or Filipino servants. "I had a couple of them that was with me at all times and I would add to them." And dressing the way a star should—like a prince—he purchased suits from Rudolph Valentino's valet after the actor's death. Others were tailor-made. "I was wearing cashmere suits that cost $1,000. From Oviatt's," he said. "Everyone wore Indian cashmere. When you were a cashmere man, you were in a different world. Certain cashmere was good for business and certain was good for romance. I knew the balance of these things."

But Fetchit sometimes used his earnings for more ambitious, creative projects. He poured a lot of his money into a production company that was established to produce a film—for colored audiences—about his idol, African American boxing champion Jack Johnson, and later another about baseball star Satchel Paige. Neither project came to fruition. And Fetchit would end up broke.

Fetchit's fame and his heady career were built on his extraordinary talent—and, for later generations, also on the industry's racist imagery. "Hol-

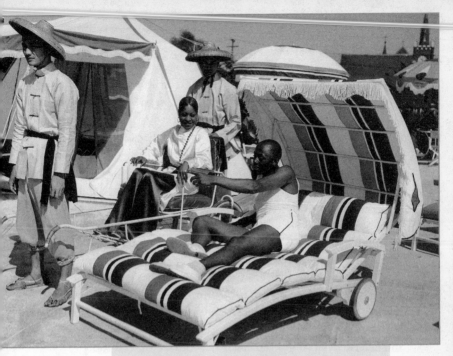

Stepin Fetchit: out of character, *a high-style day by the pool with a lady friend and a retinue of servants.*

lywood was more segregated than Georgia under the skin. A Negro couldn't do anything straight, only comedy," Fetchit later said. "I made the Negro as innocent and acceptable as the most innocent white child, but this acting had to come from the *soul*." Despite his artistry, he ultimately represented—within the context of his films—the African American as a lazy, inarticulate, shuffling, whimpering simpleton.

Yet, paradoxically, more than any other star at the time, he proved that there had to be a place for a black personality in Hollywood cinema. Moviegoers, black and white, knew him—and they went to his movies as much to see him as to see the white stars. At the close of the 1920s, his career was just taking off. He would remain—for the next five years—the most famous African American in the movies.

By the end of the 1920s, with the advent of sound, Hollywood had undergone its most dramatic transformation—and taken a mighty leap forward. Despite the stock market crash in October 1929, Black Hollywood was optimistic about its future. In 1927, Central Casting had placed 3,754 black extras in studio films—usually at a salary rate of $7.50 a day, with total wages adding up to $30,036.00. The next year, Central Casting placed 10,916 black extras, with wages totaling $89,702.89. There had been more than a 200 percent increase in placement numbers and almost a 300 percent increase in wages. In his office on Central Avenue, Charles Butler boasted that the "Negro 'extra' receives more money than any other 'extra' in the industry except Chinese. In other words, they are next to the highest paid in the industry." These numbers did not include the salaries of those fortunate few black performers who had landed contracts at the studios, some of whom earned from $25.00 a day to $300.00 a week. For the big black productions *Hearts in Dixie* and *Hallelujah*, some salaries were as high as $1,250.00 a week. Otherwise, the pickings remained slim.

Still, the more creative directors, writers, and producers in the industry were well aware of what African American performers could bring to the sound motion picture. The singers and dancers had unleashed a new kind of energy, a new rhythm that helped alter the style of Hollywood features and helped give birth to the movie musical, a distinctly American genre. The speaking voices of black actors like Daniel Haynes, McKinney, Muse, and even Fetchit also were distinct and almost aggressively *American*. King Vidor believed "that when colored drama succeeds as it does on the stage, it must also be good for the screen. At any rate it has injected some new ideas into pictures."

"One of the chief obstacles in the advance of the 'talkies' has been the voices of the actors," wrote Robert Benchley. "They have either sounded like the announcer in a railway station or some lisping dancing-master. With the opening of *Hearts in Dixie*, however, the future of the talking movie has taken on a rosier hue. Voices *can* be found which will register perfectly. Personalities *can* be found which are ideal for this medium. It may be that the talking-movies must be participated in exclusively by Negroes, but, if so, then so be it. In the Negro the sound-picture has found its ideal protagonist. . . . What White actors are going to do to compete with it is their business." The black press was just as optimistic. "In the wake of this new experiment in all-Negro pictures comes the Negro's chance to be articulate in his own behalf. Greater still, the success of these pictures shall erect the foundation of the Negro's permanent place in the cinematographic industry in California," wrote Floyd Covington in *Opportunity*.

The California Eagle created a special page devoted mostly to news about movies, the theater, and the clubs, so showbiz aspirants could read casting items and entertainment gossip on a weekly basis. Interviewing performers or visiting movie sets, columnist Harry Levette reported on the way movies were made, the way black performers were used and perceived. Bitten by the movie bug himself, Levette revealed in the 1930s that while covering the comings and goings on movie sets, he had chalked up appearances in some forty-two pictures. Other African American newspapers around the country—*The Chicago Defender, The Philadelphia Tribune, The Amsterdam News,* and especially *The Pittsburgh Courier*—started carrying news about black Hollywood performers. The press coverage endowed movie work with a relevance. It *did* mean something to the African American community that more performers were getting work.

As it turned out, neither *Hearts in Dixie* nor *Hallelujah* was a blockbuster. Seven years would pass before another black-cast movie was produced in Hollywood. And the day of the bona fide "dark star" would be long in coming. Nonetheless, in the next decade, in the midst of the Great Depression, even more African American performers would take the plunge and sail out to the city of dreams. A more cohesive Black Hollywood would begin to operate on a clear set of star attitudes, values, and status symbols, and a very defined star culture. The town itself would be invigorated and expand, its energy about to reach a fever pitch.

3

The Thirties

True, it was the worst of times. But in Hollywood, where nothing was ever quite the way it seemed, the Depression era eventually would prove to be the best of times, too.

For Black Hollywood, roles in big pictures—*Imitation of Life, The Green Pastures, Show Boat, Way Down South, Gone with the Wind*—would boost the spirits of black actors and entertainers. Radio would offer opportunities, too. New clubs would open. Old ones would be revamped and renamed. A bandleader such as Les Hite would provide nighttime entertainment for the movie people. A steady stream of restaurants, cafés, and shops would first close and then—after the initial shock of the stock market crash—flourish once again on Central Avenue. And the Dunbar Hotel would fully come into its own as Black Hollywood's most famous establishment.

An influx of new black stars—Louise Beavers, Willie "Sleep 'n' Eat" Best, Rex Ingram, Eddie "Rochester" Anderson, and Butterfly McQueen—would appear, playing supporting roles, that's true, but nonetheless invigorating American motion pictures with their unique voices, energy, and style and, in the process, helping the town to grow. Musicians from the L.A. clubs would once again head to the studios to perform musical numbers. East Coast stars such as Armstrong, Ellington, Bojangles, and Robeson all gave Hollywood a try. So did dancer Jeni LeGon and singer Etta Moten. Even Joe Louis, the heavyweight champion of the world, came to Hollywood and ended up appearing in the movies. A whole subindustry of race-movie companies would begin in Hollywood in the 1930s; black westerns, gangster tales, mysteries, and romances would create their own brand of black stars for black movie houses. For the first half of the 1930s, Stepin Fetchit would reign as the black star of stars. By the decade's end, Hattie McDaniel would assume the throne. And throughout the decade, the star who would be watched most closely by Black Hollywood would be a young woman who didn't seem interested in movies at all, an easterner on sojourn in the West, Fredi Washington.

The Depression-stricken 1930s opened with uncertainty. Seventy-four billion dollars had been lost in the stock market, three times the cost of the First World War. More than five thousand banks failed nationwide. Some eighty-six thousand businesses closed. *Fortune* reported in 1932 that approximately thirty-four million men, women, and children were without any income. Breadlines were forming. Protests were growing. Families were being evicted from their homes. When asked by *The Saturday Evening Post* if there had ever been anything like the Great Depression, the British economist John Maynard Keynes replied, "Yes. It was called the Dark Ages, and it lasted four hundred years." In L.A., the statistics were as grim as everywhere else: 20 percent of the white workforce was now without jobs. But worse, of those African Americans employed in 1930, 29 percent were unemployed by the next year. The nation held its breath, hoping its new president, Franklin Delano Roosevelt, elected in 1932, might be able to turn things around with his New Deal.

At the start of the era, the movie industry grappled with a multitude of uncertainties. Would the studios be able to master this new technological development, sound, of which audiences had become so enamored? Would great stars of the past such as Gilbert, Swanson, and Garbo still be able to draw audiences into theaters? And most pressing: Would the ordinary folks on the street be willing to shell out a dime for something as frivolous as a movie? The industry struggled to stay on its feet as a third of the nation's movie theaters folded. Studios had huge losses. For a time, only MGM was showing profits.

Hardest hit in the movie capital were, of course, the residents of Black Hollywood. Along Central Avenue, people wondered: Would fewer opportunities turn up simply because fewer movies would be made? Would the money of the stars and moguls—which had helped keep the black clubs packed as well as the servants employed (who, in turn, could pour money into the black churches and social groups)—now evaporate? Would anyone be able to afford to eat a meal in the restaurants? Or to shop? Or to have their hair styled? Or their shoes shined? Many feared that the nation's economic crisis might wipe out everything, turning the once glittering thoroughfare into a ghost town.

Early on, the clubs were in trouble. Curtis Mosby struggled to hold on to the Apex. Other niteries, shops, and restaurants did shut their doors. For "months with Nite Clubs dark and half the shops closed," wrote *The California Eagle*'s Harry Levette, "the famous block where formerly you could stand still and see the gay fraternity, resembled the 'Valley and the Shadows' of gloom."

REBOUNDING

Yet surprisingly, within a few years, the spirits and economics of the entire town rebounded. The old Fox Film Corporation merged with Darryl F. Zanuck's Twentieth Century Productions to become Twentieth Century Fox, and a powerful new studio was born. Production chief Harry Cohn and director Frank Capra revitalized Columbia Pictures and led the studio to glory.

Hollywood saw that movie houses were packed nightly. The local movie theater was a place where fears might be forgotten or allayed, where fantasies helped a nation see itself through hard times. During the Depression era, 70 percent of the population attended the movies at least once a week.

Rather than wiping out Hollywood, the Great Depression simply altered it. Hollywood stars continued to live fairly high on the hog. But gone was the more ostentatious excess of the past, the over-the-top kind of luxury and extravagance of the silent era. Images on-screen changed, too, as the talkies ushered in a new brand of realism and seemingly more down-to-earth stars. Gable. Harlow. Joan Crawford. Spencer Tracy. Cary Grant. Katharine Hepburn. Mae West. W. C. Fields. Myrna Loy. William Powell. All were glamorous, yet their screen characters were in tune with the hard-luck times. And right by their sides in one movie or another might be some wisecracking or understanding or comforting black maid or butler. In the movies, America looked more like an integrated nation than it had in the past. But that integrated world was still one in which social/racial roles were clearly defined.

An early bright spot on Black Hollywood's horizon—as well as a boon for musicians and entertainers—was Frank Sebastian's Culver City Cotton Club. Though patronized by whites and not located in the black community, Black Hollywood considered the nitery a black club, just as New Yorkers considered their Cotton Club to be. Both had a policy of showcasing black talents while rarely admitting black patrons. Much to the dismay of the black community, Sebastian had dumped Carolynne Snowden and her revues. The club then hired white entertainers. But when business fell off, Sebastian eventually reverted to his old format. Black entertainment was back in high style in Culver City.

Bandleader Les Hite was brought in. He had come to L.A. from Chicago with a vaudeville act in 1925, had joined Reb Spikes's orchestra and made recordings with the group in 1927. In 1928, he appeared at the Lincoln Theatre with Curtis Mosby's orchestra. A year later, Hite formed his first band. Becoming a fixture at the Culver City Cotton Club from 1930 until it closed in 1939, Les Hite's band soon emerged as the most popular on the West Coast. It epitomized Los Angeles–style swank and sophistication. Appearing with Hite was the young Lionel Hampton, who already was making a name for himself.

The club would sometimes hire other big-name performers to front Hite's band. That was the case when Louis "Satchmo" Armstrong made his first trip to L.A. in 1930 for a seven-month engagement at the club. Armstrong was first backed by Leon Elkins. Then, Hite took over. Louis Armstrong was already an established star, a major jazz innovator whose recordings had changed the sound and dynamic of American popular music. Hip, energetic, and the eternal optimist, Satchmo was just the kind of big name to get things rocking again.

Armstrong appeared to enjoy himself on the West Coast, where the pace was slower but the people weren't. And the West Coast folks certainly enjoyed him—and the gossip about him. During his breaks at the Cotton Club, Armstrong would often go to his car and light up a little "reefer." One evening when he and the white drummer Vic Berton were puffing away, the cops suddenly showed up. Both men were arrested and spent the night in jail. Later, they were sentenced to six months and a thousand-dollar fine. The sentence was suspended, but for several months, Armstrong and Berton had to spend their weekday nights in a hospital jail. The incident had no effect on his popularity in Black Hollywood. While on the coast, Armstrong recorded with Leon Elkins and Les Hite, performed on radio, which helped him reach an even wider audience, and was signed by Liberty Productions to appear in a musical sequence in the movie *Ex-Flame*, released in 1931. Armstrong wasn't billed in the film, and some reviewers weren't even aware of who he was. In its review, *Variety* passingly mentioned "a colored jazz orchestra" without naming Armstrong. Armstrong would return for work in films such as *Artists and Models* and *Pennies from Heaven*, with Bing Crosby.

Armstrong's L.A. appearances energized Black Hollywood. Other big-name entertainers followed him at the Culver City Cotton Club: Fats Waller, Cab Calloway, and that trumpet-blowing powerhouse Valaida Snow.

THE DUKE COMES TO TOWN

Just as exciting was the arrival of that other jazz innovator, Duke Ellington, who came to town to appear in RKO Radio Pictures' *Check and Double Check*. The film marked the big-screen debut of radio's *Amos 'n' Andy* stars/creators, Freeman Gosden and Charles Correll, who played their movie roles in blackface. Ellington was paid handsomely to provide some background music for the film—$27,500, in installments of $6,875 weekly, for four weeks' work. Not bad. Ellington quickly learned the ways of the movie capital. Once rehearsals at the studio began, the film's director, Melville Brown, decided that Ellington band members Juan Tizol and Albany "Barnard" Bigard were too light-skinned—and they might be mistaken for white! Thereafter, the band members were sent to the makeup department, where they were darkened. The *Baltimore Afro-American* let its readers know of the decision when it ran a photo of the band members with a caption that read, "They Must Black Up for Part in the Movies." A mixing of the races, even on the bandstand, was still taboo in Hollywood.

On this trip and others, Ellington, always on the lookout for talent, hit the clubs. Staying at the Dunbar, he went next door to the Apex, where he spotted the young saxophone player Marshall Royal, then working with Curtis Mosby's orchestra. Because RKO wanted a violin section in Duke's band, Ellington hired Royal to perform on violin in *Check and Double Check*. "It was a real feather in my cap," said Royal, who was then still a teenager at Jefferson High School. "It made me a pretty popular guy around school."

Ellington would return to Hollywood later in the decade for the movie

*The Duke arrives in town—with the band and
his favorite girl-singer, Ivie Anderson.*

Murder at the Vanities—and also when Mae West informed her studio, Paramount, that she wanted Ellington and no one else for a musical sequence in her film *Belle of the Nineties.* He also signed up L.A. trombonist Lawrence Brown.

Before long, Central Avenue picked up steam and began to look like its old self. In 1931, new owners took over the Apex building and renamed the nitery Club Alabam. Even more glamorous than before, Club Alabam featured local bands headed by Leon Herriford and later Floyd Ray. The club employed more than one hundred people, with a weekly payroll of fifteen hundred dollars.

Other clubs also opened their doors, "giving the loud hee-haw to old man 'Gen'l Depression,'" Harry Levette wrote in *The California Eagle* in August 1931. "The dizzy white lights are dancing daringly again, lightsome, lilting, laughter is tinkling from lips curved merrily in happy faces of white, brown, cream, or rich orange as the gay, many-colored gowns of women of all races flutter like so many butterflies."

By 1930, Los Angeles's black population had grown to 38,894. Black residents kept to their part of town. But the black neighborhoods spread out through the era.

In 1930, of Hollywood's 4,451 actors, 128 were black. Of the 2,909 actresses, only 85 were African American. The grimmest numbers were for directors, managers, officials in the industry. Of 1,106, only 3 were black. Still, by the next decade, some of the numbers would more than triple.

ENTERTAINING: FAMILY STYLE

Among the new residents were families of entertainers. From Colorado, there came a quartet of siblings named McDaniel: Sam, Etta, Orlena, and Hattie. Just about the entire McDaniel family was musical. Their mother, Susan Holbert McDaniel, had been a religious singer who had met the children's father, Henry McDaniel, in Nashville. Born into slavery, Henry McDaniel had served in the Union army and then became a minister. The couple had thirteen children, not all of whom survived childhood. From Wichita, Kansas, Henry and his wife settled in Denver. There, Henry formed his own minstrel company, which toured throughout Colorado and featured himself and his sons Otis and Sam.

Of the McDaniel children, Sam McDaniel, born in 1886, was the first to arrive in L.A.—in the late 1920s. Gregarious and full of fun, he found bits, often uncredited, in films such as *Hallelujah* and, in this new decade, such movies as *Brown Gravy, The Public Enemy,* and *A Free Soul.* He also performed on the radio show *The Optimistic Do-Nut Hour,* which made him known in Black Hollywood—and something of a player. Etta found work, also often uncredited, in movies such as *King Kong, Smoking Guns,* and *The Arizonian.* Orlena McDaniel opened a boardinghouse for Pullman porters.

By the time Hattie also decided to give movieland a try, in 1931, she had been performing for years. The youngest of the McDaniel children, she had been born in 1895, had left high school after her sophomore year, and had performed and written material for her father's company. She also worked with the Spikes Company Minstrels and traveled with Professor George Morrison's orchestra, the Melody Hounds, to Portland, Salt Lake City, El Paso, and briefly Juárez, Mexico. Sometimes billed as the "female Bert Williams," she sang with Morrison's orchestra on Denver's radio station KOA in 1925 and performed on the big-time Orpheum circuit. But work was always hard to come by. Sometimes, she took jobs performing for fraternal organizations such as the Elks and the Shriners. Other times, she entertained on the Theater Owners Booking Association circuit, known as TOBA, a group of black-owned theaters in various parts of the country. When times were really tough, she did domestic work.

These early years had been hard personally for McDaniel. She had fallen in love with a young man named George Langford, whom she married in 1922. But within months of the wedding, Langford was dead— shot to death, so the stories went. Hattie was a widow by age twenty-seven. When the Depression hit, the show in which she was appearing folded, and she was left stranded. Desperate to get a gig, she made her way to Milwaukee, where she worked at Sam Pick's Club Madrid as a ladies' room attendant. She often sang as she worked. One night, the club manager let her perform. She brought the house down with her rendition of "St. Louis Blues." Afterward, McDaniel took stock of herself. She knew that despite all she had done, all her travels, all her appearances at tiny theaters and clubs, she still didn't have much of a real career. Finally, urged on by Sam, Etta, and Orlena, McDaniel headed to L.A.

In the beginning, she again did domestic work. Then her brother Sam introduced her to *The California Eagle*'s Harry Levette. He liked her, thought she had talent, and finagled an engagement for her to sing at the Tivoli Theatre on Central Avenue. She went over well with the audience. Through Sam, she landed a spot on *The Optimistic Do-Nut Hour*. Nervous and eager to impress, she arrived that night all dolled up. She sang, did some comedy bits, and was an immediate hit. Afterward, she began making weekly appearances, earning five dollars a show, and becoming a favorite of black radio listeners. "I used to get so enthusiastic singing," she once said, "that I'd start to dance, too, and I'd dance right away from the microphone. Tom Breneman was the announcer and he'd have to lead me back to the mike. On our first show he gave me a nickname that he's never forgotten. I thought the cast would wear formal dress so I wore an evening gown. But everyone else wore street clothes, and when I arrived Tom said, 'Well, look at our High Hat Hattie.'" The nickname stuck. Later, McDaniel appeared on the *Amos 'n' Andy* and *Eddie Cantor* radio shows.

But the only movie work Hattie found in the early 1930s was bits, sometimes unbilled, in forgettable pictures such as *Impatient Maiden*, *Washington Masquerade*, and *The Golden West*. Heavyset and dark-skinned with a round face and large, expressive eyes, McDaniel knew she was hardly Hollywood's idea of a glamour girl. Nor was she—by the industry standards—a young woman. She was now in her midthirties. Still, her drive and distinct comedic talent set her apart, even during this early stage of her movie career. Moviegoers couldn't help but notice this born scene stealer in an uncredited role in *Blonde Venus* as a woman who befriends Marlene Dietrich—on the run from the law with her young son. In the age of the talkies, her great gift was her voice: It was big, loud, commanding. And she had a peculiarly American brand of aggressiveness. Audiences took one look at her and knew she was not the kind of woman to let anything stand between her and what she wanted. Still, McDaniel's rise in Hollywood was hardly immediate.

Ruby Dandridge arrived at the same time with her two young daughters, Vivian and Dorothy, and Ruby's special friend, Geneva Williams. Born in 1899, in Wichita, Kansas, Ruby had moved around. As a young woman, she married a draftsman named Cyril Dandridge in Cleveland, Ohio. But the two were no one's idea of a perfect couple. Cyril was quiet, unassuming, sensitive. Ruby was all energy and chatter, ready to talk to almost anyone, especially if she thought they could be of help to her. She already had thoughts of being a professional entertainer and was too ambitious to be a traditional pliant wife and mother. Shortly after the birth of the couple's first child, Vivian, in 1921, Ruby did the unthinkable for most women of that era: She walked out on her husband. Cyril persuaded her to come back. But while pregnant with her second child, Dorothy, she left her husband again, never to return.

Ruby took domestic jobs in Cleveland, while thinking more seriously of a career as an entertainer. She trained her daughters to sing, dance, perform acrobatics, and recite poetry. Life in the new Dandridge household changed once Ruby met Geneva Williams in church. The two women hit it off right away. Both were musical. Both liked to entertain. Having studied at Fisk College in Nashville, Geneva, whom Ruby called Neva, was a talented musician. Like Ruby, she, too, was fleeing an unhappy marriage. She soon moved into Ruby's household—and into Ruby's bed. Immediately, Ruby informed her daughters that they were to call this new family member "Auntie Ma-Ma." A strict taskmaster, Geneva further trained the girls in music and proper deportment. She also often physically punished them for the slightest infraction of any of the rules she laid down. Both were terrified of her.

By the ages of five and six, Dottie and Vivie, as the children were called, were pros, performing at colored churches, schools, and organizations in Cleveland. Then, they toured the South under the sponsorship of the Baptist National Convention, an independent federation of black churches that booked them, picked up their expenses, and paid them a salary. "Having that organization as our sponsor was, for the Negro community then," said Dorothy, "like having a deal with MGM was for white folks." The two adorable girls "were called The Wonder Children," said Vivian, "because we did acrobatic stunts."

But Ruby and Ma-Ma set their eyes on broader horizons. In the midst of the Great Depression, they came west. Always adept at making contacts, Ruby paid a visit—with her daughters in tow—to the very august Clarence Muse, now regarded as a dean of sorts of Black Hollywood. Neither Ruby nor the children nor Muse himself ever forgot the initial meeting. "Go back east, Mrs. Dandridge," Muse said, as he glanced at her daughters. "They don't stand a chance. I can't help them." "We can't go back east," Ruby said. "We got to stay." "Well, good luck," Muse told her. "But you'll never make it."

Ruby knew Muse was wrong. But she still poured on the charm and no doubt gave him a sob story about having to support the children on her own, which was indeed true. She persuaded him to lend her money. "I paid their first damn money for an apartment they lived in," Muse said years later. "And I never got my $70 back, either."

Ruby and Ma-Ma quickly adjusted to life on the West Coast. Daily, Ma-Ma continued to train the girls in a regimen of dance, voice, and piano rehearsals. To keep the family financially afloat, Ruby found various jobs as a maid. Ma-Ma also gave piano lessons to black kids in the area. When the two women felt the girls needed more advanced training, they enrolled them in Lauretta Butler's dance studio. Then, Ruby teamed Dottie and Vivie with another little girl, Etta Jones, to form a singing act. Under the tutelage of Ma-Ma, the children were groomed as a trio called The Dandridge Sisters. In the beginning, Ma-Ma also taught the children at home. But later, the girls were enrolled in elementary school. Ruby, however, never thought twice about having them cut classes to perform somewhere in and around the city. That would be the case for years to come. "Dorothy was as pretty as she could be," said Marian Patterson, who attended McKinley Junior High School with Dandridge. "But she was absent a lot, and I don't believe she ever did any work at home. I don't imagine there was anybody at home that would sit her down and tell her to do her home-

'Prepping herself for stardom: child actress Dorothy Dandridge (second from left) at dance school with her older sister, Vivian (far right).

work." The Dandridge Sisters performed locally. Ruby also took the girls to the office of Charles Butler, who liked them. Within a short period of time, they were working in musical sequences of such movies as *The Big Broadcast of 1936* and *It Can't Last Forever.*

Other talented families, such as the de Lavallades from Louisiana, also resided in Los Angeles. Carmen de Lavallade would grow up to be a major dancer with the Lester Horton Dance Company and work in movies. Her sister Yvonne would also have a brief dance career, while her first cousin Janet Collins would become a major ballerina in New York in the 1950s.

The Nicholas family also arrived: parents Ulysses and Viola; daughter Dorothy; and the two singing and dancing sons, Fayard and Harold. The boys had already become a sensation in New York: two wizards of dance with smooth tap routines who would later be known for their execution of stunning splits, spins, flips, and turns at a breakneck speed. The boys had grown up in show business. At Philadelphia's colored theater, The Standard, their parents had led the house orchestra, with Viola at the piano and Ulysses on the drums.

Fayard, the oldest, loved life at The Standard. Daily and nightly, he sat spellbound, watching the rehearsals and performances of some of the great stars of black vaudeville: Louis Armstrong, Buck and Bubbles, Adelaide Hall. By age three, he was teaching himself to dance and was entranced by the movies. When his mother gave birth to his younger brother, Fayard asked if the baby could be named after his favorite movie star, Harold Lloyd. By age five, Harold was being taught to dance by Fayard. Years later, whenever Harold was asked who had been his dance inspiration—was it Bojangles or John Bubbles or Astaire?—he always answered: "Only one person ever influenced me. My brother, Fayard." In 1931, the two debuted on radio's *Horn and Hardart Kiddie Hour*. Radio listeners had to satisfy themselves with the tap, tap, tap sounds of the brothers' feet. But it worked. The next year, the young Nicholas Brothers appeared at New York's Cotton Club, where they were to become regulars—and where they were to dazzle the rich and famous clubgoers. At the club, black entertainers were not supposed to mingle with the white patrons. But the boys were given free rein to run around, sit, or chat with whomever they pleased.

Once their Cotton Club performances made the brothers famous, the entire Nicholas family moved from Philadelphia to a luxurious apartment on New York City's Edgecomb Avenue. Hollywood came knocking on their door in the mid-1930s with an offer for the brothers to appear in *Kid Millions*, with Eddie Cantor. The whole family was seduced by L.A.'s charms. "I looked around," Fayard recalled, "and I said to my mother and my father and my brother and sister, 'This is it. Let's move here. I'm getting tired of those winters and summers in New York City.' So that was my first impression. What I really was fascinated by were the palm trees. I liked that. We didn't do much sightseeing or anything like that because we were always at the studio United Artists for this film *Kid Millions*, produced by Samuel Goldwyn. And that's when I really fell in love with Los Angeles." For Fayard, the studio "was so wonderful because everyone was so nice to us. Eddie Cantor was one of our best fans." On the West Coast, they were snapped up for performances at the Cocoanut Grove.

Leaving L.A. was like leaving paradise. But they felt they'd be coming back. Afterward, the boys toured, played the Palladium in London; performed on Broadway in *Babes in Arms*, under the direction of George Balanchine; and appeared in movies shot in New York. The brothers and their mother also returned to L.A. for an appearance in the all-star production *The Big Broadcast of 1936*, which featured some of the big stars of radio and Broadway: Bill "Bojangles" Robinson, George Burns and Gracie Allen, Ethel Merman, and *Amos 'n' Andy* stars Freeman Gosden and Charles Correll. Also in the film was the little girl whom Harold would later be dazzled by and marry, Dorothy Dandridge. But at this time, tragedy struck the Nicholas family. En route to meet his children in L.A.,

Ulysses Nicholas suffered a massive heart attack and died. Afterward, Viola Nicholas alone managed her sons' careers.

Even during these early trips to the West, the brothers became emblems of high style for the young of Black Hollywood. Viola Nicholas saw to it that both boys were always immaculately groomed and splendidly dressed, usually in suits and ties, and they were squired around town in a car driven by their personal chauffeur. No appearance, personal or professional, went unnoticed. "I was in awe of these kids who, as kids, were making more money than most adults," recalled Joe Adams, who grew up to be one of L.A.'s most popular disc jockeys and also appeared in *Carmen Jones*. "They were such perfectionists. When I was a kid, I used to go to a barbershop on Central Avenue, and they went to the barbershop when they were in town. They would pull up in a limousine and get out. Every black kid was trying to be one of the Nicholas Brothers or something like that because that was what was going on. Then Joe Louis came along, and everyone had to be a prizefighter." Upon completing *The Big Broadcast of 1936*, Viola and her sons returned east. But the Nicholas Brothers' Hollywood adventure hadn't ended. By the end of the decade, the boys returned to sign a major contract with Twentieth Century Fox.

Depression or not, Carmen de Lavallade, like other children in this city, grew up thinking of L.A. as magical. In many respects, it was still like a big country town, not at all as developed and sprawling as it would soon become. She and her two sisters were brought up by their father, Leo, who had first arrived in the city in the 1920s. He thought "it was the most beautiful place he'd ever seen," recalled de Lavallade. "You could see the mountains, always, always. And the snow on them. And the palm trees. You'd go by these orange groves when they were blooming, and oh, that fragrance. It was just beautiful. And fields of red and yellow poppies. And oleanders. And pepper trees. And big eucalyptus trees. It was wonderful." The family "little by little moved from the Eastside to the Westside. But we were mainly Eastside people. We lived in East L.A. in a Mexican neighborhood in Vernon City. Ours was a small, little house. Not a wealthy neighborhood by any means. But I kind of liked it. And there was a glass factory. And there was a little house that was a grocery store. I remember it was propped up on milk boxes. Daddy was a bricklayer, and then he became a postman. I guess he was trying to make more money. My daddy was amazing. He grew all our food. We always had food. Daddy would have chickens and ducks. He had pigeons, as long as I can remember. I must have been three or four. I remember we had a goat named Nanny. And we would have milk. And all the vegetables he grew. Rabbits, depending on which house we lived in. And, of course, in those days, it wasn't zoned. You could have your animals. You could have your food, which was wonderful. That was East L.A."

Others lived the same way. Outside the family home of Los Angeles resident Willard Brown, there were also "rabbits and goats and our vegetable garden. You'd go out in the garden. You pick some mustard greens and some corn. Or kill a couple of chickens." There were fruit trees everywhere, too. "Everywhere in the city, you could see City Hall clearly almost every day," recalled Marian Patterson, whose family moved to the city from Cleveland in the early 1930s. "There was no smog. And everyone had an incinerator in the backyard where they burned their own trash. And they had a certain day to do it and a certain time of month. And it was still clean." "It was safe," recalled another Los Angeles resident, Johnetta Jones, who grew up on East Forty-sixth Street. "My mother would send me to pay the bills, and everyplace I went to pay the bills, they were on Central Avenue. In those days, you carried cash in your hands. My mother gave me the bills with the money in the envelope, and I went around and paid all these bills. And I was never afraid. And everyone knew everyone, and everyone was concerned about everyone. Everyone had their own private family, and then the whole block was the family."

"There were not enough blacks here to have a completely segregated neighborhood," said Jones. So a neighborhood like Vernon City "was all mixed but with more Hispanic. Mainly Mexicans," recalled de Lavallade. "It was like a little Spanish hacienda." At the time, she didn't think of the racial lines drawn throughout the city. Yet African Americans and other minorities were more confined than ever. It "was a pretty town, but I didn't think much of the attitude toward Blacks," recalled Lionel Hampton, who moved to Los Angeles from Chicago in the 1920s. "It was the South in some ways." He remembered that he had to "go into the white nightclubs by the back door" and that "black musicians didn't get paid as much as white musicians—in fact, blacks got 20 percent of what whites made." There was even a separate black local unit—number 767—of the American Federation of Musicians. On public transportation, "you could sit anywhere you wanted," recalled Johnetta Jones. But for years, there were no

The Nicholas Brothers: smooth, stylish, and ready to conquer the town.

black bus or trolley drivers. Most teachers in the schools that minorities attended were white. So were almost all police officers. "The colored policemen could only work at Newton Station at Newton Street and Central Avenue. And they worked the graveyard shift for a long time," said Jones. "But Newton was not considered a black police station because the white folks worked in the daytime."

For the young, though, as for so many others, "Los Angeles was movies, movies, movies. You spent your life in movies," recalled de Lavallade. "Every Sunday when Daddy would go to work, he'd bring his mail truck, put us in there, and drop us off at the movies." She loved the glamour of Hollywood and the fact that "you knew the stars were around. In those days, it was like a fairy tale. When they would have the Academy Awards, it was like something really magical. You'd think, 'Wow! Another world!' Of course, you knew that all you saw up there were white people, except when you saw Hattie and other black actors. Maybe it's growing up in L.A. and the mystery of it all. The stars were more mysterious then. The Bette Davises. The Joan Crawfords. All the biggies. Gale Sondergaard. Anna Mae Wong. She was like Hattie with those crazy roles. But you look at those people like Hattie and Willie Best and Mantan Moreland and they did a wonderful job. They were like mystery people to me, too."

"In the Central Avenue of my childhood," recalled singer Etta James, "the black actors were heroes. They might play fools on the screen, but the folks in the neighborhood knew it took more than a fool to break into lily-white Hollywood."

Everybody also thought there was a chance of getting in the movies. Willard Brown's childhood friend Philip Hurlic was the talk of the neighborhood when he got work at the studios. "He played in a lot of movies. He was the only one in his family [who was] employed. He took care of his mother, his sister, his grandmother, and his family."

Brown also recalled the neighborhood's excitement about Billie Thomas, known as Buckwheat in Our Gang. He "lived on 109th between Central and Compton avenues," said Brown. "Buckwheat was the only child. Very, very protected. We would watch him from the playground. As far as conversation, there wasn't any conversation with him at all. We weren't allowed anywhere near inside his house." Years later Brown would open The House of Willard Brown, which specialized in "processing" hair (conking, or straightening, it) with a client list that included Nat "King" Cole, Duke Ellington, and Count Basie.

FETCHIT: STILL NUMBER ONE

But Black Hollywood—in the early 1930s—remained a one-black-star-only town. No one was better known or as steadily employed as Stepin Fetchit, who worked in such Fox films as *Cameo Kirby, Swing High, The Prodigal, Neck and Neck,* and *Slow Poke.* Still enjoying his fame and the constant buzz about him, Fetchit luxuriated in snapping the local yokels to attention with his giddy extravagance: There were tales of his spending sprees and then of his dwindling fortunes, accounts of his squabbles and battles with various women, rumors (never substantiated) of his friendship with Jean Harlow, reports (well substantiated) of his forays on Central Avenue. Musician Britt Woodman recalled an evening at a Central Avenue club when a great commotion broke out among the patrons. Word spread that "Stepin Fetchit came by with Mae West in a Rolls Royce. It was such excitement," said Woodman, "so everybody went out to the front door to see what was going on."

But with the pressures of his fame, Fetchit became difficult to work with. Stories circulated that he often showed up late on the set, that he wanted to direct himself and wouldn't take suggestions. Leaving town for a spell, he traveled, sometimes performing in small clubs and making personal appearances to pull in some money. Fetchit thought he didn't need Hollywood half as much as Hollywood needed him. Seeing his image magnified on screen, he, like so many other movie stars, appeared to believe that the world revolved around him, that he could do whatever he desired and still have hordes clamoring to be near him.

Fetchit got his first dose of serious competition when the studios started using another long, lanky actor, Willie Best, who was first known as "Sleep 'n' Eat" when he appeared in such films as *Up Pops the Devil* and *West of the Pecos.* Slow-moving like Fetchit, Best could pop his eyes, stammer, and appear befuddled or dumbfounded at the slightest provocation. Lifting Fetchit's persona, he somehow rendered it more palatable with a built-in element of self-parody. Though not the stylized performer that Fetchit was, Best nonetheless had talent. For the studios, Best also proved more manageable. He reported to work on time and didn't cause problems on or off the set. For the town, Best made good copy. Like Fetchit, he enjoyed the restaurants, the clubs, the places where he knew the fans could look him over. Yet offscreen, Best was also the complete antithesis of the character he popularized on-screen. "Willie dressed superclean and was said to have pimped some of the prettiest black girls around," said Etta James.

"White women were wild for him. Wild white women loved black movie studs." In time, he enjoyed the liquor and the dope and was known to some as a "junkie who kept high-quality stuff," said James.

BIG CASTING CALLS

Large casting calls for colored actors still made news around town. Much publicity surrounded the production *Operator 13,* primarily because of its star, Marion Davies. A tale of the Civil War dramatized in that Old South mythological style that Hollywood still loved, *Operator 13* cast Davies—opposite Gary Cooper—as a Confederate spy who gathers information by pretending to be a ditzy octoroon laundress. Davies was darkened and spoke in dialect. While in production, *Operator 13* drew good coverage from the black press, mainly because the film provided work for numerous black performers. Receiving special billing was the singing group The Mills Brothers—known for their mellow, barbershop-like harmonizing—whose bestselling records had crossed over and were snapped up by both white and black fans.

Visitors to the set were impressed by the prospects. "Not the slightest bit of burlesque of Negroes is used in the picture, the hateful word n—r is forbidden by the directors and the word wench deleted from the story," reported *The California Eagle.* "All connected with the direction are courteous to the colored players." Marion Davies was reported to keep "colored girls on hand to study their speech ways and mannerisms." Much attention was focused on Sam McDaniel, cast as the character Rufus. "During the startling action he has to scold and even handle the star Marion Davies roughly." Between shots, McDaniel, still in period costume and makeup with snow white hair, cavorted, smiled, and performed songs for an admiring crowd of fellow actors and crew members on the set—not much different from "Big" Sam Baker performing for Douglas Fairbanks's friends in the 1920s. Black actors were sometimes still expected to remain in character, to be as jovial and friendly during their downtime as they were when the cameras rolled.

On the set, too, was MGM's Harold "Slickem" Garrison, who was referred to by the black press as the assistant director on *Operator 13.* Director Richard Boleslawski reportedly consulted him about the customs, habits, and speech of Negroes in 1862. What kind of authenticity Slickem provided would be anyone's guess. But, as always, he was a mediator between the performers and studio if any problems arose.

A NEW GUILD AND A NEW NEWSPAPER

A major change in the industry came in 1933 with the creation of the Screen Actors Guild. Basic pay rates were established for extras. So, too, were work hours as well as the type of physical action actors could or could not be required to perform on-screen. An early proponent of the guild for black performers was Clarence Muse, who admonished his fellow Negro actors to join rather than to work for lower wages as scabs for independents, even if those independents were shooting black-cast movies.

Muse was working at a feverish pace. He struck up a friendship with director Frank Capra, who referred to him as his "pet actor" and cast him in the movies *Dirigible, Rain or Shine,* and later a plum role in a big hit of the Depression era, *Broadway Bill.* In 1932, he published a pamphlet "The Dilemma of the Negro Actor," in which he saw clearly that black performers were torn between waiting for serious work and accepting the financial rewards of playing clowns and buffoons for white audiences. Muse also joined the staff of *The California Eagle* as a columnist, whose articles—usually pertaining to the entertainment scene—were often carried on the front page. His association with the newspaper enabled Muse to build a power base for himself.

In 1933, *The Los Angeles Sentinel*—a new weekly newspaper for the Negro community—began publication, building up a circulation at one time of fifty-six thousand readers. Its publisher, Leon Washington, and his wife, Ruth, emerged as major figures on the L.A. scene and would be so for several decades. Like *The California Eagle* and *The Pittsburgh Courier, The Los Angeles Sentinel* covered national and international events as well as city issues. Its entertainment section proved important in promoting films and stars—and in time, in voicing criticism of the entertainment industry's depiction of black Americans. The weekly newspapers also carried articles by a perceptive entertainment writer named Fay Jackson, who became the Hollywood correspondent for the Associated Negro Press and was later a political editor for *The California Eagle.*

Born in Dallas in 1902, she had graduated from USC, where she majored in journalism and philosophy. Still in her twenties, she founded the weekly cultural publication *Flash* and the newspaper *California News.* As dramatic as the stars on whom she reported, Jackson wore her hair closely cropped, favored tailored suits, carried a briefcase, and puffed away on unfiltered cigarettes—not the standard attire or look for a young woman in the movie capital. But when singer Etta Moten commented on Jackson's boyish clothes, Jackson explained that she operated in a man's world without any intention of letting her femininity detract from being accorded respect. With Charlotta Bass as her mentor, Jackson could be tough and edgy, and she sometimes used the black star interview to focus on Hollywood's racial inequities. But she also understood that her black readers wanted sepia glamour and filmland lore. So the articles were rich in behind-the-scenes tidbits.

More than ever, the Negro newspapers helped create a sense of a more vital black entertainment community, in which everyone was aware of the activities of everyone else. Actors and actresses competed for space on the entertainment pages, with only the rare few rating a personal interview— a sure sign that a performer was considered a major player. Though coverage in the black press contributed little or nothing to the way the industry at large might view a black actor, it still raised a performer's profile in town and provided the performers themselves with a sense of accomplishment, and once more race movies were produced on the West Coast, some work could result.

AN AGENT FOR BLACK HOLLYWOOD

Black casting agents now added to the black movie community's shape and direction. Central Casting's Charles Butler remained the kingpin, though some actors felt he had too much power and was too closely aligned with the studios. Real competition for Butler came with the arrival of Ben Carter, an actor, a comic, and a choral director, who rapidly made a name for himself. Dark-skinned with large eyes and a full head of hair that sometimes seemed to be standing up at attention (as if his thumb were stuck in a lightbulb socket), Carter was born in Fairfield, Iowa, in 1910, one of four children of a barber and a maid. Musical for as long as he could remember, he received a piano from his parents on his eighth birthday. By the time he finished high school in Aurora, Illinois, he was an accomplished pianist and a fine singer. His ambition was to be a teacher, but there was no money for college.

Infatuated with the movies, Carter saved for a one-week trip to L.A. in 1933. As he roamed around the city, up and down its now famous boulevards, he couldn't get past any studio gate. "Everyone in Hollywood absolutely refused to see me," he said. Down to his last eight dollars, Carter bought a stylish, white double-breasted suit, which he wore along with a straw hat, as he strolled through Hollywood once more.

Spotting the Columbia Broadcasting Studios, he noticed that the door to the radio studio was open. He walked in. When the young receptionist who guarded the electronically locked gate inside saw him, she buzzed him in—without saying a word. Not able to let this opportunity pass him by, Carter breezed in and wandered through the halls. Suddenly, a man he didn't know grabbed his arm. "I'm certainly glad I ran into you," the man told him. "Where have you been?" Obviously, the man had mistaken him for someone else. But Carter merely said, "I just got in from the East." The man then asked him to accept a spot on one of their programs. "Just play the piano and sing a number or two. The trouble is that we can only pay you $250 a week, but we'll be thankful if you accept." Carter was thankful, too. He had his big break. Thus began his three-year tenure as a regular on the *Happy Go Lucky* radio hour. Whether true or not, Carter loved telling the story, which became part of his "official" studio bio. He also liked saying that he never found out who the man had thought Carter was.

Settling into town, Carter availed himself of every opportunity that came his way. He organized a sixteen-member children's choral group called Ben Carter's Pickaninny Choir. Carter put Eugene Jackson in the choir along with Jackson's half brother Freddie Baker and that aspiring young trio The Dandridge Sisters. Thereafter, he went into the agenting business. Opening an office on Central Avenue in 1935, Carter handled the performers Libby Taylor, Zack Williams, Hattie Noel, Ruby Elzy, Bernice Pilot, and Oscar Polk, all of whom, Carter informed the press, earned $250 a week or more. Carter collected 10 percent of their earnings. Helping the studios find large groups of extras for big pictures, he boasted of casting every black part in *Gone with the Wind* except for the characters Mammy, Prissy, and Uncle Peter. But his biggest commission—$3,000— came when he supplied MGM with the Negro performers for the 1937 Marx Brothers movie *A Day at the Races.*

When white agents noticed his booming business, they raided his clients. Protecting himself, Carter merged his company with the Bert Levy Agency. For a time, he controlled 60 percent of the black performers in Hollywood and was dubbed the "Myron Selznick of Central Avenue"— after David O. Selznick's brother, the high-powered Hollywood agent. "I haven't lost a dollar in commissions in three years," he said in 1940. "My clients know if they don't pay, they won't get work next time. Some of my clients are so grateful they want to give me more commissions than I'm supposed to get. You oughta see my house on Christmas—just full of gifts."

A master at making contacts, Carter soon enjoyed a rather lavish lifestyle. When he was feeling particularly good, he liked to summon his chauffeur to take him for a cruise "on the avenue"—Central Avenue, of course—where, like Stepin Fetchit, he appeared before his adoring fans. "I've got to put on the dog," said Carter. "I must make myself twice as successful as I really am, if I'm to command respect—especially in my agency." Yet Carter didn't hit Central Avenue too often. That might "destroy the glamor he so laboriously built around himself as an actor and agent," wrote *The New York Times*. Carter lived by a cardinal rule of Hollywood: once you've created your image, maintain it. That in all likelihood explained his marriage to an eighteen-year-old girl in the early 1940s. Carter and his bride resided in the West Jefferson section of town, not far from the residences of Hattie McDaniel, Bojangles, and Eddie Anderson. The marriage, however, was brief and probably the talk of the town because Carter was known to be at the center of early gay Black Hollywood. Opening the doors of his home for a steady flow of guests, male and female, he might have one eye on his guests, *in general,* and another on a candidate for a little mischief later in the evening.

At these gatherings, almost all the guests were *on,* laughing, gossiping, exchanging stories, eating, and always trying their best to get Carter's attention—with the hope, of course, that he might find them work. Unlike Clarence Muse's social affairs, never was there any pretense at Carter's. No lofty talk about the thee-tah. Or the cinema. Politics were important to Carter—and he never hesitated to express his political views. "Ben was very intelligent," said Geri Branton. "He was also a Marxist." But Carter, social to his bones, liked to talk about the mysteries he loved to read—and to let everyone know that his favorite exercise was sleeping. The actor he admired most: John Barrymore. His afternoons or evenings were for fun and making contacts, not for pontificating on weighty matters. The ever-ambitious Ruby Dandridge didn't miss a chance to promote her daughters *or* herself at Carter's social events. "She would come over to Ben's, and sometimes the girls would be with her, sometimes not," recalled actor Lennie Bluett. "She was always trying to get the girls in vaudeville or anything she could get for them. Pushing. Pushing. Pushing. Ruby was a typical stage mother." Her attentions to Carter proved fruitful. When he cast the colored performers for *A Day at the Races,* Dorothy, Vivian, and Etta Jones were included.

Shrewd and energetic, Carter teamed later with Mantan Moreland in a comedy act and kept pounding on the studio doors—supposedly always

*The agent who won better roles for himself than his clients:
Ben Carter (left) with his comedy partner, Mantan Moreland.*

for his clients. But Carter himself rose to play an important role, as the bartender Noah in *Little Old New York*. Originally, Twentieth Century Fox's casting office set up a meeting between Carter and the film's director, Henry King, to discuss finding a black actor for the Noah role. Sitting by King's desk, Carter described two clients he considered perfect. As Carter told the story later, King suddenly said, "You play it." "But I'm an agent, not an actor," said Carter. Of course, that wasn't really true. By then, Carter had appeared in at least eight films. "Just the same," said King, "you're going to play it." Carter was tested and played the role, much to the dismay of some of his clients, who felt the person Ben Carter was most interested in representing was Ben Carter.

Next, director Henry King wanted Carter to play the pivotal role of Hattie McDaniel's husband, the triflin' Shadrach, in a big film called *Maryland*. Carter said he pleaded with King to consider one of his clients. But the director would not hear of it. Carter ended up playing the role. But he softened the blow at his agency by persuading King to use his clients in other roles as well as his choral group. Also in the film: Clinton Rosemond, Darby Jones, Zack Williams, and those vets Madame Sul-Te-Wan and Clarence Muse. The role of Shadrach drew great attention. "Some one was smart enough to know that, next to horses, one of the most affectionate indulgences of a Maryland squire is colored folks," wrote *The New York Times*. "And plenty of these dusky worthies have been scattered all around. The funniest sequence in the picture is that of a Negro revival meeting at which Shadrach, Uncle Willie's groom, gets filled up with religion. And Shadrach, next to the horses, is the best thing in the show. Ben Carter, who plays the part, is a priceless find." Fox signed Carter to a seven-year contract. He appeared in such movies as *Tin Pan Alley, Crash Dive,* and at MGM in *The Harvey Girls,* earning about fifteen thousand dollars a year from his movie work. Some clients probably never forgave him. But Carter stayed in the agency business—and also kept his choral group going, too, always aware that his acting roles could dry up at any time.

PLAYERS NEW AND OLD

Among the new performers going from bits to roles were not only Hattie and Etta McDaniel but also Hattie Noel, Libby Taylor, Mantan Moreland, Eddie Anderson, Clinton Rosemond, Ernest Whitman, and Lillian Randolph. Veterans from the 1920s such as Louise Beavers, George Reed, and of course, the estimable Clarence Muse were still on the scene. Eyeing the contingent of newcomers, actresses such as Madame Sul-Te-Wan and Carolynne Snowden realized that they had to walk twice as fast just to keep in place. Madame held on, playing her bits as grizzled older women and occasionally lucking out with a juicy part such as that of Mustard in the women's prison drama *Ladies They Talk About.* But the bloom on Snowden's rose was gone. She hadn't appeared in a movie since *Fox Movietone Follies of 1929.* Her early dream of some semblance of movie stardom would never be fulfilled.

In 1933, Los Angeles was rattled by an earthquake that took its toll on one of Black Hollywood's glamour girls. Twenty-eight-year-old Mildred Washington, who had been the ingenue in *Hearts in Dixie,* was still plugging away in movies such as *The Shopworn Angel* and *Torch Singer*—as well as headlining in her sexy revues at niteries such as the Legion Club and Jazzland. Away from the nightclubs, she became known for her literary tastes. Having studied French and Latin, she enjoyed showing off the library at her home with its well-worn volumes of Homer and Milton. When the earthquake hit, she was rehearsing with other performers for

King Kong at the Egyptian Theatre. Running outside, she had tripped. Taken to the hospital, she suffered from appendicitis, which led to peritonitis. "Mildred Washington Dies" read the banner headline in *The California Eagle above* the paper's name in the September 8, 1933, edition. Black Hollywood grieved this up-and-coming star.

Black Hollywood knew it still needed stars—and glamorous ones at that—if it was to have any impact on the industry. The actress whose career looked most promising was Theresa (sometimes spelled Teresa) Harris, a petite, brown-skinned, Houston-born beauty with large, intelligent eyes, a sexy smile, and an endearing girlishness in her best early roles. Josef von Sternberg featured her in a musical number in *Thunderbolt* and used her briefly as a camp follower in *Morocco*. Then somehow, through grit and gumption, she landed showy supporting roles in the 1933 movies *Hold Your Man,* with Clark Gable and Jean Harlow, and *Baby Face,* with Barbara Stanwyck. Her portrayals of hip young women in the big, bad city were considered modern and forward-looking. But Harris had her share of dim-maid roles in movies of the late 1930s such as *Jezebel* and *The Toy Wife*. Later, a producer had the bright idea of casting her as the love interest for Eddie "Rochester" Anderson in *Love Thy Neighbor* and *Buck Benny Rides Again.*

Many performers kept silent about their dissatisfaction or anger over the lack of decent roles. Like the white stars, they knew bad-mouthing the industry got them nothing except a one-way ticket back to wherever they had come from. And that was the last place anybody wanted to go. But Harris—who was both outspoken and highly intelligent—didn't mince words, informing the black press of her misgivings about the plight of colored actresses. "I never felt the chance to rise above the role of maid in Hollywood movies. My color was against me," she told the enterprising Fay Jackson. "The fact that I was not 'hot' stamped me either as an uppity 'Negress' or relegated me to the eternal role of stooge or servant. I can sing but so can hundreds of other girls. My ambitions are to be an actress. Hollywood had no parts for me." Still, Harris worked into the next two decades.

WAITING FOR THE BIG PICTURE

By the mid-1930s, there hadn't been a big picture for Negroes since *Hearts in Dixie* and *Hallelujah*—and though these musicals had offered

Theresa Harris tosses her movie maid costumes aside and shows how a glamour girl should look for an evening of fun.

dramatic possibilities, they were, after all, musicals in rural settings. Talking pictures still hadn't cast Negro performers in all-out powerhouse dramatic roles. Nor had there been an important drama that provided some depiction of African Americans in a more urban, sophisticated setting.

Then word spread that director John Stahl, who had used so many African American performers in the 1927 *In Old Kentucky,* was making the rounds, hitting the colored clubs and showing up at small theaters, observing young Negro actresses. What Stahl was up to was anybody's guess. Then, in late 1933, an article appeared in *The California Eagle* with a headline—"Universal to Film Story on 'Passing for White' "—that caught the attention of all of black Hollywood. Readers learned that the studio planned to dramatize Fannie Hurst's novel *Imitation of Life.* "It is the story of a colored mammy whose daughter passes for a white girl and marries a white man."

A few weeks later, another news item appeared in *The Eagle:*

UNIVERSAL SENDS EAST
FOR COLORED GIRL
IN BIG PART

• • •

NOTED DIRECTOR ON
STRANGEST CASTING MISSION ON RECORD

John M. Stahl, Universal star director, left for New York. . . .

It is Stahl's intention and hope to find a talented young mulatto or quadroon, who could pass for white. . . . He will make an extensive quest through Harlem night clubs in New York, believing that somewhere in that renowned colored belt he will find the right girl.

A few weeks later—with the headline "Universal Still Looks for White-Negro Girl: Director John Stahl Conducts Strange Search for *Imitation of Life*"—the paper reported, "Director John M. Stahl requires in the leading role a young girl who must be of Negro blood but must be absolutely white, a 'throwback' of several generations to which there has at some time been a white father!"

Now the ears of the *entire* town perked up. Could this be the big picture about Negro life—with the big dramatic roles for black actresses?

Imitation of Life told the story of two mothers, one white, the other black, each with a young daughter and no husband, who meet and live together. Intertwined with the "woman's picture" melodramatics in the film version would be a trenchant comment on a capitalistic system that enables the white woman, Bea Pullman, to rise from poverty to economic splendor by way of a pancake mix. It's based on a recipe that has been passed down to the black woman, Delilah, by her family. The white woman packages and markets the mix, which becomes a huge national success. But heartache comes to both women as their children grow up. Bea's daughter becomes her rival in a love affair with a dashing bachelor. Delilah is devastated when her light-skinned daughter, Peola, rejects her and chooses to pass for white. The movie would climax with the heartbreaking (and prolonged) death and funeral of the black Delilah.

Signed to play the white entrepreneur Bea Pullman was Claudette Colbert. For the role of the Negro mother, Delilah—who was to be heavyset and dark-skinned—any number of actresses in Hollywood were available. Women like Etta and Hattie McDaniel were making the casting rounds. Finally, director Stahl chose Louise Beavers, who had not only the physi-

cal appearance but also that combination of warmth and a childlike vulnerability that the part demanded. But the role of the light-skinned
daughter was trickier to cast. McKinney was certainly a possibility. Neither
Snowden nor Theresa Harris was even in the running.

Though Stahl might easily have settled on a white actress for the Negro
role, he was determined to find a black one. Stahl told the press, "This girl
is the daughter of a colored mammy and this point obviously makes it impossible to use an established screen player or, in fact, any girl of Caucasian
birth. Such a thing, so to speak, would simply not 'go down' with theater
audiences." He added that the actress had to be a screen newcomer and
"though of colored birth" had to look so Caucasian "that even her own
lover would not realize the secret of her birth." Stahl also told the Negro
press, "*Imitation of Life* is now being prepared for filming, and before the
other roles are cast I will be glad to interview at the studio any white Negro
girl who fills these specifications. But she must fill them completely."

For Black Hollywood, Stahl's search for the right Negro actress for this
dramatic role—he was reported to have considered some three hundred
women—would be comparable to David O. Selznick's later search for his
Scarlett O'Hara and Otto Preminger's search for his Carmen Jones. For
weeks, casting news on *Imitation of Life* was the number one topic in Black
Hollywood.

In New York, Stahl spotted an actress he simply could not forget. Not
only was she the right complexion but she also had striking eyes that
looked by turns wounded and haunted. Stage-trained, she spoke with authority and had a distinct presence. She had already appeared in movies
filmed in New York. Perhaps most important for Stahl, she projected intelligence. The director also must have sensed that she might bring something to the role that was not necessarily written into the script—and that
she might give the character an emotional truth by drawing on some of her
own professional tensions and disappointments. After all, how many roles
would there really be for a black actress who looked white? All of this
made the young Fredi Washington the ideal choice for Stahl's Peola.

In some respects, Washington had been Peola but without the angst or
the self-loathing. "She looked like *white*. She had skin like Dresden china
and had blue eyes," recalled New York actress Maude Russell. Once, when
Washington had gone on a call for a role, the producer told her, "I expected
to see a colored girl. You look like Joan Crawford." The millionaire Wall
Street financier, Otto Kahn—openly entranced—told her, "You could eas-

ily be French." Urging her to change her name to a French one, he said
he'd pay for her dramatic education at the Theater Guild School. "But I
want to be who I am, nothing else," she said.

Born Fredericka Carolyn Washington in 1903 in Savannah, Georgia,
the oldest of nine children, Washington and her younger sister Isabel
(sometimes spelled Isabelle) had been sent from the South to Philadelphia
by their father—following the death of their mother—to study at St. Elizabeth's Convent. As a teenager, Fredi moved to the place of her dreams,
Harlem, to live with their grandmother. There, she attended high school
and then worked as a typist and secretary for Harry Pace at black composer
W. C. Handy's Black Swan Records. With no theatrical experience, she
left Black Swan to tour as a dancer in the chorus of *Shuffle Along*. From
there, she danced in the chorus at Manhattan's Club Alabam, where she
was spotted by producer Lee Shubert, who suggested her for a dramatic
role opposite Paul Robeson in the play *Black Boy* in 1926. A frequent visitor at rehearsals was a transfixed Otto Kahn. When the play closed, he introduced Washington to his son, dance-band leader Roger Wolfe Kahn,
who later hired Fredi and her dance partner Al Moiret to appear at his new
club Le Perroquet. Billed as Moiret and Fredi, the two toured Europe—
Paris, Nice, Berlin, Dresden, Hamburg. In London, she taught the latest
dance craze, the Black Bottom, to the Prince of Wales.

By then, fifteen-year-old Isabel had followed in Fredi's footsteps. Once
in Harlem, Isabel also worked after school each day at Black Swan. Later,
she sang at Connie's Inn and the Cotton Club, danced in the chorus at the
Alhambra, appeared in Wallace Thurman's play *Harlem* and in the short
film *St. Louis Blues* with Bessie Smith—as the high-yaller gal with whom
Smith fought for her man Jimmy. In 1931, she and Fredi appeared together in *Singin' the Blues*.

A darling of the theater world, Isabel was pursued by a cluster of men.
But she ignored them all to marry Adam Clayton Powell Jr.—future con-
gressman and the son of the pastor of Harlem's famous Abyssinian Baptist
Church—and then to give up her career.

Fredi, however, kept working in theater—and in films. Director Dudley
Murphy cast her as the leading lady—a fatally ill young beauty—of an elegant Duke Ellington in the short *Black and Tan*. Murphy also cast her in
The Emperor Jones as the *hincty* high-strung vamp who turns angry and
vindictive when her man, played by Paul Robeson, dumps her. But she was
so light that they darkened her for fear that audiences might think Robeson was playing romantic scenes with a white actress.

Fredi Washington, the girl with the boy's name who came west to appear in Imitation of Life.

During these years, Washington had more than her share of stage-door Johnnies. For years, rumors circulated about an affair between Washington and Paul Robeson. But "the love of her life was Duke Ellington," said her sister Isabel. Drawn to his looks and intelligence, his talent and sophistication, as he no doubt was attracted to the same characteristics in her, Washington had a discreet but passionate affair with him. Yet Washington's hopes that he would leave his wife never materialized. "I just had to accept that he wasn't going to marry me," she said. "But I wasn't going to be his mistress." At one point, a despondent Washington "left the country to get over Duke," said blues singer Alberta Hunter. "She just got on a boat and went to Paris," said Isabel, "and when she got back, Duke had taken up with a friend of hers." "It was no secret that she and my father had been involved, during and after the making of the film *Black and Tan*," said

Fredi Washington's favorite publicity still.

Mercer Ellington. "They remained close for quite some time." Washington's feelings for Ellington remained the same, but she was more in control of them.

She ended up marrying a member of his band, trombonist Lawrence Brown, in 1933. Born in 1907, the son of a minister, Brown had moved with his family to Oakland in 1914, then to Pasadena. A radio performance by a very young Brown caught the attention of evangelist Aimee Semple McPherson. Afterward, Brown ended up performing at McPherson's Los Angeles Temple on a Mother's Day with six thousand people in attendance. He moved to Los Angeles. There, his brother Harold was a well-respected pianist and—along with his wife, the engaging Nellie—outgoing and social with many friends in the entertainment business.

Fredi and Lawrence were a young and wildly attractive couple. With dark eyes, smooth skin, and a very *male* magnetism, Brown was a man whom women found irresistible. One night as future producer Jean Bach sat in a club with a group of friends, including her husband at that time, a friend shouted to the group, "Shut up! Lawrence Brown is playing. Jean's swooning over there." "If you can imagine Rudolph Valentino being black and playing the trombone," said Bach, "that was Lawrence Brown. He was *really* handsome." At first, Brown couldn't take his eyes off Fredi. He absolutely adored her. But in many respects, Lawrence was "duped" into the marriage, said Bach. It was said that Ellington sometimes "passed" his lovers on to members of his orchestra. "There were five musicians in the band who married women subsequent to their having had affairs with Ellington," said A. H. Lawrence. But the Ellington/Washington relationship appeared to be more serious. Said Jean Bach, "Duke decided and they plotted. He said, 'There's this young guy coming in from California. He's obviously not married. So you two should get married. And there would be a reason to travel with the band.' Lawrence didn't know what hit him. He just thought this gorgeous woman wants to get married." "I guess I was still trying to be as close to Duke as I could," Washington once said of her decision to marry Brown.

In the midst of this romantic dilemma, Fredi Washington's life, however, changed when she came to the attention of John Stahl. "They were testing girls all over the states," recalled Washington. "I got a call or telegram from Universal, asking me to call the studio in New York over on Fifty-seventh Street on the West Side. So I called and made an appointment. And they said they'd like to test me for this role in *Imitation of Life*.

So an appointment was set up, and I tested. And I didn't hear any more from it. I think it must have been four months or something. I forgot about it."

Scarce as serious stage roles for African Americans in New York might be, Washington believed even fewer opportunities existed for an actress like herself in Hollywood. At the time, her favorite actresses were Helen Hayes and Nina Mae McKinney. Though she liked Nina Mae McKinney's performance in *Hallelujah*, Washington believed that McKinney was the exception to the rule of the way Hollywood usually cast African Americans. She had seen the comic, wide-eyed servants. "I didn't look down on [the movies]," she said. "I looked down [on] . . . the kind of roles they were giving us. I had no interest. And I certainly was not going to do the kind of roles I had seen them give to other Negro actresses."

But while Washington had forgotten Hollywood, Hollywood—or at least, John Stahl—had not forgotten her. Universal learned she was due to arrive in Los Angeles at the same time as Duke Ellington's orchestra. "When we pulled into Union Station in Los Angeles, there was a representative from Universal at the station to meet me," Washington recalled. "Somehow he knew I was coming. And so they made an appointment then and there."

At Universal, Washington met with John Stahl. "He wanted me to do a test," she recalled. "And he wanted me to take a script home." Stahl also had an unusual request. "He wanted my reaction to the script."

Washington carefully read the screenplay, noting what was being said and what was implied, not only about the character Peola but about African Americans in general. One scene that struck her as patently false took place in a posh white restaurant where Peola, employed as a cashier, is discovered to be black. "They were able to tell Peola was a Negro by the lack of half moons on her fingers," said Washington. When she next met with John Stahl, she mentioned the sequence. "There are a few things you better get straightened out," she told him. "I am Negro, and I've got huge moons on my fingers." Showing him her nails, she asked, "Now what does that make me?" Stahl got the message. "He agreed with me." The script was changed. "Stahl decided immediately that I was the person that he wanted."

Her professional relationship with Stahl was pleasant and respectful. But Washington had more difficult meetings with Universal representatives. "We got to the point of talking about a contract. And they gave me a song and dance," she recalled. "They [intended] to sign me up for less money than I wanted. And I'd be signed up for the studio. I told them I wasn't interested." Her refusal to sign puzzled the studio. Five- or seven-year studio contracts were the goal of just about every actor and actress in town. "I don't know if I would be good in the movies," Washington told them. "And if I'm not good, I don't want to be in the movies. That's in the future. We can talk about that later. Let's talk about *Imitation of Life*. This is what I'm interested in now."

But the studio was insistent. "They haggled," said Washington, "and I told them to forget it." When they informed her that the contract was to her advantage, that they would teach and train her for a career in films, Washington said firmly, "Look, I didn't come out here to learn to act. I brought that with me. I've been on Broadway. You don't have to sell me a bill of goods, because you can't. Because I'm really not *that* interested. It doesn't matter to me whether I make this picture or whether I don't, because I know one thing—if I make it and I'm good, you're not going to have another script for me. So I wouldn't want to be thrown in a western here or this-or-that there." Washington was not going to be forced into playing some dim-witted maid because of a contractual agreement. "So let's not even discuss this."

Salary discussions also proved prickly. Universal balked that she was asking for too much. "We're not paying Beavers that," an executive told her.

"I didn't come here to talk about the contract with Beavers," she said. "Beavers takes care of her own business. I take care of mine. I don't even want to know what you're paying her."

Finally, the studio agreed to give her the salary she requested. One representative with whom she talked "turned out to be very nice. A polite little man." But her hassles with Universal hadn't yet ended. "When they decided to pay me what I wanted," said Washington, "they wanted me to sign a contract then and there." She told them, "No. I have to send this to my lawyer to look it over. And if he thinks it looks all right, then I'll be kind enough to put my signature on this piece of paper." That surprised everyone in the room. "They just couldn't get over this," said Washington. "They just hadn't dealt before with anyone like me in our race."

In the end, Universal let her lawyer review the contract. For her work on the film, Washington was paid five hundred dollars a week. "At that time, it was very good," she said.

"*Imitation of Life* to Start at Once at Universal," reported *The California Eagle* on June 1, 1934. "Unless the unforeseen happens or some undiscovered Sepia blooded luminary appears on the horizon, Fredi Washington pretty petite little tan complexioned eastern actress will play the part that makes the strange Fannie Hurst story *Imitation of Life* possible. This is that of a colored girl so white that as she grows up she not only pass [*sic*] for a Nordeic [*sic*] but marries a wealthy scion of a leading family."

"Claudette Pleased with Freddi [*sic*], Co-star in *Imitation* Film" was the headline in the next week's edition. "Mr. Stahl has made tests of more than a score of the 300 light Negro girls who have applied for the unusual opportunities of the Negro mammy and her daughter." Also reported was news that for the role of the young Peola, "Mr. Chas Butler of Central Casting bureau had several fair little girls about the age of nine or ten sent out to the studio on interview." Black child actresses Sebie Hendricks and Dorothy Black were hired to play Peola at ages four and nine.

So different were Louise Beavers and Fredi Washington that the gossips expected fireworks, perhaps like those set off by their characters in the film. Beavers: the agreeable, easygoing actress with a quick, hearty laugh and a burning desire to keep working in movies. Washington: sleek, serious, and sophisticated in a distinctly New York way and eager to make the film and return east. But surprisingly, the two became friends. By the time the picture started, Lawrence Brown was back on the road with Ellington. Arrangements were made for Washington to live at Beavers's home during filming. "I stayed with Louise because I was in Los Angeles alone," said Washington.

"She was in an entirely different position than I was because this was her living. Pictures were the only thing she knew. But what she had done before, she didn't want to continue to do. So this for her was a step-up break. Because she had done only maid roles. *Yessum* parts. Her approach was naturally different from mine. And she had a Hollywood agent. And that's a scuffle. And they had to work pretty hard at that time to get these jobs for their clients. I was from the East. I had no intentions of living in California. Had no intentions of looking to pictures to make my living. And I was married. And so I could be more demanding." Often, the women "went to work together. Sometimes, she'd go with me. Sometimes, I'd go with her."

Filming at Universal went well. Arriving at the studio early in the morning, Washington went through the daily rituals of makeup, hair, and wardrobe without showing signs of being overly impressed. Universal hired a black makeup artist—Marcia Baumann, of Ella La Blanche Cosmetology—for Washington, Beavers, and young Dorothy Black. Entering the huge sound stage, Washington looked like a young professional woman ready for the day's job rather than someone caught up in—or intimidated by—the allure of a big-time Hollywood production. Aware of the long stares and the curiosity about her, she was cordial but kept a certain distance. Throughout her life, Fredi Washington could be a socially engaging woman. But there was always a part that she kept to herself. Perhaps because of her convent upbringing and the loss of her mother when she was so young, Washington learned to shield her emotions and not to depend on anyone. That refined aloofness ultimately was part of her appeal in Hollywood, as it had been in New York. It earned her respect.

On the set, the big star was Claudette Colbert, whom Washington remembered as being "very nice to work with. As a matter of fact, the whole cast was very nice to work with." But at the end of the day, most cast members went their separate ways. "The only association I had with [Colbert] was on the set. Of course, when I finished my work, I left the studio. I left all those people that I worked with at the studio until the next day." Except Beavers.

During filming, Washington had difficulty with one line of dialogue. In a sequence in which Peola was to look in the mirror and then say that she wanted to be white, Washington bristled. "It just rubbed me the wrong way," said Washington. Finally, she told Stahl, "I cannot read that line like that, actress or no actress. This comes too close to home. I just can't read that line." Stahl asked, "How would you read it?" For Washington, the fallacy of *Imitation of Life* was its assertion that Peola simply wanted to be white, as if whiteness itself were an ideal to be pursued. "I always felt," said Washington, "that Peola didn't want to be white. She wanted *white opportunities,* the very same chance at life that her white friend Jessie, who she has grown up with, will now have as an adult." That's the way Washington wanted to play the scene. "Okay. If you feel comfortable with that," said Stahl. "Daily on the set," wrote Bernice Patton of *The Pittsburgh Courier,* "I saw him scrutinize the script religiously so that there was as little offense as possible. Throughout the screen version, he struck out the word nigger."

A significant aspect of the Peola story line, however, *was* changed. The press had publicized the fact that Peola would marry a white man. In the novel, the character, after having herself sterilized, made plans to marry an injured South American—and then leave the country. But movie audiences never saw Fredi Washington's Peola even glance in the direction of a man, black or white.

On July 1, 1934, the movie studios agreed to a self-regulatory Production Code of ethics, which specified what could and could not be depicted on-screen—and updated the old censorship rules enforced by Will Hays. Fearing the moralist groups, particularly the Catholic Legion of Decency, the industry created its own internal censorship board rather than acquiesce to outside censorship. Covering a range of topics, from crime to sex to vulgarity to "repellent subjects," the 1934 code also specified: "White slavery shall not be treated." (There didn't seem to be anything wrong with depicting good old-fashioned *black* slavery.) Most important, on the topic of interracial sex or love, the code declared: "Miscegenation (sex relationships between the white and black races) is forbidden."

Consequently, Fredi Washington's Peola, lovely as she was, was left romantically stranded.

Throughout, Beavers was told to watch her weight. The studio could not imagine a motherly black woman who was not overweight, looking as if she could literally carry the weight of the world on her shoulders. "I've got to stay fat," Beavers informed the press, sounding as if she was letting off some steam. "Yes, they want me to be plump. I couldn't have gotten the part of Delilah if I hadn't been stout. Then I went and lost twelve and a half pounds making the picture, and that was bad. It was the last part of the picture, when I grew old, that I needed to be the fattest. So they had to put a lot of extra petticoats on me."

During production, Beavers helped Washington navigate the sometimes rough waters of Black Hollywood. Though Fredi's brother-in-law Harold and his wife, Nellie, resided in town, Washington grew close to Beavers, the way people often do while working on a film. Beavers, always shrewder than she looked, knew the town inside out and was quick to let Fredi know who was who and what was what: who the shysters and charlatans were, who the gossips were, whom it didn't hurt to impress, whom it wasn't important to give the time of day to. By now, the town was in a full swinging recovery from the Great Depression with a nightlife and an atmosphere, so Fredi discovered, as distinct as Harlem's.

THE CITY JUMPS

The nightclubs were jumping. With the passage of the Twenty-first Amendment, Prohibition was repealed in 1933. And now that nighttime revelers could take a drink without worrying about a raid, the town seemed to breathe a collective sigh of relief. Club Alabam was the main spot—also patronized by white Hollywood, as the old Apex had been. Limousines drove up carrying stars like George Raft, Bette Davis, and Mae West. Club Araby drew crowds, too. In time, Curtis Mosby launched a new Apex. Other clubs followed: The Memo, the Downbeat, and another Curtis Mosby–owned nitery, The Last Word, all located within blocks of one another. Teeming with people dressed to the hilt and eager for fun, excitement, romance, booze, and some big-time entertainment, the area came to be known as Little Harlem.

Nicknamed The Stem, Central Avenue still dazzled. The hub was still at Twelfth and Central. Musician Phil Moore, who came to town in the 1930s to perform at the Lincoln Theatre, was so excited by all the energy and glamour that he thought he had died and gone to heaven. "*The Avenue,*" recalled Moore, "was astounding and magical. . . . Man, it was swingin'! I'd never seen super 'high class' show business and so many sharp ladies as I saw at the various nightclubs. Many places had real produced shows with M.C.'s, lights, microphones, a line of dancing girls, featured acts, stars, and much larger nightclub bands of higher quality musicians than I had ever been exposed to." Still pulling in the patrons, the Lincoln Theatre now featured headliners like Pigmeat Markham, Lionel Hampton, comic Dusty "Open the Door, Richard" Fletcher, the Delta Rhythm Boys, and later its master of ceremonies, Leonard Reed. Whenever celebrities left the Lincoln, Moore recalled, "Grown folks and kids would flood the street by the stage entrance to say hello and get autographs. I even felt like a celebrity when someone recognized me."

The restaurants and shops on Central Avenue were back in business, too. The Gold Furniture Company's store became the place to go for setting up a house or an apartment. And the place where everybody—common folk as well as musicians—could get a good, cheap solid meal was Father Divine's restaurant. "Father Divine was a gentleman based in New York City that had convinced quite a national congregation he was God, and preached obedience and celibacy for his flock, not for himself, 'cause he always had his personal 'angel' hanging 'round," Moore remembered. At Father Divine's restaurant, patrons were served by wholesome-looking women "in white stiffly starched nurse-like outfits." "We could eat a full dinner for thirteen cents (weekdays), and a good doin' chicken dinner with all the trimmings for fifteen cents on Sundays. And for two cents extra we could get a trowel sized hunk of hot deep-dish multi-fruit cobbler called 'The Mixed Multitude.' Damn, this was some good scarfin'!" Moore also recalled, "I don't know whether Father was God, but he was a godsend to 'hongry' show-people."

THE SMART SET

Social life was humming among L.A.'s black smart set. Still as social as ever were the servants to the stars and some employees at the studios. Invitations for their events could be hard to come by. Geraldine Pate recalled that when she arrived in Los Angeles in the early 1940s as the young bride of Fayard Nicholas, "The big deals socially were still the servants of big-time Hollywood stars. They were known all over the town and held elaborate balls or major parties." Some of the servant/studio employees shrewdly continued to move up the ranks and out of servanting.

That certainly was true of the young woman whom drummer Lionel Hampton met one evening when he was appearing at the Antique Art Club with Paul Howard's Quality Serenaders. At the time, he was looking for a new place to live. The young woman told him about her mother's boarding house on Central Avenue. Before he knew it, he moved in the next morning. "I didn't know the girl's name, and already she had made a major decision for me. That was Gladys. It was 1929. And from that day until she died, she made all the major decisions."

Born in Lehigh, Oklahoma, on an Indian reservation—she was part Native American—and having grown up in Dennison, Texas, Gladys Riddle worked in the late 1920s and early 1930s as a seamstress at the movie studios. Hampton was impressed by her style; her looks—"she was a beautiful girl—tall, light complected, carried herself well"; and the attention she lavished on him. "She'd bring home the silk drawers that she made for some guy. Either it was Douglas Fairbanks, Jr., who was married to Joan Crawford; or else it was Lord Mountbatten, who was friends with Hearst and who found out about Gladys from Marion Davies. . . . Whichever one it was liked handmade silk underwear with his initials embroidered on them, and he would wear a pair only three, four times. Well, Gladys was never one to waste anything, and so when he got rid of those drawers, she'd take them back and bring them home to me."

She also took charge of his affairs, getting him special billing at the Culver City Cotton Club and eventually negotiating record contracts. Once the two married, she continued to manage his career. Never did she back off from speaking her mind. Once, when Hampton fired the young singer Betty Carter, Gladys rehired her! She also assumed her place as an important figure on the music scene and in the social circles of black entertainers. Known as smart and tough and someone you didn't play with, she had a good, shrewd head for finance. When money came in, she would invest in real estate. "She bought a building on Adams Street in Los Angeles," said Hampton, "for twenty-seven thousand dollars." In time, she helped make Hampton wealthy. Though clearly a capable and professional woman, she was also, for Black Hollywood, one of its early Hollywood wives: those masters of social engineering who ran brilliantly managed households while always keeping an eye tightly fastened on their husbands' careers.

THE WASHINGTONS

During this era and into the next, Hazel Washington, onetime maid to Garbo and longtime assistant to Rosalind Russell, became well known in the city. Willing to try her hand at anything that might be a challenge—or fun—she became one of the early black licensed hairdressers employed by the studios to tend to the hairstyles of black actresses on such later movies as *Cabin in the Sky* and *Stormy Weather.* Like everyone else, Hazel couldn't resist a chance to appear in front of the camera. When she learned of the large number of players needed for *Imitation of Life,* she headed to Universal and won herself a small role. With her employer Rosalind Russell as her partner, she also opened a leather-goods store in Beverly Hills.

She added to her social luster with her marriage to black police officer Roscoe Washington. At a time when not many black cops prowled the beat in L.A., Roscoe became a lieutenant on the force. He also was a member of a well-known, ambitious family. His father had been a cook on the railroad and then with his own mess wagon in the mining camps in California. With his wife, Susie, and their children, Roscoe's father settled in Lincoln Heights, then "a big Italian community with a few Irish mixed in," said actor Woody Strode, who knew the entire Washington family. "To the best of my knowledge, the Washington family was the only Black family in that neighborhood."

Susie took a job as a janitor at the Avenue 19 Grammar School. Though she never went past the sixth grade, she became self-taught and filled with a fierce determination that her children grow up aware of the city and world in which they lived. Each morning, she would rise early, go out to buy the *Los Angeles Examiner,* then read the paper to her children.

The three Washington sons—Roscoe, Julius, and Edgar—all made names for themselves in the city. Julius became a fire chief, known for being a speeder. "Coming out of the garage, he'd be going ninety by the time he hit the back gate," Woody Strode recalled. One afternoon on the way to a football game, fast-driving Julius was killed after making a bad turn.

Edgar was considered the bad boy of the family. Most people called him Blue. At eighteen, he married a sixteen-year-old girl, had a son named Kenny, then left his wife to take up with another woman and then another woman and then another. "He liked the girls, the bright lights, and so forth," said Strode. Relaxed and convivial when he wanted to be, Blue headed out to the studios and found work. His career in movies, however, was cut short by his lack of discipline. "Blue was making seventy-dollars a day when guys were making ten, fifteen dollars a week," recalled Strode. "He'd get four or five days in, have $300 in his pocket and nobody would see him again until the money was gone. The Washington family was constantly looking for Blue because some director was holding up a production until he could be found."

A skilled athlete who stood some six feet five inches and weighed more than two hundred pounds, Blue tried his luck in baseball, too. He played with the Negro National League team the Kansas City Monarchs as well as the Chicago Americans.

But of all the Washington sons, Roscoe Washington, called Rocky, proved the most disciplined. "He was the only Black officer of any rank on the Los Angeles Police Department," said Strode. "There were a couple men in the detective bureau who had the rank of detective lieutenant. That was the plainclothes detail, but Rocky was the first Black uniformed officer to make the rank of lieutenant." Strode also recalled the time when Rocky was put in charge of the Central Division, in downtown Los Angeles. "The whole department was buzzing, 'If you send that nigger over here, everybody in the station will be asking for a transfer out.' " But their attitudes changed. "When they found out what kind of guy he was, every guy on the force wanted to be on the night shift with Lieutenant Washington."

Kenny Washington, Edgar's handsome son, grew up to be one of the community's most promising young heroes—as well as a heartthrob for young women in the city, especially during his days as a football star at UCLA, along with two black teammates, future actor Woody Strode and future major league baseball star Jackie Robinson. Washington was UCLA's first all-American. Stars and executives alike attended the games of Washington, Strode, and Robinson and were thrilled by their victories. How could the executives show their appreciation? Well, the big shots at Warner Bros. started by giving Strode and Washington summer jobs. It didn't matter what the guys did. It was just great having them around. "Every morning the studio would assign us to a sound stage, and we'd stand around and wait for someone to order something," Strode recalled.

The stars were as impressed with Strode and Washington as the football players were with them. "They dressed us up in brown coats with epaulets and gold-braided ropes hanging from the shoulder. We wore caps like a bellhop in a hotel," recalled Woody Strode. "We took care of the stars. Bette Davis, Jimmy Cagney, Ann Sheridan, and Olivia de Havilland were some of the big Warner Bros. stars at that time. I remember walking up to Errol Flynn and him saying, 'Oh, you and Kenny, I just love watching you guys play!' All the movie stars were football fans."

Strode always remembered one of his most embarrassing moments, "when I was told to bring a tray of food to Jane Wyman's dressing room. When I saw her sitting there in that powder-blue silk robe, one leg half out, I was mesmerized by her beauty; she had a face like an angel. She watched me come in the door, and I got so flustered I tripped on the door jamb and fell all the way inside. The food and coffee went all over the carpet. But she smoothed it over for me and helped me clean it up. She said, 'You know, I'm a big fan of yours, you and Kenny Washington. How are you boys going to do this year?' "

Washington and Strode broke the color barrier in the National Football League when they joined the Los Angeles Rams in 1946. But dazzled by the bright lights, both worked in the movies. Strode went from bits to important roles in such John Ford films as *Sergeant Rutledge* and *The Man*

Who Shot Liberty Valance. Even their old teammate Jackie, after integrating baseball's major leagues in 1947, returned to star in a movie based on his life.

SOCIAL MAVENS AND MOVIE STARS

Publisher Charlotta Bass appeared too interested in political and social issues to spend much time dressing up and sipping cocktails. In 1934, the town was stunned to learn that her husband, Joseph, had died suddenly. Already, everyone in black L.A. knew Charlotta Bass as *Mrs.* Bass. She would remain *Mrs.* Bass for the rest of her life. But never did this tough-minded lady with the thick-rimmed glasses and rather exacting schoolmarm manner seem more vulnerable and solemn than in those years right after her husband's death. Bass looked as if she would bury herself in her work, determined to keep her paper published, despite pressing financial troubles. But she made the social rounds when she deemed it necessary. Lucius Lomax remained a prime mover but still was not a part of the social life of the town's black bourgeoisie. His son, Lucius Jr., ran the cocktail lounge at the Dunbar, where he was well liked. With his brainy wife, Almena, a journalist who worked for Charlotta Bass, he launched—in 1940—the publication of a new black weekly newspaper, *The Los Angeles Tribune,* which operated out of the Dunbar. He served as publisher; Almena, as its editor.

At the apex of the black bourgeoisie's socialites stood community leaders like Dr. John Somerville and Dr. Vada Somerville; prominent physician Dr. H. Claude Hudson and his wife; the up-and-coming *Sentinel* publisher Leon Washington and his savvy wife, Ruth; and of course, architect Paul Williams and his wife, Della; as well as various business leaders. Williams won even more top commissions, and his ties to Hollywood were as tight as ever. He created sumptuous homes for Tyrone Power and ZaSu Pitts in Brentwood as well as Beverly Hills residences for William Paley, Jay Paley, and the cocreator of radio's *Amos 'n' Andy,* Charles Correll. In 1937, he designed the building for the Music Corporation of America, one of the town's leading talent agencies.

A number of the social mavens prided themselves on doing something to lift the race up. Annually, *The Sentinel* presented a Christmas show at the Lincoln Theatre. Admission was free to those who brought cans of food, which, in turn, were given to the needy.

O n occasion, the social figures socialized with entertainers, especially big names from the East. A celebrity who clearly impressed the socialites was Duke Ellington, who was a highly sought after guest when in town. He was known for forging friendships with solid members of the black bourgeoisie, the doctors and lawyers. When he returned to Los Angeles in the mid-1930s to appear in the films *Murder at the Vanities* and *Belle of the Nineties,* white Hollywood was also excited. Now MGM's bootblack Slickem proved resourceful, impressing his bosses at the studio when he arranged a special evening for the famous East Coast star at Club Ebony on Central Avenue. On hand to meet Ellington—looking suave and debonair as always in his tailored suits—were Hollywood bigwigs and MGM stars, executives, and friends: directors W. S. Van Dyke and Dudley Murphy; songwriter and future producer Arthur Freed; MGM's vice president Eddie Mannix and his wife; scenarist Sam Marx. It was a glittering evening; black and white in Hollywood socialized together—although at separate tables. Slickem sat with his guests apart from his studio bosses. But he worked the room that night nonetheless.

Paul Robeson was equally popular with the black Angeleno socialites. Even Charlotta Bass was dazzled by him. Though he was rarely in town, his comings and goings were reported in *The Eagle.* In late September 1935, the big buzz was about Robeson's forthcoming arrival in L.A.—with his wife, Eslanda—to appear for the top fee of forty thousand dollars in Universal's production of the Jerome Kern / Oscar Hammerstein musical *Show Boat,* under the direction of James Whale. En route to L.A. by train, he and Eslanda had stopped in Chicago, where she interviewed Joe Louis for a book she hoped to write. "He's as sweet as he can be and crazy about the RACE," she wrote to Carl Van Vechten. Once in town, no African American actor, except perhaps Charles Gilpin, generated as much excitement or respect as Robeson. Having already worked in films, including Oscar Micheaux's *Body and Soul,* and the British *Sanders of the River,* Robeson was now making his first Hollywood movie, playing the character Joe opposite Hattie McDaniel. Also in *Show Boat* was a star-maker role for a black actress: the important mulatto character Julie, who is exposed as she tries to pass for white. The role, everyone knew, was perfect for Fredi Washington. But Universal cast white actress Helen Morgan, who had played the part in the original Broadway production of 1927.

On the set, Robeson worked well with Morgan and the rest of the cast, including the star, Irene Dunne, and director Whale. After his rendition of "Ol' Man River," the orchestra applauded. It would indeed be a great sequence in the history of the American movie musical. Grips and technicians often jostled to see him, which prompted Eslanda Robeson to write, "We are proudest of the enthusiasm and interest of the property men and the electricians. If you can interest them, you're good." After Robeson's two-month shoot ended, director Whale wrote that he hoped to "have the pleasure of directing you in a starring vehicle." Already, Robeson had brought a script based on the play *Black Majesty* by C.I.R. James to the attention of Whale as well as Hammerstein and Kern, who bought the movie rights. "What we all three want to do is get you going in *Black Majesty*," Whale wrote Robeson. Aware the film could be shot on a low budget in England, Hammerstein believed "such an unusual undertaking will have a better chance with [producer Alexander] Korda who is a man of taste and courage, untrammeled by the superstitions and the conventional convictions of Hollywood producers." In the end, the picture was never made.

Robeson himself must have had concerns about his role in *Show Boat*. Joe was considered a lazy, good-for-nothing fellow. When Robeson had played the role onstage, he had insisted on changes. The word *nigger* was replaced by *darky*. Now, he sought final-cut approval of his scenes in the movie. But Universal's Carl Laemmle Jr. cabled the studio, "Impossible let him okay takes. Garbo doesn't even have this privilege nor anyone else." Upon the film's release, Robeson, while praised by the mainstream press for his performance, drew some harsh criticism from the black press.

Still, in the black social world of the 1930s, Robeson and Ellington were high-class acts.

Later, the most prized entertainers at big social events would be Lena Horne and Dorothy Dandridge, who—so the solidly entrenched members of the black middle class believed—conveyed the appropriate sophistication. Louise Beavers and Hattie McDaniel would be high on the social list, too. But both actresses, when doing their charity work, seemed more comfortable with showbiz folk than the black high and mighty.

Fredi Washington also had her league of admirers. Though she limited her social outings during her brief time in Hollywood, Washington was well aware of some reactions to her in this visually oriented town, which had a clearly defined beauty standard that was accepted by—and of course, mirrored that of—the rest of the nation. Bodies should be slim. Skin should be creamy. Eyes should be sparkling. Youth was prized, as well.

Just one of those ordinary *nights on the town for the fabulous Washington Sisters, Fredi (right) and Isabel.*

During sittings for photographic portraits—those lush publicity shots—all stars understood the importance of makeup, lighting, and the right photographer *and* the right retoucher. Dietrich used makeup to sculpt a face—with those startling cheekbones—for herself. Crawford learned to dress to create the appropriate look. At events, everyone assessed how everyone else looked, and sometimes one star marveled at the way another managed to create an illusion. Every public appearance had to be a calculated and calibrated visual stunner, so much so that when stars grew older and could no longer maintain a certain look, many withdrew from public life, preferring to be remembered for their earlier, perfected illusionary selves. Creating an illusion was part of the ritual, part of the game, part of the culture of movieland life and identity. Yet though beauty was almost commonplace in Hollywood, some women had such an undeniable visual power—the actual face or natural beauty under the makeup combined with the sensual glow or majestic fire coming from within—that other personalities as well as industry leaders could be truly stunned by seeing them. That happened whenever Garbo appeared. Or Dolores Del

Rio. Or later, when Elizabeth Taylor came into a room. Or when industry people actually saw Lena Horne and Dorothy Dandridge in the flesh. Later, when Hollywood had to rethink its beauty standards, Cicely Tyson would have a similar effect. Washington's looks had the same power over people. Discussions about her were usually centered on her skin color and her blue-green eyes. In Hollywood, white *and* black were as fascinated as New York's sophisticated theater circles had been. Washington took it all in stride, having learned to live with it, rather than to thrive on it, at an early age.

mitation of Life was ready for release by December 1934. Word of mouth spread quickly within the industry: reactions at early screenings indicated that *Imitation of Life* was a highly moving and emotional film, even then viewed as a classic tearjerker. Within black Los Angeles, curiosity grew. Advance preview screening invitations were hard to come by. A writer for *The Pittsburgh Courier* was so angered that representatives from the black press were not invited to the première at the Pantages theater that the paper believed this incident another sign of the town's basic bigotry. Swept into the controversy was Louise Beavers. Generally, Beavers courted the African American press and considered herself an important member of Los Angeles's black community. But she clearly did not come off at her best when she supported the studio. "I'm getting a lot of publicity and I'm not worried about it," she said. Universal, however, admitted Bernice Patton of *The Pittsburgh Courier* to a special screening. Once the film opened, black patrons had to go to the Pantages to see it. Not until February 1935 did *Imitation of Life* open at the Tivoli on Central Avenue.

The film was acclaimed by the mainstream press, which more often than not singled out Washington and especially Beavers for their performances. "Picture is stolen by the Negress, Louise Beavers, whose performance is masterly," commented the reviewer for *Variety*. "This lady can troupe. She took the whole scale of human emotions from joy to anguish and never sounded a false note. It is one of the most unprecedented personal triumphs for an obscure performer in the annals of a crazy business. Fredi Washington as the white-skinned offspring was excellent in the funeral scene when overcome by remorse."

In the pages of *The California Eagle*, Charlotta Bass herself praised the film as "the best picture of the year." "*Imitation of Life* is a presentation of

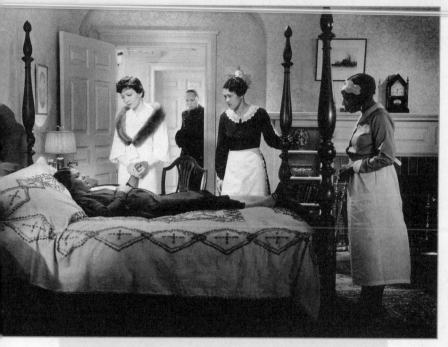

The death scene that launched a million tears: Louise Beavers in Imitation of Life *with Claudette Colbert, Hazel Washington, and that grande dame of early Black Hollywood, Madame Sul-Te-Wan.*

the social problem that is on trial in this Nation today," wrote Bass, who also commented on the aspect of the film that she found so compelling, the conflict between a submissive mother and a rebellious daughter, both of whom are torn apart by a nation's racism. "The colored woman was content with her lot in life but the colored daughter, which part is very ably played by Fredi Washington, is a tragic picture of what happens every day in real life." In *The Pittsburgh Courier,* Bernice Patton wrote that at the film's preview, prominent critics were in tears, including Louella Parsons, "who cried openly as I did, and others. I felt that a new high in humanitarianism had been reached among those great thinkers, and a better condition for the Negro is bound to come." Fay Jackson wrote that "Fredi Washington expresses the desire for freedom and equal justice . . . that is more convincing than any mere performer could have voiced. True to her own life, the injustices of color and race prejudices have retarded and prohibited a fuller life and freedom of expression." Yet others had mixed feelings about *Imitation of Life's* messages. In *Opportunity,* black critic Sterling

Brown wrote that it required "no searching analysis to see in *Imitation of Life* the old stereotype of the contented Mammy and the tragic mulatto; and the ancient ideas about the mixture of the races." The criticism marked a shift in attitude within the African American community. Roles for black performers were now being examined more closely.

Black Angelenos nonetheless were excited by the use Universal had made of familiar talents not generally seen in the movies. For the funeral scenes, seven local lodges were used. The choral group was Frieta Shaw's Etude Ethiopian chorus. The quartet that sang during Beavers's death scene was from Sarah Butler's Old Time Southern Singers. Sarah Butler herself—still the wife of Charles Butler—also appeared in the film, along with local minister the Reverend N. P. Greggs.

LOUISE BEAVERS, MOVIE STAR

mitation of Life established Beavers as Hollywood's most important African American actress. Born in Cincinnati, Beavers had graduated from high school in Pasadena. When she was appearing in Los Angeles's Ladies Minstrel, a scout for Universal asked her to come out to the studio. She was cast as a mammy character in *Uncle Tom's Cabin*. Afterward came roles in such movies as *Ladies of the Big House, What Price Hollywood?* the Mae West feature *She Done Him Wrong*, and scores of others. None of these roles had indicated her dramatic powers. If anything, they were a sign of her drive to win speaking parts in a competitive town and to deliver her one-liners effectively enough to get attention and to give some sense of a *person* under the movie-maid costumes.

Now there was even Oscar talk. After the columnist and radio announcer Jimmy Fields promoted Beavers, *The Pittsburgh Courier* called Fields "a brave white man. He has been telling the world over the air every week that Louise Beavers has turned in the best performance of the year." But to no avail. *The Courier* wrote that although "everyone else heard him and thousands agreed with him, the 700 Academy members evidently wore their ear mufflers." When the list of nominees for Best Actress was presented, Beavers's name was not included.

Even then, Washington realized that *Imitation of Life* might be the high point of Beavers's career. "You see that one thing that happened with Louise was that her agents immediately, when she made such a hit in the picture, upped her salary beyond what anyone was going to pay for the

Louise Beavers, flawless skin and a luminous smile.

type roles they had for her. I told her at the time, I just don't think this is wise. But of course, they were her agents. She didn't do too much after that, really, because they priced her out of the market." Though Beavers would appear, by some counts, in almost two hundred films, such as *Bullets or Ballots, Wives Never Know,* and *Rainbow on the River,* no other comparable role came her way in a career that lasted into the early 1960s.

Still, as far as black America was concerned, Beavers had already secured her place in motion-picture history. "Louise Beavers Makes Screen History Here" was the headline in *The Eagle* on December 7, 1934. Universal sent her on a promotional tour to big cities like Chicago, Atlanta, New York, and Pittsburgh, where she was interviewed and celebrated by the black press as well as African American social groups. "Louise Beavers, Hollywood's most outstanding actress for 1934, and the woman who helped to 'steal' the smash cinema hit, *Imitation of Life,* is coming to Pittsburgh!" wrote *The Pittsburgh Courier.* "The whole town knows it and the whole town's talking!" Usually, Beavers stepped off trains in those cities wearing a stylish hat, a fur coat, and a broad smile, a far cry from the dowdy Delilah. She also let the white press know that she might not be considered a glamour queen, but she wasn't a maid who happened to act. "I've worked with most of the stars, yes, but only at the studios, not in domestic service," she said, aware of the patronizing way in which the mainstream press sometimes treated African American performers. "I know that's what they say, that I work between pictures for the stars. But I never have done that, except for Miss [Leatrice] Joy. I don't mind. I just figure it's for publicity." Obviously, Louise *did* mind. She was an *actress*! And she wanted everyone to understand that!

Back in Los Angeles, she was a mighty queen bee in black entertainment circles. For some years, she resided in a modest yet beautifully tended home on Twenty-ninth Street off Western Avenue. Active in charity groups, she was the subject of much discussion. Though Beavers always had an eye for a dashing fellow, her love life rarely seemed to go right. Her first marriage, to man-about-town Bob Clark, fell apart. The joke among Beavers's crowd was that Beavers, the ideal domestic on-screen, apparently hated housework and, of course, knew next to nothing about flipping pancakes. "I am the worst cook in the world," she was quick to say. "No, I never did have to cook. And that's lucky, too, because nothing I cook ever tastes right." One could even catch a brief bit in *Imitation of Life* of Beavers, while flipping a pancake, doing it incorrectly. Eventually, Beavers moved to Hobart Avenue, a grand, wide, tree-lined street with spacious homes with landscaped lawns and lush gardens.

Despite the film community's curiosity about Washington, no studio came up with any great follow-up role for her. The truth: she was too light and glamorous to play the designated *colored* roles (the maids), yet no way would any studio cast her as a white woman. Even casting her as the mulatto Julie in *Show Boat* seemed too daring for Universal. Later, Fox hired her for *One Mile from Heaven*. Directed by Allan Dwan and starring Claire Trevor, *One Mile from Heaven* cast Washington as a "Negress" who raised a white child as her own and found herself in the middle of a publicized court battle. "Film marks reappearance of Fredi Washington, as the Negress nurse," wrote *Variety*, "and she is splendid. Has looks. Good voice and real acting ability. She's deserving of a better chance than this picture offers." Always the realist, Washington stuck to her plans, refusing to languish in all the pretty sunshine while waiting for work. She returned to

New York, where she had yet to decide whether she liked the handsome Lawrence Brown enough to stay married to him. The marriage disintegrated. "I don't think it took him long to get unglazed and for a lightbulb to go on," said Jean Bach. "So he got mad at Duke and stopped speaking to him," she added. In time, "Fredi and Lawrence despised each other. They could have killed each other very happily and gone to prison the rest of their lives knowing they had done something worthwhile!" The two divorced, and after many contentious years, Brown left Ellington's band. He spent his last years in Los Angeles, living quietly and grumpily next door to singer Nellie Lutcher.

In the 1940s, word leaked out that Washington was being considered for a role in a big picture, *The Foxes of Harrow*. But in the end, the part went to another actress. "I think it hurt my sister," Isabel Washington Powell said, "that they didn't put her in other things. She didn't talk about it. But I always believed that was how she felt." In New York, Fredi helped found the Negro Actors Guild and also wrote reviews and articles about the plight of black actors for her brother-in-law Adam Clayton Powell's paper *The People's Choice*. Most in New York felt she had been too smart for those people out west. But Washington's fate in the movies was a great loss for Black Hollywood.

AN OLD STAR IN A NEW ERA

By the mid-1930s, Stepin Fetchit was welcomed back to Hollywood with open arms—and what Fox Pictures considered plum assignments in such films as *David Harum, Carolina*, and *Judge Priest*. Fox's publicity department put out the word that its star had reformed from his high-living, temperamental ways. "The Negro comedian, recently brought back to Fox Film, has played roles in three recent pictures without making a single miscue," reported New York's *Evening Post*. "Fetchit hit the peak of his career four years ago when he 'went Hollywood,' owning three automobiles, employing as many liveried chauffeurs, with epaulets topping off a sandy uniform, boasting fifty suits of clothes, living in the finest home in the 'colored' colony and entertaining like a prince. Prosperity went to his head and it interfered with his work. . . . He is back in the fold and watching his step . . . and is saving his money, or, rather, the studio is saving it for him."

Despite Fox's efforts to create a new image for its star, Fetchit remained

A forlorn Fetchit, when the Hollywood good times were about to end.

as demanding and difficult as before. "He was a fabulous character," recalled actor Ralph Cooper, who worked at Fox in the mid-1930s and witnessed up close Fetchit's bad-boy ways and the wily manner in which the comedian maneuvered his way around the studio bosses. "He would arrive at the studio every morning when on a shoot, in two Cadillacs," said Cooper. "The first one carried his supply of near beer, which he drank like water all day long. Riding along with the near beer was his valet and his footman. Step rode to work in the second car. As soon as they pulled into the lot, Step's footman would jump out with a footstool and run to open the door of the second car for Step. Step's valet meanwhile would emerge from the first car carrying a gold hanger from which was draped the raggedy old costume Step would wear in that day's shoot. The footman would open the door for Step."

"Step hit the floor fuming," recalled Cooper. "And every day it was the same argument—why did the studio insist he arrive at seven when he wasn't going to be needed until two?. . . . It was my guess that the studio did it on purpose, just for laughs in the morning. Step hated the telephone, and he refused to get one for the very reason the studio said he had to have one—so they could get in touch with him when they needed to. Finally, the studio insisted. . . . Step agreed, but Fox had to pay for it."

Cooper also recalled that whenever studio chief Darryl F. Zanuck asked the actor to do something, Fetchit would listen quietly but then say he had to discuss the matter first with his manager, Mr. Goldberg. The next day, he would report to Zanuck that Goldberg had approved the studio head's request. Finally, an exasperated Zanuck told Fetchit, "I don't have time to wait for you to talk to him tonight and get back to me tomorrow. . . . What's his damn phone number?" Fetchit confessed, "Well, Mr. Zanuck, I guess you had to find out some day. *I'm* Mr. Goldberg." Zanuck seemed amused. Or perhaps he simply endured the actor's antics because—for a spell—he didn't feel he had much choice.

Yet now not only was the comedian Willie Best working regularly, but another African American entertainer—a headliner from vaudeville—had come west and was about to score a coup in pictures. Fox had signed dancer Bill "Bojangles" Robinson to appear with Shirley Temple in the Old South drama *The Little Colonel*.

BOJANGLES COMES TO TOWN

Surprisingly, Robinson's role in *The Little Colonel* had come about because of a note D. W. Griffith—his Hollywood heyday long over—had sent to Twentieth Century Fox executive Winfield Sheehan. "There is nothing, absolutely nothing, calculated to raise the goose-flesh on the back of an audience more than that of a white girl in relations to Negroes," wrote Griffith. Exactly what Griffith was trying to say is hard to guess. Yet, surely, Griffith had something in mind other than what ended up on screen with Temple and Bojangles. "What weight Sheehan accorded the Griffith suggestion is unclear, but not what he did," said Shirley Temple. "Traveling to New York, he scouted black tap dancer Bill 'Bojangles' Robinson, then on the Paramount Theatre stage."

In New York, Robinson was a major star, every bit as famous and celebrated as Ethel Waters and Paul Robeson. Born Luther Robinson in Richmond, Virginia, in 1878, he was orphaned as a child and raised by his grandmother, a former slave. His brother was actually named Bill. But legend had it that one day, Luther punched him and said he was taking the name for himself. Around the age of eight, he ran away to Washington, D.C., where he worked in a racing stable. To supplement his meager income, he danced for pennies in saloons and on street corners. For a time, he also danced with a partner.

Once on his own, he delighted audiences with the lightness of his tap and his unique style. Critics noted that he didn't use his hands much. Often, the hands would be on his hips. Nor did he often move the upper part of his body: Usually, the action would be from the waist down. Dancing upright and on his toes, he would kick one foot up and over the other. Added to this unique style was a breezy manner and attitude. He exuded an almost palpable sense of optimism and enthusiasm. The style might best be called *copacetic*, a word he helped popularize, which meant that everything was cool, just fine and dandy. His artistry and sheer joy in dancing would give Depression audiences the impression that, tough as the times were, life ultimately was what you made of it. In vaudeville, Robinson was a headliner who commanded four thousand dollars a week. In theater, he starred in the musicals *Blackbirds of 1928* and *Brown Buddies* and later in *The Hot Mikado*. In 1930, he performed a movie number in the Technicolor musical *Dixiana*. But Hollywood hadn't called since.

Offstage, his career and idiosyncrasies were well publicized in New York. He boasted of his daily diet of ice cream. For breakfast, he ate ice cream along with eight to ten buttered biscuits. Lunch was ice cream, too—and nothing else. Dinner: again, ice cream, along with steak or chops or fried fish and more hot buttered biscuits. That didn't sound particularly life-enhancing. Yet his physician said the Bojangles daily ice-cream diet didn't affect his health. "Organically, Bill Robinson is perfect," said the doctor in 1934.

Ice cream even changed his personal life. Once, having left a pool game to look for ice cream at a Walgreens store in Chicago, he met a pretty clerk named Fannie, then working to pay for her studies as a pharmacist. "I didn't pay too much attention to the dapper, carefree man who kept coming in and out of the store to indulge his great weakness for ice cream," said Fannie. "He was a hanger-on in the poolroom a few doors away and when he wasn't trying his skill on the green tables, he was rolling the dice fast and furiously. The drug store was new and shiny and the soda fountain where I worked was beautiful. Bill admired the new fountain and then, seemingly, I began to come in for some of the admiration. He began conversations with me." The conversations led to a courtship, and before Fannie knew it, she was Mrs. Bill "Bojangles" Robinson.

Afterward, the two were a very social couple. He was "Big Bo," and Robinson nicknamed her "Little Bo." Geri Branton, who knew the couple in the early 1940s, always believed Fannie was too sophisticated for Bojangles. Yet Fannie proved to be the ideal showbiz spouse. Outgoing, ami-

Enjoying everything the movie capital had to offer,
Bill "Bojangles" Robinson with his wife, Fannie, one of the early
well-known Black Hollywood wives.

able, well informed, a smart dresser, and easygoing enough to put up with her husband's demands and temperament, she understood that at public outings, she should always be by his side but never take any attention away from him. Not yet a Hollywood wife in the classic sense—the type whose whole life was wrapped up in the industry and who might be hell-bent on impressing everyone with her knowledge of the best place settings and who would be tough enough to fight to keep her title of *Mrs.,* as Nat "King" Cole's wife, Maria Cole, would be in the 1950s—Fannie, like Gladys Hampton, was one of the first wives of a black star to be a key player in the Hollywood social scene.

Once signed for *The Little Colonel,* Robinson traveled to L.A. with Fannie—by train. Though he'd been in the city before, he and Fannie were as entranced as everyone else by those clear blue skies, blood-red sunsets, and even the balmy weather. On the Fox lot, the two were introduced to Shirley Temple by Fox executive Sheehan outside her cottage. "The first thing I noted was the way his arms and legs moved with a silky, muscular grace," said Temple. "He was square-jawed and shiny-cheeked, his great round eyes showing whites all around. I was instantly attracted."

The gang's all here to keep Little Shirley happy:
Willie Best (left) and Bill "Bojangles" Robinson with
Shirley Temple in The Littlest Rebel.

Famous for his staircase dance specialty—he'd tap his way up a flight of stairs—Robinson was asked by Fox to teach the routine to Shirley. They worked together splendidly in rehearsal and eventually on screen. Shirley called him Uncle Billy; he always called her "darlin'." "Most relationships spawned on movie sets are thin as a slice of film," Shirley Temple recalled, "but Uncle Billy and his wife, Fannie, had been frequent guests at my parents' Sunday buffet dinners. Although I had never been invited to their home, it was a social curiosity not particularly strange as our guests seldom invited us back anywhere." At the end of filming, Shirley—as a way of thanking him for teaching her the intricate dance number—presented Robinson with a gift: a brand-new Ford automobile, so *The California Eagle* reported.

Audiences around the country were enthralled by the two in *The Little Colonel*. No need to worry about any harm coming to little Miss Curly Top in this post–Old South melodrama. Her Uncle Billy was there to protect, soothe, comfort. Fox loved the hefty box-office receipts and the press coverage: Bojangles was considered a class act from the East, not the kind of nouveau riche Hollywood trash that Fetchit—with his over-the-top ostentatiousness—now seemed to personify.

The studio brass decided to put Robinson into its new Temple movie, an Old South drama—*The Littlest Rebel.* He was cast as Shirley's faithful butler who has nothing better to do than remain by her side throughout the Civil War. Also cast was Fetchit in a typical role: as a bewildered, dopey servant who doesn't seem to know his right foot from his left. Having already appeared in the Shirley Temple movie *Stand Up and Cheer,* for Fetchit the new feature was work as usual, but he understood the importance of appearing with the nation's number one box-office star. What Fetchit didn't realize—at least, not at first—was that the studio viewed his black costar, Robinson, as his future replacement: in the eyes of Fox, Robinson was the first real Negro box-office star to come along since Fetchit.

But when Fetchit took a better look at the script for *The Littlest Rebel,* he no doubt quickly realized that Bojangles had the better role, while his character looked like little more than colorful background flavor. During the filming of a party sequence, Fetchit clashed with the director, David Butler, letting it be known that he didn't have enough to do in the scene. When word reached the executive offices, Fox tried to appease Fetchit. But he wasn't willing to listen. He walked off the set. He returned. But then he left again. Finally, the news hit the press. Fetchit "quit cold last Thursday in the midst of the filming of *The Littlest Rebel,*" reported *The California Eagle,* "and went home, upsetting the whole production schedule."

Fetchit must have assumed that Fox representatives would cajole and charm him into returning to work. But Fetchit overplayed his hand and made a critical mistake: Not only had he publicly ruined a production schedule, but he failed to realize he was no longer such a unique star. Someone suggested that Fox check on Willie Best's availability. Best "was caught at home by phone and given a rush call to come and take Step's place," *The Eagle* reported. "This he did."

The incident may have marked the beginning of the end of Fetchit's Hollywood career. Fetchit appeared in other Fox films, including *Dimples,* starring Shirley Temple, but by decade's end, he was deemed passé. He left town, perhaps hoping to be called back as he had at the start of the decade. But the call never came. Fetchit traveled, again making personal appearances and taking work where he could find it, in clubs. But as was true of so many former stars, Fetchit never seemed to realize that the parade had passed him by. In exile from Hollywood, he still believed he was the greatest colored movie star. Jean Bach recalled meeting him in 1938 in New York when she attended the theater one night to see John Bubbles perform. Fetchit noticed her in the audience. At intermission, a very short employee known by everyone walked over to her and politely said, "I have a note for the lady." "It said, 'Stepin Fetchit says if you come around backstage [at the club where he was appearing] tomorrow, he'll give you his autograph.' And I thought, 'That is the dumbest thing I ever heard. That's so crazy. Who would do a thing like that? Who would want the autograph?' In those days, the NAACP line was that you hated that whole concept of this shuffling, terrible guy. But I did go backstage because I was curious to meet him." Surprisingly, she found him interesting and ended up going out with him "a couple of times." Fetchit might tell tired old stories that sounded as if they belonged to another era. But he himself was hardly anybody's idea of a meek, scared-of-his-shadow simpleton. He had an assistant whom he constantly humiliated and really treated like his personal slave. "Step was also insanely Catholic and had all sorts of stuff around his neck," recalled Bach. Even though he was old enough to be her father, "he looked young. That's what surprised me. He was marvelous-looking. Every time I saw him, he had the most gorgeous cashmere suits. He was very chic. And great-looking. And a pretty good sense of humor."

For a time, the mainstream press reported on his brushes with the law. But eventually, even the comic run-ins were of no interest.

BOJANGLES: DANCING TO STARDOM

Bill "Bojangles" Robinson kept working in films: in the melodrama *One Mile from Heaven,* with Fredi Washington, and in two other features with Temple, *Rebecca of Sunnybrook Farm* and *Just Around the Corner*. Fred Astaire also paid tribute to him, donning blackface for a number called "Bojangles of Harlem" in *Swing Time* in 1936.

Basking in his position as Hollywood's new Number One Negro Star, Bojangles also experienced the uglier side of the industry's racial politics. When he appeared in *Rebecca of Sunnybrook Farm,* Bojangles motored to The Desert Inn in Palm Springs to teach Shirley Temple new dance routines. The Desert Inn—a series of cottages with a main building, all at the foot of the spectacular San Jacinto Peak—was a refuge for the wealthy and

Bill "Bojangles" Robinson
with actress Jeni LeGon.

Paul Robeson and his wife, Eslanda.

privileged L.A. set, including the Hollywood stars. "A staff of two hundred attended the needs of two hundred guests," recalled Shirley Temple. But those guests didn't include blacks or Jews. Temple always remembered the way Bojangles was treated in Palm Springs. Once she and Robinson had completed rehearsing their routines in her Desert Inn cottage, she asked him where he was staying. He didn't want to answer. Finally, he told her that he was staying above a drugstore on the entry road to the inn.

"But that's where the chauffeurs sleep!" said Shirley. "But *you're* not a chauffeur."

"Now, darlin', don't you fret. I've got a secret," he told her. "I may be staying in the chauffeur quarters but *my* chauffeur is staying there too!"

Shirley Temple recalled another incident that occurred during the filming of *Just Around the Corner*. "We were performing in the movies for the last time, a moment which may have escaped us both. Leaving one final kiss on his shiney cheek, as I always did, I headed for my cottage and he toward the commissary. Later I was told that inside he paused to chat at the first circular table, where some other dancers urged him to sit. Declining with a customary chuckle, he had picked a single table against the back wall and eaten alone." Robinson understood the studio's unwritten racial codes. Blacks and whites did not mix in the commissary.

For black America, Robinson, however, had a reputation of being too eager to please whites, of remaining silent *and* smiling in those situations when he could have spoken up. "I like white folks to like me," he told a reporter. Later, he amended the statement: "I like white people to like me." Most black people, upon hearing the comment, simply shook their heads. Did he know what he was saying? As far as Lena Horne was concerned, Bojangles "was the biggest Uncle Tom in show biz," according to her daughter Gail Buckley. He was "poisonous to Blacks and truly believed in the wit and wisdom of little Shirley Temple."

But while Bojangles appeared far easier to work with than Fetchit, he proved difficult in other ways. Fellow performers gossiped about his foul temper, his penchant for gambling, the thirty-two-caliber gold-inlaid, pearl-handled revolver he carried. He was also said never to have walked away from a fight. One of the most publicized incidents occurred in 1938 when he got into an altercation with a white student athlete from UCLA, who said the dancer pulled a gun on him. When the student, with a friend, was driving back to his fraternity house, he attempted "to wedge his roadster between Robinson's limousine and a truck." The vehicles almost collided. At the wheel of his car with his chauffeur in the passenger seat, a furious Robinson got out of the car and argued with the young man. "He called me abusive names," said the student. "Then he pulled out the gun. I thought it was a blackjack and began to defend myself with my fists. He pounded me over the head with it." The young man was left with "seven gashes an inch long on his scalp." A strapping two hundred–pound center for UCLA's football team, the student was then twenty-one years old. Robinson was sixty. The press reported that a crowd gathered, "unaware of the dancer's identity, and muttered threats against him."

Robinson was booked on "suspicion of assault with a deadly weapon" and ordered to appear in court.

"It seemed to me that the matter was entirely due to racial prejudice," said Robinson. "He had no reason at all for talking to me as he did. No one's going to talk back to me that way."

Other incidents sprang up throughout his life: He was shot four times and, so he let the press know, "slashed by knives and razors a dozen times, but never stabbed." At another time, while in Pittsburgh, he was shot by a policeman who mistook him for a purse snatcher whom Robinson himself was pursuing. His fights and quarrels away from the studios were perhaps the sign of a restless man who, having suppressed so many emotions and much anger, found release in exploding over seemingly minor incidents.

For a time, Bojangles commuted back and forth to New York, where he and Fannie lived in high style in a seven-room apartment in one of Harlem's most luxurious buildings. He was chauffeured around town in a Duesenberg limo with a license plate number that read BR6. But soon, he was seduced by the opulent California lifestyle. Bojangles delighted in every jam-packed moment of the West Coast showbiz scene: the wild mix of people; the casual but elegant style of dress; the fellow entertainers who courted, fawned over, and played up to him, endlessly reminding him that he was still the King of Tap. Frequently spotted with Fannie at the race-track—looking like a well-heeled, older playboy in his snazzy white slacks and his sporty dark jackets and white hats—he loved betting on the horses. With Fannie by his side, he also showed up at charity events and benefits on Central Avenue as well as nightclubs and theaters, which he loved. And he delighted in the gorgeous young women—the showgirls, the playgirls, the models, and even the wives of friends—who flattered and fawned over him. Not one single thing—especially, not one single young woman of interest to him—ever passed him by. The city—and the vast attention movieland brought him—rejuvenated Bojangles. And he enjoyed making movies: all the attention from the grips, the cameramen, the directors, the actors. Fannie helped prepare him. Nightly, she'd read him Shirley's lines so that he could learn his own. On the set, he became known as "One Take Bill."

Before the 1930s ended, the couple moved into a spectacular Westside home designed by Paul Williams. The stately red-brick and white-clapboard structure—surrounded by a wrought-iron fence—took up half a block at the corner of Thirty-sixth Place and Catalina. Outside were lush and densely landscaped citrus trees and shrubs. A garden walkway led to an adult "playroom" with the latest in L.A. interior design: bamboo furniture throughout, along with bamboo walls and ceiling—and a well-stocked bar. Inside the main house, guests gushed over the spacious master bedroom, which opened to an adjoining dressing room. Big Bo and Little Bo had a policy of open house. So the place was always packed. Among the first visitors was—perhaps unsurprisingly—Clarence Muse, who let all his readers know about the fabulous home in his column for *The Eagle*. In town for a visit, Fredi Washington was invited over, along with her sister Isabel and Isabel's husband, Adam Clayton Powell. Not easily impressed, Bojangles seemed dazzled by Powell and his wife, who were on the top tier of the East Coast black bourgeoisie.

The studios kept Robinson working in such movies as *In Old Kentucky* and Paramount's *The Big Broadcast of 1936*. But by the end of the decade, his appeal waning, Fox dropped him.

TOILING IN GREEN PASTURES

During the era, *The Green Pastures*, based on the hit Broadway play by Marc Connelly, also employed hundreds of black performers. The first all-Negro picture produced by a major Hollywood studio, Warner Bros., since 1929, *Green Pastures* was a fantasy with a portrait of an all-colored heaven presided over by a majestic Baptist-preacher-style De Lawd. Key roles went to Rex Ingram, George Reed, Edna Mae Harris, and Ernest Whitman, with music by the choral group the Hall Johnson Choir. Much like *Imitation of Life*, the production drew the attention of those locals who generally didn't pursue movie work. Russian-born studio composer Dmitri Tiomkin liked the Hall Johnson Choir and hired it to perform in Frank Capra's *Lost Horizon*. But a studio executive told Tiomkin, "Who the hell ever heard of niggers singing Russian music."

THE THIRTIES ■ 165

Tiomkin, however, refused to drop the group, which later was heard in such films as *Swanee River* and *Cabin in the Sky*. Its arranger, Jester Hairston, also began a twenty-year association with Tiomkin, becoming the arranger for such films as *Red River* and *Duel in the Sun*.

MILLION-DOLLAR MOVIES

Not since the days of the Lincoln Motion Picture Company had independent production of colored movies generated as much attention as a new movie company on the scene, Million Dollar Productions. One of its founders was Ralph Cooper, a transplanted New Yorker. In 1934, Cooper had launched the Apollo Theater's famous Wednesday-evening shows— Ralph Cooper's Original Harlem Amateur Night—at which a young Billie Holiday was so popular that the audience wouldn't let her leave the stage until she sang the only two songs she knew *again*. When visiting New York, Hollywood stars like Mae West and Joan Crawford—and later, Marilyn Monroe and Elvis Presley—headed uptown to watch the Apollo amateurs make a bid for the big time.

Tall, broad-shouldered, light-skinned, with almost jet-black hair, Cooper was sometimes called the Dark Gable. He was not only an actor but a dancer and a comic. In the mid-1930s, Twentieth Century Fox hired him to choreograph the Shirley Temple movie *Poor Little Rich Girl*. Once Cooper got to town and everyone had a chance to look him over, the studio brass offered him a five-year contract and enrolled him in its in-house training school—along with Tyrone Power, Alice Faye, and Jack Haley. Fascinated by Hollywood, Cooper nonetheless knew it had no place for a black leading man. So at Fox's training school, he learned as much as he could about working behind the scenes: "directing, script writing, lighting, set designing—everything you needed to know about filmmaking," he said. He put that knowledge to good use in 1936, when he and George Randol formed Cooper-Randol Productions to produce the black-cast melodrama *Dark Manhattan*. Cooper wrote and starred in the picture.

Afterward, Cooper formed Million Dollar Productions with brothers Harry and Leo Popkin, who were eager to crack open a growing race-movie market. By now, there were theaters that catered to black moviegoers in urban areas and black belts in the South. Shooting on tight schedules and shoestring budgets of about fifteen thousand dollars, Million Dollar Productions turned out fast-moving genre pictures loaded with steamy sirens and pugnacious gangsters. Many of Hollywood's black stars saw the potential of Million Dollar Productions right away. Louise Beavers signed on to play a widow rearing two sons in *Life Goes On* and a sensitive probation officer helping wayward boys in *Reform School*. Theresa Harris also saw a chance to put to rest—albeit temporarily—her servant roles with a glamorous turn in the company's *Bargain with Bullets* opposite Cooper.

Harris told Fay Jackson of the Associated Negro Press that she enjoyed working in the race movie "because in the picture I have the chance of wearing clothes." Fay Jackson added, "She means a beautiful wardrobe that is usually denied colored women in white movies."

Jackson also took honest stock of the state of Harris's career, noting that just a few years earlier Harris had been one of the town's top black actresses, appearing in hits with Jean Harlow and Barbara Stanwyck. But now "the breaks in Hollywood films seem to have deserted her. She has turned to the all-Negro company as an outlet."

Harris told Jackson she was taking a chance with her "reputation in joining pioneer companies." "But the opportunity of playing in roles otherwise denied one in white pictures is a great relief in the aspiring Negro motion picture artist."

Million Dollar Productions' big coup came when Cooper—looking for an actress to appear opposite him in the musical melodrama he had scripted titled *The Duke Is Tops*—decided to cast a young beauty he had met at the Cotton Club in New York: Lena Horne. But when he tried to reach her, Cooper learned she had married, moved to Pittsburgh, just given birth to a baby, and considered herself retired from show business. "Only after hours of phone calls and help from mutual friends, including a columnist on the *Pittsburgh Courier,* did Lena finally accept my offer." As far as Cooper was concerned, *The Duke Is Tops* would be his baby. Though Leo Popkin was billed as the director, Cooper always maintained that he wrote and directed the feature.

Lena Horne may not have realized it, but *The Duke Is Tops* came at the right time. Her life had long been troubled and lonely. Having grown up in Brooklyn, the daughter of an aspiring actress, Edna, and a handsome father, Teddy Horne, who came from a socially progressive middle-class family, Horne spent her most stable childhood years living in the home of her paternal grandparents. Her grandmother was an early suffragette and a community leader. But after her parents separated, Lena was taken by her mother to live in a series of different homes, traveling from one place to another in the South. Often, her mother left the girl with strangers as she sought work in other areas. "There is an awful sameness about living with strangers and being a stranger yourself all the time," Lena Horne once said of those years.

When her mother remarried, mother, daughter, and new stepfather returned to New York. By then, Horne was developing into a strikingly beautiful young woman with dark hair and the café-au-lait copper coloring that audiences and journalists would discuss endlessly. At age sixteen, with prompting from her mother, Horne became a chorus girl at the Cotton Club. Nightly, her mother sat in the dressing room, always ready to ward off the randy sharks who might hanker for young Lena. After the Cotton Club, Horne—sometimes billed as Helena Horne—toured as the girl singer with Noble Sissle's Society Orchestra.

When Horne's father introduced her to a young man named Louis Jones—the son of a minister in Pittsburgh *and* a college graduate—she fell in love and soon married. But hers was hardly wedded bliss. Money problems drained her, as did the demands of a husband whom she found controlling, headstrong, and overbearing. The birth of her daughter Gail in 1937 gave her hope that her marriage wouldn't crumble. At this time, she received a call from New York agent Harold Gumm, who told her about the musical *The Duke Is Tops*, soon to be filmed in Los Angeles. "Gail could not have been more than four months old," Horne remembered. The movie, she learned, "was being produced by some shoestring independents, the Popkin Brothers, and they wanted me for a part. The shooting schedule was only ten days. Louis and I needed money, but it never occurred to me to leave my baby." But Gumm was persistent. "Maybe you can buy a few things you want," her husband, Louis, told her. "Maybe I'll be able to pay some bills," Horne thought. She accepted the offer.

"Louis immediately insisted that I must look like a star, so we went into debt for a fancy outfit and I climbed on a plane—my first one—and took off for Hollywood, which I had never seen," said Horne. Upon her arrival in Los Angeles, she was met by an unenthusiastic Ralph Cooper. "I had put on weight, having the baby, and he was disappointed at the way I looked." Horne herself felt she looked all right. But Horne was now exposed to a dictum upon which Hollywood, white and black, insisted: Leading ladies were required to be thin.

For Horne's stay in Los Angeles, Million Dollar Productions did not book her into the Dunbar Hotel. The budget was too small. Instead, Horne stayed at the home of character actress Lillian Randolph. She and her sister Amanda Randolph were both struggling to find roles and keep their heads above water. Later, Lillian Randolph became best known for her radio work as the maid Birdie on *The Great Gildersleeve* and her television appearances as Madame Queen on *Amos 'n' Andy*. Much as Louise Beavers had done with Fredi Washington, Lillian Randolph helped Horne get to know the town.

Throughout, the production was plagued by money problems. The producers struggled to keep their heads above water.

In long-distance phone calls, Horne and Jones argued about the film. Though he wanted her to leave the production, she knew she couldn't. "He knew nothing about the protocol of show business, which demands that you not walk out, especially when walking out could cost other people their jobs." None of these conversations made it easy for Lena Horne to enjoy her time out west in the sun. Nor did the fact that this was her first movie role. There was much to learn about performing for the camera. For later generations, she would appear mighty stiff.

Years later, she recalled the one bright spot of her first experience in black Hollywood: Lillian Randolph. "She was the best sort of woman," said Horne, "who afforded me stability and human warmth at a time when I desperately needed them." Also important was her association with black composer Phil Moore, who arranged the music for *The Duke Is Tops*. The two would work together for years. Moore helped her develop her style for nightclubs and recordings. Horne made another important contact with the dancer/choreographer Marie Bryant, who "was to become a best friend."

Completing the picture, Horne promptly returned to Pittsburgh—without ever receiving full payment for her work. Her husband assumed that her career was now officially over. But at private parties in the homes of Pittsburgh's wealthy white set, Horne occasionally performed with black pianist Charlotte Catlin, which brought Lena some much-needed money, especially when she and Jones later became parents of a son, Teddy. Little did she know then that her marriage was just about over. Nor did she realize that already—with her glossy image and her highly discussed beauty—her brief time in L.A. marked the dawn of a new day in the movie industry, for she would, in the next decade, usher in a whole new image for African Americans in Hollywood. Once Lena Horne became known for her mainstream studio films, *The Duke Is Tops* was retitled *The Bronze Venus* and redistributed with splashy posters—and with her name above the title.

Million Dollar Productions also kept its eye on the other young woman who would lead to a real image change: the teenage Dorothy Dandridge. By the late 1930s, her mother, Ruby, saw some of her dreams come true for her daughters. Along with Etta Jones, the girls—as The Dandridge Sisters—had appeared at the Cotton Club in New York, toured England, performed on Broadway in *Swingin' the Dream,* and worked in such movies as *Going Places,* with Louis Armstrong, and *A Day at the Races,* with the Marx Brothers and Ivie Anderson. But Dorothy—who, like Horne, was emerging as a celebrated beauty—was already restless with ambitions to be a dramatic film actress. An important step forward was a lead role in another Million Dollar Productions film, *Four Shall Die,* which was shot early in the next decade.

THE SEPIA SINGING COWBOY

Other independents flourished on the West Coast, providing Black Hollywood with more work. A handsome young singer from Detroit named Herbert Jeffrey arrived in L.A. in the 1930s with energy and ambition to burn. Having begun his career in Detroit speakeasies, he had also performed with the bands of Erskine Tate and Earl "Fatha" Hines. When he recorded "Blue Because of You" with Hines, the printer misspelled his name as Herb Jeffries. Thereafter, he used the name professionally.

Light-skinned with dark, wavy hair and a sporty mustache, and sometimes mistaken for Latino, Jeffries—with his baritone voice and smooth delivery—became a heartthrob in nightclubs and on recordings. "He was *so* handsome," recalled actress Ruby Dee. Now, he wanted to make movies. Rather than hitting the studios, Jeffries headed for Gower Gulch, the part of the city near Sunset Boulevard and Gower Street where independents produced low-budget B movies and westerns. Already a raconteur with confidence and a jaunty savoir faire, Jeffries persuaded white producer Jed Buell to make a colored western with himself as the singing star, an ebony version of popular singing cowboys such as Gene Autry and Roy Rogers.

Teen divas: The Dandridge Sisters, featuring Etta Jones (left) and Dorothy (center) and Vivian Dandridge.

Transporting his cast and crew to Victorville and Saugus, producer Buell and director Sam Newfield shot *Harlem on the Prairie* in about ten days. With a story by Fred Myton, the film had additional dialogue by Flournoy Miller, who years before, with his professional partner Aubrey Lyles, had not only performed in a comedy act but also had written the book for the Eubie Blake / Noble Sissle groundbreaking all-black Broadway musical *Shuffle Along*. Miller appeared in *Harlem on the Prairie* along with his new comedy-act partner Mantan Moreland, Connie Harris, George Randol, the singing quartets The Four Tones and The Four Black-

As dashing as they come, Herb Jeffries—
vocalist with Ellington and black cowboy star.

birds, and Maceo Sheffield, a former police officer who provided security at the Dunbar Hotel.

Decked out in spurs, Stetson, and fancy pants, Jeffries cut a dashing figure, especially when he sang the title song and the tune "Romance in the Rain." *Variety* predicted that *Harlem on the Prairie* would have "much box office promise from several angles. As a novelty, for the colored theaters, it's surefire. As a novelty for the ofay houses it likewise has its exploitation appeal." The paper added that the film, which looked as if shot on a budget of twenty thousand dollars, "could be made very amusing for subsequent bookings in major houses, after the producer has exhausted its legitimate market. One idea would be to pare the 54 mins [*sic*] running time down to half, and offer it as a hokum novelty."

Harlem on the Prairie—called "the first Negro musical western"—launched a new genre. Afterward, Jeffries was tapped by another independent producer, Richard Khan, to star in *Two-Gun Man from Harlem*.

"In those days," Jeffries recalled, "whites used the word Harlem to identify with Blacks, Negroes then." Jeffries persuaded Kahn "not to use the word Harlem" on a later film. Instead it was called *Bronze Buckaroo*. "Maybe that didn't work as well because our next movie was *Harlem Rides the Range*." Jeffries also remembered the basic movieland formulas of his films. "They were just like white Westerns. The family mine was being foreclosed. There was a fight over water rights. A pretty girl had been kidnaped." Usually, they lifted the story lines "from white movies and just changed names." White crews were used because "blacks couldn't get into the unions." Yet the actors were members of the Screen Actors Guild.

The black cowboy sagas helped lead to a flurry of race-movie activity in L.A. that provided work for performers such as Mantan Moreland and Flournoy Miller and for a writer/director such as Spencer Williams, who helmed such features as *The Blood of Jesus; Go Down, Death; Dirty Gertie from Harlem, USA;* and *Juke Joint.* One enterprising company, Globe Pictures, enlisted boxing champ Joe Louis to appear as a boxer in *The Spirit of Youth*, which was actually a thinly veiled biopic on the champ himself. Alongside Louis were Clarence Muse, Edna Mae Harris, Clarence Brooks, and Cleo Desmond. Springing up were other companies like Dixie National Pictures, Hollywood Productions, Toddy Pictures, and George Randol Productions. Some made a film or two, then closed up shop. But in the late 1930s and early 1940s, Black Hollywood hoped that the new companies would lead to new representations of African Americans on-screen. The Negro press was quick to laud the efforts of the race-movie market as well as black performers.

"Our wages are satisfactory but in many technical matters, we are still struggling," Theresa Harris told reporter Fay N. Jackson. Yet she believed if a company like Million Dollar Productions succeeded, Hollywood might rethink its depiction of African Americans and make films with more varied roles. "And in the meantime, many more top notch actors now unemployed will be cast in roles commensurate with their real abilities as actors."

Million Dollar Productions stayed in business for a few more years. But eventually, the pressures of financing, distribution, and exhibition led to the company's demise. Cooper returned to New York. "I never did hit the bigtime in Hollywood," said Cooper. "But I'm proud of the movies I made because they constituted the new cycle of blacks in modern-day portrayals."

MR. MUSE, FILMMAKER

$\big($ eeing the black moviemaking activity, Clarence Muse decided to join the fray. But shrewdly, Muse sought backing from mainstream Hollywood. By now, he had become Black Hollywood's self-appointed spokesman, its seemingly erudite cultural ambassador, its clever sophisticate eager to pontificate and show the locals how to live and work with style. At social affairs, he turned up well dressed, well groomed, well mannered. At a special memorial for actor Will Rogers, who had been killed in a plane crash in 1935, Muse joined a lineup of stars, white and black, including Stepin Fetchit and Hattie McDaniel, to pay tribute. Through his column in *The California Eagle*, Muse still wielded influence, if not power, within Black Hollywood. Muse made it his business to meet anybody who was anybody. When *The Eagle* snagged an important interview with Paul Robeson, in town to do the film *Show Boat*, the paper's reporter made sure to let readers know that it was Clarence Muse who had arranged the interview. On movie sets, Muse remained, to his credit, observant and outspoken. When he appeared in King Vidor's *So Red the Rose* as a rebellious slave, Muse balked at doing a certain scene. Years later, director Vidor remembered Muse's determination to play the scene in *his* own particular way.

When Muse headed the Negro branch of the Federal Theatre Project in Los Angeles, he was just about at the top of his game. He also struck up a friendship with Langston Hughes, who arrived in L.A. in late 1938. The two ended up working on a movie script together. Fortune, or so it seemed at the time, had smiled on Muse when he staged a very successful production of the Hall Johnson musical *Run Little Chillun* for L.A.'s Federal Theatre. Movie producer Sol Lesser saw it and was impressed. Afterward, the producer talked to Muse about creating a film project for white child star Bobby Breen. Muse knew this was the vehicle on which he and Hughes could collaborate. Hughes quickly wrote an outline for a possible film titled *Pirates Unawares*. Lesser, however, rejected it. Yet he wanted Muse and Hughes to continue working to see if they could come up with something else. Finally, an agreement was reached for the two to write a story for Breen—set in the South in an earlier age; they would each receive $125 a week to write a screenplay.

Black Hollywood must have been optimistic about the forthcoming production. But ultimately, the experience proved a humiliating ordeal for Hughes, who, unlike Muse, was unaccustomed to the industry's now no-

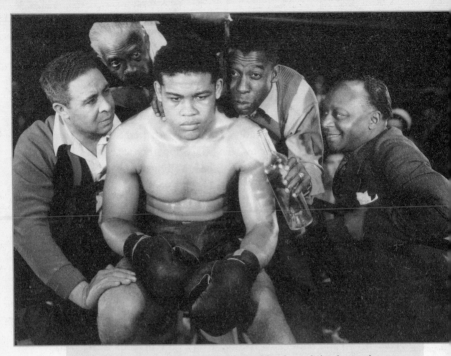

The Brown Bomber arrives in town and lands a role in the movies:
Joe Louis with Clarence Brooks (far left), Clarence Muse (right of Louis),
and Mantan Moreland in The Spirit of Youth.

torious lack of respect for its writers. Four or five people might work on a script before it went to the screen. Writers had to please directors, producers, stars, and studio heads. A black writer with a deal at a major studio was a true oddity, and Hughes, although acclaimed in New York, was treated as such. On one occasion, when Hughes was to lunch with a studio executive, the executive refused to enter the restaurant with him. Hughes had to eat a sandwich outside—"under the broiling California sun." He also had to adapt to the industry's work schedule. "Never take a Hollywood job," he once said. "They vary from nothing to do at all, to rush! rush! rush! No nice in-between kinds." But he also found it "amusing and not unprofitable working for Hollywood." Most likely, he enjoyed the sunshine, the stars, and the opulent lifestyle as much as everyone else.

Finally, a screenplay—acceptable to Lesser—was completed. Set in the Old South, the film *Way Down South* told the story of a dear little young white master, played by Breen, upset because his "contented," "happy" slaves are about to be sold. Cast to play a key role as the kindly Uncle

Caton was none other than Mr. Clarence Muse. Throughout production, he relished his role—what actor wouldn't want to write his own dialogue and create his own scenes?—as well as his forthcoming screenplay credit. On the set, he assisted director Bernard Vorhaus in handling the cast's white stars Breen and Sally Blaine as well as black actors Lillian Yarbo and Matthew "Stymie" Beard and more than three hundred other African American performers. Released in 1939, *Way Down South* made Muse more important than ever in Black Hollywood. He had completed a production for a major company. The credit read: "Story and Adaptation by Clarence Muse and Langston Hughes." Muse and Hughes had also written spirituals for the film.

But *Way Down South* did little for Hughes's reputation. Earlier, he had said that no Hollywood studio "had dared make one single picture using any of the fundamental dramatic value of Negro life. . . . On the screen we are servants, clowns, or fools. Comedy relief. Droll and very funny." Those words may well have come back to haunt him. Though *The Los Angeles Times* considered the drama "picture-perfect," other reviewers were less charitable. Calling the film "slow-going" and "tiresome," *Variety* commented, "The business possibilities do not appear bright, and there is no question what will happen below the Mason-Dixon line." *Way Down South* was also criticized as being little more than a replay of black movie stereotypes. Hughes's friend Louise Thompson wrote him of reactions in New York. "Everybody says they cannot understand how you could have written such a scenario or if they changed it why you permitted it to come out under your name. I tell you this unpleasant news because I know you want to know what they are saying about the picture here."

The reactions may have been a blow to Hughes's reputation but Muse, accustomed to the vicissitudes of life and work in Hollywood, took it all in stride. Nor did the criticism deter him from future behind-the-scenes film endeavors. In 1940, he coauthored and starred in the very entertaining race movie *Broken Strings,* the tale of a very proper, very pompous classical violinist who, having become paralyzed, must reevaluate his life and his views on popular music.

As the 1930s were drawing to a close, members of the black press stepped forward, openly questioned the roles of African Americans, and demanded changes. One of the most vocal critics was Earl Dancer. The former manager of Ethel Waters and an all-round New York theater impresario of the 1920s and early 1930s, Dancer had closed up shop in the East and moved west, where he hoped to reinvent himself. At first, he managed dancer Jeni LeGon, a rare female tap-dancing star. Dancer made the right connections, which resulted in wide coverage for LeGon in the Negro press and also a movie contract and roles in *Hooray for Love*, with Bill "Bojangles" Robinson, and such later films as *Arabian Nights, I Walked with a Zombie*, and *Easter Parade*. But the energetic, pixieish LeGon seemed out of step with those nurturing, full-figured women such as Beavers and McDaniel and never became a hot item in the movies.

Growing more resentful of the movie companies' casting of black performers—and, so some would say, of his lack of a place within the industry—Dancer wrote the column "Light and Shade" for *The California Eagle* and became the paper's drama editor. In an article, he attacked the industry. For twenty-five years, Dancer wrote, black America and its press had poured millions into publicizing movies. But what had they received in return? His answer: a collection of movieland Aunt Jemimas and Uncle Toms. "There has been more of them than anything else." There had been musical sequences in films in which "they make us contort ourselves in grotesque make-up and caricatures that they label authentic characterizations." There had also been *Hearts in Dixie*, which he believed "very few Negroes sat through," and *Hallelujah*, not much different from *Hearts in Dixie* and "the great, great granddaughter of *Uncle Tom's Cabin*." Occasionally, an artist like Bill Robinson had been signed to a contract, he wrote, for which Hollywood expected black America to be grateful. But, said Dancer, the worm would eventually turn and now "we are demanding what is rightfully ours." He called for "more sympathetic roles . . . authentic and not caricatured" and for the studios to use more black Americans in their technical departments. Finally, he demanded that Negro composers be given "credit for their music, instead of white composers who take their tunes for two bits and sell them in the studios for thousands." Forceful and angered, Dancer was insisting on a new day for African Americans in Hollywood.

The tone and temper of Black Hollywood was about to undergo a change—which would come to maturation during the war years.

THE BIG PICTURE

till, nothing could curb the town's excitement as production began on the era's big film—in production at the same time as *Way Down South*—

David O. Selznick's *Gone with the Wind*. Based on Margaret Mitchell's bestselling novel about the Old South, the Civil War, and the Reconstruction era, *Gone with the Wind* generated great publicity from the start. While the mainstream press pondered over who would play Rhett and Scarlett, Black Hollywood focused on the important Negro roles of Prissy, Pork, Uncle Peter, Big Sam, and especially, Mammy. Photos of three contenders for the role of Mammy—Louise Beavers, Georgette Harvey, and Hattie McDaniel—ran in *The California Eagle* on February 17, 1938.

By sheer will of being, McDaniel had now climbed her way to showy roles in such movies as *Alice Adams, China Seas, Show Boat,* and *Saratoga,* and she'd worked side by side with major stars such as Harlow, Gable, Stanwyck, and Hepburn. She always held her own, belting out her lines, sometimes charming audiences, other times ruffling their feathers with a feisty, aggressive attitude that pumped up even the most innocuous dialogue.

Just as charismatic offscreen as she was on, she became a leading social figure in Black Hollywood. Intelligent and resourceful, she was able to clearly differentiate between the characters she played and the woman she prided herself on being. By the late 1930s, she had earned enough money to buy herself a modest home on Thirty-first Street on the Westside, which was featured in the pages of *Silhouette* magazine and *The California Eagle*. Readers of *The Eagle* were informed that the home's furnishings came directly from the Gold Furniture Company's store on Central Avenue and Washington Boulevard. This was clearly a celebrity endorsement in the days long before such endorsements became commonplace for African Americans.

McDaniel took pride in showing the press around the house, especially her dining room, which was decorated in burnt ivory and russet—with a table that was usually set with expensive Spode china, imported damask linens, the finest crystal and silverware. Using her den as an office, she reviewed scripts or answered letters there with the help of her secretary, Ruby Berkley Goodwin, an African American reporter who had first met McDaniel when interviewing her on the set of *Show Boat*. Throughout the den were show-business mementos and autographed pictures of stars with whom McDaniel had worked: Harlow, Gable, Bojangles, Crawford, Mae West, Barbara Stanwyck, Glenda Farrell, Alice Faye, and Margaret Sullavan. Often, her quiet hours were spent reading, and early on, she began collecting books on Negro history and culture. Parked inside her garage was a splashy Packard sedan, which she drove *or* in which she was driven around town. Everything about McDaniel's home and the way she lived served as an explicit counterimage to her movie-maid roles. "She had the most exquisite house I've ever seen in my life. The best of everything," Lena Horne said of McDaniel. "I have a family I have taken care of very beautifully," McDaniel told Lena Horne. "I'm a fine Black mammy [on screen]. But I'm Hattie McDaniel in my house."

She hosted parties and also enjoyed lively evenings on the town. Like Beavers, she was not—offscreen—some nonsexual nurturer tending to the needs of others rather than herself. Having lost one husband, she married a second, Howard Hickman, in 1939, then dumped him that same year and was on the lookout for another. She obviously was not easily satisfied.

Ambitious as ever, McDaniel knew that she had been impressive in her roles, and she no doubt loved *The Eagle*'s comment that she "rates number one box office" and that the managers of local theaters "report that Hattie McDaniel's presence in a picture is a guarantee of full houses and enthusiastic audiences." Yet McDaniel also knew she still hadn't found the big career-defining part, the way Beavers had with *Imitation of Life.* With that in mind, she became determined to play Mammy. The stakes were high; the competition, fierce. *Gone with the Wind*'s original director, George Cukor, interviewed various candidates. Women such as Madame Sul-Te-Wan and Bertha Powell were considered. First Lady Eleanor Roosevelt even contacted Selznick saying she knew the perfect person to play Mammy: a black woman who worked as a cook at the White House. An early supporter of McDaniel was Bing Crosby, who wrote Selznick that the actress in *Show Boat* looked just right for the role. But McDaniel understood that her chief competitor was Beavers, who had already worked under Cukor's direction in *What Price Hollywood?* McDaniel signed with the big white agency MCA, clearly with hopes that it would help her land the part.

Finally, along with Louise Beavers and Hattie Noel, she tested for Selznick on December 6, 1938. One can only imagine the response of Selznick and director George Cukor as they viewed the footage. In the famous scene in which Mammy must persuade Scarlett to eat before attending the Wilkes barbecue, Beavers was a sweet and cheery servant with a vague air of befuddlement and exasperation. Noel almost seemed intimidated by her Scarlett. But Hattie was formidable, as sturdy as her bulky frame, as commanding as her powerful voice. On January 27, 1939, Selznick offered McDaniel a contract. She would start work on February 1 for a renewable fifteen-week period at $450 a week. Butterfly McQueen, who had scored a success on the New York stage, was cast as the ditzy ser-

In a city becoming car-crazy, Hattie McDaniel
takes tender, loving care of hers.

vant girl Prissy. Oscar Polk was signed to play Pork. Eddie Anderson, who now had found success on radio as Jack Benny's manservant Rochester, signed to do Uncle Peter. Playing Big Sam would be Everett Brown. A multitude of other black actors—including Edgar "Blue" Washington— were used in bits or as extras. At first, there were concerns about the dialects of the black performers. They had to be comprehensible. Yet Selznick International hoped for some type of authenticity. Daily, the studio provided one car to pick up McDaniel and the other black actors for each day's shoot.

The Negro press as well as black leaders kept an eye on the production. The NAACP's executive secretary Walter White wrote Selznick, suggesting that the writers, director, and various production people read W.E.B. Du Bois's *Black Reconstruction.* He also wanted the producer to hire an African American to be present on the set during the filming to give advice. Selznick showed some sensitivity to the concerns of the African American community. In Margaret Mitchell's novel, there had been a sequence involving the Ku Klux Klan. In the film version, the Klan was dropped.

Selznick paid attention to the criticism of black writer Earl Morris at *The Pittsburgh Courier.* In his pamphlet "Sailing with the Breeze," Morris argued for the film's deletion of the word *nigger*, which had been used in Mitchell's novel. McDaniel also wanted the word deleted. Selznick complied. Shrewdly, Selznick arranged for Morris to come to Los Angeles during the filming. Selznick's assistant Marcella Rabwin said the best way to combat some of the criticism of the black press was by sending information on the characters played by the black actors to black newspapers. Selznick International would be viewed as "treating these actors as stars of the picture. In other words, we would let our actors in GWTW do our work for us in the colored newspapers across the country."

Selznick also wrote Walter White that aside from removing the word *nigger*, he had "left no stone unturned in our efforts to eliminate from our picture any possible objections which the Negroes of America may have had to portions of the novel, *GWTW*." He added that the film would be free of "anti-Negro propaganda" and that the primary black characters would be presented as "loveable, faithful, high-minded people." Also aware of the situation in Europe that might lead the United States into war, he added, "I feel so keenly about what is happening to the Jews of the world that I cannot help but sympathize with the Negroes and their fears, however unjustified they may be about material which they regard as insulting or damaging."

One incident of which Selznick may have been unaware but that African American actor Lennie Bluett said occurred during filming was that signs were put up indicating "Colored" and "White" lavatories for the extras. Despite protests, Bluett said the signs were not removed. Finally, one day he saw Clark Gable on the lot. Studio protocol forbade extras from approaching stars. But Bluett walked over to Gable and voiced his anger about the lavatory situation. Gable was also outraged. Once the star expressed his feelings to the studio, the signs were removed, said Bluett.

McDaniel enjoyed a good relationship with Gable, with whom she had recently worked in *Saratoga*. Before she was signed, Gable had told Selznick that she was his favorite for the role of Mammy. Their scenes together would be those of two strong personalities (on- and offscreen), one (Gable's Rhett) seeking the approval of the other (McDaniel's Mammy). Little was said about McDaniel's relationship with actress Vivien Leigh, who was so consumed with her character and so strained by the pressure of the production that she tended to be easily ruffled. She had her differences with Victor Fleming, who replaced Cukor as the film's director. By McDaniel's account, she and Leigh worked well together and sometimes kidded each other. Staying in character once the cameras stopped rolling, Leigh asked one day, "Mammy, may I go to lunch?" "Whea ya going?" McDaniel answered, staying in character also. After Cukor was fired from the production, Leigh and Olivia de Havilland stopped by his home to work on their interpretations of their characters. McDaniel, who had key scenes with both actresses, was apparently not included in these sessions.

Throughout production, observers on the set had spread the word that McDaniel, as well as McQueen, were turning in remarkable performances. A big, glamorous première was set for *Gone with the Wind* in Atlanta with all the major stars in attendance. In Selznick's offices, there was discussion about McDaniel's possible appearance in Atlanta. Finally, it was decided that because of attitudes in the South, she should not attend. Thus, the movie had its grand opening without her. On printed programs for New York and Los Angeles, McDaniel's photograph was run with those of the white stars. But her portrait did not appear on those printed programs for Atlanta and the rest of the South.

The completed *Gone with the Wind* had its critics within the black community. "If for nothing else but its distortion of the Reconstruction Period," wrote African American dramatist Carlton Moss, "*GWTW* ranks as a reactionary film." But the Civil War epic engendered none of the outrage that had met *The Birth of a Nation*. Once Oscar buzz for McDaniel started, black newspapers like *The Pittsburgh Courier*, *The Chicago Defender*, and the *Baltimore Afro-American* were in full support. When she was finally nominated for the Oscar as Best Supporting Actress, all of Black Hollywood held its breath. Competing with her for the honor was *Gone with the Wind*'s Olivia de Havilland.

On Oscar night, February 29, 1940, McDaniel and her escort, black actor Wonderful Smith, entered the Cocoanut Grove ballroom of the Ambassador Hotel, along with Selznick; his wife, Irene; and the stars Gable, Leigh, and de Havilland; as well as some of Hollywood's most famous personalities—with a total of some twelve thousand people in attendance. Wearing white gardenias in her hair and dressed in a light blue gown with an ermine shawl, McDaniel had the glow and posture of a confident star. Individual tables were set up for the crowd. McDaniel spent some time at Selznick's table. But on this night, Hollywood still drew its racial lines. For most of the evening, she and escort Smith were seated at their own table— apart from the group. Yet when Fay Bainter came to the podium to present

On the set of Gone with the Wind, *Hattie McDaniel, with friend, looks through the black publication* Flash.

the award to the winner, the entire room broke into spontaneous applause when McDaniel's name was announced. Gossip columnist Louella Parsons wrote that the ovation for McDaniel "will go down in history as one of the greatest ever accorded any performer in the annals of the industry. En masse, the entire audience, stars in every place, stood and cheered their beloved Hattie McDaniel. Tears came to Mammy's eyes as she made her way to the stage to accept the award."

McDaniel accepted the award with a speech (rumored to have been written by Selznick's staff) that moved the audience. "Fellow members of the motion picture industry and honored guests, this is one of the happiest moments of my life, and I want to thank each of you who had a part in selecting me for one of the awards. For your kindness, it has made me feel very, very humble, and I shall always hold it as a beacon for anything that I may be able to do in the future. I sincerely hope that I shall always be a credit to my race, and to the motion picture industry. My heart is too full to tell you just how I feel, and may I say thank you and God bless you all."

Olivia de Havilland admitted that she was disappointed at losing, stating later that on that night, "I found I couldn't stay at the table another minute. I had to be alone. So I wandered out to the kitchen at the Ambassador Hotel and cried." A couple of weeks later, she came to her senses and "suddenly felt very proud," she said, "that I belonged to a profession which honored a Black woman who merited this [award], in a time when other groups had neither the honesty nor the courage to do the same sort of thing."

Black Hollywood was ecstatic. McDaniel's achievement seemed to signal a new era for African American actors and actresses. But ultimately, another reality—a war in Europe—would have a greater impact than this particular Oscar night.

4

The Forties

During the opening months of this new era, the great topic of conversation was Hattie McDaniel's Oscar win. But by the end of the following year, the jubilant mood would fade and the town turned jittery, stunned by the news of the bombing of Pearl Harbor on December 7, 1941. As America entered the Second World War, President Roosevelt's warm fireside chats of the 1930s would be replaced by calls to action. During the war years, movie attendance remained high as a nation sought to fortify itself with popular escapist fantasies, lush melodramas, and action-packed war tales of valor and victory. Stars black and white would do their part to boost the war effort.

Black Hollywood would also undergo a surprising transformation. On the one hand, an established generation of stars would further stretch the boundaries of the town itself. Yet those same stars, most still playing servants (Hattie McDaniel, Louise Beavers, Willie Best), would find themselves struggling to hold on to their careers while a younger generation—the composed musical performers such as Lena Horne and Hazel Scott—would usher in new images. And by decade's end, when mainstream Hollywood would see the emergence of postwar actors such as Kirk Douglas, Burt Lancaster, and Montgomery Clift and the rise of actresses such as Ava Gardner, Jennifer Jones, Deborah Kerr, and Susan Hayward, dramatic black actors such as James Edwards and Juano Hernandez would also play major roles. And with their arrival would come a new lifestyle—a new attitude and point of view—for Black Hollywood.

THE NEW BLACK ELITE

cDaniel's success marked the first signs of a rising Black Hollywood elite that saw itself as far more accomplished than its predecessors. The emerging elite—which included McDaniel, Bojangles, Louise Beavers, Ben Carter, and Eddie Anderson—prided itself on being very much a part of the life of the town and having name recognition among the studio casting directors. Louise Beavers was still known for her performance in *Imitation of Life*. Anderson's appearances on Jack Benny's radio show made him one of the nation's most popular personalities.

More than ever, Black Hollywood became socially stratified. In public, stars liked to mingle with stars. Or with prominent black Angelenos. Stars also had their entourages or their "people" around them, those hangers-on who would do just about anything to be near the glamour, the fame, the fun. Offscreen, too, those performers who had played servants never let an opportunity pass to show they were intelligent and well spoken. In interviews with the white press, they might play themselves "down," coming across like ordinary folks and even conforming to some racial stereotyping. But among the Negro establishment, they were eager to reveal themselves as cultivated and sophisticated—with servants of their own.

This emerging elite maintained lavish but sedate bourgeois lifestyles. Though Hollywood remained, for black as for white, a town of conspicuous consumption, no one in Black Hollywood wanted to exhibit the gaudy ostentatiousness of Stepin Fetchit. In the past, black stars had lived well—but in neighborhoods where there was a mix of social classes and professions. Stars now prided themselves on maintaining beautiful homes in more prosperous neighborhoods and on proudly showing off their personal collections: of books or antique dolls or miniature train sets or whatever.

THE NICHOLAS FAMILY:
FAYARD, HAROLD, AND MOTHER NICHOLAS

oining this emerging Black Hollywood elite—and helping to solidify it—were Viola Nicholas and her two talented sons, Fayard and Harold. After their Hollywood movies of the 1930s, the brothers had returned to their base in New York, always under the watchful eye of their mother. Viola could zip through a contract without missing a beat *and* without overlooking the details in fine print. Highly disciplined, she could be exacting and tough-minded. She understood how her sons should be billed, and she knew what projects were best for them. "She knew all the angles of managing and talking to the different people," Fayard Nicholas recalled. "She had a great mind. You could give her certain numbers and ask her to add, subtract, divide. And she'd do it all in her head without writing it down—then give you the right answer. She did all the business. And she seemed to be getting better with this." Part of the business was also still being on guard for her sons' welfare, especially protecting them from all those pretty young things—those predatory girls on the prowl. Actually, it was the girls who should have been on guard!

During the Nicholas Brothers' engagement at New York's uptown Cotton Club in 1938, they had met The Dandridge Sisters, also appearing on the bill. Before Viola knew it, Harold had fallen in love with young Dorothy. Viola couldn't do much about that. Nor had she appeared threatened. After all, The Dandridge Sisters would be touring and eventually returning to their home in California while the Nicholas Brothers remained East Coast–bound.

In 1939, the Nicholas Brothers went on tour, traveling to Rio de Janeiro. Once the brothers were back in New York, Viola was informed of Hollywood's renewed interest in hiring her sons for movie work. This time around, it was Twentieth Century Fox. "The William Morris Agency called us and said, 'Fellows, we'd like for you to do a movie test,' " said Fayard. "So we went to some studio in New York . . . to do this movie test. Now when we were in Rio de Janeiro, we learned all these Brazilian songs, these melodies, which were similar to Spanish ones. We knew that this film was going to be *Down Argentine Way*. That would be Spanish. So we sang this song 'Brazil' which we learned. Naturally, we did the dancing and the songs. About a week later, the William Morris Agency called and said, 'Fellows, you're on your way to Los Angeles.' "

At Twentieth Century Fox, Fayard and Harold worked with the choreographer Nick Castle for their appearance in *Down Argentine Way,* starring Betty Grable and Don Ameche. The brothers were such a hit that Fox offered them a five-year contract, which, unlike contracts for other black performers, didn't require them to play roles. The brothers yearned to have speaking parts but none of those gawking, wide-eyed comic-servant roles. Instead, they would appear basically as themselves, performing sensational numbers in the years to come in movies such as *Tin Pan Alley, The Great American Broadcast, Sun Valley Serenade,* and *Orchestra Wives.* Audiences would be astonished by the flips, the twirls, the turns, the somersaults, the

Manager, musician, and negotiator—and determined to do the best for her boys, Viola Nicholas with her sons, Harold (left) and Fayard.

leaps, and the startlingly energetic dances that had them running right up the side of a wall and that seemed to defy gravity—echoing some of the giddy optimism of the town itself. Their Fox contract, which left them free to appear at theaters and clubs around the country and abroad, became big news in Black Hollywood in 1940. No other black stars had ever had one quite like it.

Viola Nicholas shrewdly took stock of her life and her sons' and of their careers. Movie work would only increase their fame and ensure more lucrative deals offscreen. Harold and Fayard liked life in the West. So did Viola. She decided to relocate to Los Angeles. Daughter Dorothy remained in the East to continue her education at Howard University, in Washington, D.C. Though the new Nicholas house had none of the posh grandeur of their New York apartment on Edgecomb Avenue, it had great charm, a pure Southern California–style bungalow in a neighborhood of "many races," said Fayard. "There were whites and Latinos. And blacks. You name it." "It was a nice little house," recalled Fayard. "I think it had two bedrooms, a living room, kitchen, bathroom. Had a little den. It was nice for my mother. And she was so neat." "It was lovely," recalled Geri Branton. Outside were the clear skies and the palm trees that Fayard loved.

Viola's sons were now old enough to live and work without her. "We were going to the studio every day," said Fayard. "So she didn't have to be around that much." But it was not easy for their mother to relinquish control. At home, she saw to it that clothes were laundered and pressed, that meals were prepared, that appointments were made and kept. "She even made sure our shoes were shined," said Fayard, "even if she had to do it herself. Mother did everything for us." And she was determined—in this rough-and-tumble atmosphere—to keep her sons *and* herself grounded. "Mother read her Bible nightly," Dorothy Nicholas Morrow recalled.

Quickly, Viola became known within the movie community as a remarkable woman who carried herself like a proper but savvy young East Coast matron. "Everyone liked Mother," recalled Fayard. "She had a particular knack and facility for having people around," said Dorothy Nicholas Morrow. "She was a charmer." "She was very, very proper in the old-fashioned way when you hear about real proper ladies," said Byron Morrow, who married Dorothy in the late 1940s. "That's what she was. A lady. She had been to England. She liked the way they spoke. And she spoke that way." "She had a gift for words," said Fayard. "And she always wanted us to speak beautifully. I can remember when we were in the Broadway show *Babes in Arms* in 1937, and there was a song that Richard Rodgers and Larry Hart composed called 'All Dark People Is Light on Their Feet.' We didn't like the song at all. That's the only song we didn't like 'cause they wrote such songs as 'The Lady Is a Tramp,' 'Where or When,' 'My Funny Valentine,' 'Johnny One Note.' All these wonderful songs and they give this song to us. And so opening night, my mother said, 'Listen, when you and your brother sing this song, don't say "All Dark People *Is* Light on Their Feet." Say "All Dark People *Are* Light on Their Feet."' And the stage manager said, 'Wait a minute. You sang those lyrics wrong.' And so the next day, we did it their way. We did it for about a week. And then we went back to . . . 'All Dark People *Are* Light on Their Feet.'"

Viola herself was not like most stage mothers, who tended to be dowdy, preferring to dress down so their precious babies could have the spotlight to themselves. Often, stage mothers wanted to look as nonthreatening as possible, so when they moved in for the kill—"You've *got* to hire my child"—they might catch a producer or director off guard. Of course, that was never really the case. Everybody was suspicious of stage mothers and stayed as far away from them as possible. But Viola herself was a style maven who looked like an actress or a designer or an interior decorator, a woman with flair. Because she sometimes didn't have time to actually shop for clothes in department stores, Viola also "had persons who had dress shops who were able to come to your house to take orders for making clothes for you," said Dorothy Nicholas Morrow. "This was quite exceptional. If she had something made, she'd have a dress made for me as well. Mother knew how to sew, too. She did crocheting and knitting and everything. So she was quite accomplished."

Nothing was ever out of place. Everything was beautifully coordinated: the right jewelry, the right gloves, the right scarves, the right shoes, the right handbags, the right colors, and always, for Viola, the right attitude. "I never saw her any other way but meticulously coiffed," said Byron Morrow. "I never saw her out of what you saw when she went to church. That's the way she was all the time. That's the way she dressed. The way she made up. That's the way she looked." Though she stood about four feet eleven inches, she entered a room like a statuesque fashion model, the kind who made all heels snap to attention and all heads turn in her direction. Viola Nicholas understood that stepping out of the house could never be a casual affair; in show business, it was a Public Appearance.

Aware of the importance of being seen around town, she'd arrive at gatherings, sometimes with her sons, sometimes with an escort. Once inside, her eyes would quickly survey the club, still on the lookout for any overly aggressive young women who might set their sights on *her* Fayard or *her* Harold. And Los Angeles was full of them. What girl wouldn't want to be with the hottest black entertainers of these early years of the era?

Handsome, with a rich brown coloring, a full face, a full head of hair slicked back, and a rakish mustache, Harold was short with a compact, sturdy muscular frame. At nineteen, he lived like a young monarch, incredibly pampered, accustomed to having his way and being the center of attention, with a doting mother and an older brother always nearby. Already, he was a dapper ladies' man about whom all sorts of tales and gossip had circulated. "He was a great talent but arrogant," said Etta Jones, "and spoiled by all those showgirls at the Cotton Club." The girls were all over Harold. And Harold was all over them. Yet though Harold liked the roar of the adoring female crowd and enjoyed performing, he could also be moody, distant, aloof, and withdrawn, always reserving a private part of himself for himself. "He was the most selfish man I ever met," said Geri

Branton. Others who knew him echoed that sentiment. Harold saw through the superficiality of show-business life, its fascination with appearances, and its lack of understanding as to what lay beneath. But it was also hard for him to express his deepest feelings.

Fayard was just the opposite: relentlessly outgoing, gregarious, and high-spirited, a born optimist and a raconteur with a zest for life. He, too, liked the chorus girls and pretty fans. Yet Fayard was easier to understand and perhaps to like. "He was always himself," said Rigmor Newman, Nicholas's third wife. "He never tried to be someone different when he was in different situations." Basically, you knew who Fayard was the minute you met him. It took far longer even to begin to understand the more complicated Harold. Fayard was called Big Moe; Harold, Little Moe.

During these years when movie stars were expected *always* to look like movie stars, neither brother appeared anywhere—at a club or a restaurant or on a golf course or on stage or screen—without being dressed to the nines. From the time they were children, said Fayard, their mother "would always take us to tailors. And we ordered different styles of suits. She said, 'Fellows, when you're on that stage, you must always be dapper.' We had tails and tuxedos in all different colors. White tails. Black tails. Brown tails. Tan tails. You name them. Blue tails. And shoes to match. My mother was the one who made all this possible. She wanted us to look beautiful on that stage." As they hit the clubs or restaurants in their spiffy suits and casual slacks and shirts, they had a hip but more traditional sporty East Coast style than was generally seen in Black Hollywood. They wore their clothes well, aware of what worked for them, what didn't. Shirts, cufflinks, ties, belts—all those male accessories that could make or break the *look*—were carefully selected and coordinated. Their style influenced a new generation of young male stars such as Sammy Davis Jr. and Bobby Short.

Usually, the Nicholas Brothers toured for months at a time. Once back in L.A., they maintained disciplined schedules for their film work. Fayard worked most closely with the choreographer Nick Castle at Fox. Harold hated rehearsals, looking as if he would rather be somewhere else, but he had trained himself from childhood to pick up on all the important discussions about camera angles and movements, cuts, and lighting. Once the cameras rolled, he and Fayard both were fully concentrated on their work and, of course, performed brilliantly.

At Twentieth Century Fox, the brothers were regarded differently from the black character actors. Like Bojangles, they were considered high-grade stars *from the East*. Yet at Fox's commissary, they ran into problems. Studio commissaries were hotbeds of industry chatter and gossip and clearly divided by class. MGM's served lunch to about twelve hundred people daily. Different groups came in different shifts. At all the commissaries, supporting players—often dressed in their costumes for whatever film they were working on—sat with other supporting players. Publicity people often gathered at a publicity table. The same was true of the wardrobe people. The executives, the writers, and the directors also had their section of the commissaries. Stars mingled among the higher-echelon personnel. Some, such as Garbo at Metro, had lunch served to them in their dressing room. Fox's commissary, the Cafe de Paris, was elegant and pleasing to the eye, with paintings of the studio's stars lining the main room. It also had the reputation of having the best food in town.

During their past experiences in Hollywood, the younger Nicholas Brothers had thought nothing of eating in commissaries. But one day, when Harold and Fayard were about to enter the Fox commissary, they were stopped. "I think it was when we were doing *Orchestra Wives*," Fayard recalled. "We were with Nick Castle. And we went over to this commissary to have lunch like everybody else. And we could see all the extras were going in there. And then, as we approached the doorman, he called Nick Castle over and started talking to him. I didn't know what was going on. And Nick came back. And I said, 'What's going on?' He said, 'You guys can't go in there.'"

Angered, Fayard and Harold asked, "What do you mean? All the money we make for this studio, and we can't go in there. Look at all the extras. They're going in there. Just 'cause their faces are white, they're going in there." "Don't worry," Castle told them. "I'll take care of it." Fayard remembered that "he went and talked to the boss, Darryl F. Zanuck. And Darryl F. Zanuck said, 'The Nicholas Brothers *will* go in there.' So we go there with Nick Castle, and everything was fine. But you have to speak up." Geri Branton recalled that the brothers would sometimes dine in the executive dining room.

Still, Fayard remembered that later, while at Fox filming the black-cast musical *Stormy Weather*, the actors were consigned to "a special little restaurant. And that's where they wanted us to go." The restaurant was "totally separate," not even on the main floor of the commissary. "But we said, 'No. We're not going there.'"

YOUNG DANDRIDGE

In the early 1940s, L.A. was a playground for Harold and Fayard during their downtime. Harold hit the clubs, the after-hours joints, the restaurants, the parties, enjoying the full network of gatherings and get-togethers of show-business life. Staying up until all hours of the night and sleeping late in the mornings, he played cards with buddies and soon enjoyed what would be his first love among leisure activities: the golf course. "My brother could never get enough of golf," said Fayard. Fayard also enjoyed the showbiz camaraderie as well as the breezy California lifestyle.

Not long after settling into L.A., the Nicholas's family life changed. That was primarily because Dorothy Dandridge was there. Having been separated because of their various touring schedules, Harold and Dottie were now together, free to explore the city and to see each other constantly. More and more, L.A. was becoming a car town. The days of hopping onto a trolley to get to the studios were fading. And there were outdoor restaurants where you could park your car and a waitress would come out to take your order. Harold bought a sporty blue Chevrolet in which he and Dottie took jaunts to the movies, to restaurants, to the clubs, to the get-togethers in the lobby of the Dunbar Hotel, and for long moonlit drives through the hills overlooking the city. Harold loved being seen with the young Dandridge, who was developing into a lush, dreamy beauty, known all over Black Hollywood.

Viola watched the relationship closely. So did Ruby Dandridge and Ma-Ma. By now, as Ruby worked more regularly on radio and in small parts in movies, she was very much a part of the Black Hollywood scene: socializing with other performers, gossiping like mad in her inimitable high-pitched voice, and always in search of a better part for herself or her daughters, mainly Dorothy. Vivian was as outgoing as her mother, but without Ruby's calculations and manipulations. But Ruby knew that Dorothy had the drive and focus that could lead to stardom and *something else*. At the sight of Dottie and Harold together, both Ruby and Ma-Ma had stars in their calculating eyes. If she became Mrs. Harold Nicholas, Dorothy would stand at the top of Black Hollywood's social circles. Both even envisioned her becoming a part of the Nicholas Brothers act. Of course, Viola Nicholas had other ideas.

More entranced than ever, Harold proposed. But Dorothy held off. By now, she had left The Dandridge Sisters trio to venture out on her own. "Our last performance," said Etta Jones, "was at Frank Sebastian's Cotton

Club." Always on the go, Dorothy used every opportunity to work, to be seen, to be heard. It might be a benefit such as the 1940 Christmas show at which she performed along with Bing Crosby, Sunshine Sammy, Mantan Moreland, and the King Cole Trio, featuring the young Nat "King" Cole. Or it might be her appearances with the Floyd Ray Orchestra at the Orpheum or other theaters in nearby cities. She was also finding roles in movies such as *Sundown* and *Lady from Louisiana* and the female lead in the Million Dollar Productions race movie *Four Shall Die*. For Ruby and Ma-Ma, the plum assignment came when Harold and Fayard suggested to Nick Castle that Dorothy dance with them in the "Chattanooga Choo-Choo" number in *Sun Valley Serenade*—to give the sequence "some sex appeal," said Fayard. He was well aware that, unlike Fred Astaire and later Gene Kelly, he and Harold danced only with each other without that added appeal of a young female knockout by their side. Castle agreed, and the "Chattanooga Choo-Choo" number became a classic: three dazzling performers entranced with one another and their ability to entertain—the perfect kind of high spirits for a war-torn age. While shooting the sequence at Fox, the brothers and Dandridge were visited on the set by Darryl F. Zanuck. Taking one look at Dandridge, Zanuck remarked, "You're very pretty." He wouldn't forget her.

Without thinking about it, Dandridge personified, possibly more so than any other black actress of the era, the hardworking, ever-ambitious aspiring young star, aware of the racial lines in Hollywood as well as studio politics but plowing ahead nonetheless. "She had been bred for stardom," said Harold Nicholas, who could also have been speaking of himself. She turned up in two innovative, progressive revues of the prewar 1940s. First came a performance in the white show *Meet the People*. When comedienne Virginia O'Brien left the show, Dorothy decided to go against the odds—and audition for the role. Her decision paid off. The idea that a colored girl could try out for and then win a non-Negro role in a non-Negro show was considered novel, to say the least. Barely eighteen years old, she won raves. Then came Duke Ellington's *Jump for Joy*.

JUMPING FOR JOY

No theater production of the early 1940s drew as much attention from Hollywood, both black and liberal white, as Duke Ellington's *Jump for Joy*. Nor did any other production before the war better indicate a shift in ideas and perceptions—and a unique coming together of progressive Hollywood, both black and white—to begin reassessing itself. The idea for the show had come about during a trip Ellington made in the early 1940s to the West Coast, where he continued to have a legion of fans, many in high-powered positions. Ellington made the usual rounds of the clubs and gatherings. One evening, he and his collaborator Billy Strayhorn ventured out to Culver City to attend a party at the home of MGM writer Sid Kuller. The place was packed with movers and shakers. Mickey Rooney, John Garfield, and screenwriter/novelist W. R. Burnett were among the guests at what was a rollicking evening.

Everyone had so much fun, they decided to do it all over again the next week. Ellington returned to Kuller's, again with Strayhorn as well as such Ellington band members as saxophonist Harry Carney and drummer Sonny Greer. In attendance this time around was MGM's young glamour girl Lana Turner, who, away from the cameras and the eyes of the public, didn't seem at all bound in by America's ideas on proper racial deportment. She asked Strayhorn to dance. When he politely turned her down, she asked Greer, who promptly complied. The drinks kept flowing. The food kept coming. The music played on. The revels went on into the early hours of the morning. An ecstatic Kuller is reported to have said that the place was really jumping, to which Ellington added, "Jumping for Joy!" Before the party ended, the two talked about collaborating on a show together.

That wasn't just idle party chatter. Soon, Ellington and Kuller were putting together a revue unusual both in content and in contributors. Calling itself a "Sun-Tanned Revu-sical," *Jump for Joy* was Ellington's first major theater project: a series of sketches with plenty of music and satire. The composer wanted to take the black musical in a new direction by, for the time daringly, poking holes in the entertainment world's accepted depictions of African Americans. Ellington said that "a team of scholarly Hollywood writers decided to attempt to correct the race situation in the U.S.A. through a form of theatrical propaganda. This culminated in meetings at which the decision was made to do *Jump for Joy*, a show that would take Uncle Tom out of the theatre, eliminate the stereotyped image that had been exploited by Hollywood and Broadway, and say things that would make the audience think." Kuller wanted to go against the grain of "black humor performed by blacks for white audiences from a white point of view. Our material was from the point of view of black people looking at whites."

Originally, the first act was to end with a skit titled "Uncle Tom's Cabin

Is a Drive-in Now." Here, that old faithful dupe Uncle Tom lay on his deathbed, going off to some kind of afterlife reward, heavenly or otherwise. But old images don't die easily. At Tom's side stood a Hollywood and a Broadway producer, each hoping to revive him with a shot of adrenaline! Nearby was a chorus of blacks saying farewell: "He lived to a ripe old age. Let him go, God bless him!" Another skit was titled "The Sun-Tanned Tenth of the Nation." "Brown-Skinned Gal in the Calico Gown" paid tribute to tan beauties.

Everything about *Jump for Joy* was all-star—and aside from the cast, integrated. Music was by Ellington and Hal Borne with lyrics by Paul Webster and music arrangements by Ellington, Strayhorn, Borne, and Mercer Ellington. Among those writing additional music and lyrics for the show were Langston Hughes, Mickey Rooney, and Sid Kuller. Fifteen writers also contributed to the show, with credits going to Kuller and Hal Fimberg. Among the backers, supplying the cold cash needed to mount a production with a large and talented cast, were John Garfield, Hollywood producer Joe Pasternak, and W. R. Burnett. The casting director was Ben

Carter. Staging the production was the choreographer Nick Castle. Directing the sketches were Sid Kuller and Everett Wile. The production was produced by Henry Blankfort.

For the cast, Ellington gathered a vibrant group that included his favorite girl singer, Ivie Anderson (spelled "Ivy" on the program); the comedian Wonderful Smith; the act Pot, Pan, and Skillet; the Hi-Hatters; actor Roy Glenn; and Ellington's heartthrob vocalist Herb Jeffries. Also included were choreographer/dancer Marie Bryant, Sonny Greer, and the glamour girls Avanelle Harris, Lucille Battle, and Alice Key. Joining the show later was blues singer Big Joe Turner. And in the role of the pert ingenue was teenage actress Dorothy Dandridge. At the time of rehearsals, she was working on the film *Sundown*. The producers were so eager to have her that rehearsals were arranged around *her* schedule. Ellington led his band from the orchestra pit.

Opening night at the sixteen-hundred-seat Mayan Theatre on July 10, 1941, was a glittering affair that generated more buzz than any other black theater production on the West Coast. In the theater were the backers Garfield and Rooney as well as such stars as Marlene Dietrich and Fayard Nicholas. Langston Hughes flew in for the opening. "The audience itself was of unusual composition," said Ellington, "for it included the most celebrated Hollywoodians, middle-class ofays, the sweet-and-low, scuffling-type Negroes, and dicty Negroes as well (doctors, lawyers, etc.). The Negroes always left proudly, with their chests sticking out."

The Eagle's ecstatic reviewer John Kinloch wrote that the show was "not only a hit but a home-run!" "The Duke is tops!" he proclaimed. The real surprise was *Jump for Joy*'s wit "and sparkle, the uncompromising exile of Uncle Thomas and his cohorts, the daring satire of white society by a dusky brother." Praising the cast, Kinloch singled out Ivie Anderson, who was showcased singing Ellington's "I Got It Bad (and That Ain't Good)." "Anderson's dramatic moments in Langston Hughes touching 'Mad Scene from Woolworth's' reveal a striking dramatic talent. A certain sense of conviction seems to hang about this lady; there is a private dignity which she never sacrifices." Of the revue's teenage ingenue, he commented: "Dorothy Dandridge is beautiful. Don't know whether she can sing or dance or wot [*sic*]. But she's beautiful. YEAH MAN!"

Los Angeles's mainstream press was also impressed. "The performance of two acts and more than 30 scenes moved with speed and colorful variety," wrote Florence Lawrence in the *Los Angeles Examiner*. "One or two of the acts may have to be cut, but let us hope not that amusing item on loan sharks, billed as 'Human Interest,' nor the equally clever satire of the soldier and the President in which Wonderful Smith touches on some pertinent political subjects."

Once *Jump for Joy* opened, nightly meetings were held after each performance in which changes were made for future shows. Skits that didn't work were tossed out. New ones were added. Always there was a free flow of ideas going back and forth. One evening, Orson Welles gave suggestions. "We were always on guard against the possibility of chauvinism creeping in, of saying the same things about other races we did not want said about Negroes," said Ellington. "The show was done on a highly intellectual level—no crying, no moaning, but entertaining, and with social demands as a potent spice." Ellington added, "The show was a smash."

Despite the enthusiasm of the critics and liberal Hollywood, *Jump for Joy* ran only three months, 101 performances. Ellington said the war scooped up "most of our young show-stoppers." Others felt that *Jump for Joy* was ahead of its time. But some of those Hollywood creative talents who saw *Jump for Joy* were starting to see Negro entertainers in a different light.

TWO WEDDINGS, TWO YOUNG HOLLYWOOD WIVES

While the mothers Nicholas and Dandridge kept a guarded eye on the relationship of Dorothy and Harold, Fayard surprised everyone when he suddenly married. One evening during the brothers' appearance at the Regal Theatre in Chicago in late 1941, they met a young woman who for years had been reading about the Nicholas Brothers "in magazines and papers like *The Chicago Defender.*" Captivated by their talent, she admitted, "I had decided I was going to marry one of the Nicholas Brothers." Born Geraldine Pate in Jackson, Tennessee, but called Geri by everyone, she was one of three daughters. She had been a dutiful convent lass in New Orleans, where she studied at Xavier Prep, which was "the place that all upper-middle-class Catholic blacks tried to go to," said her second husband, Leo Branton. Afterward, she attended Lane College, then went to stay with relatives in Chicago while she studied at DePaul University. She had once wanted to be a chorus girl but felt she wasn't sexy enough. But now she had other plans. "I was going to work for the Catholic church as a social worker," she said.

She had gone to the Regal to sell tickets for a benefit for the African American sorority Delta Sigma Theta. In the lobby, she was spotted by the brothers' chauffeur, Lorenzo Hill, who walked over and engaged her in a conversation. Hill was always on the lookout for pretty girls. "He wanted Fayard to have a girlfriend because Harold had Dorothy," said Geri. "And he was trying to help Fayard out." When Geri and Fayard met, one of the first things he told her, said Geri, was, "You're the prettiest thing I've ever seen in my life. If I had a soup spoon, I'd eat you like soup." "Silly stuff," said Branton. Was Geri excited by meeting him? "Heaven's no," she said. "He was an interesting person. He traveled a lot." But she had "absolutely no interest in him." Her studies were uppermost on her mind.

But a dazzled Fayard felt differently. Completely unlike the women he had known in New York and Los Angeles or on his travels, this well-bred beauty was articulate and well read with a sharp mind, an interest in politics, and impeccable manners. A voracious reader and a fascinating conversationalist who could discuss just about any topic, she glided with ease through social circles high and low. Fayard recalled that one evening after "I was getting ready to leave her place to go back to the Regal Theatre, I said to all the guys, 'I'm going to marry that girl.' It was love at first sight. I liked the way she carried herself. I could see how intelligent she was. It was something that I never experienced from other girls because all the time I had said, 'I don't want to get married. I just want to be a bachelor.' That was it. But when I saw her, I made up my mind. 'I'm going to marry that girl.' " Geri, however, still had other ideas.

Fayard, along with chauffeur Lorenzo, persisted. "They bothered me every day about coming to Los Angeles." Not letting up on his pursuit of her, Fayard proposed. He wanted to marry her right away. Of course, Viola Nicholas, also in Chicago, was not about to hear of any such thing. "Fayard's mother hired a private detective to check on my background," said Branton. But the private detective appeared to be almost as entranced as Fayard. After investigating her, he brought Geri the report "to let me read it and to let me know what she was doing. And the end of the report said, 'If I were not a married man, I would ask this young lady to marry me. She is an absolutely perfect lady.' " Once Viola Nicholas actually met Geri, "she just fawned all over me. She was very sweet." But Geri couldn't forget that Viola had her followed.

Finally, Fayard, Harold, and Lorenzo persuaded Geri to make a trip— on her own—to Los Angeles. But en route, when the train made a stop, "they met the train and had me get off," she said. "The conductor came. Lorenzo was maneuvering everything." "Well, we're going to get married," Fayard told her. So she got off the train and was married to Fayard in early

1942 by a justice of the peace, with Harold as best man and Viola and Lorenzo in attendance. Geri said the marriage took place in Las Vegas. Fayard said it was Pasadena. Nonetheless, she married him in part because of her anger that his mother had a detective investigate her and in part because "he was interesting. And I also wanted to protect him. I thought he was being taken advantage of." The couple settled in Los Angeles—in Viola's home. After the wedding, the nineteen-year-old Geri informed *her* family of the marriage.

Geri Pate and Fayard Nicholas were an odd pair. Perennially boyish and optimistic, he was devoted to having fun and happy times. Even after their marriage, he was also always interested in other women. Yet Fayard experienced a true sense of identity—and reality—mainly when he was on the stage. "He only thought about one thing—dancing. He was interested in clothes and how he looked. But he was just cued in on dancing." The dance became his *truth*. Geri, however, was always grounded in the here and now. She didn't mince words with anyone or deny the realities of the world around her. Or the reality of who her husband was. "He was an artist," she once said. "And artists really shouldn't marry because they have to give everything to their art. It isn't right to hold them back. Let them fly." Most unusual about this young woman poised to make her way through the corridors of the entertainment capital was that she was without ambitions to be a performer. That surprised almost everyone she met in the heady and competitive factory town.

By the time Geri and Fayard were settled in Los Angeles, America had entered the war. But life in L.A. was not yet greatly affected. Geri was immediately introduced to Dottie—"She came to meet me"—and the rest of the Dandridge household. Geri detected that Ruby Dandridge and Ma-Ma were suspicious of her. "They thought that I would join the Nicholas Brothers as a dancer and then that would cut Dottie out," said Geri. "Dottie didn't have those feelings." She liked Dandridge right away. Like many in show business, Dottie was often self-absorbed. Yet Geri saw that she possessed other qualities rare to showbiz personalities. "I never met anyone who had the same kind of generosity. She was the sort of person who if you were in need, she would get out of her bed and [help] you. She took a stove out of her house once because somebody got put out of their apartment and they were going into another apartment. She gave them the stove. It was a spirit. It was the heart." Nor did Dandridge "talk against people." The same was not true of Ruby and Ma-Ma, though.

How did her mother-in-law, Viola, take to Geri and the marriage?

"Well, she liked her. She thought she was a nice little girl," said Fayard. "But she wasn't too happy about it. But she had to accept it. She didn't want her favorite son to get married." Of course, her favorite son was then twenty-seven years old. "She was afraid that I would do something that would interfere with her relationship with Fayard," said Geri. "Her sons provided her livelihood. And I think she was scared of me at first."

Not long afterward, in September of 1942, Dottie and Harold married. Their wedding was one of Black Hollywood's most talked-about events. The guest list was restricted. In attendance were only close friends and family: Viola Nicholas; Ruby; Ma-Ma; Vivian, who had married a young man named Jack Montgomery; Etta with her husband, the musician Gerald Wilson; Geri and Fayard; and such luminaries as Hattie McDaniel and choreographer Nick Castle. The two young Nicholas brides then took their place at the very top of Black Hollywood's social ladder.

At first, Dottie and Geri, though cordial, were not great friends. But the two came to know each other better because the brothers spent so much time together. Their relationship changed after Dorothy was in a car accident. Geri visited her in the hospital. The two talked at length over several days, and Dottie opened up, confiding her family secrets and some of her own doubts and fears. By the time of her release from the hospital, Dandridge told Fayard, "Geri is my best friend." The two young women would remain lifelong friends.

On the surface, Geri and Dottie seemed almost as different as Fayard and Geri. Dreamy and romantic, Dottie wanted life to conform to her hopes and her fantasies. Despite early problems in her marriage to Harold, Dandridge was madly in love with him. Both women realized how hopelessly spoiled their husbands were and how both men always had an eye for other women. Harold—even more so than Fayard—was a perennial philanderer. A steady stream of beautiful women flowed through his life. They pursued him—and Fayard—while the brothers toured. Harold's affairs and encounters, pursuits and seductions, were open secrets in Black Hollywood. Still, Dandridge "wanted to have a white picket fence and really be a good wife," said Geri. Geri, however, eventually discovered "that I didn't love Fayard. I loved his dance, his art. I appreciated everything he did for me—the places I got to see, the remarkable people I got to meet. But I realized I didn't love him." Though she endured his affairs for years, she had no illusions.

The women had different styles. Geri's style was more subdued. She wore her collars buttoned at the top, dressed in skirts and blouses, and

*The marriage of the year when Black Hollywood's
young prince takes a bride.*

didn't see herself as sexy or on display as an actress always knows she is. Dandridge, however, with her natural sensuality, was always watched, studied, scrutinized, and eventually pursued by an array of men of all races, ages, and classes. Yet Geri, with her lively, intelligent eyes, her warm mouth, and her wit, was never without her admirers. Her intelligence made her an ideal dinner guest. Still, some in Hollywood couldn't figure her out. "Geri talked above them. And they couldn't understand her," said Marilyn Williams Hudson, daughter of architect Paul Williams. "They just didn't know what she was talking about. If you had an intellectual conversation, they weren't geared to that." Geri exposed the young Dandridge to books and new ideas. Because Dandridge had traveled and worked so much as a girl, "she didn't read until she was quite old, about four years prior to my meeting her," said Geri. "She had missed a lot. She had a hunger for knowledge. When [she realized I had] read a lot, she would just, for hours, talk to me and make me analyze [the books] for her. And we'd analyze together and so on. This thirst for knowledge was just insatiable." She began devouring books of all sorts, especially on psychiatry and psychology. "She was like a sponge," said Geri. "And she was a quick study."

If Geri and Fayard were to have a life of their own, she knew they'd have to move out of Viola's home into one of their own. So "when Fayard bought me a convertible, I sold it," said Geri, "and bought a house in a mixed neighborhood" not too far from Viola. Still, Viola Nicholas "didn't like it too much. But she had to accept it," said Fayard. "I could see it in her face. But she accepted it because I'm married now. This is my wife. I can't stay with her all the time. So we found a place." Later, they bought Viola a home on Fifty-first Street between Main and Broadway. And with her sons off on their own, Viola ended up having at least two new husbands: a short-lived marriage to producer Earl Dancer and then a union with a handsome former boxer named Charles Early, who was known around town for his looks and his perfect physique.

Of Hollywood residences, the anthropologist Hortense Powdermaker once wrote, "The myth of enormous and elaborate homes set in the midst of big estates turns out to be generally untrue. Beverly Hills, Bel-Air and the others are quite charming, conventional, well-kept upper-class suburbs, not too different from the Roland Park of Baltimore, the Shaker Heights of Cleveland. The actual Hollywood-situated homes seem less ostentatious, since many of them are in an informal, modern style. A home surrounded by an acre or less may be dignified as an 'estate,' while 'ranch' is frequently used to describe any informal house with only an acre or less of land." Those comments applied, of course, to homes in Black Hollywood, too. The great lavish estates had belonged to the stars of the silent era and a Black Hollywood star such as Fetchit. But those days were now gone. Throughout movie-colony history, there would always be a few select stars who would dazzle even Hollywood by living on a truly grand scale, be it Elizabeth Taylor or to a certain extent Frank Sinatra and Dandridge in the early 1960s. But their particular personalities and their celebrated approach to living would always supersede even *their* homes.

During this era, Harold and Dottie moved into a modest residence nearby on Twenty-seventh Street between Arlington and Cimarron. Pure California-style, their home looked more like a large bungalow with a small, well-tended lawn in the front, a good-sized front porch with beautiful palms and shrubs on both sides of the entryway to the house, and a large lawn in the back. Inside the one-level house, there were a living room, dining room, kitchen, two baths, and two spacious bedrooms. With an interest in interior design, Dottie decorated it stylishly. "She had wonderful taste," said Harold. "She had thick white white carpeting, lovely drapes," said Geri. "They spent a lot of money on redecorating it," said Fayard. "A beautiful little house. Just made for them." It was considered a cozy dazzler of a residence, all the more so because of the events that took place within its doors.

The two Nicholas wives sometimes accompanied their husbands on tour and, back home, entertained often. Hollywood wives were expected to know how to entertain: what china and silverware were appropriate, what type of menu their guests would appreciate, what type of small talk would best bring out a shy guest, although in show-business circles, most guests were extroverted and talkative. So the Hollywood wife was also expected to know when to keep quiet and let the guests shine as well as when to flatter and cajole.

For Geri and Dandridge, who loved to cook and entertain, the evenings at their homes glittered with sparkling nonstop conversations, plenty of laughter, and California-casual-style glamour. Because the weather allowed Californians to entertain as much outside as in, Dandridge's large lawn was just right for backyard parties where plenty of tables and chairs as well as barbecue grills could be set up for friends. Much to the delight of their proud husbands, the two young wives would greet their guests looking sensational in their casual hostess outfits. One night, Count Basie's entire band came for dinner at Harold and Dorothy's. Or Herb Jeffries might breeze in. Other times, Louis Armstrong, who had known Dottie since the days when he and The Dandridge Sisters appeared in *Going Places*, showed up, full of laughter and high spirits and a joint or two as well. Dandridge always called him Pops.

Bill Robinson, who had known the Nicholas Brothers from the days at the Cotton Club and Dottie from the time when The Dandridge Sisters performed in *The Big Broadcast of 1936*, also visited both Geri's and Dottie's homes. "We spent a lot of time with him. Uncle Bo," said Geri. He had taken Hollywood by surprise when he divorced the much-admired Fannie. "He had had a lovely wife," said Geri. "And then he left her when he met this chorus girl, Sue." Bojangles completely controlled his young wife, dictating her every move and even the way she looked. "We were really friendly with his second wife," said Geri. "He called her Sue. Her real name was Elaine. And he was a funny guy. He couldn't stand her nose. And he had it fixed. That was unusual in those days. And if she talked too much or said something he didn't like, he would say, 'I'm going to break that nose I give you.' But, see, Uncle Bo meant it. He wasn't kidding. She

*A typical day in sunny L.A.: Dandridge and
Geri Nicholas (Branton) at a drive-in restaurant.*

was so much younger than him. We were all in our twenties in those days.
He was seventy then."

Eddie "Rochester" Anderson lived nearby, as did Mantan Moreland,
who made his name playing the chauffeur Birmingham Brown in the
Charlie Chan mystery movies, and his wife, Hazel. Nearby, too, was Hattie McDaniel, who took the town by surprise in early 1941 when she
eloped with a real estate dealer named James Lloyd Crawford. Upon their
return to Los Angeles, a big reception was held for them with five hundred
guests in attendance and so many cars heading toward the house that there
was a traffic jam. Everyone wanted to look the guy over. By now, Black
Hollywood was swarming with attractive gentlemen callers, out to make
their mark not on the screen but rather in the boudoirs of available
women. Already the town questioned whether Crawford might be such a
gentleman caller. But McDaniel was too much in love to have such
thoughts herself—at least, not yet.

During these years, Geri found the black entertainment community
tighter and closer than it would be in the decade to follow. Because there
were still few big names working in the movies and because of the racial

lines still drawn at the studios and throughout the city, the entertainers tended to be all the more bound together by their experiences. Though the city wasn't like the apartheid South with its "Whites Only" signs and Jim Crow laws, everyone still knew where he or she was or wasn't welcomed. In essence, "Los Angeles was completely segregated then," said Geri. Performers entertained frequently at their homes. And the nightclubs remained great meeting and mingling places. "In those days of segregation, you only had each other," said Geri. "Every once in a while, Tyrone Power and, of course, Carole Landis and Rita Hayworth and a few daring whites would mingle with us. But we would hang out in the clubs. After people worked, they'd finish and they'd come over to the Dunbar Hotel. And the Club Alabam."

The black elite of Hollywood had its own social lines. With their husbands, Geri and Dottie represented the successful new young Black Hollywood, the kind of glamorous, attractive young couples the town had not seen before. Invitations poured in daily—for dinners, for parties, for receptions. But Dorothy's sister Vivian, who performed sporadically while struggling to hold on to some semblance of a career, was relegated to the lower end of the social ladder. "In show business, there's so much snobbishness," recalled Branton. "While we would go to Hattie McDaniel's parties and people who worked regularly, Vivian hung out with chorus girls. That wasn't our crowd. It wasn't by choice. But it was just the way people separated. And we'd see Billie Holiday and Hazel Scott and Duke Ellington and Cab Calloway and people like that. They were the ones that came to my house. Or Dottie's house."

Because of the Nicholas Brothers' status in the industry, the two couples' social circles also extended at times beyond the borders of Black Hollywood. They became friendly with white actress Carole Landis and "were often invited to Gene Kelly's and his wife Betsy Blair's," said Geri. "And we'd go to [dancer] Eleanor Powell's on Sunday afternoons. We'd be the only black people there. But everyone would be friendly."

The Nicholas wives also grew friendly with Ben Carter, that ingenious actor/agent who was part of politically liberal—as well as sexually liberal—Hollywood. Smoothly maneuvering his way through various sectors of Hollywood, he picked up the secrets and peccadilloes of any number of stars. Gay Hollywood, black and white, remained fairly separate but not exclusively so. Though Carter would never be invited to the Sunday brunches of famous gay director George Cukor, he did mix and mingle with important white stars, albeit clandestinely. At his "open" parties, as

ABOVE:
Geri Nicholas (Branton) with her son Tony.
AT RIGHT:
Happy days at their enchanted bungalow: Dandridge and Nicholas with their daughter, Harolyn, outside their home.

opposed to his exclusively gay gatherings, Geri and Fayard and Dottie and Harold would be invited as well as a performer such as Katherine Dunham. "Tyrone Power and Cesar Romero, [who] were having a big affair, [were] there. Ben was a part of that crowd. Burt Lancaster. Archie Savage," recalled Geri. "Of course, we didn't smoke. And we weren't big drinkers. We weren't a part of that. Lena was a more daring lady in that regard. But the four of us [Harold, Dottie, Fayard, and myself] had fun together."

Hattie McDaniel at her wedding reception at her home with her groom—her third husband—James Crawford.

Guests might see Joel Fluellen, then a struggling actor and always an ambitious social climber, who, like Carter, came to know an array of major stars, black and white. For years, Fluellen had trouble keeping himself afloat. But he loved show-business life and would do anything to be a part of it. An attractive man—tall, solidly built, brown-skinned—an excellent cook, a good conversationalist, and intelligent and well read, he understood he could be a valuable social asset: the perfect dinner guest when a hostess was one man short.

Born in Monroe, Louisiana, in 1910, Fluellen came to Hollywood by way of Chicago, where, enraptured by the worlds of entertainment and the arts, Fluellen struck up friendships with a rich variety of people coming to the Windy City. He studied acting with the actress Abbie Mitchell, met actor Canada Lee, and so impressed poet Countee Cullen that he invited Fluellen to New York. But the dramatic change came when Fluellen, then working as a clerk in a department store, found himself staying at the same hotel as Louise Beavers, then promoting *Imitation of Life.* Beavers liked him and suggested he come to L.A.

In early 1936, he arrived in the city, his head in the clouds with glamorous notions about Hollywood's black stars and with visions of the Hollywood he had seen in photographs on the wall behind the counter at

Bridesmaid Dorothy Dandridge (center, front row) at the wedding of the Los Angeles Sentinel's *society editor, Jessie Mae Beavers.*

Walgreens drugstore. Stepping off the Great Northern train, he hopped into a cab and asked to be taken to the Dunbar Hotel. But during the ride—as he gazed out the car window at a rather ordinary but lively city street—he asked the driver, "When are we going to get to Central Avenue?" "You're on it," the driver told him. He discovered that the Hollywood that black performers inhabited was hardly the one of his imagination. He was surprised that Beavers lived modestly, yet well, then still in her home on Twenty-ninth Street. When *Green Pastures* was being filmed, Fluellen joined the extras who were picked up by a studio truck to go out to Warner Bros. Finding it hard to adjust to the city, he briefly returned to Chicago, but the lure of the klieg lights soon brought him back to L.A. The second time around, he was determined to work in movies and be near the center of the action. Mostly, he did bits—in the beginning—and also designed hats and catered parties.

Like Ben Carter, Fluellen was very much a part of gay Black Hollywood. At one time, he had an affair with a wealthy older white man who kept him dressed in the latest fashions and entertained with giddy nights

Lena Horne, the new girl on the coast, with Black Hollywood's high and mighty: Hattie McDaniel and her husband, James Crawford; Geri Nicholas (Branton); Fayard Nicholas; Eddie "Rochester" Anderson and his wife, Mamie; Ben Carter and Nick Stewart (bottom row).

on the town: the best parties, the best receptions, the best restaurants for dinners or lunches; the best secret gatherings of top men in the industry. At another time, he dallied with one of Hollywood's big athletic stars.

Fluellen's friendship with Beavers gave him his entrée into Black Hollywood's top social circles. Adept at reassuring troubled women of their appeal and allure, he stayed for a time at the Dunbar Hotel, where he became friends with a boozy Billie Holiday and an even boozier Nina Mae McKinney. For a time, he and McKinney lived together, as friends, not lovers. He also grew close to Hattie McDaniel. At the McDaniel and Beavers parties, Fluellen was the most accommodating of guests: He was quick to empty an ashtray or fix a drink or gossip and dish the dirt. To his credit, he could also confidently hold up his end of an informed conversation on the arts or literature. Fluellen never permitted himself to be what he might call pure Hollywood lowlife trash. He respected actors such as Robeson and later Sidney Poitier. He understood the aesthetics of the

Joel Fluellen: social arbiter, master chef, gossip, snob, and fearless fighter for the rights of black performers.

dance style of Harold and Fayard. He came to admire Lena Horne's class and sophistication. Keenly aware of the racial politics of the town, he could be an outspoken fighter for the rights of black performers and later would help lead the call at the Screen Actors Guild for better roles for black actors. But Fluellen could also be a ruthless snob. If you weren't in the business or important in some arena, he usually couldn't care less about you. For years, he cozied up to Ruby and Ma-Ma, quick to flatter them both. He enjoyed gossiping with Ruby, who could be useful by informing him of the films that were about to go into production, the ones that needed black actors, and the ones about which he should confer with Ben Carter.

But Fluellen had another reason for his friendship with Ruby: He was dazzled by her daughter Dorothy, whom he first saw in the lobby of the Dunbar Hotel. That day, she was wearing ballet shoes, and at first, he thought she was a ballerina. "Dorothy was the loveliest . . . the most delicate" woman he had ever seen. Awestruck, Fluellen did everything conceivable to be near her. If Harold were out of town on tour, Fluellen made it a point to get to the Nicholas home to keep Dandridge company, to shop with her, to cook for her, sometimes to massage her, and always to flatter her endlessly. Fluellen would know many famous people, but none ever affected him as Dandridge did. "He *obsessed* on my sister," said Vivian.

Yet Fluellen was also impressed with Geri, who, before long, had vast social and political contacts in Hollywood, both white and black. "He would come around me and go to the kind of parties I'd go to with Helen Gahagan Douglas. I could get in a lot of those places because of the Nicholas Brothers," said Geri. "They knew I knew other stars. And they used that. This is a *using* town. You have no worth if you can't produce." Nonetheless, Fluellen later won roles in such important movies as *Friendly Persuasion* and *The Learning Tree* and was a part of the Black Hollywood scene for decades, up to the time of his death in 1990, when, old and frail, he put a gun to his head and pulled the trigger.

THE WAR COMES TO HOLLYWOOD

When America entered the Second World War, Hollywood, like the rest of the nation, joined the war effort. Stars such as Clark Gable and James Stewart took leave of their careers and joined the armed forces. Henry Fonda and Gene Kelly served in the navy. Comedian Bob Hope traveled more than a million miles to entertain the troops. Fearing that Harold and Fayard would soon be drafted, Twentieth Century Fox rushed them into *Stormy Weather*. As it turned out, Harold was too short for military service. But Fayard was drafted and then shockingly put on kitchen duty at Fort Huachuca in Arizona.

The Office of War Information established the Bureau of Motion Pictures. With movies now openly viewed as being a powerful form of propaganda, the studios were encouraged to do their patriotic part *on-screen*—indeed, to make movies that supported the war effort and that also saluted the ideal of America as the land of the free and home of the brave. Scripts were submitted to the Bureau of Motion Pictures. The Office of War Information then might make suggestions for changes. All of this ultimately affected Hollywood's images of African Americans. Heading a special wartime filmmaking division, director Frank Capra worked with the young black scriptwriter Carlton Moss to create *The Negro Soldier*, a tribute to the contributions of black military personnel throughout the nation's history. Another tribute, *The Negro Sailor*, was also filmed.

The NAACP's executive secretary, Walter White, became more vocal about the inequities on-screen. On two occasions, White traveled to Hollywood with Wendell Willkie, the NAACP's counsel and a onetime Republican presidential candidate as well as a board member of Twentieth Century Fox. Both men attended an Academy Awards dinner, went to studio commissaries, and sought meetings with studio executives to discuss movie roles for African Americans. At a Hollywood luncheon, Willkie delivered a speech that strongly criticized racial stereotypes. Throughout his visits, he "pointed out the incalculable harm that continued picturization of Negroes, Asians, Africans, and Latin Americans as either savages, criminals, or mental incompetents was doing both abroad and in the United States." White also made his case, urging "the film industry to use more courage and imagination in the handling of roles of dark-skinned minorities." White wanted to see Negro extras in scenes depicting everyday American life—blacks on city streets or in restaurants or at train stations. In this way, the diverse fabric of American life would be revealed. White also grew increasingly critical of the roles played by Hattie McDaniel. Some studio executives chose not to meet with White. But Darryl F. Zanuck and Walter Wanger were among those who did. David O. Selznick and Zanuck agreed to new guidelines for using extras and also agreed to bring more blacks into the studios in technical and craft positions.

Los Angeles Sentinel publisher Leon Washington criticized the industry for the roles assigned to black actors—just as writers such as Earl Dancer, A. J. Rogers, Earl Morris, and Fay Jackson had been doing since the late 1930s. Jackson once complained of a studio that had used its bootblack as a consultant on the topic of black history for a film production. Could that have been anyone other than Slickem? Now the war galvanized the more progressive segment of Los Angeles's black community. And around the country, the black press called for a double V: victory over the enemy abroad *and* over Jim Crowism at home.

Within Black Hollywood, those actors and actresses who made their living playing servant roles grew fearful that they would no longer have a livelihood. Discussions flared up in homes, in restaurants, at openings, even at the clubs. A wave of change had begun.

Daily, Los Angeles was also undergoing a transformation as more and more African American workers came in search of jobs. "When the war broke out," lifelong L.A. resident Johnetta Jones recalled, "people used to come here off the train and bus and get the U streetcar that ran down Central Avenue. And they'd get off the streetcar with their suitcases and go door-to-door, trying to rent rooms. They came to work in the defense plants and the shipyards. That's when people began to move around the city." Trumpet player Clora Bryant recalled that she stood awestruck upon her arrival at Union Station in January 1945. The sun was shining, and there was energy everywhere. "I'd never seen anything like that. My eyes popped. I looked at all the trains coming and going and backing up and pulling out." Bryant came to study at UCLA while her father found work in the shipyards. Their very first night in town, she and her father had dinner at the home of Ben Carter, whom her brother actor Mel Bryant knew. Bryant remembered that Carter "lived in this fine, big two-story house that was white stucco. It was really decorated. Ben had a maid who had been married to a member of Ellington's band. She had also been a cook for actor Joseph Cotton. She fixed dinner for us with roast pork and lemons." The lemons came from Carter's lemon trees. "It was a point in my life that I will cherish," Bryant recalled, "because there was something exciting happening just about every day." Between 1940 and 1945, the city's population increased from 75,000 to 150,000, and black L.A. began stretching its boundaries farther west.

THE NEW FACE IN TOWN

Just before the war, the first sign of a new day came with Lena Horne's return to town. In Pittsburgh, Horne finally accepted the fact that her marriage to Louis Jones would never work. Not knowing what else to do, she returned to show business. She appeared in the theatrical production *Blackbirds of 1939*, and performed as the girl singer with the band of white orchestra leader Charlie Barnet. Finally, Horne made a name for herself when she appeared at Café Society Downtown, the very chic Manhattan supper club run by Barney Josephson that also headlined such performers as Billie Holiday, Josh White, Teddy Wilson, and Hazel Scott. According to writer Helen Lawrenson, the club—in a basement at 2 Sheridan Square in Greenwich Village—was founded on New Year's Eve 1938 to raise money for the Communist Party. Café Society became a great hangout for liberals and progressives. Not only were there Negro entertainers onstage, but black patrons, the ordinary along with the celebrated, were welcomed in the audience. Among the famous patrons were Paul Robeson, Eleanor Roosevelt, Lillian Hellman, Budd Schulberg, and S. J. Perelman. Barney Josephson also opened a sister club called Café Society Uptown. At Café Society, where she became a darling of sophisticated New Yorkers, Horne, unlike other black singers, didn't perform blues or spirituals or jazz numbers. Mainly, she sang show tunes and pop standards.

While at Café Society, Horne received word from her agent, Harold Gumm, that Felix Young, who ran a very chic L.A. supper club called Le Papillon, wanted her to come west to appear in a revue at his new club, The Trocadero. Ellington, Katherine Dunham and her dance troupe, and Ethel Waters were scheduled to perform. Barney Josephson was opposed to her going. What could the West Coast—Hollywood—offer her? Others in New York, however, believed that Horne might find work in the movies. That included the NAACP's Walter White, who, having known her grandmother, met her through Paul Robeson. White believed that Horne might be able to change the image of black women in the movies. Instead of being cast in ditzy-maid roles, she might usher in portrayals of polished and poised women. Horne had her doubts about leaving New York. But in the summer of 1941, she packed her bags and, with daughter Gail and her cousin Edwina, boarded the Twentieth Century Limited at New York's Grand Central Station. In Chicago, they changed to the Super Chief, which carried them to Union Station, in downtown Los Angeles. Her daughter Gail said the family later learned that real movie stars never got off in L.A., exiting instead at the earlier stop in Pasadena. Such were the ways, they soon discovered, of the movie capital. Her son remained with his father in Pittsburgh.

The palm trees didn't seem to elicit from Horne the same sense of wonder that they did from other new arrivals. She focused mainly on preparations for the Trocadero opening as well as adjusting to the social life out west. There were problems on both fronts. Felix Young had let Horne stay in an apartment he had on Horn Avenue, which was just above Sunset Boulevard. Residents in the apartment building and the area were not accustomed to seeing a Negro resident, although they weren't sure what to make of Horne. Some thought she was Latin. Still, there were always stares. Horne didn't feel comfortable at all.

But the other problem with the Trocadero engagement was that there was no such club. Felix Young's nitery burned down. Eventually, he opened his club in a smaller building, which he called The Little Troc. But times were hard for a while. Katherine Dunham and most of her troupe "were living in a little house down the Strip," recalled Lena Horne, "and now they were forced to cook their meals, and wash their clothes in communal pots, and sit around waiting for Felix to get together the rest of the money he needed to open."

Before coming west, Horne had run into Phil Moore, the young arranger on *The Duke Is Tops* who was now employed at MGM. In New

York on a break, Moore had gone to Café Society Uptown to hear Count Basie. In walked Barney Josephson with a young woman. "Damn, she was a knockout," Moore recalled. "Gorgeous face with Egyptian fresh honey and almond complexion and nice neat little freckles, flashing intelligent eyes, 'fondable' nearly straight hair, irresistible promising smile, fascinating mouth with fresh snow-white teeth—for days—and a sculptured groovy figure. Kinda skinny legs but who the hell cared. She had class to spare that was not affected, just there. The great thing about this lady was that the whole added up to about ten times the total of the components. On top of that she looked familiar."

"Aren't you the guy that wrote the music for *The Duke Is Tops?*" she asked. Only then did Moore realize it was Horne. "I was really amazed at the transformation from her being a new mother, to the way she now looked," he recalled. "We all decided to go to Monroe's up in Harlem and hear some music. Basie, Lena, me, and a bunch of guys went and had a ball. Way late in the morning, Lena leaned over the table and asked me, 'Next time I come to California, will you write some arrangements for me?' A pretty wasted Phil said, 'Oh, sure, Baby, sure.' "

Back in L.A., Moore received a call from Felix Young, who "asked me if I could come out to meet someone, and talk about work," said Moore. "I walked into his place and lo and behold, there was that young beautiful Lena Horne." Moore recalled, "Felix said Lena had assured him that I would make some arrangements for her. I seem to remember [that] what music she had had was burned up in the fire."

With his duties at Metro, Moore didn't have much time to write. But he agreed to bring in his trio to perform, and he'd sketch some arrangements and help her build a repertoire. "It's kinda hard," he said, "to imagine the Lena Horne we've now known and admired for so many years, once being out of a job, vulnerable, anxious for approval, and scared of what was going to happen, or not happen, next, but at this juncture, that's the way it was. I gotta say, she went through this drought period like a champ, and not like a whiner, as I've seen so many times when folks had to pay their dues. Maybe it was because her father, like mine, was a gambler, and she too had seen that winning, losing, and dealing a new hand, were all part of the game called life."

Moore also recalled, "Often when I start to work with a stimulating talented woman, it seems like I fall in love or get a severe crush on them." That's how he felt about Lena. But Horne, focused on her career, was "wise enough to quell my ardor into friendship." Among the songs he arranged for her during these years were some of the most famous in her repertoire: "Deed I Do," "Embraceable You," "The Man I Love," and "Stormy Weather." Her new friend Billy Strayhorn also arranged "Honeysuckle Rose," "There'll Be Some Changes Made," and "Blues in the Night."

Finally, The Little Troc opened. But Ellington and Ethel Waters were no longer on the bill. In the beginning, Lena was an added attraction for an audience that came primarily to see Katherine Dunham, along with her troupe, including her star dancer, Archie Savage. Between the Dunham shows, Horne performed sets, backed up by Moore's trio. The "joint was packed every night with the creme de la creme—if there's such a thing in Hollywood," said Moore. Upstairs on the second floor was a gambling den, which certainly didn't hurt the nightclub's appeal. The Little Troc was also in an ideal location. Next door to the club was the plush dress shop of the Hollywood designer Adrian, which catered to some of the industry's biggest stars and social figures. But inside The Little Troc, Dunham's troupe barely had room to move. "Actually the room was much too small for an artist of Miss Dunham's scope, name and reputation," said Moore, but because it "was such a prestigious engagement, where she would be seen by everybody who was anybody, she took the job as a 'pas a deux.' "

The small setting, however, worked to Horne's advantage. "At first the audience *liked* her, I guess partly because she was so sensual and yet had class, and was the most striking black woman they'd ever seen," said Moore. "But, as time went on, they *loved* her because she was turning into a great singing entertainer. After a few weeks patrons and celebrities were returning just to see her, making encore requests of numbers they liked, and bringing their friends." Reservations were being made weeks in advance, said Moore. Comedian Milton Berle became so excited by Horne that he sat ringside yelling out requests, disrupting her performances. An angered Felix Young banished the comedian from the club.

Then, Katherine Dunham had an argument with the owner, and she left. "And the owner was asking me, we were trying to get Josephine Baker. Any star that we could get, that he could get," said Moore. "I said, 'Felix, look I think we got a star here.' " Horne became the headliner. "The business was just overwhelming," said Moore, "and she was knocking people out, and from then on, she was it. She had a great kind of charisma, a great kind of command. She didn't speak much then, at all, between songs, or anything like that. But she did another type of material then than most black artists were doing. We did most of the standards: Gershwin. Cole

Porter. Rodgers and Hart. And that sort of thing. It was really sophisticated material." Nightly, celebrities like Marlene Dietrich, John Barrymore, Cole Porter, Artie Shaw, and Shaw's former wife Lana Turner sat in the club. Horne's favorite actress, Greta Garbo—with her friend Mercedes D'Acosta—also came to The Little Troc.

MGM COMES CALLING

MGM's Roger Edens also stepped into The Little Troc to see Horne—more than once. At MGM, Edens was a highly regarded composer/arranger who worked with producer Arthur Freed to create some of the most successful musicals in movie history: such movies then and later as *Babes in Arms, Meet Me in St. Louis, The Harvey Girls, The Band Wagon, An American in Paris,* and *Gigi.* Edens brought Horne to the attention of the studio. She recalled that within a few days, Al Melnick of the Shurr Agency accompanied her to MGM for discussions about possible movie work. Even before the car drove through those hallowed gates, Horne was already moving Black Hollywood in a new direction, more into the mainstream of the moviemaking process: working with a top white agency, appearing successfully at a chic club away from Central Avenue, and living in Hollywood outside the restricted confines of the Negro community. Some of these things had been done before, but Horne did them all—and in her own distinctive way.

At MGM, Edens greeted Horne and Melnick: "I heard you sing and liked it so much. Would you sing for us?" Horne was then ushered into the office of Arthur Freed, who initially was not interested in seeing her. "I'll give her fifteen minutes," Freed had told agent Melnick. "Then get her out of here. I got work to do." But once she performed the song "More Than You Know," it would be some four hours before Freed let her leave. He asked her to sing for the head of the studio, the all-powerful Louis B. Mayer.

"He was a short, chubby man and by now everyone is familiar with the tales of his temperament," Horne recalled. "But on this occasion—as upon most of the very few others that I dealt personally with him—he seemed very genial and fatherly to me." After she sang, Mayer left the room, only to return with actress Marion Davies. Would Lena sing for her, too? Famous for her stammer and sweetness, Davies said afterward, "L-l-lovely, my dear." Lena also saw director Vincente Minnelli, another transplanted talent from the East, who told her he hoped they would work together.

*MGM, the studio with "more stars than there are in heaven,"
gets its sepia one, Lena Horne with Roger Edens.*

Not long after that afternoon, negotiations began for Horne to sign a contract with MGM. Having recently bought the rights to the stage musical *Cabin in the Sky,* the studio considered casting her in the role of Georgia Brown. Nervous about dealing in this world of high-powered white male executives, Horne asked her father to come west to help in the negotiations. Seated in Freed's office with a group of studio executives, Teddy Horne was frank about his concerns for his daughter. Handsome and confident, Teddy Horne informed the studio brass that all he had seen of black women in movies were as maids to white actresses. Teddy Horne was assured by Mayer himself that his daughter would be handled differently.

Signing a seven-year contract, Horne was guaranteed a salary of $350 a week for forty weeks a year. The other twelve weeks enabled her to work at nightclubs and other venues, including the Loew's theaters, the chain of movie houses owned by the same parent company that controlled MGM. Later, recalled Gail Buckley, when it was publicized that Hazel Scott, another performer from Café Society, had signed a contract at $5,000 a week at another studio, a contract negotiated by Barney Josephson, MGM was embarrassed into increasing Horne's salary to $900 a week with yearly raises of a hundred more weekly.

Though Nina Mae McKinney and Fredi Washington had been considered glamour girls, Horne was in a league of her own. "Lena was the first one," said Phil Moore, "that was really given a star treatment, in terms of having special designer gowns, eating in the stars' part of the commissary, and really associating with the upper echelons of the studio. The upper-middle echelon. You know, the heads of departments and things like that." Having a major Hollywood studio behind her, Horne enjoyed a number of perks. For personal appearances, she could borrow clothes—those gorgeous gowns in which stars were seen when about town—from the studio's wardrobe department. The studio publicists also pushed for coverage from mainstream media.

Long sessions were devoted to studying the best ways to light her and to make her up. A special makeup—called Light Egyptian—was created specifically for her by the legendary Max Factor. But it proved a bust: much too dark and used, so Horne said, only on white actresses playing mulattoes, such as Hedy Lamarr in *White Cargo,* in a role that, ironically, Horne would have loved to play. Ultimately, it was decided to light and photograph her as any white actress would be. A greater dilemma for MGM was how to style her hair. The head of Metro's hairdressing department, Sydney Guilaroff, who would be known over the decades for creating hairstyles for every great star from Garbo and Crawford to Monroe and Taylor, recalled, "No hairdresser at the studio would touch Lena's hair." Guilaroff himself did the styling. But because he couldn't be on the set every day, he informed the studio that it had to hire a black hairstylist. "MGM hadn't had one before that," said Guilaroff. Nonunion black hairdressers were brought in. In time, Noelia Tiny Kyle did Horne's hair. Eventually, Hazel Washington was brought in as the studio's first licensed black hairstylist. And in makeup, the department head, Jack Dawn, did Horne's makeup himself, much as Guilaroff had done.

Within a short period of time, Horne grew even more chic: in looks, in dress, in attitude. Like other female stars, she slimmed down and easily slipped into high-fashion gowns with hair stylishly coiffed and with high-gloss, perfectly applied makeup that accentuated her dramatic eyes. Yet offscreen, Horne would never look like a Beverly Hills lady who lunched; instead, her basic style would be that of an East Coast sophisticate with nods to European haute couture.

While waiting to put *Cabin in the Sky* into production, MGM used

Lena: dream girl of the war years.

Horne in the films *Panama Hattie* and *Thousands Cheer,* in which she appeared in "specialty numbers," sometimes set in a nightclub, performing a song or two, then disappearing. "She wasn't given any kind of roles in the films, except musical things that could be deleted if it was sent down South," said Phil Moore. Lena Horne's great disappointment was MGM's refusal to cast her in an important dramatic role, especially in its 1951 remake of *Show Boat* as the mulatto Julie. Ironically, when MGM had the perfect Julie under contract, it cast Ava Gardner, whose singing had to be dubbed.

Horne, however, was viewed suspiciously by Black Hollywood. Those performers who did extra work or played bits as maids or butlers feared she was part of an NAACP revolt that might lead to less work for Negro performers. An apprehensive Horne met with some of the actors. "Walter White and Paul Robeson wanted to break the power of this group," Horne's daughter, Gail Lumet Buckley, said, "but it was Lena who came face to face with them at their 'protest' meeting." Their anger was real. Horne found herself in a terrible situation.

But actor Eddie Anderson proved supportive, as did Hattie McDaniel, who "sent me a note to come to her house," said Horne. Aware of the problems any black actress faced in Hollywood, McDaniel encouraged Horne to continue working, despite any criticism from Black Hollywood. "You've got two babies. You've got to work. Just do what you have to do." Horne never forgot McDaniel's graciousness during this difficult time.

Still, not feeling comfortable in Hollywood, Horne returned to New York whenever possible. During such a visit, she confided to Count Basie that she planned to give up movie work. "Basie told me," said Horne, "after I had been there [in Hollywood] three miserable months, 'You've got to stay because they don't choose us, and you've been chosen and whether you like it or not, you've got to go.'"

Returning to Los Angeles, she adjusted to her new life. She became closer to dancer/choreographer Marie Bryant and struck up a new friendship with Hazel Washington, who still reigned high in Negro social life. Upon Horne's initial arrival in L.A. in the 1940s, Duke Ellington suggested that his master composer and collaborator Billy Strayhorn—there during the run of *Jump for Joy*—take her around town. The two met during the overture for *Jump for Joy* when the young composer slipped into the empty seat next to her. "I'm Billy Strayhorn," he said. "I've been sent to see if you're all right." Other nights, he squired her around town to "the Negro section." They'd hit the after-hours haunts "to hear the great singers and musicians who always seemed to be playing there. It was there, for example, that I heard Winonie Harris, one of the legendary blues singers, for the first time. The guys from Duke's band would come in, and some of their wives, whom I also knew from New York. And I ran into some of the girls who had been at the Cotton Club with me and even some of the girls who had been in that little quickie picture I had made, *The Duke Is Tops*. They helped to make me feel a little less lonely and strange." She and Strayhorn developed a close relationship.

Horne found herself in a "privileged" position that brought her to the attention of white Hollywood—*and* taught her the ways of the game in town. "In Hollywood my first party was at Cole Porter's house," said Horne, "and it was something of a social *coup* to invite the latest singing sensation to the party. Nothing was said about money, and, ostensibly, I was a guest, but it was perfectly understood that I would sing for my supper. I didn't want to, but Felix Young thought it would be good for the club and good for me. Cole Porter was, as always, perfectly charming, and I was to be a guest in his home many times later." But Horne never forgot the condescending attitude of southern-born actress Miriam Hopkins and opera star Grace Moore. Though she liked Tallulah Bankhead, she didn't fail to see how Bankhead, who spoke of cute little pickaninnies and the "non-Negro-ness" of Horne's features, was also clearly a product of the South.

In time, Horne felt more relaxed as she socialized with Vincente Minnelli, Gene Kelly, and Kay Thompson, all easterners under contract to Metro, along with producer Fred Finkelhoffe and his wife, singer Ella Logan; lyricist Ira Gershwin; and composer Harold Arlen. A lively friendship also developed with the earthy Ava Gardner. For a time, Orson Welles showed a keen interest in her. But much as she admired this wunderkind, Horne wasn't interested in a romance. Not lost on Hollywood—during these years and those that followed—was the fact that Lena Horne was also a colored star receiving mainstream press coverage. *Life, Time,* and *Newsweek* all ran stories on her. So did the publication *Liberty,* which referred to her as "the girl with the flashing smile, the tawny skin, and the voice that makes the 'I Love You' songs sound as though she really means you." The publication *Motion Picture* ran her as its cover girl in 1944, marking the first time a Negro star had appeared on the cover of a fan magazine.

Perhaps not unsurprisingly, Horne was pursued by one of the industry's most powerful men, Twentieth Century Fox's Joseph Schenck. When she worked on loan out at Fox, Schenck sent word that she was invited to join him for lunch. Neither had much to say. But he invited her to a dinner party a few weeks later. In attendance were a few MGM executives and some young women. "After an extremely formal dinner during which the men discussed grosses," said Horne's daughter, Gail Buckley, "the butler passed cognac and coffee and everyone settled down to watch a movie. Joe Schenck beckoned Lena to sit next to him on the sofa and reached for her hand. Lena pretended her hand did not belong to her and stared stonily at the movie screen until it was over. She went home unmolested and never received another Schenck invitation." Of course, beautiful young women in Hollywood, black and white, were always considered accessible *and* disposable items.

Eventually, Horne moved into a home of her own on a steep hill on Horn Avenue. "Our house, which rested against the side of a mountain, was a typical Southern California Mexican-style house," recalled Gail Buckley, "with white stucco walls and a terraced terra-cotta roof. There was the smell of eucalyptus everywhere—and azalea, bougainvillea, and red and pink geraniums. The nights were cold and the crickets were thunderous.

"Below our hill was Hollywood and the Strip—Disneyland before its time," said Buckley. "There were restaurants in the shape of sombreros, bowler hats, and old shoes. There were Swiss chalets, Bavarian schlosses, Kentish cottages, Spanish haciendas, and the Garden of Allah, which looked like Christmas in Bethlehem. Christmas in Hollywood was often more exotic than traditional. Beverly Hills pioneered the dyed Christmas tree—usually shocking pink, or gold."

Yet even in this fantasy setting, racial realities always surfaced. When Horne's son, Teddy, came to stay with them, he and Gail were the only black children in their school. Some neighbors drew up a petition to have the Horne family kicked out of the area. But right across the street from them were Humphrey Bogart and his wife at the time, actress Mayo Methot. Down the way resided actor Peter Lorre and writer Vera Caspary. "Fortunately, our allies were stronger than the bigots," said Gail. "When the petitioners rang Bogart's bell, he told them to get off his property or risk being shot at." Lorre and Caspary also would have nothing to do with such a petition.

Otherwise, there were happy memories. "My California was pre-freeway and pre-coaxial cable," Gail Buckley recalled. "I can see the field of orange-red poppies that grew wild at the end of Sunset Boulevard. . . .

Grown-ups always wore sunglasses and scarves. The pre-smog climate was Edenic. Our lemon trees produced fruit the size of grapefruit, and gardenias bloomed by the garden door."

For a time, Lena resumed a romance—which had started in Pittsburgh—with heavyweight champ Joe Louis, who was in and out of L.A. and at the time still had a well-publicized marriage to Marva Louis. Their romance was a hot topic of discussion: two major African American celebrities, young, attractive, accomplished. "Oh, everybody knew about it," said Geri Branton. Fayard Nicholas recalled seeing the two together one evening at the Mocambo. "You make a pretty couple," he told them. How long did their relationship last? "It didn't last long," Nicholas laughed. Yet Louis once commented that he "was so carried away" with Horne that "it wasn't proper." Their relationship was also often stormy. "Lena would fuss with me about not coming to see her on the MGM lot," he said. But Louis steered clear of the studio because "there was another star there, Lana Turner, asking me why I didn't come out and see her." Louis said he was in love with Horne yet didn't want to leave Marva.

But the Louis/Horne relationship came to an end shortly after a heated argument on the telephone. "She started giving it to me hot and heavy," said Louis. "Told me I'd been in town for a couple months and hadn't bothered to call her but a few times. She hinted about knowing that I'd been seeing other movie stars, too." An angered Louis drove to Horne's home. "Well, then Lena started cursing me like nobody ever had. Before I knew it, I hit her with a left hook and knocked her onto the bed." Fortunately, Louis came to his senses—when a relative of Horne's threatened to call the police. "I stopped. I left and went to my hotel. I was so scared I was shaking," he said. "End of romance." Years later Horne denied that Louis had ever been violent. "I have a temper," she said, "and I've never allowed anybody to strike me without a terrible kind of reaction. But Joe has never been unkind to me."

PHIL MOORE: THE MAN WHO MADE MUSIC

Other new arrivals altered the atmosphere of Black Hollywood. Now residing in L.A. was composer Phil Moore. Born in 1918, orphaned, and placed in a county hospital in Portland, Oregon, he had been adopted by a gambler, George Moore, and his homemaker wife, Irene, whom everyone called Jimmy. Growing up, young Phil was exposed to his father's wide range of acquaintances in Portland, Seattle, and other cities. George

Moore had been a backer of the hit black Broadway show *Shuffle Along* and later managed boxer Henry Armstrong. George and Jimmy Moore saw to it that their precocious son was well educated. Playing the piano at age five and later attending Seattle's Cornish Conservatory, Phil always believed he had a kind of all-American boyhood "because I was the only black kid in my grammar school and the only one in my high school, and then we moved to Seattle and I went to the University of Washington." There, Moore studied orchestration.

"When I went to Seattle, I started playing professionally, when I was thirteen," recalled Moore. "Playing for singers a lot in speakeasy-type places around there. One was the Bucket of Blood, and the other was the Black and Tan. I would work from nine o'clock at night until schooltime in the morning. And most of the time, I was playing for singers. Seven nights a week. That was perhaps the best college I ever went to."

"But I had a very good thing that doesn't happen to very many black kids. And I attributed a lot of my background to that. My mother never told me what I couldn't do. And if I'd go to my mother and I'd say, 'Hey, Mom, I think I want to be president,' she said, 'Well, you gotta be good to be president. You gotta be smart, and you gotta work.' So, therefore, I always had that attitude. That was a big advantage that I had because my eyes were never at the ground. They were always at the horizon and in the skies, looking for whatever's out there."

Moore had first come to Hollywood with a friend in the 1930s for a three-week performance at the Lincoln Theatre. His obvious talent and energy, along with some of his father's associates, helped him make contacts and quickly rise up the ranks of Negro entertainment. Through comic Flournoy Miller, Moore was recommended as an arranger for a radio appearance of Ruby Elzy, one of the original stars of *Porgy and Bess.* At the Lincoln, he came to the attention of headliner Ethel Waters. When Waters's arranger had to leave the city because of an emergency in New York, she decided to give Moore a chance. After a rehearsal, she asked him, "How old are you, kid?" "Seventeen," he told her. "Who taught you how to play that way for singers?" "Oh, I worked with a lot of demanding lady singers in Seattle clubs." When he mentioned a Miss Zelma, Waters asked, "You mean Noodles Smith's Zelma?" "Uh, huh." "Honey, that mean old evil heifer sure taught you somethin!"

At the end of the three-week engagement, Moore felt sad about leaving the city. With a friend, "we drove all over town and ended up late in the evening on Mulholland Drive, a road that runs along the very tops of the hills that split L.A. asunder. I always like to find the highest lookout point where I travel, usually at night, so I can look the situation over. We stopped at a very special vista point where we could survey most of the sparkling city lights of L.A., Hollywood, Beverly Hills, and Bel Air, and looking the opposite direction, we could view the thousands and thousands twinklins of the entire San Fernando Valley. Surveying the magnificent L.A. scene, I really was impressed and liked what I saw. I didn't have to own a big house in Beverly Hills or Bel Air, all I wanted was a chance to have a little niche, and a little taste of the magic. There just had to be a part for me in this scene."

Returning to Seattle, "I got to be the second best-played pianist in these joints, and I said, 'Okay. I'm ready for Hollywood now.' And so that's when I matriculated and took the trip. I worked my way down the coast to Los Angeles. It wasn't Hollywood then that black people came to, it was L.A., because black people didn't live in Hollywood at those times." Moore recalled that "black musicians couldn't play in the white parts of town. Otherwise, stink bombs would be thrown in because there was a white union and a black musicians union. Things were very different then. I remember Marian Anderson came out to sing, not at the opera house but the auditorium, or something like that, and she had to go to a hotel in a freight elevator. Same with Paul Robeson. And this was a highly segregated area, Los Angeles. . . . The only time we went to Hollywood was to work. But I came to L.A., and I worked on Central Avenue at the Dunbar Hotel." Eventually, Moore's parents moved to Los Angeles, too.

Moore became the musical director for *The Duke Is Tops* and worked on a musical sequence of MGM's *A Day at the Races* with the Marx Brothers, Ivie Anderson, and The Dandridge Sisters. Along with another L.A. newcomer, Nat Cole, he arranged music for The Dandridge Sisters. Moore also appeared with the trio in the MGM short *Snow Gets in Your Eyes.* At Metro, he "met some people in the music department, so I later applied for a job there." An appointment was set up for him to meet the music department's head, Nat Finston.

Moore never forgot his appointment. "At about five minutes to ten I presented myself to the gate guard, received my pass and was instructed how to get to Finston's office," said Moore. "His secretary sat at her desk behind a short fence with a gate so she could get in and out easily. This anteroom was quite small, walls encrusted with stills of films, and some chairs against the wall facing the secretary. The doorway to Mr. Finston's office was right next to the chairs, so that anyone entering his office would have to pass directly in front of the sittees." Moore spent hours sitting—and waiting. Late in the day, the secretary informed Moore that Finston couldn't see him. That was a Monday. She gave him a pass to come the next day. The same thing happened on Tuesday, Wednesday, and Thursday. "I became a chronic sittee," said Moore. But he kept coming back. On Friday of that week, Moore—carrying an armful of scores and music—was finally led into Finston's office, where he expressed his interest in becoming an arranger at the studio.

"What else can you do? Do you play any instrument?" Finston asked. "Can you play for singers—in all the different keys?"

"Yes, sir," replied Moore.

"Can you play for dancers and make musical notes for a choreographer?"

"Yes, sir."

"Can you read well?"

"Yes, sir, practically anything."

Finally, Finston told him, "I can't put you on as an arranger, but we do need a good rehearsal pianist. If you want that job, you can start Monday morning."

"I didn't get the job I was looking for," said Moore. "But I was the first black person hired on a steady basis in the music department of the studios of Hollywood." That proved to be "a shock down at the old segregated black musicians' local. They couldn't believe MGM had hired a black guy." Moore was aware that before his arrival at MGM, black composer William Grant Still had been hired by the studio. "But it didn't work out due to the fact that he was very classical and couldn't orient himself," said Moore. "People in Hollywood don't like this particularly. But doing music for films is like cutting bologna. You know you have to cut it so much, and it has to fit so many things. It's a craft problem. . . . Since I'd had so much experience with singers, they kind of put me in charge of going to New York with their stars who would make personal appearances at the Capitol, which was called the flagship of Loew's theaters at that time."

Moore had made it to the majors. The studios of the thirties, forties, and fifties "were mammoth factories developing talent, personalities, images, films, and selling these films through their own distributors and theaters," recalled Moore. "In the golden age they had large staffs in various departments all working toward enhancing the talent and the final product. There were drama coaches, singing teachers, choreographers and dance teachers. Each studio had its own extensive sound department, a pool of arrangers, a slew of music copyists, and up to one hundred top quality musicians under contract, not to mention all the public relations people, writers, directors, cameramen, and technicians, and office staff they employed. They were really something else!"

At MGM, Moore worked with top stars like Judy Garland, with whom he was never left alone in a room. "They'd always send a chaperone along. I guess they thought I was about to rape her," he once said. "But pretty soon they got over those fears." After a year or so, he began orchestrating for MGM. Then, he was called into Finston's office. "Kinda gave you a rough time when you first came here, didn't I?" Finston said. "Phil, I just had to do it that way, because I had to get a feeling of your attitude and disposition. No matter how talented you were, if I hired you, you were going to be the first Negro on our lot. I couldn't protect you, or nursemaid you. Do you understand?"

"Upon becoming a full-fledged arranger at Metro, I learned the studio system of working with arrangers," said Moore. "The music director of a film would choose the arrangers he would use for a particular score. He then would assign us each certain sections of the film according to our specialities. Sometimes, when he wished to have someone work very close to him, that man would become his 'assistant.' During the next few years I guess I was just about every music director's assistant. You could call it 'an official ghost,' meaning one who did a hell of a lot of music sketching and arranging, but very rarely getting any credit." He also recalled, "After I graduated to orchestration, they wouldn't even let me write for strings for almost a year. A black man wasn't supposed to be able to do that, even if he had studied at the University of Washington. But I became an instant authority on Africa, exotica, South America, jungles."

Away from the studio, Moore continued to arrange and write compositions for the bands, black and white, of Duke Ellington, Jimmie Lunceford, Charlie Barnet, Tommy Dorsey, Gene Krupa, Harry James, and others. He also wrote the pop hit "Shoo Shoo, Baby," which he said was inspired by Lena Horne. On the Sunset Strip, he performed with his trio at the white clubs such as Ciro's, Le Papillon, and the Mocambo. Like Lena Horne, he was extending the boundaries for black artists and making the town a less segregated place.

At MGM, Moore never fit the stereotyped conception of what a Negro should be like. Always well dressed, usually in suit and tie, he sometimes

*The man who made music and helped build careers:
arranger/composer Phil Moore with Lena Horne.*

wore glasses, smoked a pipe, and spoke of music in cerebral terms. "He was a well-spoken man," singer/pianist Bobby Short recalled. "I think a little cautious sometimes. . . . His manners were impeccable. And yet Phil had a kind of wild side. He would wear funny hair-gear. When the hair began to really go, he'd wear those bandanas." Socializing with whites and blacks, Moore, recalled Bobby Short, "was just so unlike any kind of black man they had ever seen. That I had ever seen. Smooth. Elegant. Sophisticated. Not bound in by the old boundaries."

With his round face, a receding hairline, and stocky build, Moore was hardly considered handsome. Yet women gravitated to him. Perhaps it was all his highfalutin but unpretentious talk about music and art. Perhaps it was his interest not only in a woman's physical charms but also in the way she thought and spoke, the way she viewed herself and the world. He tended to like the women who walked off the beaten path, breaking down barriers in their own distinct ways, just as he did. He had several wives, one of whom was Jeni LeGon, the dancer who had arrived in Hollywood in the previous decade. Together, they wrote the song "The Spring" for Lena Horne to sing in her debut MGM film *Panama Hattie*. "Phil brazenly, without any regard for convention at all, was also out with any number of white women at all times, long before it became accepted," said Bobby Short. "It was like living outside the whole accepted boundary of being a black person." In time, Moore got over his crush on Lena. But later, he fell madly in love with the woman many considered Horne's rival, the younger Dorothy Dandridge.

For Moore, studio life ultimately had its drawbacks. On loan to Paramount Pictures to work on *The Birth of the Blues*—starring Bing Crosby, Mary Martin, and Jack Teagarden and featuring Eddie Anderson and Ruby Elzy—he found it rather absurd that Paramount would do a movie about the blues that starred whites. "The title song, though much loved by white folks," said Moore, "is an ersatz Hollywood Tin Pan Alley concoction, that had been a big hit, but certainly was *not* a blues." Moore thought Brian Donlevy, cast as a jazz trumpet man, "probably didn't know which end of a trumpet you put in your ear."

Moore also clashed with a music executive. When a cast album for *The Birth of the Blues* was to be recorded by Decca at its studio on Melrose Avenue in Hollywood, Bing Crosby, who recorded for the company, had Moore hired to do arrangements. Coming from New York to supervise was a top executive, "a self-made man of self importance, in his self-made plastic world," said Moore. When the executive griped that Moore's "hep" version had to be changed because it didn't have a melody, Moore complied. Unknown to the executive, Crosby himself had asked Moore to do the special arrangement. When Crosby heard the new version, he asked, "What's the matter, Phil, don't you like *your* arrangement?" Moore let Crosby know that the "company" didn't like it. "I don't think it's commercial," the executive said. Bing then informed him, "Well, I like it, and if you don't like it, you can get another boy singer!" Then, he walked out of the recording room. The first version stayed. But the executive "never spoke to me again in [his] life," said Moore, "and tried to see that any songs I wrote were *not* recorded by Decca. However, a little later, my song 'Shoo Shoo, Baby' was a big hit for the Andrews Sisters on Decca. So there!"

At MGM, there was also an incident with high-powered producer Arthur Freed. Phil had written background music for a Freed production that the producer complained "didn't seem to catch the feeling of the scene." Another composer was then assigned to create a new number. Afterward, Freed had the film screened, along with the two different recorded versions, then told Phil he was sorry but he had to go with the new composition, presumably of the white composer. What he didn't know, recalled Moore, was that the score he had selected was actually the one Phil had written. "Later on, someone must have told him," said Moore. Like the Decca executive, "Mr. Freed never spoke another word to me again in his life."

Though Moore worked on more than forty films at MGM—including *Ziegfeld Girl, Panama Hattie, Presenting Lily Mars, Cabin in the Sky,* and *Kismet*—and on loan to Paramount Pictures scored such films as *This Gun for Hire, My Favorite Blonde,* and *The Palm Beach Story,* he rarely received credit. "I made many recordings with Phil on his own records," said musician Gerald Wilson. "He worked at MGM all the time." But it was "like ghostwriting. I've never seen his name on the screen. They did him really a bad deal. I kicked because they didn't put my name on *Where the Boys Are* and the other movies I scored for. I kicked. That was in the late fifties. But this guy was already writing music for MGM and other studios, too. Not only him—Calvin Jackson wrote many scores at MGM, man. I'm not speaking like one or two or three. I'm talking like ten or fifteen. Heavy, heavy scores."

After toiling at MGM, Moore asked for a promotion. Again, he was called into Nat Finston's office. "I was up in the front office discussing your promotion," Finston told him. "I, as well as a couple of your colleagues recommended you highly, but they just refuse to have a colored person in that position." After having been at MGM for five years, Moore left.

For years, he was bicoastal, traveling back and forth between L.A. and New York. He formed the Phil Moore Four, which performed successfully at Café Society Downtown. He also coached or arranged for a gallery of stars: Horne, Hazel Scott, Mae West, Jane Russell, and later, Joyce Bryant; Pearl Bailey; Ava Gardner; Marilyn Monroe, in preparation for *Gentlemen Prefer Blondes;* Dandridge; and Diahann Carroll. The women all noted his sensitivity, his ability to help them work through their insecurities and vulnerabilities. "He gave me confidence in my own ability," Marilyn Monroe once told *Ebony,* "and made me realize that people would be willing to listen to me as well as to look at me."

Moore later managed Bobby Short. "I think he was immensely talented. I think he was a damn good musician," said Short. "He was a loner. . . . You didn't find Phil hanging out with a bunch of jazz musicians, chewing the fat or discussing this or that. He had no time for that. He was in his office trying to get something done. He was kind of before his time. You know, there are many black musicians today who have offices and who approach their business the way Phil did all those years ago. Forty years ago.

Fifty years ago. Phil was doing this in the 1940s. Back in those days, for him to sit down and score for a symphony orchestra was rare. And he went to MGM and often did movie scores for films without getting credit for them. He composed a number of interesting things and got contracts to record them with big orchestras. I think he was the musical director for a record label at some point. He was a first in many, many, many ways. I mean, there are many black men around today . . . who can lay claim to things like that. But back in those days, Phil's position was really quite rare. And, of course, it meant denying himself a lot of things that one takes for granted today.

"He was subjected, of course, to things like the rest of us—discrimination and segregation and so forth. And he survived that and pushed his way through all of it and made it possible for a lot of the rest of us to do it. My first residence in New York was Carnegie Hall. And I got in there because Phil Moore had a studio in Carnegie Hall. He didn't get me in. I got myself in. But the notion of my even living there came about because I had stayed at Phil's studio in Carnegie Hall.

"He had no time for those restrictions. It's not fair to live with those fences around you. So when it came to making his life, he didn't start out looking for an apartment in Harlem. He started out looking for an apartment in midtown where his business was. You must hail a person like that as a champion. He was remarkable. He was a great influence in my life."

Moore recommended that MGM hire another black arranger/composer/pianist, Calvin Jackson, in his place.

LET'S HEAR IT FOR THE NEGRO TROOPS!

Upon first hearing the news about the war, the town seemed shell-shocked. Lena Horne recalled being with Billy Strayhorn at the time. Everything seemed to stop or move in slow motion. But soon, any number of social events revolved around war efforts: the rallies at which stars appeared or performed, the Victory Committee meetings and galas, the USO clubs, the war bond drives. If anything, the war seemed to intensify the town's energy and heighten its mood. The idea was obvious and simple: Enjoy today or tonight, because who knew what tomorrow held. Many on the West Coast feared a Japanese invasion. Like others, Hattie McDaniel stocked up on canned foods in preparation.

Always, Hollywood felt that support had to be shown for the troops. At one of the big USO benefits, there was a big to-do when Joe Louis joined Bing Crosby, Jimmy Durante, and other stars for a celebrity golf tournament. Much of the industry threw its weight behind the Hollywood Canteen. Founded by Bette Davis and John Garfield in 1942 with financial support from Jules Stein, the head of the powerful Music Corporation of America agency, the Hollywood Canteen was the West Coast's answer to New York's Stage Door Canteen, a club where servicemen could come to be entertained for free and mix with show-business stars. Frank Sinatra, Dinah Shore, and Bing Crosby were among its biggest supporters. Big stars like Marlene Dietrich, Betty Grable, and Hedy Lamarr served as hostesses and would dance with ordinary soldiers. Nightly, name orchestras would entertain. One memorable evening, Duke Ellington performed a duet with virtuoso harmonica player Larry Adler. Also on the bill that night: Bette Davis, comedy team Abbott and Costello, and singer Rudy Vallee.

At a time when the armed forces were still segregated, no one expected to see black soldiers dancing with one of the white female stars. Yet whereas the USO was segregated, with separate clubs for white and Negro soldiers, the Hollywood Canteen, like the East Coast Stage Door Canteen, was as open and integrated as possible at the time. Geri Nicholas Branton and Dorothy Dandridge were among the Hollywood wives who served coffee and doughnuts to the boys in uniform. Other young black women were dance hostesses—with whom some white soldiers didn't hesitate to dance. Occasionally, black soldiers danced with white women. There were complaints, however, about the races mixing. Bette Davis's anger over such reactions was reported in the January 6, 1943, issue of *The Pittsburgh Courier* with a headline that read: "Bette Davis Overrules Objections to Mixed Couples at Hollywood Canteen." Davis insisted that there be no racial discrimination at the Canteen and that Negro soldiers be permitted to mingle with everyone in all sections of the Canteen. After all, she believed that Negroes got the same bullets as whites. So why should they be treated any differently?

Lena Horne could always be counted on, even on holidays. Bette Davis recalled that Christmas Eve "was always a difficult night. Patriotism or no, this is a family night and we always worked on skeleton crew with a paucity of entertainment." One Christmas when several performers canceled their appearance, a call was made to Horne, who asked, "Are you sure the boys aren't tired of me?" "Half an hour later her incandescent smile was brightening up the Canteen and the Christmas of hundreds of soldiers," reported *Liberty* magazine. "It was after midnight when she returned home, to the remnants of her own Christmas party."

Some within Black Hollywood naturally questioned the war effort. "A rough estimate of the total number of Blacks in the armed services during World War II," wrote historian John Hope Franklin, "places the figures in the neighborhood of 1 million men and women." Many believed that black GIs were traveling abroad to fight for the freedom of others while Negroes at home were still disenfranchised citizens. Most of the town, however, supported the war and believed that much should be done to boost the morale of the Negro soldier. Stars such as Horne, Eddie Anderson, Phil Moore, Ellington, Count Basie, L.A.'s well-known trumpeter Gerald Wilson, Lionel Hampton, orchestra leader Benny Carter, and—on a special occasion—Joe Louis performed on *Jubilee*, the armed forces' radio show, broadcast primarily for the benefit of black military men and women. Becoming the musical director for the Armed Services Radio, Phil Moore produced musical shows for the United States military all over the world. Frank Capra was the head of his division. Moore had his own primarily black show *eelibuj*, which was *Jubilee* spelled backward. He also liked to boast that a B-25 was named after his song "Shoo Shoo, Baby."

Black Hollywood's titular queen, Hattie McDaniel, emerged as a driving force in wartime activities. A captain in the American Women's Volunteer Service, McDaniel headed a subcommittee of the Hollywood Victory Committee. At her home, she met with other committee members, such as Eddie Anderson, Leigh Whipper, Louise Beavers, Mantan Moreland, Fayard Nicholas, Ben Carter, and Lillian Randolph. Friction and controversy swirled within Los Angeles's black community about McDaniel's subcommittee, which was criticized by *Sentinel* publisher Leon Washington as being too conservative. He noted that most of these performers (with the notable exception of Nicholas) made their living off playing stereotyped roles. Still, McDaniel held a massive benefit at the Shrine Auditorium in July 1942 to raise money for black military groups. She hit the USO clubs, toured to sell war bonds, and entertained the troops.

During Lena Horne's travels to army bases, she clearly realized that a battle still had to be waged at home. Two incidents lingered in her memory. On one occasion, the army arranged for her to attend the graduation ceremony of the Tuskegee flying school—where the all-Negro 99th Pursuit Squadron underwent its training, in Tuskegee, Alabama. Horne ar-

Lena Horne, speaking out for the troops.

rived in Alabama in the early hours of the morning, where she waited for a connection to take her to Tuskegee. Cold and tired, she saw a lunch counter that was still open. "I know I'm in the South," Horne was reported as saying to an attendant, "and I don't want to cause any embarrassment but I'd like a cup of coffee. Do you think it would be all right for me to go in there?" Told that she could enter, Horne went inside the lunchroom and took a seat—only to be ignored by a waitress who served the other customers without so much as looking in Horne's direction. Finally, the waitress asked what Horne wanted. Horne simply requested a cup of coffee. "I'm sorry," she told Horne, "but I can't serve you." "But I was told it would be all right." "Well, if you'll go around back to the kitchen, I'll see what I can do." Horne told her not to bother. Then a young boy, the son of the waitress, said, "Say, aren't you Lena Horne?" He asked her to autograph a menu. She signed and walked out of the lunchroom.

Upon her arrival at Tuskegee, Horne was given a rousing reception by the black military men. Just as white GIs posted photographs of Betty Grable and Rita Hayworth on their lockers or inside their military backpacks, Horne had become a pinup girl for African American soldiers. And no doubt for some white ones, too—though they may not have wanted to admit it. She was the perfect dream girl for a soldier's long, lonely nights away from home, just the kind of pretty ideal for which he believed he was fighting. That night at Tuskegee, the white commanding officer introduced her as evidence that "the charm and beauty of womanhood are not confined to any one race." During her visit, she was praised and pampered, adored and adulated—all treatment befitting royalty. Yet Horne remained frank and honest with herself about her position and—despite the incident at the lunch counter—some of her privileges. "It doesn't flatter me," she said, "to be treated well simply because I'm the 'famous Lena Horne.'"

She became enraged when the army sent her to entertain at Camp Robertson in Arkansas. As always, the white commanding officers were courteous and admiring, even chivalrous. But when Horne took her place onstage, she faced an all-white audience. Where are the Negro soldiers? she asked. Told that if she wanted to entertain them, she would have to go to the Negro mess hall; she headed in that direction, only to arrive and see a group of German prisoners of war seated in front of the black soldiers. She walked out. "Take me to the NAACP," she told an aide, whereupon she was taken to meet Daisy Bates, a pioneer of the civil rights era. The story about Horne's walkout in Arkansas made its way back to Hollywood, and it was one of the incidents that led the more conservative members of the movie colony to view her as a rebel and even a troublemaker.

During the war years, racial incidents also flared up in the city. "I saw several very, very unattractive incidents," recalled Bobby Short. "On the sidewalk during that period, white soldiers up from the South for the first time brushing with black people, I've seen some dreadful things. I remember a black man—very, very well dressed—was on a bus riding out to Hollywood, as I was. And he fell asleep. And his head fell over on the man's shoulder next to him, who was a young GI. He jumped up and screamed, 'Why, this goddamned nigger!' It was a very, very difficult time. You had these bucks, young whites, up from the Deep South, where segregation ruled. And for the first time in their lives, they were sitting side by side with black people in movie theaters, on the bus, on the sidewalk, on the streetcar. And to many of them, it was just unbearable."

Short also remembered that throughout the war years, black Angelenos couldn't even go to a decent beach for a swim. "The beaches were highly

Hazel Scott.

segregated," he said. "If a black person wanted to go to the beach, you went to some awful place at Santa Monica where it wasn't even the beach. You were on the coast off the sea. But it wasn't even the beach."

STUDIO LIFE

For the duration of the war, life at the studios was affected in unexpected ways. Roles gradually changed. At Warner Bros., Michael Curtiz's *Casablanca* cast Dooley Wilson as the easygoing, iconic Sam—who performed what became a wartime anthem for lovers, "As Time Goes By." Also at Warners, John Huston's *In This Our Life* featured serious-minded Ernest Anderson as the young Negro who hopes to be a lawyer but is falsely accused of a hit-and-run accident. Playing the young man's saddened mother was a surprisingly restrained and beautifully modulated Hattie McDaniel. These were early attempts to present audiences with the New Negro.

Two major black-cast films went into production. At MGM, *Cabin in the Sky* was filmed under the direction of Vincente Minnelli with a cast

*Mellow and moody: Billie Holiday with
Louis Armstrong and Barney Bigard (right) in* New Orleans.

that included Ethel Waters, Lena Horne, Eddie "Rochester" Anderson, Rex Ingram, Louis Armstrong, Butterfly McQueen, John "Bubbles" Sublett, Mantan Moreland, Willie Best, Ruby Dandridge, Kenneth Spencer, and in a deluxe cameo, Duke Ellington. MGM also lent Lena Horne to Twentieth Century Fox to appear in the other big black-cast film, *Stormy Weather*, with its all-star cast, which included Bill "Bojangles" Robinson, Fats Waller, Katherine Dunham with her dance troupe, Cab Calloway, Ada Brown, Dooley Wilson, Ernest Whitman, and in the film's most spectacular climactic sequence, the Nicholas Brothers. Black choreographer Clarence Robinson was also signed for the production. Benny Carter led the orchestra. There had not been two big-studio black productions in the same year since the release of *Hallelujah* and *Hearts in Dixie* in 1929.

At the studios, top musicians also came and went: Count Basie, Louis Armstrong, Duke Ellington in such movies as *Stage Door Canteen, Atlantic City, Reveille for Beverly,* and *Hit Parade of 1943.* Most significantly, Hazel Scott signed to do a series of films: *I Dood It, Something to Shout About, Rhapsody in Blue.* A Trinidad-born child prodigy who had grown up to be-

All-star black-cast lineup: Lena Horne and Bill "Bojangles" Robinson in Stormy Weather; *to Robinson's immediate left, Avanelle Harris.*

come a teenage sensation at Café Society, Scott had created a unique style of jazzing up the classics, turning standard classical music into boogie-woogie. Café Society's Barney Josephson, who negotiated her movie contracts, specified she could not be cast in any derogatory manner. "No bandana on her head," said Josephson. "No apron upon her waist. And they took her. They wanted her that much." Instead, Scott, splendidly gowned and coiffed, usually appeared as herself in a nightclub or theater setting—a stunning emblem of youthful glamour and style. Known as a clotheshorse, she showed up at rehearsals dressed in the most elegant casual style: tailored slacks and blouses or suits with a fur coat resting on her shoulders. As the second wife of Adam Clayton Powell, now a New York congressman, Scott became one of the town's social darlings.

The dancers and singers were thriving. Katherine Dunham and her troupe appeared in films. On his own, Harold Nicholas appeared in *Carolina Blues* and *The Reckless Age*. The Berry Brothers performed in *Panama Hattie*. Later Billie Holiday played a rather dim maid in *New Orleans*. But in the musical sequences with Louis Armstrong, Holiday's mellow, moody style was on brilliant display.

Some stars also appeared in soundies: short films, running five minutes or so, precursors to music videos, which were shown on jukeboxes that had tiny monitors, resembling primitive television sets. A soundie was often shot in one day at a small studio in L.A., recalled Avanelle Harris. The pretty girls such as Harris would audition. According to Harris, the man in charge then "just went down the line and picked the face he wanted." The pay for the pretty girls was twenty-five dollars a day. Featured on the soundies were performers white and black, such as Armstrong, Dandridge, The Mills Brothers, and Nat "King" Cole.

WORKING IT BEHIND THE CAMERAS

More African Americans were walking through the studio gates to work behind the cameras. At MGM, Calvin Jackson—the young Philadelphia-born pianist and composer recommended by Phil Moore—worked as an orchestrator on such films as *Bathing Beauty, Music for Millions,* and *Her Highness and the Bellboy.* Local guys such as Gerald Wilson also headed to the studios. In the 1930s, Lee Young had been hired to teach Mickey Rooney to play the drums for the film *Strike Up the Band.* Young also worked at Warners, Paramount, and the Hal Roach Studios. Later, he was put on the staff at Columbia. But as before, black musicians rarely received credit for their work.

The same was true of Marie Bryant. "Another backdoor choreographer," said Bobby Short. A light-skinned, long-legged dancer with expressive eyes, a lush, full mouth, and hair that was usually cropped short, Mississippi-born Bryant might have stayed in the South had not her family decided it was better to get her out of town. Trouble sprang up when southern neighbors discovered that Bryant's mother had frequently shopped at a white grocery market, usually with little Marie by her side. No one had questioned their race. But one day, a little white boy—aware of their ruse—taunted Marie, calling her a "nigger." She pounced on the boy and punched him. That night, her mother and father—a chef on the railroad—had a long discussion. Fearing some type of retaliation from their neighbors, they left Meridian, Mississippi, two days later and headed west.

In Los Angeles, Marie took dance lessons from the well-known dance teacher Mary Bruce, who Bryant said instilled her with a sense of racial pride. "She would bring out little glasses of white and chocolate milk," recalled Bryant. " 'Taste the milk,' she would say, 'and tell me which tastes nicer and also, which looks nicer. Now if you feel bad about being colored, remember this test.' I used to feel lots better after drinking the chocolate milk." Bryant also studied Katherine Dunham's dance technique.

Still young, Bryant danced in nightclubs in the late 1930s and early 1940s. Her appearance in *Jump for Joy* caught the eye of Hollywood, white and black, as did her mellow vocals in the "Sunny Side of the Street" number in Gjon Mili's moody short art film *Jammin' the Blues,* which featured Lester Young, Illinois Jacquet, Jo Jones, and Red Callendar. She also had a sensational bit with Harold Nicholas in *Carolina Blues.* Duke Ellington proclaimed her "one of the world's great dancers." Soon, Bryant landed studio jobs, assisting choreographers Billy Daniels and later Jack Cole, who trained such dancers as Bob Fosse and Gwen Verdon. When an entranced Gene Kelly, who called her "one of the finest dancers I've ever seen in my life," needed "just a little something" for his "Slaughter on Tenth Avenue" number in *Words and Music,* he phoned Marie and asked her to come to MGM. There, she worked on the number with young dancer Vera-Ellen. Afterward, actress Paulette Goddard asked Bryant to choreograph her shimmy number in the 1949 version of *Anna Lucasta.* Once Betty Grable and husband Harry James saw Bryant perform at the Florentine Gardens Cotton Club show, they asked her to choreograph Grable's numbers in *Wabash Avenue* in 1950. Bryant ended up appearing in the film, too.

Bryant hopped from one studio to another. At Paramount, she staged an Indian dance with Bob Hope. At RKO, she worked with Lucille Ball. At Columbia, she gave limbering exercises to young star John Derek. "They're pretty shocked when I first check in," she once said. "Much looking, double takes, eyebrow arising and all that. Still, when they see what I teach and the results I get, they accept me quickly." Ava Gardner as well as the wives of such Hollywood stars as John Garfield and Richard Conte took private lessons for a fee of fifteen dollars an hour, then a large sum. "I've never had to sell Marie to anybody," said choreographer Billy Daniels. "Stars usually ask for her."

Bryant became known within the industry for her "controlled-release" technique. "This consists in finding the natural line of each body," said Bryant, "and the favorite ways it likes to move about—then controlling these movements. For instance—in ballet dancing, the body is tight. In boogie-woogie, the dancing is loose and free. I learn any routine that becomes popular: boogie, modern dancing, primitive, ballet. Then I learn the muscles that control these dances—and that's controlled release. My danc-

Choreographer Marie Bryant, whom Gene Kelly called one "of the finest dancers I've ever seen," shows her moves to Harold Nicholas in Carolina Blues.

ing is described by some as the kind of dancing 'only Negroes can do because it's sexy and kind of lowdown.' But that isn't so. My work is controlled and artfully routined and within this framework I dance the popular movements people pay to see."

Extroverted, outspoken, wickedly clever, and all high energy and effervescence, Bryant could shoot the breeze with just about anyone. "She was all bubbles," said Bobby Short. "So much fun and so down. And funny. And yards and yards of talent. A wonderful singing style and danced beautifully." For years, she lived with her mother on the Eastside. "We'd often go to her house after work, late at night, and have drinks," Bobby Short remembered. "You can't imagine how wild it was. Not wild but just, you know. And Marie was always equally at home with black and white people."

Jean Bach recalled a story Bryant gleefully recounted one afternoon. "Marie was in St. Louis, and there was a movie with Clark Gable that she wanted to see." Bryant hopped into a cab to the white part of town. The cab driver told her, "Ma'am, I'll have to let you off just six blocks away, and you'll have to walk the rest of the way because I can't go up there." Bryant went into the movie theater but decided not to sit in the balcony where blacks were seated. Instead, she sat in the orchestra section, enjoyed the movie, and afterward got up from her seat. "There was an usher standing near the door," said Bach. "And she rushed up. He said, 'Yes, Ma'am, what can I do?' 'Would you say that I was colored?' He said, 'Well, no, Ma'am!' " Bryant then gleefully announced, "Well, I am!" Said Bach, "And she ran out of the theater, and she ran all the way back to the hotel. And that was her moment of triumph!" Once, when Bach visited Bryant's dressing room at a club in Los Angeles, she saw "pictures on her dressing table of Norman Granz and John Garfield. So you could tell what kind of guy she fancied."

Bryant also helped popularize the term *buns,* which was considered funny and mildly risqué at the time. "She always refers to the fannies of her pupils as 'buns,' " said choreographer Billy Daniels. When she worked at Fox with Grable on a difficult routine, no one in the rehearsal hall forgot Bryant's comment once Grable mastered the number: "That's it, Betty. Those buns are great. Oh, those buns!" Bryant appeared on camera as a nightclub singer in such features as *They Live by Night* and *Tiger by the Tail*—into the 1950s.

Also working at the studios was alto saxophonist and arranger/composer Benny Carter. When he arrived in town in the early 1940s, his reputation was already well known to Black Hollywood but not to studio executives. But before the decade ended, he would be one of the most successful behind-the-scenes musical artists. Born in 1907, Carter had started performing in Harlem in the 1920s. For a time, he was a member of Fletcher Henderson's orchestra. Leading his own band from 1932 to 1934, he also became—over the years—an admired arranger/composer for such major orchestra leaders as Ellington, Benny Goodman, Tommy Dorsey, Chick Webb, Artie Shaw, and Cab Calloway. In 1935, he headed to Paris, later London, Denmark, Sweden, and the Netherlands. Upon returning to New York, he appeared at the Savoy in Harlem, the ballroom known as the Home of Happy Feet. His performance on the Savoy's radio broadcasts made him nationally known. In 1942, he embarked on a cross-country tour that ended with an engagement at Billy Berg's Swing Club on Las Palmas Avenue in Los Angeles. "That two-week engagement stretched into fifty-two years," said Carter, who became a lifelong L.A. resident.

Carter played L.A. nightclubs and theaters—Casa Manana, the Hollywood Club, and the Million Dollar Theater—and then, in January 1943, he went to Twentieth Century Fox to arrange numbers for *Stormy Weather*. Performing with the studio's orchestra, he played solo and ensemble sax as well as trumpet on the sound track and cowrote a song with Fats Waller. Impressed with Carter, Fox's music director, Alfred Newman, gave him assignments on three other Fox films. Carter also worked at MGM, his career stretching from the 1940s, with films such as *A Song Is Born* and *Thousands Cheer*, in which he performed with Lena Horne, into the 1950s, with *An American in Paris* and *The Snows of Kilimanjaro*. In the 1960s, he composed for such television shows as *Ironside* and *The Name of the Game*. "Benny opened up the eyes of a lot of producers in studios so they could see that you can go to blacks for other things outside of blues and barbecue," said Quincy Jones. "I know that whatever problems I had, even as late as the '60s, Benny's must have been 10 times rougher." Away from the studios, Carter kept an ensemble group going in the 1940s with such innovative new talents as Max Roach, Miles Davis, and Dexter Gordon. He also played and arranged for Billie Holiday, Ella Fitzgerald, Sam Cooke, and Nat "King" Cole.

till, despite what many hoped were new attitudes in the executive offices of the studios, disputes, debates, and disagreements flared up on the sound stages during and after the war. Hazel Scott—high-minded and haughty—clashed with Columbia Pictures mogul Harry Cohn over stereotypes in a film on which she worked. An angered Cohn swore she'd never work in Hollywood again. She had already signed to do *Rhapsody in Blue* at Warners. But "then he was as good as his word," said Scott. "I never made another Hollywood film." When *Tales of Manhattan* was released, Paul Robeson was so outraged by the final product—featuring himself, Ethel Waters, and Eddie Anderson as naïve, overly religious sharecroppers—that he denounced the film and said he'd never appear in another Hollywood feature. He didn't.

Possibly the most talked-about star explosion occurred on the set of *Cabin in the Sky*. Ethel Waters—now an older, heavier star (she was then

Ethel Waters—all peaches and cream—with Duke Ellington and director Vincente Minnelli, before *her explosion on the set of* Cabin in the Sky.

forty-six)—believed that the glamorous, younger Lena Horne was getting preferential treatment from director Vincente Minnelli. Horne was alerted by Minnelli of possible problems with Waters, who still had a reputation for a quick temper and repeated outbursts. Minnelli told Horne the only way to compete on-screen with Waters—one of the most charismatic and talented stars of the twentieth century—was basically to do nothing. "Be real small," he said. "You can never be stronger than Ethel. Just be vulnerable and coquettish."

Horne stuck to the plan. But when she injured her foot—shortly before her big scene with Waters was to be filmed—Waters believed that it was a ploy to get attention. An infuriated Waters exploded at a rehearsal, criticizing nearly everything about the production. But she went further. "She flew into a semi-coherent diatribe that began with attacks on Lena, and wound up a vilification of 'Hollywood Jews,'" said Gail Buckley. "You could hear a pin drop. Everyone stood rooted in silence while Ethel's eruption shook the sound stage. She went on and on. Freed, [Eddie] Mannix, and Ethel's agent all appeared on the set." But no one could calm her down. Finally, Minnelli told everyone to go home for the day. Later, the sequence was filmed without any incident. But Waters said her career suffered. There had "been conflict between the studio and me from the beginning. For one thing, I objected violently to the way religion was being treated in the screen play," Waters recalled. "But all through that picture there was so much snarling and scrapping that I don't know how in the world *Cabin in the Sky* ever stayed up there. I won all my battles on that picture. But like many other performers, I was to discover that winning arguments in Hollywood is costly. Six years were to pass before I could get another movie job."

LIFE AS USUAL

In other ways, social life went on as before. Still flourishing was the cluster of clubs—the Club Alabam, The Last Word, Club Memo, and the Downbeat Club—in the section known as Little Harlem on Central Avenue in and around Forty-second and Forty-third streets. New clubs appeared. So did after-hours joints. And places for the sporting crowd. The Brown Bomber and the Bird in the Basket, which trumpet player Clora Bryant remembered as the best place in town for musicians to jam, were always packed. On West Adams Boulevard, Dynamite Jackson's cocktail lounge became a hot spot, too. Herb Jeffries opened the doors to his nitery, appropriately called The Black Flamingo, on Avalon near Vernon. There were also radio broadcasts from Bird in the Basket and the record store Dolphin's of Hollywood, on Vernon Avenue off Central.

Over on East Vernon Street and Central Avenue, musicians as well as some folks from high places liked to hang out at Ivie's Chicken Shack, the restaurant run by vocalist Ivie Anderson. Having suffered for years from asthma, Anderson realized that the grind and pressures of her tours with Ellington hadn't helped her condition. Finally, she decided to give up traveling and settle in L.A. There, she opened her Chicken Shack. Anderson herself was the hostess, assisted by her husband, Marque Neal. "He was a good-looking man," recalled Bobby Short. "Very thin. Looked somewhat Oriental. But he wasn't. But, of course, we all look like so many things. He was always there." The restaurant itself "was a small room. Very tastefully, very, very well done inside. Simple. And nice, easy banquettes to slide into and a spinet piano," said Short. "And she had some wonderful, wonderful piano players there. She had Charles Brown as a young man who just began his career, probably at Ivie's Chicken Shack." In the evening, patrons "could go there and have drinks. You found a lot of so-called upper crust sitting in there. And she welcomed the white trade." "She kind of ran short because all these big-shot Hollywood types would come in and say, 'Put it on my tab.' And they owed her," producer Jean Bach recalled. "She should have been tougher about that."

The Lincoln Theatre showcased new acts such as the King Cole Trio and the Will Mastin Trio with the young Sammy Davis Jr. and a true sensation such as Peg Leg Bates, a dancer who had lost a leg and used his wooden peg leg to tap up a storm. Bates had sold-out performances. The Elks Hall at Thirty-fourth and Central and the YMCA at Twenty-eighth also remained centers of activity. "Central Avenue was still like Lenox Avenue and 125th Street," said Short.

"It was people going in and out of everywhere, out of the clubs, out of the restaurants, the stores," recalled Clora Bryant. "There were all kinds of stores up and down the street, like furniture stores, five-and-ten-cent stores, doctors' offices, dentists' offices, restaurants, barbecue joints." There was just as much going on the street as there was in the clubs. In the day, the scene was all black, but at night, "I saw Rita Hayworth, Cesar Romero. Alan Ladd. . . . Ava Gardner," said Bryant. "There were always some fine cars lined up outside the clubs on Central Avenue from the movie stars or people just from Beverly Hills."

The hangout of hangouts on the avenue, recalled Short, was still the Dunbar Hotel, with its plush and expertly run bar where revelers exchanged not only gossip but stories about the war, while the drinks flowed. Well-heeled men pursued gorgeous young women. And well-heeled women were on the lookout for the dream dates. Stargazing—even among stars—was part of the evening's adventure, too. Was that Lena over there? Or was that really Harold Nicholas talking to that pretty girl who was not his wife? The fun went on until the wee hours of the morning. Once the nightclub shows ended and things slowed down at the Dunbar, most of the crowd was ready to head back home and laugh about the evening. But some all-night partyers liked to drop by other places. So did many performers, who, upon completing their shows at the clubs, liked to head for small, intimate settings to unwind and mix with other show folk.

The most popular after-hours joint was Brother's. "Brother was legitimately employed at the Dunbar Hotel as a bartender," said Bobby Short. Standing behind the bar, he'd be immaculately dressed "in a white vest jacket and black tie and black trousers. . . . Closing time during the war was midnight. Or 11:30. And he'd sort of glide and say, 'Oh, see you later.'"

Rarin' to break loose and go out on his own: Sammy Davis Jr. with Will Mastin (right) and his father, Sammy Davis Sr., in their act, The Will Mastin Trio.

That meant the party hadn't ended. "Brother would quickly leave that job when it closed and rush to his house on Adams Boulevard. A nicely furnished house. And it operated all night long as an after-hours club." If you were a patron at the Dunbar, you would linger there for a bit "and drink your drink. And you'd go out and find your car and drive around to East Adams Boulevard to this white house and knock on the door. And Brother would appear in complete Chinese drag or something. Or a high Russian something." Said Short, "Some kind of drag. Some kind of exotic look. And a little makeup," with a smudge of mascara or a smidge of whatever. Herb Jeffries also recalled that as "you walked into Brother's, Brother had his makeup on and his Chinese gown on and the whole thing."

Brother's was not the kind of place to which any ordinary Joe Schmo could expect to gain entry. Even showbiz folk couldn't be sure the doors of Brother's would be open to them. "Supposed to be on the Q.T. But everybody knew about it," said Short. "If he didn't like you or know you, you didn't get in. He decided who got in and who didn't," said Short. "If he didn't want a particular person in his home, he might softly say, 'I'm sorry, we're closed tonight' or 'I'm sorry, you can't come in.' " If he did like a guest, a grand and gracious Brother might greet the guest in a soft voice, saying, "Oh, hi, Miss Brown." Or he might be more accommodating if it was a guest such as handsome Herb Jeffries. "When he met you at the door," recalled Jeffries, "he would say, 'Hello, darling, how are you? Come in.' "

"It was quite dark in there," said Short. "And every room was a sitting room, you know. Soft music. And there might be someone playing the piano. Mostly, people just sat around. In those days, you got dressed up. People were sitting around during the war in furs and jewels, and dresses and dark suits. Dressed! Heavy perfume. Sitting in there smoking and drinking and having a little plate of food if they liked. It was grand."

Many nights, Fayard and Geri Nicholas, along with sister-in-law Dottie, would stop by. "Harold would drop us off," said Geri. "He'd go his way. The three of us would have fun." Other times, when the Nicholas Brothers were on tour or during Fayard's time in the military, Geri Branton and Dorothy Dandridge on their own "would often end up at Brother's," said Branton. "Sitting in a room with pillows around. And they'd sell breakfast and everything."

The crowd was mixed. "Black and white," said Jeffries. "People like Tyrone Power and Cesar Romero. Or Rita Hayworth," said Geri Branton. Recalled Bobby Short, "I must say in all the after-hours places, it was nothing at all to see the place half filled with white people." "The biggest names in the city went down there to Brother's," said Jeffries. "It was nothing to see Orson Welles sitting in there. Lena Horne sitting in there. Great musicians coming in there. It was nothing to see Charlie Barnet. I mean the biggest names in the business." When Lena Horne arrived in L.A. in the 1940s, Billy Strayhorn introduced her to Brother's. "It would be crowded and hot and funky, and yet muted and wonderful, and I know those were some of my happiest, most feeling moments," Horne recalled. "Lena always lived in a white neighborhood," said Geri Branton. "But she would always come across town after the shows. That's one reason I'm sorry that there's integration, because when there was segregation, you just met with everybody."

Some nights at Brother's, with both Lena Horne and Dorothy Dandridge in attendance, patrons weren't sure where to look, so dazzling did they find each woman. Later, the press would depict them as rivals. The two stars "would be friendly," recalled Branton. "But nothing big. I would get invited to Lena's house. But they didn't invite Dottie to Lena's house. Lena [was] quite a hostess. A good cook." Even at this time, patrons at Brother's seemed to understand that these two women would come to define two distinct eras in Black Hollywood's history.

For Black Hollywood in the 1940s, Brother's was always the quintessential *in* showbiz gathering place. "Oh, it was marvelous," said Short. "Any entertainer from out of town coming west heard about Brother's and went there. . . . Usually, people just sat around and talked and drank and joked and laughed. Oh, it was something! Before you knew it, you were leaving and going outside, where it was dawn."

Social clubs, charity organizations, and civic causes also flourished. "You know, in black society, there are so many social clubs," said Bobby Short. "And with French names. I remember one club called Les Dames d'Aujourd'hui." For the young set, there was the riding club Crop and Tails, its most prominent member being Mrs. Harold Nicholas. Along with Geri Branton and at times Harold, Dandridge also attended benefits and rallies for social causes of the day.

For the older establishment—the wives of the doctors, lawyers, and teachers—the Links was the best known. For the older entertainment crowd, organizations such as the Thirteen Aides Charity Club and the Allied Arts Club were popular. Taking center stage among such groups was the Doll League. Bobby Short learned of the group when he first came to L.A. in 1943 and stayed at the home of pianist Harold Brown and his wife, Nellie, who was a member. "It had been founded by a woman who was very political. And she formed this club of young colored matrons. And it was called the Doll League because they were going to manufacture dolls to be passed around to needy black girls at Christmastime. . . . She asked Louise Beavers to be her cofounder," said Short. "I knew Mantan Moreland because his wife, Hazel Moreland, belonged to the Doll League. Hazel was very social. Just *dressed* [all the time]. And very, very social, you know. *'I'm Mrs. Mantan Moreland!'* Well, the Doll League had a couple of galas every year. And they had a big function every fall to raise money to buy dolls for these girls."

AWAY FROM CENTRAL AVENUE

During these years, some black performers moved out of the Central Avenue niteries for appearances at major white clubs where all of Hollywood might show up. Billy Berg's jazz clubs, at one time on La Cienega, at another time right on Hollywood Boulevard and then on Vine, were great hangouts. Black and white patrons could sit with drinks while they listened to the moody, mellow sounds of Billie Holiday or Lionel Hampton's band or Berg's house band, led by Lee Young, the brother of legendary tenor saxophonist Lester Young. Holiday also performed at Berg's club The Trouville; there, too, nightlong jam sessions rocked, with Young on the drums and Nat Cole on the piano. In 1945, Dizzy Gillespie brought his sextet to Berg's Hollywood club, and patrons could now listen in fascination to the new bebop sensations such as Charlie Parker, Ray Brown, and Milt Jackson—as well as Dexter Gordon and Illinois Jacquet.

Also popular was the integrated nitery Shep's Playhouse, located in the part of the city known as Little Tokyo, an area where many Japanese Americans had resided. But when many of these citizens were interned in camps during the war, others moved into the area. The master of ceremonies—for a time—was local favorite Leonard Reed, and nightclubbers could hear the sounds of another new jazz star such as Coleman Hawkins. The white nitery the Louisiana Club—previously the Wilshire Bowl—also showcased a black band: Les Hite's group, with such musicians as Gerald Wilson and Charlie Mingus. In Watts, the Brown Sisters opened Little Harlem. Comedians Redd Foxx and Slappy White also appeared at local clubs.

Let the good times roll:
Lionel Hampton,
June Richmond, and
Canada Lee.

Swing
CLUB

HOLLYWOOD AND LAS PALMAS BLVDS.

HOLLYWOOD

And the studio scouts still were coming to the clubs to spot black talent. Frank Sebastian's Cotton Club was revamped into Casa Manana, now a club with mostly white entertainers but some black headliners, too. Warner Bros. music director Ray Heindorf caught Jimmie Lunceford's band—when Gerald Wilson was still a member—at Casa Manana, and soon, the orchestra was working on the studio's 1941 film *Blues in the Night*. Gerald Wilson—and three other trumpet players: Snooky Young,

Jack Trainor, and Walter Williams—performed, along with the Warner Bros. orchestra, with the black dancers in the 1943 *This Is the Army*.

Some nightclubs—such as the Swanee Inn on La Brea, the Plantation in Watts, the Little Eva on Sunset—offered ersatz Old South–style nights on the town. With its decor that featured scenes from *Uncle Tom's Cabin*, along with images of Mississippi River steamboats, the Little Eva Club served southern-style dinners. Niteries such as The Bal Tabarin and the Stork Club specialized in presenting "colored revues" with plenty of light-skinned "Creole"-looking chorus girls. The Plantation, which publicized itself as "California's largest Harlem nightclub," had such top bands as Count Basie's, Jimmie Lunceford's, and Billy Eckstine's and was packed with black music lovers. Yet many of these spots would, by the war's end, start to look old-fashioned.

More sophisticated and forward-looking nightclubs occasionally head-lined the new talents. Of these clubs, few were more glamorous—and few more frequented by the Hollywood establishment—than the Mocambo. Run by Felix Young and Charlie Morrison and described as a "cross be-tween a somewhat decadent imperial Rome, Salvador Dali, and a bird-cage," the Mocambo opened on January 3, 1941, on the fabulous Sunset Strip, where all the hip, chic clubs, restaurants, and bars were packed nightly. The Mocambo had a Mexican motif: colorful, "exotic"-looking walls painted by Jane Berlandina; flaming red columns; and lacquered trees. The centerpiece was an aviary with live birds. All of Hollywood made its way to the club: Marlene Dietrich, Lana Turner with her various husbands, Henry Fonda, James Stewart, Hedy Lamarr, Louis B. Mayer, Cole Porter, Cary Grant, Lucille Ball and Desi Arnaz, and Norma Shearer. Occasionally, some members of Black Hollywood such as Fayard Nicholas also enjoyed the club's entertainment.

Occasionally, a black performer would headline at the club. In July 1942, before she filmed *Cabin in the Sky*, Lena Horne was booked by Young and Morrison into the Mocambo with Phil Moore as her arranger and musical director. Horne's glittering engagement helped confirm her club appeal and stardom and clearly convinced MGM of her uniqueness.

Some black performers appeared at the offbeat Café Gala, which sat at the bottom of Horn Avenue and Sunset Boulevard, the location later oc-cupied by Wolfgang Puck's first Spago. Run by a dapper former New Yorker named John Walsh, the Gala was known at first as a gathering place for Hollywood's gay elite. Its talent was always innovative and, for the time, rather cutting-edge, leaving behind the prewar brand of enter-

A star on the rise, Nat "King" Cole, with Jean Bach (left) and producer Norman Granz (third from left) at the first of the Jazz at the Philharmonic concerts on the West Coast.

tainment in favor of what was new in song, dance, and comedy. In a very short time, the Gala became a very *in* club for industry people, too—straight, gay, and otherwise. Famous stars, directors, writers, and producers would come to see the fresh and the unusual. African Americans were welcomed onstage and off, although it was primarily a white club. "John Walsh always had black people in the room. Now, they were a particular kind of black people. First of all, black people with the guts enough to walk in," said Bobby Short. "Jeni LeGon went there with Phil Moore. When the Dunham kids came to town, they couldn't wait to get to the Café Gala." Lena Horne performed at the club as did Zero Mostel and the Jack Cole Dancers.

Bobby Short recalled the glorious fun of the Gala's after-hours parties when big names would gather around the piano. "We would just close down the place and keep the bar kind of secretly going. And we'd have a good time. I mean when you've got Roger Edens, Conrad Salinger, and Kay Thompson and Lena Horne and God knows what else sitting out

JIM DOLAN *presents*
at

Cafe gala

THE SONGS AND
INIMITABLE PIANO STYLINGS
OF
BOBBY SHORT
Commencing . . .
**WEDNESDAY
AUGUST 8th**
1 9 5 1
With . . .

8795 SUNSET BOULEVARD

*Bobby Short, lighting up the club and
social scene in the 1940s and early 1950s.*

there, all drinking their heads off, and the place closes. And there are two
grand pianos. A lot of wonderful things happened." In the early and mid-
1940s, Hollywood was slowly becoming more integrated. Still, Bobby
Short recalled that there were restaurants where Horne "didn't feel welcome, nightclubs where she didn't feel welcome." Horne once yearned to
dine at the restaurant Trader Vic's but knew it was "notoriously segregated." Finally, when her friend Barney Josephson came to town, he took
her there. They were met by Humphrey Bogart, Robert Benchley, and
others. Management at Trader Vic's said nothing.

But years later in a Beverly Hills restaurant, a man called her a "nigger."
Horne threw an ashtray, a lamp, and just about whatever she could get her
hands on at him. "I guess she was delighted to go to the Café Gala because
people just fell down for her there," said Bobby Short.

STILL THE ARCHITECT TO THE STARS

The career of Hollywood's grand architect Paul Williams remained in
full swing, with important, groundbreaking commissions. Once the
nation entered the war, he served as an architect for the United States
Navy and created a war housing project of some 125 units at Fort
Huachuca in Arizona. The postwar years saw him embarking on some of

his most ambitious—and famous—creations. "The glamour was back in Hollywood, and I was thrilled to be a part of it as my office bristled with steady commissions," said Williams.

In 1947, he designed the Palm Springs Tennis Club. For the movie-colony elite, Palm Springs, just a couple of hours' drive away from Los Angeles, remained the perfect escape from the competitive, gossipy, backstabbing atmosphere of Hollywood life. Stars spent their weekends or their downtime between pictures in the slow-paced desert city. But Palm Springs establishments such as The Desert Inn and the Ingleside Inn still had a restrictive policy. Both Jack Benny, who was Jewish, and Eddie "Rochester" Anderson, obviously African American, were denied rooms at The Desert Inn. They stayed instead at El Mirador. The Racquet Club opened its doors to patrons regardless of race. In the postwar era, Palm Springs gradually changed. Williams's tennis club provided the ideal spot where stars could relax, mingle with friends, casually lunch over a drink or two, and pound out their frustrations on the tennis court.

Williams also designed the W. & J. Sloan Department Store in Beverly Hills, one of those establishments such as his earlier Saks Fifth Avenue design, where stars made up and dressed up to go shopping.

Then came stellar commissions. Since its opening in 1912, the Beverly Hills Hotel had stood on Sunset Boulevard—on twelve acres of land and at an original cost of $500,000—as a dazzling emblem of Hollywood at its most powerful and luxurious. The mission-style revival building, called the Pink Palace because of its pink stucco exterior, originally had 325 rooms, along with bungalows and restaurants. As the perfect setting for important business deals, weddings, receptions, clandestine romances, and the visits of dignitaries, the hotel had a long, glamorous history. Handsome Francis Taylor opened an art gallery at the hotel in the late 1930s. Debonair and courtly with impeccable taste, Francis discovered in the postwar years that his clients were not only interested in browsing the gallery for work by the masters but were also hoping to catch a glimpse of his beautiful teenage actress daughter Elizabeth. Later, his daughter would spend honeymoons with various husbands in the hotel's famous bungalows. Marilyn Monroe and French star Yves Montand would conduct their not-so-secret love affair in one of the bungalows.

Few hotels better represented the allure of Hollywood. At its epicenter was the famous Polo Lounge, where moguls, stars, directors, and writers conducted business as ostentatiously as possible. Being seen or paged at the Polo Lounge was akin to an all-important Personal Appearance. But truth be known, the Beverly Hills Hotel was in need of some serious sprucing up by war's end. Paul Williams won the prized commission to update the Polo Lounge and the Fountain Coffee Shop for a new generation. He redesigned both in 1949, giving them a sparkling new modern look. He also created the Crescent Wing of the hotel—with his signature architectural swirling curves in the lobby. "It was a very loose, very elegant post–World War II modern style," said architectural historian David Gebhard. "The style was a decided contradiction to the original building, but both styles existed well together because of Williams's sense of scale and detailing."

The same year of the Beverly Hills Hotel commission, Williams, with Norman Bel Geddes, created additions and alterations for another of Hollywood's legendary edifices in need of a face-lift: The Ambassador Hotel. Having opened in 1921 with gardens and fountains throughout, The Ambassador, which could accommodate some three thousand guests, was the site of the Academy Award ceremonies in the early 1930s. Williams also redesigned an old structure to create the Regency revival–style restaurant Perino's. With its black-and-white tiled entry and the palms that led to the oval dining room, Perino's was considered one of the city's most elegant establishments: the place for Hollywood's most powerful executives and stars.

During the postwar years, Williams still designed or sometimes redesigned luxurious residences for the stars. He altered the home of Jennifer Jones in 1946. A year later, he designed yet another home for Tyrone Power in Bel Air. In the 1950s, he created homes for Lucille Ball and Desi Arnaz in Palm Springs; for singer Julie London in Encino; for Dave Chasen, the owner of the elegant Hollywood restaurant Chasen's. In 1958, he was one of the designers of the Los Angeles International Airport. A year later, he created additions and alterations for the Flamingo Hotel in Las Vegas.

Most talked about was the very hip, technically state-of-the-art bachelor pad he designed in 1956 for Frank Sinatra with push buttons to open drapes, to raise and lower a movie screen. Assigned to create the interior decoration was Williams's daughter Norma Harvey, a talented design artist who worked as a color consultant on various of her father's projects. Williams's other daughter, Marilyn Hudson, recalled that Sinatra trusted her father enough to leave everything in Williams's hands. "Sinatra never saw that house until they gave him the key," said Hudson. "Norma went up to San Francisco, bought all the linen, the china, and everything for the house. Sinatra was in between wives then. But Nancy Sinatra was the one that had contact with Norma." The house was featured on national television when Sinatra was interviewed by Edward R. Murrow for the television show *Person to Person*.

Williams never lost sight of the irony of his unique position as one of the town's very top architects. "Once again I found myself designing places that would not welcome me had I not been Paul Williams, architect," said Williams. "Some things change, some things remain the same."

During the postwar years, he also authored two books: *Small Homes for Tomorrow* and *New Homes for Today*, which emphasized the need for affordable single-family dwellings in this postwar economy. In all likelihood, the most personal of his new buildings was the Broadway Federal Savings and Loan, the oldest black savings and loan west of the Mississippi, which he designed in 1964. Williams served as a vice president and director of the company, which helped African Americans in Los Angeles to acquire mortgages and purchase their first homes. "For too long white-owned banks had kept Negroes and other minorities from getting home loans, a practice called redlining," said Williams. "I spent my entire adult life designing homes for others and believed that the survival of a community depended on home ownership. I desperately wanted Negroes to be able to own their own homes." Sadly, the building was destroyed during the disorders and civil unrest in Los Angeles in 1992.

Socially, Williams and his wife, Della, remained among the most prominent members of the black bourgeoisie. On occasion, they socialized with a client such as Bill Robinson as well as Walter White and Mary McLeod Bethune. At their home, stars such as Lena Horne and Clarence Muse were among the guests, as were W.E.B. Du Bois, Olympic star Jesse Owens, Adam Clayton Powell Jr., Ralph Bunche, and William H. Hastie, the first black governor of the Virgin Islands. Della Williams remained active in the Links, the sorority for high-powered, civic-minded black women. At Links events, the women were dressed to the hilt: mink for those cool L.A. nights, sedate sleek gowns, and those tasteful matronly coiffures. No matter how high the members of the bourgeoisie—the doctors, the lawyers, the political figures—might climb, still, in these postwar years, the bourgeoisie felt a responsibility to the African American community, to foster scholarships for needy students, to help the underprivileged, always to do whatever possible to keep the race moving upward. Williams himself was active with such black men's groups as the Omega Psi Phi fraternity and the Pacific Town Club.

On weekends, the couple preferred more intimate, family gatherings with perhaps a few close friends: barbecues with their grown children and their spouses, and later with the grandchildren. Weekends were also spent at their home in Lake Elsinore, a fashionable spa area, where, like Martha's Vineyard on the East Coast, there was also a black enclave. "We went there every summer because my sister had asthma," said Marilyn Williams Hudson. "When we started going, there were people who owned homes up there, and a lot of them would rent them out to people in the summer. Later, my folks bought a house on the other side of the lake. It was pretty big, and it had lots of ground." Nearby, Williams's close friend Dr. H. Claude Hudson had a summer place, too. "Family meant so much to my father," said Marilyn Williams Hudson. "He never brought his work home. If he had an incident at the office, we never heard about it at home. When he came home, he shut the door at the office, and he became a father. He was *really,* truly a family man." For Della and Paul Williams, family life was extended in 1946 when their daughter Marilyn married Elbert Hudson, the son of Dr. H. Claude Hudson, in one of the big social events of the season.

MOVING UP AND MOVING OUT

During and after the war, Black Hollywood pushed beyond its past residential borders. Some stars boldly moved outside the areas to which African Americans had long been confined, moving even farther west into once-restricted parts of the city. When musician Benny Carter arrived in Los Angeles in 1942, he rented a home once owned by Tyrone Power. But he had to do so in the name of a white friend. That same year, Hattie McDaniel—still flush with her Oscar triumph—moved into a home on Harvard Boulevard in the West Adams Heights area. Around the corner from McDaniel, on Hobart Boulevard, Louise Beavers settled into a home that had once been owned by a mayor of Los Angeles. Longtime New Yorker Ethel Waters also purchased her first home *ever,* at 2127 South Hobart, on December 12, 1942—just around the time she was filming *Cabin in the Sky.* Actor Joel Fluellen, Ellington band member Juan Tizol, actress Frances Williams, bandleader Noble Sissle, Wonderful Smith,

Zutty Singleton, the president of Golden State Insurance Company Norman Houston, and others moved into the neighborhood, originally known as Blueberry Hill but eventually called Sugar Hill.

"I guess you might call Sugar Hill or Blueberry Hill the Westside," said Bobby Short. "But it was sort of an offshoot in an area that had rather grand houses that had been left behind, and so Negroes with enough money bought these houses. And some of them were movie people who had made enough money to buy a large house and live grandly. And some were enterprising ladies who rented out rooms Harlem-style, you know. But they did live on Hobart Boulevard." A haven for the Hollywood-style black middle class, Sugar Hill became the ultimate status symbol. The first to move to the area—at 2133 South Harvard Boulevard—had been Ben Carter, in 1942.

Most residents, however, found themselves locked in lengthy battles and litigation to maintain that lifestyle—*and* their homes. The long-held restrictive housing covenants in Los Angeles, which for decades had limited the rights of white homeowners to sell to whomever they chose, had always ensured that homes could not be sold to African Americans. "Restrictive covenants!" said Bobby Short. "Every device known to keep blacks in one position. And there was even, I recall, a real estate firm called boldly White and Christian." On those occasions when black Americans had been able to purchase homes in such designated areas, they usually had to pay above the market price. In the case of performers such as McDaniel, Beavers, Waters, and Frances Williams, once they had bought their homes, they were threatened with eviction by white property owners in the neighborhoods, who stated that the stars were residing in the areas illegally. Their claim was that no one had had the right to sell them homes in the first place!

That happened in and outside Sugar Hill. When Benny Carter purchased a home on Kenwood Avenue on L.A.'s Westside, it caused a round of protests not too different from those of Lena Horne's neighbors on Horn Avenue. One resident attempted to have Carter evicted. Carter went to court and won. But afterward, when he purchased another home, on Hollyridge Drive in Beechwood Canyon, his new neighbors protested as much as his former ones. Singer June Richmond and nightclub owner Dynamite Jackson also went to court to fight the covenants.

Many black homeowners hired attorneys to represent them individually, but without much success. The battle against the covenants turned hot and fierce during and after the war and ultimately galvanized Black Holly-

Louise Beavers, long on the lookout for the right fellow, surrounded by a bevy of slick dudes, including Clarence Muse (right).

wood in this pre–civil rights era. Actress Frances Williams began holding Saturday workshops at her home in an effort to strategize ways in which, as a group, blacks might fight in the courts. Finally, the African American attorney Loren Miller worked on behalf of McDaniel, Beavers, Waters, and others jointly to fight the suit of the white property owners. On December 6, 1945, Judge Thurmond Clark issued a decision on the case: "This court is of the opinion that members of the Negro race are accorded, without reservations and evasions, the full rights guaranteed them under the 14th Amendment of the Federal Constitution." He added that the "rights of citizens shall not be abridged because of race, color, or previous condition of servitude." Three years later, in the case *Shelly v. Kramer,* the United States Supreme Court banned restrictive covenants, freeing African Americans in the city to live wherever they chose.

The court decisions forever changed the residential boundaries of Black Hollywood as well as black Los Angeles—and were an early sign that the city would be forced to integrate itself in these dawning years of the civil rights movement.

HIGH ON SUGAR HILL

ugar Hill's tree-lined boulevards, its spacious homes, and its expansive landscaped lawns became potent symbols of African American progress. The residents were eager to show the way they and their friends lived. At her three-story Craftsman home on Hobart, Louise Beavers was known to entertain frequently. "People did go there for a cup of tea. I remember seeing Ethel Waters there one day," recalled Bobby Short. "I liked Beavers very much. She was very, very warm. Very sweet and very easy and down-to-earth."

Some of Beavers's passions would have surprised her fans. She liked baseball, prizefights, and a good game of poker. Guests were gleefully led upstairs to the third floor, where card tables were set up and where the refreshments were plentiful. They dealt hands, dined lavishly, exchanged stories, gossiped, and laughed into the early hours of the morning. Beavers still did not spend time in the kitchen. She had a husband who could do that. She had found love—at long last—and married Leroy Moore, an interior decorator who had come to Los Angeles from Gainesville, Texas, in 1942. Seven years younger than Beavers, Moore prepared and helped serve the food and drinks for the poker partyers. In those early-morning hours as the games were winding down, Beavers might be puffing on a cigarette while her guests could gaze out her windows at spectacular views of downtown Los Angeles with its entrancing ribbon of lights. There she was— Louise Beavers, one of the screen's favorite servants—sitting with the city laid out before her. Not the Hollywood Hills, true. But not chopped liver either.

Still, always resourceful and clear-headed, Beavers may have felt that her financial good fortune could come to an end at any time. Even though she had been in the movies for almost twenty years, Hollywood was a fickle town. It never hurt to be prepared with a few extra bucks. Her home was more than large enough for just herself and her husband. So she began taking in other entertainers as boarders, one of whom was singer-organist Earl Grant, who lived on the second floor. "To take in roomers was a little bit déclassé," said Bobby Short. "One did not boast about that."

Also living in high-bourgeois style was Ethel Waters, who was thrilled to purchase her very first home. "Twenty-five is a long while for a girl to live out of a trunk, and Uncle Albert Bauman, who was in the real estate business," said Waters, "had been urging me to buy a home in California. After looking over a few homes I fell in love with one located in Southwest

Around town: Louise Beavers outside her home.

Los Angeles. It had ten sunshine-filled rooms on three floors. There were two stately old trees in front and a neatly trimmed lawn, and some green stuff was growing over the door like a bower. I had my furniture brought from New York." Waters recalled she "shook with happiness" on "that first evening I walked into my house. During the day the moving men had brought my things, and when I saw that they had placed each chair and table exactly where I wanted, I burst into tears. 'My house,' I told myself. 'The only place I've ever owned all by myself.' But 1942 was the year World War II gave sharks' teeth to the always hard-hitting internal revenue boys, and they took a sixteen-thousand-dollar bite that annum out of my bank roll. Just the same, I felt I was sitting on top of the world. I had a home at last." Still, Waters commuted to and from New York and hit the road—where all the money was. She would never make a decent living waiting for movie roles. Unlike Beavers and McDaniel, she was too big a name to live off playing comic-maid parts. Besides, her outburst on the set of *Cabin in the Sky* had left her unemployed in Hollywood. And her income-tax problems were only beginning. But for a time, Waters lived well without thinking about tomorrow.

Around town: Ethel Sissle, wife of bandleader Noble Sissle.

Also in the area on Adams Boulevard was a new hotel for African Americans, the Hotel Watkins. Purchased by William "Bill" Watkins, the hotel opened its doors in 1945. Later, it could boast of the Rubaiyat Room, which was designed by Paul Williams's daughter Norma Harvey. The nephew of jazz pioneer King Oliver, Watkins had a lineup of social contacts. Eventually, his hotel's guests included such stars as Duke Ellington, Ella Fitzgerald, Nat and Maria Cole, Dinah Washington, and Fats Domino. A sign that Sugar Hill loomed large in the imagination of L.A.'s black community was the 1946 play *Sugar Hill*, with music by James P. Johnson and a book by Flournoy Miller.

In the surrounding area—on cross streets or adjacent to the center of Sugar Hill life on Harvard and Hobart boulevards—were the homes of other celebrities. The actress Laura Bowman and her husband, LeRoi Antoine, lived on West Thirty-fifth Street. Kenny Washington bought a home a few blocks away on the same street. The composer William Grant Still and his wife and two children lived in a modest bungalow. Inside, Still had a carpentry shop where he made toys for his children. Out back was a

Around town: Celebrating a brand-new Buick.

garden where the couple grew vegetables. Nick (or Nicodemus) Stewart resided at 3409 Walton. Later, he opened the Ebony Showcase, a theater where movie folk and newcomers alike could appear in vehicles Hollywood wouldn't touch. James Baskett settled into a place at 3442 South Arlington. On Van Ness were the residences of Geri and Fayard Nicholas as well as Sam McDaniel and his wife. Mantan and Hazel Moreland settled into a home on Kenwood. And Dorothy Dandridge and Harold Nicholas, despite the fact that their marriage was falling apart, still lived in their modest home at 2272 West Twenty-seventh Street.

Residential areas continued to stretch. Bobby Short recalled that "in 1949, I moved into a garage apartment of a large, sprawling old house on Arlington Boulevard. Arlington for a few blocks between Pico and, dare I say, Wilshire had lots of grand, grand, grand, grand houses. And through that ran a street called Country Club Drive. Well, Negroes had begun buying houses in that area. And the house that I lived in was owned by a prominent black lawyer." Also on Country Club Drive were the homes of composer Andy Razaf and actress Lillian Randolph.

SUGAR HILL'S GRAND MATRIARCH

But the grand matriarch of Sugar Hill was Hattie McDaniel, who, in the postwar years, discovered that the maid roles in movies were drying up. But she was thriving on another medium: radio. In 1947, McDaniel starred as the comic maid on the radio sitcom *Beulah*. Ten million listeners tuned in to each broadcast. Her spirits buoyed—her career wasn't over after all—McDaniel entertained lavishly at her Harvard

Hattie McDaniel with her one-time rival Olivia de Havilland and Jean Hersholt at the 1949 Academy Awards ceremonies.

Boulevard home, both for formal gatherings and the more frequent informal ones with friends such as Louise Beavers, Frances Williams, Carlton Moss, and Wonderful Smith. In her thirteen-room, green-tiled Mediterranean-style home—with its sweeping arches and large bay windows—she played hostess twice a year to a large gathering of entertainers, black and white, with Hollywood's gossip columnists Hedda Hopper and Louella Parsons among the guests.

Proudly displayed in her music room was her Oscar, along with her wide assortment of antique dolls and figurines. Also on view were her books on African American history and culture. Usually at the parties, McDaniel liked preparing the food herself. But there was always help around. A chauffeur drove her for her appointments. A housekeeper ensured that everything in the residence was kept in order. And McDaniel still employed Ruby Berkley Goodwin, the former journalist, as her personal secretary/assistant. Goodwin herself was something of a status symbol: here was an educated black woman, at one time outspoken about

Hollywood's roles for black performers, keeping McDaniel's busy schedule in order and advising her at times of crisis.

Marking the one-year anniversary of her performance in *Beulah,* McDaniel staged an elaborate party for a cross section of guests that was covered by the press, black and white. Dramatically greeting her guests, McDaniel was dressed stylishly in a light tailored suit with her hair pulled back. Not the expected Hollywood flash. Instead, she looked like the very proper, sedate wife of a successful businessman, something of a Beverly Hills matron. Or, as Hattie would let people know, a Sugar Hill one. MGM's swimming star Esther Williams showed up smiling broadly, along with actress Agnes Moorehead, comedienne Joan Davis, radio star Arthur Blake, and hat designer Mildred Bount. Perhaps most surprising was the arrival of Dr. and Mrs. E. Franklin Frazier. A highly respected sociology professor at Howard University on holiday on the West Coast, Frazier was later the author of the groundbreaking study *Black Bourgeoisie,* which examined the mores, values, and behavior of America's black middle class. One can only wonder what new insights E. Franklin Frazier might have gleaned from Hattie's gatherings.

Also in attendance were the cast members of *Beulah,* including Ernest Whitman and Ruby Dandridge, who played Beulah's friend Oriole on the show. Feeling his oats, Whitman asked Joan Davis's daughter to join him in a jitterbug. Though interracial mingling of a certain type was still frowned on in the industry, no one seemed to think twice that afternoon about this interracial jig, perhaps because Whitman, old enough to be Davis's father, seemed like such an amicable, nonthreatening gent. Talking loudly and energetically was Ruby Dandridge, who was now working regularly in movies and on radio. Once her daughters were out of the house, Ruby seemed to come into her own. Financially, things were on the upswing for her. She and Ma-Ma moved into a new home, where Ruby was as much the hostess as McDaniel. Still a social climber and as chatty and aggressively friendly as ever, Ruby—decked out in a large hat and colorful dress—moved among the guests at the McDaniel soirée, quick not only to let them know what she was up to but also to inform them of the activities of her daughter Dorothy, who was still mainly known as Mrs. Harold Nicholas but who, Ruby still believed, could be the biggest of all Negro stars. Of her other daughter, Vivian, still struggling to find work at clubs, Ruby had little to say.

McDaniel lived like a Hollywood star—with a love life that was watched closely. Eyebrows were raised in 1944 when Louella Parsons reported that McDaniel—then fifty years old—was pregnant. At the time, she was still married to real estate agent James Lloyd Crawford. "Betty Grable, Lana Turner, Maureen O'Hara, Gene Tierney and the rest of those glamour girls have nothing on me," McDaniel told the columnist. "I, too, am taking time out to welcome the stork." Many wondered if the Academy Award–winning actress was mistaken or delusional. But McDaniel excitedly made preparations for the new arrival. It was almost all she could think or talk about. Ultimately, her physician informed McDaniel that hers was a "false pregnancy." Afterward, she slipped into a lengthy depression.

McDaniel's marriage to James Lloyd Crawford ended in divorce *and* headlines. "He thought because he was married to me he didn't have to work," McDaniel testified. "When I insisted that he get a job, he got one he thought would humiliate me, and said if I didn't like it he would kill me."

But McDaniel didn't give up on finding her true love. Two years later, in 1947, she married interior designer Larry Williams in Yuma, Arizona. Returning to California, she was as eager as before to introduce the new husband to Black Hollywood. But a little over a year later, she was back in divorce court. This time around, she told the judge of quarrels and humiliations, including an incident that occurred a little more than a month after their marriage, at a picnic/barbecue for the NAACP. "There was a lot of meat left. I asked the cook, could I take some to my dogs. Well, my husband said, 'Here I am, in a million dollar decorating business and you a radio star, wanting to take scraps to the dogs!' I told him people with millions ask to take scraps for their dogs. . . ." Complaining that Williams refused to escort her to her friends' parties, she said he wanted only to be seen at the big premières or concerts. During their four-month marriage, he gave her sixty-five dollars. "I'm not going to ask you for any money," he told her, "but if you want to give me some, I'll take it." "I got so I couldn't sleep, and I couldn't concentrate on my lines," she testified. "I couldn't eat. I'm a real hearty eater, but I got so all I could eat was a little soup to keep me going. I lost a lot of weight—10 or 12 pounds." McDaniel was granted the divorce. Would she marry again? Hedda Hopper asked her. "I've been married enough," said McDaniel. "I just prefer to forget it." All of this was fodder for the press, which made McDaniel—still grandly residing in her spacious home on Harvard Boulevard—look all the more like a star.

Eddie "Rochester" Anderson, the most famous black movie actor of the 1940s.

MAN ABOUT TOWN

While McDaniel remained Black Hollywood's premier female star, the top black actor was clearly Eddie Anderson. Down Western Boulevard, just off Thirty-sixth Street, an entire block was referred to as Rochester Lane, simply because Eddie "Rochester" Anderson lived there. By 1942, he was earning $100,000 a year and, for a time, was the highest-paid black actor in Hollywood. He was born in Oakland in 1906. His father, Big Ed Anderson, had been a minstrel performer; his mother, Ella Mae, had been a circus tightwire walker until an accident ended her career. Still young, he sang, danced, and did comedy bits in L.A. clubs and theaters.

The big break came at Frank Sebastian's Cotton Club in 1937. Anderson heard that comedian Jack Benny was looking for a black comic to appear as his valet on his radio show. Anderson auditioned and got the part. For his first appearance on *The Jack Benny Program,* he took home a paycheck of seventy-five dollars. He was an instant hit. Soon, his performances on radio and then in movies with Benny—such as *Buck Benny Rides Again* and *Man about Town*—made him a household name. Playing the clever servant Rochester, known for always outsmarting his boss, Benny, Anderson became so identified with the character that he was billed henceforth as Eddie "Rochester" Anderson. His most distinctive characteristic: his gravelly voice, which sounded as if someone had run sandpaper over his vocal cords. Short, energetic, quick-witted, he seemed the most self-assured of little guys, able somehow to transcend life's daily dilemmas without losing his composure. In Anderson's mind, his character Rochester was the king of the Benny home, who unfortunately had to endure the simp antics of his "boss." Lena Horne considered him the first modern black comedian.

Throughout the 1940s, his fame grew. And his dwelling became something of a black tourist attraction. Locals loved to point out Anderson's house to visitors: it was the large fifty thousand–dollar white colonial-style home with dark green shutters. At the time Anderson moved in, the area was hardly a haven for the black bourgeoisie. His presence transformed the neighborhood. He—or rather, his wife, Mamie—entertained frequently. Though generally outgoing, Anderson could also be withdrawn. The couple's home became a showplace with a large dance floor for parties and a theater for viewing movies. During the war years, the downstairs became a bomb shelter. Upstairs were a library and Anderson's leather-trimmed den, each overflowing with books, magazines, papers, and mementos. Mamie liked informing the press that she belonged to the Book-of-the-Month Club. Because some commentators joked that stars knew almost nothing outside Hollywood life, performers were eager to let the public know that was hardly the case. Everyone in Hollywood seemed to collect something—the rarer and more unique, the better. For Rochester, it was model railroad trains and old rocks, which were housed in his basement. In his garage was a trio of old automobiles. Outside was a large swimming pool with cabanas and showers. Neither Mamie nor Rochester was known to have ever taken a dip. Could it have been that neither could swim?

Often seen about town, Rochester and Mamie, like Bill and Fannie Robinson, hit the racetrack, usually Santa Anita. Anderson liked horses so much that he set out to become a breeder/trainer of racehorses, joining an exclusive club of powerful Hollywood men with dreams of their horses'

Anderson and his wife, Mamie, at the racetrack, cheering for his horse Burnt Cork.

winning the Kentucky Derby: among them, moguls such as MGM's Louis B. Mayer and Warners' Harry Warner, director Mervyn LeRoy, and actors George Raft and Don Ameche. Anderson called his first thoroughbred Mustard Seed. Another, Up and Over, was injured in a fall. Told that the horse would have to be put to death, a shaken Anderson said, "Don't shoot my horse. Leave him to me." Studiously reading all he could on horse anatomy at the library of his studio, Paramount Pictures, he consulted a surgeon who became interested in the animal's condition. Somehow—miraculously—Up and Over was able to romp again. His other thoroughbred, Burnt Cork, had some success. But horse racing did not prove to be a money maker for him.

Nor did his other endeavors. His nightclub tanked in a short time. Later, he opened a factory in San Diego to manufacture pilot chutes. A pilot chute was an apparatus attached to a parachute. Needless to say, Anderson did not have much luck with this venture either. But he was proud of being the employer of forty colored workers at his factory. "Even if it doesn't turn out to be a sound investment," Anderson's manager said, "at least it's an enterprise that helps worthwhile men and women of his race. And it's good publicity."

The town liked hearing stories of Anderson's business forays. And he was able somehow to remain in solid financial shape. In the early 1940s, he enjoyed strolling along Central Avenue with his pockets bulging with money, passing out five-dollar bills. He and Jack Benny were such friends that Benny was said to have personally negotiated Anderson's contracts, even insisting on his being able to approve or disapprove of his lines. Roles were tailor-made for Anderson, who rarely endured the on-screen demeaning antics of a Stepin Fetchit. Known for his tardiness, however, Rochester showed up late so frequently at the radio studio that Benny instituted a fine of fifty dollars to be paid whenever Anderson failed to arrive on time. And the whole town heard of the occasion when Anderson was scheduled to go to New York for appearances with Benny and the show's cast. Out late the night before, he couldn't be awakened by Mamie the next morning. Hundreds stood at Union Station to give the Benny cast a send-off. When Anderson arrived, the Super Chief was pulling out. With Mamie and his business manager, he raced in his station wagon to Pasadena, where the train had its first stop. A motorcycle contingent of L.A.'s finest escorted him. He made the train.

The press doted on Anderson. Not only did a new publication such as *Ebony* report on his comings and goings, but in 1950, he and Benny appeared on the cover of *Look*. Yet the mainstream media, while admiring of his talent, could sometimes be condescending. In its major feature on him in 1943, *The Saturday Evening Post* referred to him as "a drawling, shuffling little colored man with a quip on his lip." For black America, though, there was no star like him.

During these years, African American entertainers still all knew one another, a sign of the cohesiveness that Geri Branton had enjoyed so much. Bobby Short recalled an evening when he was looking for the home of actress Lillian Randolph on Country Club Drive. "I didn't quite know the address," Short recalled. "I went to a house that I thought was her house. And I rang the doorbell, and I could hear soft music inside, and I thought I was . . . at Lillian's house. Oh, no. To the front door came Hattie McDaniel. Back in those days, life was very, very [informal]. You didn't call. You just dropped by. And this goes for any day of the week. And on Sunday particularly. And Hattie came to the door. Hair all done up. Good makeup job. I remember a brilliant house gown of silk in a wonderful pale orange to the floor. And her jewels. It was Sunday evening. And I'm sure she hoped somebody [would stop by]. So she came straight to that door. A big smile. And said hello. I said, 'I'm Bobby Short.' She said, 'Yes, I know who you are.' And she said, 'Come right in.' I said, 'Well, I'm afraid I can't stay because I'm looking for Lillian.' " "Oh," McDaniel said and then gave Short directions to Randolph's home.

Throughout the 1940s, stars such as Anderson, McDaniel, and Beavers were considered integral and respected members of L.A.'s black community. Playwright Barbara Roseburr Molette recalled her childhood years as a neighbor of Rochester. After the war, her family moved from San Diego—where there had been work in the aircraft factories—to Los Angeles's Westside. "During the war, when they pushed the Japanese out of their homes, black people bought their homes. And by the time the war was over, there were a lot of blacks on the Westside where the Japanese had once been. And when the whites, who had also bought the Japanese homes, moved out after the war, they sold to blacks. When the Japanese came back in after being interned, they bought on the Westside again. At that time, for blacks, Crenshaw was the western boundary of the Westside. Blacks hadn't yet gone further west. The eastern boundary was Figueroa." Molette also recalled that "when we first moved there, Adams Boulevard was the north/south dividing line. . . . North of Adams, which was where Hattie McDaniel lived, was where the mansions and larger houses were. South of Adams were the bungalows."

Rochester's home, though large and considered grand, was south of Adams. "It was actually a half block west of us," said Molette. "I could walk out of my backyard and go over to my neighbor's backyard, and then I would be facing the front of his house. At that time, I asked myself, 'Why does this man have this wonderful house—the largest and most expensive and the poshest home—why does he have it in this neighborhood?' And, of course, it was because of the restrictive covenants. I'm sure all of the adults understood." When he built his house, he could not build north of Adams. Molette recalled that the neighborhood "was very eclectic and racially mixed, with Asians and a few white holdovers who tended to be older. But there were no white children in the neighborhood. It was economically integrated among blacks and Asians. Among blacks, there were teachers and doctors and lawyers. Everybody lived in the same neighborhood if you were black."

All the neighbors knew Rochester's home. "There was a swimming pool

Anderson's son on the diving board of the swimming pool where the neighborhood kids could take a dip.

in the back. And he would let neighborhood kids swim in the pool," said Molette. "We used to see him all the time at the grocery store or outside walking. . . . He always smiled and spoke." For the young Barbara Molette, these were wonderful childhood memories. There were others.

"I had a dear friend, Loma. We were inseparable. And one day, she said, 'I know where Hattie McDaniel lives.' I said, 'You do?!' 'Yes,' she said. 'Do you want to go over?' " When Molette answered yes, her friend Loma explained that they'd have to get up very early to go, because, otherwise, her grandmother might stop them. "So to avoid that, we got up at 5:30 in the morning." The two girls hopped on their bicycles. "Everybody who has ever been a child in Los Angeles knows about the Arlington Dip. To get from Adams to Jefferson Boulevard, if you were going down Arlington, you would go down a steep hill, and then it would be flat for about three hundred yards, and then you'd go down another steep hill, and then you'd be at Jefferson. That's why it was called the Arlington Dip. To get to Hattie's house, we'd have to ride our bikes *up* Arlington, up this steep hill."

When the girls arrived at McDaniel's home, the maid answered the back door. "May I help you?" she asked. "We're here to see Hattie McDaniel," the girls said. Very patiently, the maid told them, "It's a little early. She's not available." "Can we come back another day?" The maid said sure. "We came back the next day, and the maid invited us in. I imagine she probably talked to Hattie McDaniel and told her she had had these visitors. We sat at the kitchen table. And she gave us cookies and milk. We went back other times. We never met Hattie." But on another visit, the maid showed them around Hattie's living room. "It was a beautiful, spacious place with lots of antiques. But it seemed sort of lonely. There was nobody there. This was around 1949. We had heard she was ill. That actually prompted one of our later visits. We went to see how she was, and we asked the maid, who said she was resting. . . . The maid gave us a signed picture of Hattie and cast members of the *Beulah* radio show."

Maintaining the home was costly. Eventually, McDaniel sold it and moved to a smaller eight-room "cottage-style" home on Country Club Drive.

NEW OPTIMISM, NEW FEARS

Once the war had ended, the town was swept up on a wave of optimism. The clubs were packed nightly. On Central Avenue, the restaurants were full. The shops were busy. The thoroughfare was still bustling. Yet nightlife entertainment on Central Avenue seemed to have peaked in the early and mid-1940s. It drifted into its first stages of decline in the late 1940s. Many factors led to the fall of Central Avenue and the decentralization of old Black Hollywood. During the postwar years, more whites had frequented the Central Avenue clubs, joining African American patrons for evenings of lively entertainment. Yet old-timers recalled the attitudes of the Los Angeles Police Department's chief William H. Parker. "Under Parker—a puritanical crusader against 'race mixing'— nightclubs and juke joints were raided and shuttered," said Los Angeles historian Mike Davis. Those Central Avenue businesses that had been patronized by whites were harassed. "That was the whole program with Police Chief Parker," said Clora Bryant. "He didn't want those white stars coming to the Eastside. The white clubs like the Mocambo didn't like it either because they were losing money. But Parker was a redneck from the get-go. They didn't want whites there, dropping their money. And they didn't like these white girls with black guys."

The economic life of the avenue suffered for other reasons. The new-comers who had arrived, suitcases in hand, looking for rooming houses at the start of the decade and then found work in the defense plants were, now that the war had ended, the victims of huge layoffs. No longer did they have the weekly paychecks that had helped to keep many establishments in business. Gradually, Central Avenue started to look decrepit and beaten down. Gradually, the stars, white and black, looked elsewhere for fun and excitement. So did the everyday patrons of clubs and restaurants.

Some turned their eyes to the Sunset Strip. In the late 1940s, the big clubs on the Strip were opening, albeit gingerly, their doors to black patrons. Though Duke Ellington had appeared at Ciro's in 1945, and Nat "King" Cole would perform there with great success in 1948, Bobby Short recalled that the club nonetheless "was considered taboo. So was the Mocambo. And in 1947, I had a very good friend—white. She used to give me jobs playing for fashion shows at the May Company, where she was a fashion director. And one day she said, 'cause I was there [at her house] all the time, 'Let's go to Ciro's tonight and have supper and watch the show.' And I thought to myself, 'Ummm.' " Short decided to go, changed into a tie and jacket, and together, they walked into Ciro's. "And had a great table, sat there, and had dinner and watched the show," said Short.

Later, Short told his friend vocalist Evelyn Myers, wife of saxophonist Marshall Royal, about the evening. "She was totally incredulous. She said, 'You're just full of shit.' She said, 'You ain't been to no damn Ciro's last night.' And I said, 'Ha! Evelyn, I was there.' 'Oh, don't give me that shit. That's a damn lie.' I said, 'Evelyn, I was there.' 'All right. All right. But you weren't there. I know that.' That's the way it was in those days. You just did not go to Ciro's.

"And from that moment on, I went to Ciro's," said Short. "And one night, around 1949, 1950, I wanted to go to the Mocambo. And I simply called up the Mocambo, got a reservation, and showed up. Now this is to show you the levels of black society. Down from where I lived on Arlington in the garage apartment was another grand house owned by the Weavers. Mr. Weaver had the concessions at Mocambo. When I say concessions, I mean he was a black man. His employees parked the cars, did all those things. And inside, his wife had the check room and the cigarettes, and the girl who walked around with the tray, selling the stuffed pandas and so forth. So I pulled up in front of Mocambo with my date, Ruth Cage. And we just were taken in there, had dinner, saw the show and danced and left. No problem."

Los Angeles resident Marian Patterson remembered that after the war, the Mocambo opened its doors for private parties for certain African American social clubs. Of course, the big shift would come in the next decade with a series of sensational openings of black stars on the Strip. But the Sunset Strip's gain would be Central Avenue's loss.

THE OLD GUARD

n the early postwar years, the old-guard Black Hollywood also faced tough new realities. Protests from the black press and the NAACP along with new postwar attitudes within black America led to the demise of the old, contented comic-servant roles. At the Oscar ceremonies in 1947, a special Oscar was awarded to actor James Baskett for his role as Uncle Remus in Disney's 1946 *Song of the South*. But the award came amid controversy. Before the presentation, the Oscar committee had a heated debate. Some complained that dear old Uncle Remus was a pathetic, dated stereotype. And many were cognizant of the protests within black America against the film and its central character. Others, however—notably, gossip columnist Hedda Hopper, known for her political conservatism— led the side for the presentation of the award. Once presented, the award hardly had the impact of McDaniel's win less than ten years earlier. It struck some as the height of self-righteous movieland condescension. By then, the studios were becoming more sensitive to such criticism.

A leader in the fight for better roles for African Americans was that social arbiter of the era Joel Fluellen, who went before the board of the Screen Actors Guild. Since 1938, SAG had collected articles—from the Negro press—on "The Negro Question." Lena Horne and Rex Ingram were brought onto the SAG board in 1944. Then, in 1946, Fluellen introduced resolutions to SAG, asking the organization to form a committee to study and change the situation for African Americans in Hollywood. Actress Betsy Blair, wife of star Gene Kelly, proposed a resolution that read:

> WHEREAS, Negro actors have a long and honorable history in American theatre and in the motion picture industry and played an important part in the formation of our Guild, and
>
> WHEREAS, unemployment among our Negro Guild members has reached a point more alarming than at any time in Guild history, and
>
> WHEREAS Negro parts are being omitted from a great many screenplays and are, in many cases, actually being cut out of books and plays when

adapted to the screen, in several instances producers have even gone to the length of using white actors in Negro roles,

NOW, THEREFORE, BE IT RESOLVED that the Screen Actors Guild use all of its power to oppose discrimination against Negroes in the motion picture, and

BE IT FURTHER RESOLVED that a special committee be set up at once to implement this policy and to meet with representatives of the Screen Writers Guild and the Screen Directors Guild and the Motion Picture Producers Association in order to establish in the industry a policy of presenting Negro characters on the screen in the true relation they bear to American life.

The proposal was passed, and an Anti-Discrimination Committee was formed in November 1946. It was dissolved "at a board meeting on March 10th, 1947, the same meeting which saw Ronald Reagan elected as S.A.G. President," said Blair. But that was not the end of the story. The committee was revived with Warner Anderson serving as chair and members that included Clarence Muse, Betsy Blair, Boris Karloff, and actress Marsha Hunt. Hunt recalled that the group urged casting departments at the major studios to change their policy in the depiction of all minorities, "to show that not all Blacks were servants, nor all Filipinos houseboys, not all Chinese ran laundries, not all Japanese were gardeners, not all Indians had been scalpers, not all Italians were gangsters." The group was told that casting decisions were in the hands of producers and directors. The casting directors offered to help but stressed that no one should expect miracles. Yet occasionally "there was a surprise piece of casting," said Hunt, "pointing the way to a better and fairer day. . . . And Joel Fluellen deserves to be remembered and honored for his early efforts to 'overcome.' "

The racial climate in the nation itself was changing. As black GIs returned to the States after having fought abroad, they became more vocal— as did African American community leaders—about injustices and inequities in their own country.

In late 1947, Hattie McDaniel confided to Hedda Hopper that she had gone two years without any movie work. Actors such as Willie Best, Mantan Moreland, and Louise Beavers found movie roles similarly scarce. Even the venerable Clarence Muse was no longer steadily employed. Some turned to radio—and in the next decade, television. In her *Los Angeles Times* column, an indignant Hopper informed her readers that Hattie's career problems had not so much been the result of the industry's attitudes. "But the details I picked up weren't pretty," wrote Hopper. "Hattie, I discovered, had not been victimized by Whites. She had been attacked by certain members of her own race, simply because she had tried to 'earn an honest dollar' by playing roles those critics thought degrading to Negroes. Her part in *Song of the South* caused many theaters to be picketed."

At another time, that comment might have gone unchallenged. But a fired-up writer with the byline C.A.B. protested in *The California Eagle*. While agreeing with Hopper that McDaniel was a fine artist, the writer C.A.B. believed Hopper's other comments—the way in which she attacked Negroes for the problems in McDaniel's career—were an old ploy of "the political enemies of the Negro." In essence, Hopper was blaming the victim. "It is not Miss McDaniel that the Negro people find fault with. It is the policy pursued by producers and directors in prescribing stereotyped parts and bits to Negro actors and actresses that reflect discredit on the entire race," wrote C.A.B. "Neither the NAACP, the Negro newspapers, nor individuals are fighting Miss Hattie McDaniel. For your enlightenment, we are fighting a damnable system that keeps Miss McDaniel and the rest of us second class citizens." C.A.B. was none other than the *Eagle*'s publisher, Charlotta Bass.

A NEW POSTWAR GENERATION

In 1947, the town was struck by the arrival of the black-cast drama *Anna Lucasta*, which told the story of a young prostitute in conflict with her family and herself. In the touring version that came to L.A., the original Broadway star, Hilda Simms, had been replaced by young Ruby Dee.

Also in the cast was her husband, Ossie Davis, and such Los Angeles performers as Laura Bowman, Lawrence Criner, and Monte Hawley. A hit in the East, "*Anna Lucasta* was the play that took the black experience from a segregated existence in Harlem," recalled Ossie Davis. "We were the cast that integrated the theater." *Anna Lucasta* opened at a "top-flight theater [the Belasco] in downtown Los Angeles. And we were *the* theatrical event," said Davis. "Downtown Los Angeles was important. The freeways hadn't been built yet. And downtown was alive and vital.

"For twenty-four hours, we, too, were the toast of the town," said Davis. "When the curtain went down, Charlie Chaplin, Thomas Gomez, and some other outstanding performers came up on the stage. And they were hugging us, and they were embracing and talking about the play. Talking about some of the situations and the characters. And Chaplin was assuring us that this was something that Hollywood would have to do, and that this had to be made into a picture. His enthusiasm just lifted everybody. None of us had come to Hollywood looking to get into pictures." But it looked as if *Anna Lucasta* would come to the big screen with an all-black cast.

Davis noted that "Hollywood's lavish opening-night welcome did not extend to hotel accommodations." One of the few cast members put up at a hotel was Ruby Dee. "The other actors stayed with people in the community who functioned as a kind of a floating hotel for entertainers who would come there," said Davis. "I wound up on San Pedro, down near the railroad station, where there was lodging for railroad sleeping-car porters."

During the run of *Anna Lucasta*, Dee and Davis were constantly meeting people. Herb Jeffries was always at the theater. Anthony Quinn introduced himself to everyone, too. "I didn't realize how big a deal it was until they began carrying me around town for these publicity things," Ruby Dee recalled, "and I didn't have such a thing as a wardrobe person to dress me or prepare me. I'd never done it before. I'm thinking about names of people like Bogart and Van Johnson and all the stars I read about all my life. So many of those people were coming to the theater. It was a Hollywood night to come and see us." Memorable for Davis was meeting comedian Willie Best. "He came backstage and he's not an articulate man. But the way he looked at us and the way he talked and the pride he felt and [it seemed like] sort of an apology for what he was doing. All of that was expressed somehow in just the way he looked and the way he related to us. I was touched by him because he didn't have that Hollywood bubble at all. He just came in very quietly and seemed to be deeply appreciative."

And there was a nonending round of gatherings and parties. "All the way across the country, one of the things we always experienced [was that] there was—in all the communities where we stopped—a group of people every night when the show was over. [They were] waiting to put you in the car and take you to their homes and give a big entertainment in their homes every night. In Hollywood and Los Angeles, it was *high art*. The doctors would do it." Stars like Dorothy Dandridge and Louise Beavers also invited cast members to their homes. "I remember these gorgeous homes," said Ruby Dee. "It was my first realization that living in Hollywood, black actors like Beavers—even though she played maids mostly and things like that—this was what life could be like for her. To live in a fine house and to have a fine car." Much as Davis liked Beavers, there was a part of her that was closed off, in the way that stars frequently held on to some personal sense of identity that they would not share with the public. "I felt welcomed at her house," said Davis. "But I really had no idea of who she truly was."

Dee had "the feeling that Louise Beavers and Hattie McDaniel and that whole layer of black actors—that they knew how to remain employable in Hollywood and how much of themselves really to let loose and show. I felt that they knew that white America was not mature enough to understand that black people were just as human as anybody else, that they had survived so long because of a certain determination to make it through the job market so that they could accomplish the things that they wanted to later." She believed that was true of Nick Stewart, who opened Ebony Showcase, which put on serious black theater productions.

Los Angeles actor Lawrence Criner invited the entire company to "his mother's farm, which was out where Disneyland is now [in Anaheim]," said Davis. "It was Lawrence's people," recalled Ruby Dee, "who owned the land [that became] Disneyland. They didn't get such a good deal to get off the land."

The cast also enjoyed "all the goodies and glories of Central Avenue," said Davis. Of the clubs, Davis said, "We went to every one [of them]. [But] I don't remember the name of a single one. The Dunbar Hotel I remember," said Davis. "But somebody would always be waiting. And they would say, 'We're going to this one tonight. We're going to that one.' You'd get dressed. And you'd get into the car. And you'd be there.

"I remember where I lived on San Pedro, it was easier to get to Central Avenue. And there was what you now call a soul food place on Central. And the lady who owned the place adopted me because she fell in love with my capacity to eat and appreciate her cooking. She said, 'I'm going to come and see that play.' I said, 'Well, come right on, honey.' I kept inviting her. One night I came downstage [during my performance], and she was sitting right in the first row. She said, 'Knock me out, honey.'

"Hollywood didn't have that same meaning as it subsequently had," said Davis. "Black folks out on Adams and Western boulevards and on Central Avenue—there was a substance and city pride and sort of an organized social society." "It was a whirlwind," said Dee. "I was awash in alcohol," Davis remembered. "It was aglow for me from one party to the other."

As it turned out, *Anna Lucasta* was made into a movie in the late 1940s but with an all-white cast—and Chaplin's former wife Paulette Goddard as the star! Still, the success of the play *Anna Lucasta* may well have influenced the way Hollywood would cast black actors in the near future.

Slowly, a new generation of black actors was being employed by the studios. James Edwards played a prizefighter in *The Set-Up*. Canada Lee appeared as a physically and emotionally battered prizefighter in *Body and Soul*. Football star Kenny Washington and Suzette Harbin appeared in *The Foxes of Harrow*, based on a novel by black writer Frank Yerby.

In 1949, a few select films—labeled Negro Problem Pictures—focused on the race problem. Young maverick movie producer Stanley Kramer's *Home of the Brave* became Hollywood's first feature to focus on racism in America—and within the military, at that. Outside Hollywood, Louis de Rochemont produced *Lost Boundaries*, the tale of a Negro family passing for white. Cast as a new-style articulate young black man who befriends the son of the troubled family was New York actor William Greaves. At MGM, director Clarence Brown selected veteran actor Juano Hernandez to play his fiercely independent hero Lucas Beauchamp in an adaptation of William Faulkner's *Intruder in the Dust*. And at Fox, Elia Kazan directed *Pinky*, the story of a young black woman so frustrated and humiliated by racism in her southern community that she decides to leave and live as a "free" white woman in the North. Playing the young woman's grandmother was Ethel Waters. Her old employer Fox chief Darryl F. Zanuck had her test for the role under the direction of John Ford. But once Waters won the role, she clashed with the director. "It was a professional difference of opinion. Ford's Negroes were like Aunt Jemima. Caricatures," said Zanuck. "I thought we were going to get in trouble," said the producer. Ford was replaced by New York stage director Kazan. Ethel Waters walked off with an Oscar nomination as best supporting actress of 1949. Soon afterward, she returned to New York, where she had her greatest stage triumph in Carson McCullers's *The Member of the Wedding*.

Some of the new actors didn't take seriously the idea of having movie careers. Actor Canada Lee came to town, did his work, and then headed back east. James Edwards and Juano Hernandez, however, settled in town. Considered something of a loner, the older Hernandez, greatly respected, appeared less social, more reflective and philosophical, and not one to countenance fools easily. Though he was *in* Hollywood, most felt he was never quite *of* Hollywood. But Edwards—handsome, headstrong, moody, and sexy—became a part of the new postwar generation of black actors, eager to make a place for himself in movies and in Hollywood life.

Postwar optimism: Dorothy Dandridge (third from left) throws a pajama party with her sister-in-law Dorothy Nicholas (second from right).

A NEW MOOD

The war raised the political consciousness of a segment of Black Hollywood. Now was the time for the film colony—and the nation—to examine its values and long-standing racial divisions. Among the most outspoken and politically active was Geri Nicholas Branton, who, along with her sister-in-law Dorothy Dandridge Nicholas, had worked with the Hollywood Democratic Committee during the war years to support victory abroad and the presidency of Franklin Roosevelt at home. The two had also participated in a round of fund-raisers, blood drives, war bond sales, rallies, and benefits, some of which supported the election of progressive politicians. Along with Lena Horne, Branton and Dandridge became involved in the Hollywood Independent Citizens Committee of Arts, Sciences, and Professions (HICCASP). Horne was elected to the organization's board and also promoted the Fair Employment Practices

Commission in California. By the end of the era, these activities would be viewed suspiciously by conservative politicians and conservative members of the industry.

Once the war ended, Branton saw the political climate of the town change even more—and also the racial climate at the studios. The Nicholas Brothers' Fox contract had come to an end. Though they appeared in MGM's *The Pirate* with Gene Kelly, their speaking parts were cut out, and there was no other movie work in Hollywood for them. Like comic black character actors, black tap dancers seemed relics of the past. Europe, however, welcomed the Nicholas Brothers with open arms. Both Branton and Dandridge shuttled to and from Europe, traveling abroad with their husbands as the men toured, then returning home to tend to domestic matters. By then, they had both become mothers: Dorothy, of a daughter, Harolyn; Geri, of a son Tony and later a second son Paul. When in the States, Branton immersed herself in a flurry of political activities. By now, she had become a part of Hollywood's liberal community, which included such stars as John Garfield; Bette Davis; Humphrey Bogart; Katharine Hepburn; Myrna Loy; Betsy Blair; Melvyn Douglas; and Douglas's wife, Congresswoman Helen Gahagan Douglas.

Like much of liberal Hollywood, Branton noticed—and later became alarmed by—the rise of a new politician, Richard Nixon. Surprisingly, Nixon won the support of Lionel Hampton, who helped him navigate his way through black L.A. and, in a sense, through Black Hollywood, too. When Nixon ran for a congressional seat, Hampton did all he could to assure his victory and set up introductions to important community leaders like Norman Houston of the Golden State Insurance Company. Nixon was also taken to meet members of the fraternal lodges, the Elks and the Masons. Because black votes were important, Hampton worked on a Republican black voter registration drive. "We had a big rally," said Hampton. "He got something like twelve thousand black votes, and that was enough to put him over."

Hampton also campaigned for Nixon in his bid for the senate against Helen Gahagan Douglas. "I was assistant campaign manager again. Kenny Washington, the ex–football player, was also working for him," said Hampton. It was a long, nasty battle. Supporting Helen Gahagan Douglas was Branton, who was appalled, like the rest of liberal Hollywood, by Nixon's tactics. Hampton, however, said that Nixon "must have decided Central Avenue was lucky for him, because the night of the election he was sitting in a little bar there, called the Last Word, drinking beer." Nixon won the senate seat.

Fearing that Geri's politics were left of center, Ruby Dandridge advised her daughter to stay away from her. "She'll just get you in trouble," Ruby warned. Ruby was just "a damn Aunt Jemima," recalled Geri. But Dorothy didn't pay any attention to her mother's comments. Branton and Dandridge, along with their friend Jean Seroity, also struggled to keep *The California Eagle* from folding. "Mrs. Bass always had problems meeting the payroll," said Branton. "Dottie, Jean, and I did all we could to help her financially."

T he town's mood was also affected by the actors from New York—already under the spell of a new acting technique, the Method. For hours, East Coast actors could sit discussing their Craft, their Art, and their Integrity. That was happening with West Coast acting students, too, at the Actors Laboratory. Established by Morris Carnovsky and Phoebe Brand, two former members of the famed Group Theatre, the Actors Lab was a very progressive—and some said very political—acting school located at Sunset Boulevard and Laurel Avenue, right behind the famous Schwab's Drug Store, the place where aspiring starlets had sat, hoping to be discovered. The Lab taught the famous Stanislavski Method as well as exercises to heighten an actor's concentration. Drilled into students' heads was the idea of Technique. Joseph Papp, then known as Joseph Papirotsky, was among the teachers at the Lab, along with Anthony Quinn, Hume Cronyn, and Aline MacMahon. No doubt most in Black Hollywood regarded the Lab as exclusively a white actors' club. But in the mid-1940s, the young Dorothy Dandridge, with a dream of being a dramatic film actress, had joined the Lab—in all likelihood its first black student—in hopes of getting the best training possible. She participated in such Lab productions as *A Doll's House* and *The Philadelphia Story*. But even at the progressive Lab, she was dropped from an important production because it was thought that white audiences might not accept her in the role. All those who saw the young Dorothy Dandridge—venturing out on her own—were aware of her ambition and drive, although most were so struck by her beauty that they could think of little else. Anthony Quinn considered her one of the most beautiful women he had ever seen. Actor Joel Fluellen pressured the Actors Lab to admit other black students, such as Juanita Moore, Juliette Ball, and Davis Roberts.

At the close of the 1940s, Black Hollywood appeared uncertain yet hopeful about its future. Would more dramatic roles be offered? And where did young black women fit into the equation? The lead role in *Pinky*—of the troubled young black woman—had been played by a white actress, Jeanne Crain. And when MGM would remake *Show Boat* in 1951, the role of the troubled mulatto Julie would go to Ava Gardner. But just as 1929—with the black-cast films *Hallelujah* and *Hearts in Dixie*—had altered the perspective of the town and even changed the way entertainers lived, 1949 marked a shift, the most significant in Black Hollywood's history, in roles *and* in lifestyles.

5

The Fifties

During the new decade, the mood was cautiously optimistic. There would be an influx of talented performers: Sidney Poitier, Harry Belafonte, Eartha Kitt, Ruby Dee, Ossie Davis, Frank Silvera, and William Marshall. Locals such as James Edwards, Juano Hernandez, Carmen de Lavallade, Juanita Moore, and Woody Strode would also head out to the studios. Having relocated to New York, Ethel Waters would return to Hollywood for major roles in *The Member of the Wedding* and *The Sound and the Fury*. Stepin Fetchit would come back to town to work in *Bend of the River* and *The Sun Shines Bright*. And those successful battles against the restrictive housing covenants heralded a new era when black Angelenos presumably could live anywhere they chose, free of discrimination.

But along with the optimism, there would be devastating changes in the industry that would affect everyone in town. The House Committee on Un-American Activities, which had held hearings in 1947 to investigate "the extent of communist infiltration in the Hollywood motion picture industry," would hold new hearings in 1951. Those members of the film colony, black and white, with questionable political activities and associations of the past would find themselves blacklisted from movie and television work. Hollywood would also be rocked by the government antitrust suits of the late 1940s, which would force the major movie companies to sell off their movie theaters. Long-term contract stars such as Gable and Tracy, Crawford and Davis would eventually find themselves free agents, going from one studio to another to appear in films. The new stars such as Marlon Brando, Elizabeth Taylor, Marilyn Monroe, James Dean, Kim Novak, Audrey Hepburn, Montgomery Clift, and Grace Kelly—all exuding old-style Hollywood glamour that would mark them as the last of a dying breed—would fight to maintain their independence, not only from the studios but from long-standing Hollywood protocol and the traditional politics and culture of stardom. By the era's end, Hollywood would see the death of the studio system itself.

Many in Hollywood, as in the rest of America, would stay home in the evenings, seated in front of a little box with a tiny screen. Central Avenue and those other areas where black performers had always gathered for fun, relaxation, and sexy adventures would also find business dropping. By the close of the era, the very contours and boundaries of the old Black Hollywood would be disappearing, soon to vanish forever. Gone would be the center of Black Hollywood life, probably best symbolized by the death of two Black Hollywood veterans and the withdrawal of another, all of whom had helped define the town for its black residents. And ironically, the stars who would be viewed by old Black Hollywood as its greatest hope for the future—Dorothy Dandridge, Sammy Davis Jr., and Nat "King" Cole—would ultimately help create a far more integrated movie capital, not only at the studios but in the way black stars lived and socialized.

NEW FACES IN TOWN

nvigorated by the wave of postwar optimism—and the box-office success and critical appeal of those Negro Problem Pictures—the more progressive filmmakers believed that Hollywood, like some European filmmakers, especially the Italian neorealists, had to address social issues and psychological tensions. Some sought to create more modern representations of African Americans—sometimes in low-budget films; other times, in big-budget studio productions.

At Twentieth Century Fox, producer Darryl F. Zanuck and director Joseph L. Mankiewicz began production in 1949 on *No Way Out*, a contemporary urban drama about a young Negro doctor falsely accused by a bigot of killing a white patient. The obvious choice for the lead was James Edwards. But Mankiewicz selected a young actor from New York, Sidney Poitier. Also brought west for supporting roles were: Mildred Joanne Smith; Frederick O'Neal, one of the founders of the American Negro

Theater; and a talented acting couple, Ruby Dee and Ossie Davis, whom some of the town knew from their appearance in the play *Anna Lucasta*.

Ossie Davis recalled the excitement of "taking the train, not to California, not to L.A., but to *Hollywood.*" "Ruby and I had both been on Pullman cars before, the last time in *Anna Lucasta,* but this time was different. This trip felt like a wedding journey, our first joining to a job in Hollywood."

Much the same was true of twenty-two-year-old Sidney Poitier's feelings about his first trip to Los Angeles. Raised on Cat Island in the Bahamas, Poitier had been a young drifter unsure of what to do with his life. Leaving home early, he lived in Miami, then went to New York, where he struggled to adapt to the cold weather and to keep himself financially afloat. When he saw an ad—"Actors Wanted by Little Theater Group"— in the black newspaper *The Amsterdam News,* he was naïve enough to think this might be a way of getting himself employed. Little did he understand that the ad was for an audition with the American Negro Theater in Harlem. When Poitier read from a script—in a thick West Indian accent—he was almost hooted off the stage by Frederick O'Neal.

But he was now hooked on acting. Listening to the radio nightly and repeating phrases, he worked diligently to lose his accent, a marvel of concentration and perseverance. He joined the American Negro Theater, drew attention in small roles in theater, notably in an all-Negro version of *Lysistrata,* starring Fredi Washington and Etta Moten. He toured in *Anna Lucasta,* though he was not with the cast during its Los Angeles engagement. Set to appear in the stage musical *Lost in the Stars,* Poitier learned of an audition at Twentieth Century Fox's New York office for *No Way Out.* He made two screen tests in New York. On the second test, he was directed by Joseph Mankiewicz, who offered Poitier one of the starring roles. He would be paid $750 a week, quite a contrast from the $75 a week he would have earned in *Lost in the Stars.*

As a boy in Nassau, Poitier had grown up loving the movies, especially westerns with stars such as Bob Steele, Gene Autry, and Roy Rogers. "I was transfixed by their every move—I accepted them as real." As a boy in Georgia, Ossie Davis also went to cowboy movies. "Some were talkies and others were silent," he remembered. "In my fantasy, I was always on my horse, riding to the rescue of some white girl, just like Tom Mix, Hoot Gibson, and Art Accord. Often these films had Negro characters in them, people like Stepin Fetchit, who were always the target of our ridicule. We'd talk back to the screen and join the white audience laughing."

*Bursting with energy and hopes for the future:
the young Sidney Poitier.*

Now Poitier, Davis, and the others arrived in the city where their child-hood fantasies had been created. When his train pulled into downtown Los Angeles, Poitier recalled, "I was beside myself with excitement. The anticipation was almost unbearable."

Their stay in the city was far different from that of earlier black stars such as Fredi Washington, Lena Horne, and Duke Ellington. No longer was the Dunbar Hotel the lone important establishment that would take them. Upon Poitier's arrival in the summer of 1949, Fox made arrange-ments for him to stay at a hotel in Westwood. "After I checked in, it didn't take much exploring to discover I was in an all-white hotel—in an all-white neighborhood. And, as I expected, I soon found that living exclu-sively among white people with no other blacks around was like being a visitor in a foreign culture, on the alert and at the ready twenty-four hours a day."

The agent for Ruby Dee and Ossie Davis made arrangements for them to stay in a home on Western Avenue that came with a guest house *and* a

Newcomers Ossie Davis and Ruby Dee, greeted by veteran
actress Laura Bowman, upon their arrival in Los Angeles
for the stage drama Anna Lucasta.

caretaker on the property. The couple settled in, comfortable in the new surroundings. This time was Davis's fondest memory of Los Angeles. "The closest we had to a honeymoon was then," said Davis. "I had this house with Spanish tiles. [And I loved] going to the store and buying wine. Just the two of us." "Early mornings, riding through the city to the studio was a breathtaking experience," said Dee. "We'd make our way to Pico Boulevard, which was in walking distance, and take one of those beautiful red streetcars that were, at that time, the pride and joy of the city. All this was before the freeways had been built, before the auto companies had persuaded the city fathers to rip up the tracks, and get rid of the non-polluting streetcars. We passed block after block of beautiful homes and estates as we headed westward on Pico toward 20th-Century-Fox. The grass was very green, and the trees looked as if their leaves had been waxed—I'd never seen anything like it."

"The California sky was pure blue," recalled Poitier, "the streets were clean, the humidity was low, and everybody seemed to be on vacation. All of which prompted me to think to myself: hey, this place is all right, boy."

But the actors had not been at Twentieth Century Fox very long before they saw some of the contradictions of the town. "At the studio, we were immediately struck by the fact that we didn't see any black people working anywhere," recalled Dee. "No technicians, no grips, no electricians, no props people. We didn't see any dark skins in the makeup and wardrobe departments or as hairdressers. From the minute we entered the gate in the morning till the time we left, we were in an all-white world, and that reality was hard for us to ignore."

Sidney Poitier was dazzled by the stars in the studio commissary. But all he saw of blacks, other than cast members of *No Way Out*, was "an occasional kitchen worker or janitor." "Twentieth Century–Fox was not untypical of Hollywood studios in its almost complete exclusion of minority workers on all levels." Of other studios, he recalled, "I made films when the only other black on the lot was the shoeshine boy—as was the case at Metro."

Like Lena Horne, Dee spent time having various makeups tested on her before the studio decided simply to make her up as little as possible with just a bit of powder. But when it came to styling her hair, no one seemed to know what to do. Finally, Dee approached director Mankiewicz and asked whether she could perhaps have a black hairdresser to do her hair. "I didn't know in those days," said Dee, "that you weren't supposed to go to the director and ask about that kind of thing. But Mankiewicz was very nice and said he'd have arrangements made." That very afternoon, Fox brought in the black stylist Elizabeth Searcy. Still, Dee believed she detected subtle racism in the wardrobe department when one of the matrons appeared not to want to touch a pair of shoes that Dee had worn. "I felt the blood rise to my face." Dee grew "uncomfortable because I felt those in wardrobe straining to be normal, working with people that, were it not for their jobs, they would not touch."

But Dee and Davis found director Mankiewicz and the crew sensitive and easy to work with. Yet the contradictions of the production were apparent. "Every day at work on *No Way Out*, I was conscious of the film's political and social themes," said Dee. "I was also vividly aware of the discrepancy between the fictional world of the film and the reality of racist discrimination on the lot, and in the film industry. The people responsible for getting us before the camera became more gracious and efficient, but remained unaware that they helped form the scaffolding of racism on which bigotry and exclusivity grows." When Dee asked a technician about the fact that there were no blacks in the unions, he "said—and I believed him—that he hadn't given it much thought." For the most part, neither Dee nor Davis discussed their feelings with those at the studio. Davis recalled that because film work was so new to him, he was eager to learn as much as possible, and often, he wanted to please.

The couple also spent time seeing the town and getting together with some people they had met in 1947. Davis felt Central Avenue wasn't what it had been just a few years earlier. But "there was definitely still a *community* there among the black actors." Completing *No Way Out*, Dee and Davis went back to New York, their base throughout their long careers. Yet both returned to make films and television dramas, especially Dee, who was called back to appear in *The Jackie Robinson Story* and then in *Tall Target*. Poitier also headed back to New York, but not before Mankiewicz recommended him for the antiapartheid drama *Cry the Beloved Country*, to be filmed in South Africa. For years, he, too, remained New York–based with his wife, Juanita, and their young daughters. But he returned to Los Angeles to do other films, often staying at the Chateau Marmont on Sunset Boulevard.

CARMEN DE LAVALLADE: LOCAL GIRL MAKES GOOD

L.A.'s Carmen de Lavallade found the postwar atmosphere in Hollywood promising, although in a more limited way. From the start, she wanted a career in dance. Her role model was always her cousin Janet Collins, who had studied with Lester Horton's dance company and then gone on to New York. There, in 1951, she became the first black prima ballerina at the Metropolitan Opera House—four years before Marian Anderson's celebrated operatic debut. "I patterned myself after Janet," said de Lavallade. "She was the first person in the family that went out into the theater. She was always in and out of the city. And when she came, it was always like Auntie Mame. Janet's coming! Whoooo! That was like a big occasion when Janet would breeze in, and boy, would she breeze!" When de Lavallade studied with Lester Horton, whose company was the most important for modern dance on the West Coast, he singled her out for dance stardom.

After her 1950 debut with the company—at age nineteen—de Lavallade became one of the most talked-about dancers in the city. Lena Horne came to see her perform, and the press dubbed her Lena's protégé. "I can't remember how it happened," said de Lavallade. "But it helped." With the Horton troupe, she also performed at Ciro's and found work at the studios.

Tall, slender, and shapely, with a light brown complexion and flashing brown eyes, she performed in a spectacular dance sequence in *Lydia Bailey,* choreographed by Jack Cole. She danced in *Abbott and Costello Meet Dr. Jekyll and Mr. Hyde, The Egyptian,* and *Carmen Jones* and won a role in the ancient-Rome spectacle *Demetrius and the Gladiators,* which starred Susan Hayward, Victor Mature, and Anne Bancroft and featured black actor William Marshall in a showcase turn as a noble Nubian gladiator.

From the start, she was entranced by the movie studios. "It's something about walking in those big barnlike places, the back lot, where all you could do was dream. You hear about these places. You see photographs. And to actually be on the set and you're looking around to see if you see a movie star. And watching how they work. I always find that fascinating. I'd rather be on the set watching. Some people don't even know how brilliant they are at what they do. Moviemaking is a special kind of art form. It's absolute magic. And some people just bring magic with them. It's like they're born for it."

But she also saw some of the absurdities at the studio when she and other black actors appeared in *Lydia Bailey.* "The day of shooting, the first thing you have is makeup. James Truitt, also from the Horton company, told me about this special makeup, Negro Number Two, because he did *Mighty Joe Young,* which had African dancing. I laughed at him and told him, 'It's not true.' And he told me, 'You just wait.' And sure enough, I saw all these makeup things, and I looked up and saw a makeup labeled Negro Number Two. The director had looked at us all, and he picked the darkest guy, a beautiful black guy, and he said, 'I want them all that color.' Well, we all kind of looked at each other. There was one lady, Florence, who had green eyes, and she was very, very fair. Well, when they put that stuff on our skin, we looked green. It was so funny. And at that time, Alvin Ailey was supposed to be my partner in this voodoo dance. And he got sick. And Jack Cole said, 'I'll do it.' And the thing is, he looked better than anybody else, because the makeup was made to cover pale skin. He came out a nice color. You put it on black people with all kinds of skin tones, and you get that green and yellow and this and that. Oh, my goodness, if we didn't look weird. And we started laughing. And we'd find each other walking down the studio street, and it was so embarrassing, and we'd start laughing."

De Lavallade quickly learned studio politics and star-system protocol. The old casual and carefree days were clearly gone. Some stars could be friendly and relatively congenial, quick with a joke over a flubbed line. But many, no doubt tense about their own work, said little to supporting play-

Ballerina Carmen de Lavallade with Susan Hayward in Demetrius and the Gladiators.

ers. If you were among the one or two black players in an otherwise all-white film, feelings of isolation could easily creep in. Black filmmaker Carlton Moss once observed that black performers on movie sets always had that moment just before the cameras rolled when they seemed to stop moving, when Moss believed he detected their sense of isolation in what was usually an all-white setting of fellow actors and crew. "It happened even with big stars," said Moss, "like Sammy, Pearl Bailey, and Dandridge."

On *Demetrius and the Gladiators,* however, de Lavallade remembered when Susan Hayward, like the stars of old, crossed the line of star protocol. Cast as a handmaiden to Hayward's character, Messalina, de Lavallade found Hayward professional and cordial. But next to nothing was said on the set. Then, one day, the cast went to the back lot to shoot a sequence. "It was a little trek on the way out there," de Lavallade recalled. At the end of the long day, de Lavallade quietly waited for a studio bus to pick her up. "I had to drag all this stuff back," de Lavallade recalled. Then she saw Susan Hayward pull up in her car and ask, "Would you like a ride? Get in." De

Lavallade climbed in. "I'm sitting next to her on the front seat. We didn't say very much of anything at all." But Hayward must have seen something about this young dancer, just starting out, that reminded her of herself at an earlier time. "I just blanked out," said de Lavallade. "Susan Hayward, a great star, driving in her car and giving me a lift. I've never forgotten that." De Lavallade knew it was something stars generally didn't do.

Though she liked movie work, she knew there wasn't going to be a career for her in Hollywood. Gene Kelly wasn't going to cast her as his dancing partner. But Gene was an admirer. He "wanted to use me in something, but evidently, he couldn't. I remember whenever I'd see him, he was very warm. I think he knew the history of the theater. I was doing very well and never got anything. When I look back on it, there was probably no way." New York, however, was a city for a young dancer on the rise. She traveled east with Horton's troupe. On the stage, de Lavallade appeared in *House of Flowers* with Pearl Bailey, the young Diahann Carroll, and a Trinidadian-born dancer, Geoffrey Holder, whom she married. Again following in her cousin Janet Collins's footsteps, de Lavallade became a star ballerina at the Met in productions of *Aida* and *Samson and Delilah*.

THE STRIP

I n the early 1950s, the nightclub scene—away from Central Avenue—appeared better than ever for the new black music stars making a name for themselves. Now the two big-name clubs, both located on the Sunset Strip, the fierce competitors the Mocambo and Ciro's, headlined black stars. Three breakthrough openings set the town on its ear. Dorothy Dandridge and Sammy Davis Jr., each of whom came to epitomize a new kind of Black Hollywood stardom, packed the Mocambo and Ciro's. And an old-timer, Josephine Baker, came to town and showed she still had what it took to be a star.

AT THE MOCAMBO: DOROTHY COMES OF AGE

A t the start of the 1950s, Dorothy Dandridge was struggling to pull her life and career together. For Dandridge, the immediate postwar years were a time of depression over the state of her marriage—and anxiety and near desperation over the condition of her daughter Harolyn, who was called Lynn. Born in 1943, Lynn had developed slowly, still unable to talk by age four, then five. "Dottie tried everything," said Geri. "She took Lynn from one doctor to another." Finally, a female physician informed Dandridge that Lynn would never learn to talk, never develop like other children. Her daughter had been born severely brain-damaged. "It broke Dottie's heart," said Geri. "She always blamed herself," said Harold Nicholas. Dandridge decided to end the marriage.

She had never really stopped working in the 1940s, having appeared in films—often in musical numbers with stars such as Count Basie and Louis Armstrong and in bits and supporting roles. Still ambitious to be a dramatic film actress, she continued her studies at the Actors Lab. In the meantime, she had to make a living. Turning her attention to nightclub work, she struggled to put together an act but was getting nowhere until she ran into Phil Moore. The two talked. Moore always believed that Lena Horne was the queen of nightclubs. But there was a place for Dorothy. Both he and Dandridge understood that nightclub appearances might bring her to the attention of the industry and, in turn, lead to movie roles. Soon, Moore was coaching her and writing special arrangements that played up her vocal assets and downplayed any limitations—much as he had done for Lena. He also sought to highlight her as a stunning visual creation in the clubs. Endless sessions were devoted to her look: her gowns, her makeup, her hairstyles.

Moore was impressed with Dandridge's drive and ambition, dazzled by her beauty and sensuality, and moved by her vulnerability. He had long carried a torch for her; now, he was wildly in love. The two became lovers. Moore urged Dandridge to give up the house on Twenty-seventh Street and move to Hollywood itself, a more central location for interviews and auditions, the place where all the action was. She found a duplex on Hilldale Avenue, which she shared with Moore. During the early 1950s, unmarried stars still didn't openly live together. Moore occupied the upper level of the duplex; Dandridge, the lower. Her one-bedroom apartment had a fireplace with a large piano in the living room. A fine cook, Dandridge made good use of the small kitchen. Outside was a garden, where she entertained friends. Dandridge's move to Hilldale marked a continued widening of the residential boundaries for Black Hollywood—and also a widening of the social boundaries.

On Sundays, Moore hosted musicales, sophisticated gatherings for some of Hollywood's more artistically progressive, black and white. Moore would be at the piano. Dorothy, unsure of herself, often would simply watch as others performed. Glittering figures came and went. Ava Gardner, whom Dandridge knew, came to Moore for vocal coaching in prepa-

Even during their private time, away from the studios, movie stars like Dandridge were expected always to look like movie stars.

ration for her role as Julie in MGM's remake of *Show Boat*. A fragile and nervous Marilyn Monroe, whom Dandridge had known from the Actors Lab, also studied with Moore. Some evenings, Monroe would visit Dandridge just to talk. "Dottie had a little white rug in front of the fireplace," said the actress Juliette Ball. "And Marilyn used to lie on that rug. And many a night, she cried. Mostly about relationships."

Small club bookings brought Dorothy Dandridge attention, as did supporting roles in the low-budget films *Tarzan's Peril* and *The Harlem Globetrotters*. When she performed at the El Rancho Hotel in the growing postwar entertainment center of Las Vegas, she was introduced by actress Marie Wilson to a *Life* magazine photographer, who took pictures of Dandridge in hopes of publishing them in the magazine. But nothing would appear for a year.

Then came Dandridge's appearance at the Café Gala, the small club perched on a tiny hill at the base of the big, steep hill on Horn Avenue. By the early 1950s, the Café Gala, where Lena Horne had performed so successfully, had become even more of a haven for the more avant-garde and creative talents. Into the 1950s, stars such as Horne still came to the club to catch the new performers—and also to hang out for those informal gatherings around the piano. The crowd at the Gala wanted the new, the daring, even the experimental in this relaxed social setting where black and white could openly mix. The patrons were "mostly ex–New Yorkers out there visiting," said Bobby Short. "It was a very, very New York / European kind of atmosphere. It was chic."

Accompanied by Moore on piano on her opening night in February 1951, Dandridge, known for her great insecurities when appearing before a live audience, was wobbly and nearly frightened out of her wits. But by now, Moore knew her so well that midway through the performance, he started talking to her, coaxing her out of her shyness and doubts, drawing her out of herself. Nightclubbers sat in rapt attention. A sexy psychodrama was unfurling right before their eyes. Loosening up and moving about the small room, Dandridge soon sang each and every song as if she owned it. The songs themselves—much like Lena's material—weren't gospel, nor jazz, nor rhythm and blues. Instead, she sang standards and show tunes such as "It's a Woman's Prerogative" and "Harlem on My Mind." Her training as a girl in the Lauretta Butler dance school showed: She moved like a dancer. As part of her act, she also tossed a coin in the air. Would she catch it? Most times, she did. When she didn't, she could simply shrug her shoulders as if to say, "What the heck. Let's keep on with the good times anyway." "She was perfection," said Dandridge's former sister-in-law Dorothy Nicholas Morrow. "She was peaches and cream," recalled Bobby Short. "She was just so frigging pretty that when she walked out in front of the audience with that low-cut dress and those boobs and that little waist, she was just a killer. Just a killer."

In the February 24, 1951, edition of the *Los Angeles Mirror*, entertainment editor Dick Williams raved: "She leans there on the piano at the end of that room that has the feel of a Manhattan style intimate supper club, eyes closed, lips parted, her hands thrown in front of her, the fringe of her tight white dress flying as she huskily intones 'Got Harlem on My Mind.' . . . This is Dorothy Dandridge, the most exciting new sepia singer I've spotted since Lena Horne." *Variety* also praised her: "A new showbiz career looms brightly for Dorothy Dandridge. She's been around before, but never with the window-dressing and guidance Moore has dished out and she looks like a cinch chick." Crowds lined the street to see her. "That was the first time she had ever really been important on her own, because she got press that you would not believe," said Bobby Short. "You couldn't get in to see her."

Black Hollywood knew it had a major star in the making. Already she was being compared to Horne, and the black press would publicize a supposed rivalry between the two women that in actuality didn't exist. But where would she go from the Gala? Other beautiful Negro women such as Carolynne Snowden and Nina Mae McKinney had heated up the Los Angeles nightclub scene without attaining major stardom. It all depended on what happened next. As it turned out, the next stop for Dandridge was the Mocambo.

A couple of years earlier, Dandridge had gone to see Charlie Morrison, one of the Mocambo's owners. Though Morrison didn't then think she was ready for the big time, he had seen something utterly unique and indefinable in her. When she mentioned Phil Moore, Morrison phoned him. Thereafter, the hard work—with demanding rehearsals and endless strategizing—began. Now, after the Gala opening, Morrison booked her into the Mocambo—and then hyped up the May 1951 opening to the point where it became one of the town's most talked-about events. The hit Mocambo engagement also marked the beginning of the end of the Dandridge/Moore relationship. No longer was there talk about Moore and his protégé. Now it was about Dandridge and her arranger/accompanist Moore. The two sailed for England for an engagement at the supper club

Dandridge: dream girl of the Eisenhower era.

Café de Paris in London. She had another smash. Back in the States, the entire town was talking about her.

Signing with the powerful MCA agency, Dandridge was soon on a major nightclub tour that led to an opening at New York's La Vie en Rose on January 21, 1952. Dandridge and Moore both understood the new ground rules for stardom for a Negro goddess in Hollywood. She had to succeed in New York. Horne had come from New York. So had her predecessor Ethel Waters. Tough and brutal as the East Coast critics could be, New York was the base of the major press, the place where the right buzz would impress Hollywood all the more. Her engagement at La Vie en Rose was another triumph, which led to media coverage in the pages of *Time, Theatre Arts, Quick,* and *Cue. Look* ran a photo of her on the lower part of its cover. Moore hired a young pianist/arranger, Nick Perito, to be the musical director for her tour. "Don't forget," he cautioned Perito, "she's my girl!"

But by then, her relationship with Moore was over. He spent most of his time now in New York at his digs in Carnegie Towers. Yet Jeanne Moore Pisano, who later married Moore, once said, "I really think Dorothy was the love of his life." In 1953, Dandridge would return to the Mocambo for an even more spectacular opening as Charlie Morrison rolled out the red carpet—and launched a media blitz that played on the success of the recent publication of Alfred C. Kinsey's *Sexual Behavior in the Human Female.* Dandridge was publicized as a "volume of sex with the living impact of the Kinsey report." Morrison had his Mocambo cigarette girls sell copies of Kinsey's book at an inflated price of fifteen dollars each. Hollywood turned out: Peggy Lee, Joel Grey, Gordon MacRae, Maureen O'Hara, Ella Logan, as well as black actor William Marshall and black comedian Slappy White. Dandridge would also play the big clubs in Vegas. But most important, the studios took notice. MGM signed her for the lead role as a sensitive schoolteacher in *Bright Road.* Before the era ended, she returned to London to appear at the Savoy. There, at a reception, the Duke of Edinburgh, the future Prince Philip, stood among a group of admirers and quietly asked for an introduction.

LA BAKAIR: BACK IN THE STATES AND IN TOWN

The other big news in 1951—and an event for which Hollywood turned out in full force—was the appearance of Josephine Baker at the RKO Hillstreet Theatre. At age forty-five, Baker was the legendary heroine of a story that read like a modern fairy tale: She was the little girl, born out of wedlock and dirt-poor in St. Louis in 1906, who had started performing as a teenager and then, at nineteen, had conquered Paris in *La Revue Nègre* in 1925. Afterward came triumphs in the Folies Bergère and at theaters throughout Europe. Icon status was bestowed on her: She was idolized as a towering *exotique*, the most glamorous and alluring woman alive. What a wonderful revenge, she once said, for a girl whom America had considered an ugly duckling! Having worked with the French underground during the war, she was awarded the Medal of the Resistance with Rosette in 1946. Charles de Gaulle sent her a letter of congratulations. In 1950, she appeared in Havana, then was offered an engagement at the Copa City in Miami.

Fired up with postwar optimism, she decided that now was the time for a return to the United States—on her own terms. Outspoken on civil rights, Baker insisted through weeks of negotiation that her contract stipulate that black patrons be admitted to the club. She turned down an offer of ten thousand dollars a week until her demands for an integrated audience were met. At a time when Jim Crow laws were staunchly enforced (blacks in Miami Beach had a 6:00 P.M. curfew—after which, policemen could stop them and ask for identity cards), Baker was booked into Miami Beach's *whites-only* Arlington Hotel and was squired around town in a deluxe automobile driven by a white chauffeur. "This is the most important moment of my life. It's the first time I've been in my native land for twenty-six years," said Baker, "because the other times don't count." Engagements in New York, Chicago, Boston, and Los Angeles followed.

Long ticket lines formed for her two-week appearance in L.A. For members of the film colony, who were immensely curious about her, Josephine Baker represented old-world European glamour, more sophisticated and extravagant than general American fare. Onstage, Baker sang in French and English as well as Spanish, Portuguese, and Italian. And she dressed in a two-hundred-and-fifty-thousand-dollar wardrobe with gowns by Balenciaga, Balmain, and Dior. On hand was a French maid to assist in her costume changes. Everyone knew her as a champion of rights for black Americans. At one performance, an audience member shouted, "Why don't you go back where you came from?" From the stage, Baker shouted, "I am back where I came from. And you—where do you come from?" The crowd went wild with applause. Never had Hollywood, black or white, seen a goddess like this one.

Offstage, Baker also made news. After her final L.A. performance in

July 1951, she dined downtown at the plush Biltmore Hotel. When she heard a man say, "I won't stay in the same room with niggers," she angrily rose from her table and phoned the police. Told that they could do nothing because they were not present when the remark was heard, Baker, at their suggestion, made a citizen's arrest! Later, a municipal judge found the man—a forty-five-year-old salesman from Dallas—guilty of disturbing the peace. Sentenced to ten days in jail or a one hundred–dollar fine, the man paid the fine.

Rumors swirled that Baker hoped to find movie work in Hollywood. "It isn't a question of whether the movies want Josephine," her manager told the press, "but whether they want her enough to make the kind of movie consistent with her way of thinking on the matter of segregation." Baker didn't find a movie role in Hollywood. But no one would forget she had been in town.

SAMMY ARRIVES AT CIRO'S

ammy Davis Jr.'s appearance at Ciro's in 1951 also altered Hollywood's nightclub scene. Like Dandridge, Davis had been in show business since childhood. Born in 1925, the son of two entertainers, Sammy Davis Sr. and his wife, Elvera "Baby" Sanchez, Davis had been left in the care of his paternal grandmother while his parents traveled with entertainer Will Mastin. When the couple's marriage fell apart, Davis Sr. turned his sights to his precocious son. At age two and a half, young Sammy won first prize in an amateur dance contest at Philadelphia's Standard Theater. At three and a half, he was a pro. Sammy could sing. Sammy could dance. Sammy could mug. Sammy could do comedy. Sammy had perfect timing. And Sammy loved performing. Little Sammy was taken on the road as part of the act, eventually known as the Will Mastin Trio. From the start, the pint-sized Sammy was the trio's energizing spark plug.

By 1933, having made a name for himself in vaudeville, the eight-year-old Sammy was cast in the movie short *Rufus Jones for President*, in which, despite some painful stereotypes, he danced energetically and poignantly sat on Ethel Waters's lap while she sang him to sleep. In the early 1940s, Davis spent his adolescence on the road, performing at small clubs and theaters, dives and pit stops, that chain of black nightspots known as the chitlin circuit. During the war, he was drafted into the army. Sheltered from real life, as the Nicholas Brothers had been, he was now exposed to racism in its most blatant form. Assigned to one of the first integrated bar-

Bringing her high-voltage glamour and Old World sophistication to the film capital, Josephine Baker with Arthur Freed, Gina Lollobrigida, and Vincente Minnelli.

racks, he was taunted and teased unmercifully by the white GIs. On one occasion, they wrote "I'm a Coon" and "Nigger" on his chest and face. On another occasion, they broke his nose. (In total, Davis's nose was broken five different times.) But Davis performed in army camps where, he later admitted, he worked hard to "neutralize them [the white bigots] and make them acknowledge" him. "My talent was," he said, "the way for me to fight."

After his stint in the army, Davis went back on the road with the Will Mastin Trio, performing at small clubs again but also at important black theaters such as the Apollo in New York and the Lincoln in L.A., as well as in Las Vegas. Davis now had a reputation as a one-of-a-kind entertainer, the type of star who, like Ethel Waters, seemed to be able to do everything: sing, dance, perhaps even play dramatic roles. Skilled pros that his father and Mastin were, they now seemed like backups for Sammy. All eyes were on the kid. Sometimes, his comedy bits smacked of soon-to-be-dated prewar routines. Davis would perform with exaggerated *cullid* dialects, especially in a bit about a southern tobacco auctioneer. He did impersonations, including one of Stepin Fetchit. But he also played the drums and could put any song across, and in 1947, he signed with Capitol Records. For most of his life, he was painfully aware that he had almost no formal education, though at one time, he took a ninety-dollar-a-year correspondence course from the Calvert School in Baltimore. His onetime business partner, Sy Marsh, once said that Davis "till the day he died could sign his name, but he couldn't write. He never personalized autographs to anyone because he couldn't spell people's names and he was embarrassed." Davis also never felt himself attractive (he spoke of wanting a nose job during these early years). But otherwise, he seemed every inch the confident budding young star: charismatic, fiercely outgoing, always *on*. Sometimes, he didn't seem to know when to turn it off. Whereas Dandridge was considered the type of private woman who would be the first to leave the party, Davis was the kind of guy who'd be the last to go.

As word of his talent spread to white Hollywood, Davis became the kind of performer of whom hip white stars were aware. The same was true of the young comic Redd Foxx. But Sammy wasn't immediately accepted by the public at large. When he appeared on comic Eddie Cantor's television program *The Colgate Comedy Hour,* some viewers objected to seeing him in their living rooms and sent hateful letters to the network. "Dear lousy nigger," read one letter, "keep your filthy paws off Eddie Cantor he may be a jew [*sic*] but at least he is white and don't come from africa [*sic*] where you should go back to I hope I hope I hope. I won't use that lousy stinking toothpaste no more for fear maybe the like of you has touched it. What is dirt like you doing on our good America earth anything."

Some venues were closed to Sammy. Finally, an offer came in 1951 for a booking at Ciro's, run by Billy Wilkerson. Like the Mocambo, Ciro's had epitomized swanky Hollywood sophistication since its opening in 1940. The club's ultramodern exterior had been created by George Vernon Russell; its baroque interior, by Tom Douglas. Inside, the walls were draped with reseda ribbed silk. Along the walls, there sat ribbed red silk banquettes. The ceiling was painted red. Bronze columns and urns provided lighting above the bandstand. Advertisements for the club's opening had proclaimed: "Everybody that's anybody will be at Ciro's." That proved true, as stars such as Lana Turner, Paulette Goddard, and Olivia de Havilland glided through its entrance.

At Ciro's, the Will Mastin Trio would open for the headliner, Janis Paige. The weeks and days before the engagement were tense for young Davis. Perhaps no other star of the twentieth century craved an audience's approval and acceptance—even needed and thrived on its "love"—as much as he did. Entertaining was Sammy Davis Jr.'s reason for being, his highest form of gratification.

With a powerful buzz running throughout Hollywood, opening night was packed with excited patrons and stars. Janis Paige had no idea what lay in store for her. The Will Mastin Trio came onstage and just about ripped the lid off the place. Or Sammy did. Considered daring, here he was, a black entertainer whose impersonations of such white stars as Frank Sinatra, Humphrey Bogart, James Cagney, and James Stewart along with African American legend Louis Armstrong had the Ciro's crowd, as Sammy later recalled, "pounding on the table so hard I could see the silverware jumping up and down." His dancing had them tapping their feet in approval, while the energy level in the club reached an almost fever pitch. "Everybody was at Ciro's," said columnist James Bacon. "I was sitting at a table with Clark Gable and William Holden and the Humphrey Bogarts, and the Will Mastin Trio came out with Sammy Davis. Sammy went into his imitation of white stars, like Jimmy Stewart and Jerry Lewis, and those people were in the audience. They were only supposed to do 20 minutes, but every time they'd go off, the audience would start to yell. They did close to an hour." That night, the audience didn't want to let Sammy and company leave.

By the time Janis Paige appeared—after the intermission—everyone was just about ready to go home. "We'd taken eight bows," recalled Davis. "Janis Paige was in the wings waiting to go on to close the show. She was so upset she sang off key for fifteen minutes. She couldn't even get the audience's attention." The next morning, the press heralded Davis's breakthrough performance. "Once in a long time an artist hits town," wrote Paul Coates in the *Los Angeles Mirror*, "and sends the place on its ears. Such a one is young Sammy Davis Jr. of the Will Mastin Trio at Ciro's." "It was such a big night for Sammy that Janis Paige told George Schlatter [a producer at Ciro's], 'You better put them on as headliner,' " said James Bacon. In essence, Paige became *their* opening act. "Sammy Davis was made after that," said Schlatter.

Davis was off on his mighty ascent to major American stardom. He returned to Ciro's for another triumph in January 1955, one that helped catapult him into the big time. In November 1954, Davis, had been in a terrible accident. After his performance at the New Frontier in Las Vegas, Davis had taken off for Los Angeles with his driver in the early hours of the morning, so that he could record music for the movie sound track of

New stars for a new age: Diahann Carroll and Sidney Poitier.

Six Bridges to Cross. But midway on their journey, with Sammy at the wheel, their car collided with another in a violent, bloody crash. In shock, Davis crawled from the vehicle onto the highway. He felt something hanging on his cheek. It was his left eye. Afterward, he spent months in recuperation—and in a state of deep depression. He discovered he had lost his basic coordination—and had to learn to walk *and* dance all over again. Unsure whether he could ever perform again, he struggled to hold himself together. Finally, he agreed to make his first appearance—again, as part of the Will Mastin Trio—at Ciro's. Opening night—with stars such as Humphrey Bogart and Lauren Bacall, Cary Grant, June Allyson and Dick Powell, Spencer Tracy, Gary and Rocky Cooper, and Edward G. Robinson in attendance—Davis had another rousing triumph, which now made him appear like a larger-than-life star who had faced death and beaten it on that highway, and now was back in full glory.

The nightclub and theater appearances of Davis, Dandridge, and Baker signaled a new era in the town. A star such as Nat "King" Cole had appeared at Ciro's in 1948. But the huge success of the engagements at the Mocambo and Ciro's meant that the Sunset Strip itself was *officially* no longer off-limits for black stars. Eartha Kitt, Pearl Bailey, and Billy Eckstine also opened at the clubs, packing in audiences and wowing the critics. And Lena Horne continued to perform, exuding her one-of-a-kind glamour and a rather icy sex appeal. In fact, the most talked-about nightclub performers—those by whom the industry seemed most interested in being entertained—would now often be the black headliners whose energy and styles transformed the mainstream club scene.

Yet oddly, though no one quite realized it, the classic nightclub scene was teetering on its last leg. As the studio system slowly slipped into decline, stars no longer felt the pressure to be seen at the clubs or even around town. Though a later young Hollywood would always have its nightspots, the giddy, glamorous haunts of the past would eventually close up shop. By the end of the decade, the nightclub scene would be just about dead.

THE LITTLE TUBE

Television experiments had begun as early as the mid-1920s. But after the war, manufacturers had finally come up with a moderately priced version of this box that would enable millions of Americans to own one. From the late 1940s into the 1950s, television sales rose year by year as TV became a potent cultural force in American life. Television meant more work for black performers on the variety programs in New York, where most early television productions were based. On everything from *The Ed Sullivan Show* to *The Colgate Comedy Hour*, stars such as Pearl Bailey, Sammy Davis Jr., dancer Peg Leg Bates, Eartha Kitt, Nat "King" Cole, Marian Anderson, and Dorothy Dandridge all were now coming into American households. From the East Coast, Hazel Scott briefly hosted her own program. TV helped kill the clubs and eventually would siphon off a large percentage of the movie audience.

Yet television kept the careers of Black Hollywood's old guard alive. Influenced by radio programming as well as movies of the 1930s and 1940s, the tiny tube broadcast sitcoms that were often harried tales of domestic life: husbands and wives, children and relatives, caught up in daily dilemmas. On hand to provide the families with cheery support were black servants. In New York, *Beulah* became a TV series starring Ethel Waters, Dooley Wilson, and Butterfly McQueen. But after little more than a season on *Beulah*, Waters left the show. The production set up shop in Los

The new medium that saved old careers: Spencer Williams (right) and Tim Moore on the set of TV's Amos 'n' Andy.

Angeles, first with Hattie McDaniel as the star until she took ill, and then with Louise Beavers. Also on the show were Ruby Dandridge, Ernest Whitman, and in some episodes, the very young Leslie Uggams.

Servant roles in the TV series *My Little Margie* and *The Stu Erwin Show* enabled Willie Best to keep his career afloat. Lillian Randolph, who had played the housekeeper Birdie on radio's *The Great Gildersleeve*, repeated the part in the television series. Her sister Amanda portrayed a similar character on *The Danny Thomas Show*. Eddie Anderson continued to play the crafty Rochester on TV's *The Jack Benny Show*. And when CBS aired the controversial television version of the radio hit *The Amos 'n' Andy Show*, a lineup of old-time performers was working regularly: Tim Moore; the Randolph sisters, Lillian and Amanda; Johnny Lee; Ernestine Wade; Alvin Childress; Jester Hairston; and Spencer Williams. Williams and Moore had actually retired, thinking their careers were over, until they were called back to Hollywood for the roles.

TV work kept the actors busy and the town alive whenever the stars made appearances along Central Avenue or around the city. But life in Black Hollywood had undergone yet another transformation. For decades, Black Hollywood had fought for more work and a more respected place in the industry as well as for roles in films centered around black life in America. But now that a new day appeared to really be near, the industry's long-standing distortions about African American life also had to die. The movie studios understood the new realities before the television networks could grasp them. But eventually, TV's comic-servant roles—and the old-guard performers—would fall by the wayside.

JAMES EDWARDS: LOST HEARTTHROB

Throughout the 1950s, Sidney Poitier's slow but steady climb to stardom—in such films as *No Way Out, Edge of the City,* and *The Defiant Ones*—had an impact on audiences, critics, and the way the studios viewed black characters. Yet no one in town really thought of Poitier as a personality who was part of movie-capital life. He was yet another easterner on sojourn like such East Coast–based white stars as Montgomery Clift, Paul Newman, and Joanne Woodward. Surprisingly, other actors, such as Marlon Brando and James Dean, came to symbolize a new attitude in Hollywood: the rebels from the East, who ultimately contributed to the town's postwar culture and life. They became heroes for future generations of aspiring young actors who wanted to make it in the movies and yet still appear to be holding on to their ideals and integrity. Yet though rebellion became a fashionable pose, black male rebellion or outspokenness in Hollywood would never be accepted or tolerated. That was certainly the case with James Edwards.

During the opening years of the new decade, no black actor's career was watched more closely than that of Edwards. Six feet two inches tall, lean but muscular, with a rich brown coloring, chiseled features, and dark brooding eyes, Edwards appeared to enjoy his role as Black Hollywood's heartthrob. Yet he was a serious actor with lofty plans to write and direct a black musical for Broadway and to tour the South, taking theater to black audiences. His appearance in Hollywood had come after years of hard work and troubled times.

Born in Muncie, Indiana, Edwards worked his way through high school and college, doing everything from cutting grass to babysitting. A skilled athlete, he ran track and played baseball. By age eighteen, he was a professional boxer, earning a dollar a day plus a small bonus for each fight. But

James Edwards, Hollywood heartthrob and rebel.

after a bloody match, his horrified mother told him, "No more fights. From now on, you concentrate on your education." Edwards enrolled in Indiana University but left, so he said, because of its racial attitudes, to study at Knoxville College in Tennessee, where he majored in psychology. With his strong political consciousness, he became a labor organizer in the steel industry in Calumet, followed by a two-year stint on the War Production Board and army service.

After Edwards suffered massive facial wounds in an automobile accident, surgeons had to reconstruct his face, even rebuild an ear, so he later told the press. Lying in a hospital room, with a white soldier who was also a patient, Edwards was visited one day by his mother. When she spoke to the other patient, the young man said nothing and turned away from her. Edwards explained to his mother that the soldier, who was from North Carolina, had never said one word to him. As she was about to leave at the end of the day, Edwards's mother gave the white soldier a book and a box of candy. "I hope you feel better," she told him. After she left, Edwards and the soldier still said nothing to each other. Finally, the soldier broke the silence, saying, "You've got a wonderful mother, buddy." The two men became close friends. Ironically, the incident could easily have been included in at least two of Edwards's best-known films, *Home of the Brave* and *Bright Victory*. In both, he played sensitive black military men who became close friends with fellow white soldiers but only after suffering the torment of racial bigotry.

As part of his therapy at the hospital, Edwards was advised by a psychiatrist to take public-speaking courses at nearby Northwestern University to help him rebuild his confidence. The classes excited him and led him to think of an acting career. "I did Romeo to at least 20 Juliets," said Edwards. "I also played the prince in *Death Takes a Holiday*, one of the toughest roles an amateur could undertake. Later, I appeared in *The Little Foxes, The Skin of Our Teeth*, and *The Petrified Forest* when they were presented at Northwestern. If it hadn't been for the Army, I guess I never would have become an actor."

Edwards later performed with Chicago's Skyloft Players and also traveled as part of a singing group. While on the road, he received a telegram asking him to come to New York to audition for a Broadway drama called *Deep Are the Roots*. Arriving in New York, Edwards was dressed in "a purple zoot suit, a yellow coat, a yellow feather in my hat, a long watch chain dangling at my side and a flashy necktie." But, he recalled, "I didn't have time to think about clothes. This looked like the biggest thing to come my way. As soon as the train got to New York, I rushed over to the producer's office. When I walked in, Elia Kazan and Kermit Bloomgarten were there. They must have thought I came to try out for a part in *Carmen Jones*. Before they would let me read for the part, they asked me to remove my jacket. But even that did no good. I didn't get the part."

Edwards, however, was hired as the understudy and eventually played the role on Broadway, then traveled with the production to Los Angeles. He loved the town, and though the odds were against his finding movie roles, he stayed, appeared in the films *Manhandled* and *The Set-Up*, and joined a theater group. Playing a seventy-five-year-old man in the play *The Torch Grows Dim*, Edwards recalled the closing Saturday night of the short-lived production when the fifteen people onstage played to an audience of eight. That evening, a young man came to his dressing room and asked Edwards to come to his office the next Monday at 10:00 A.M. But the Saturday night before, Edwards and some friends went to Tijuana for some fun and stayed until late the next day.

When he missed the Monday-morning meeting, his manager called and asked what had happened, threatening to come to Edwards's place and drag him to the appointment. By twelve noon, Edwards was in the young man's office. It was producer Stanley Kramer, who informed him of his plans to make a movie about racism in the American military. But first he had to find the right black actor for the pivotal role. "I told Mr. Kramer, I'd play the part just for three meals a day and a place to sleep," said Edwards. "Money was unimportant. This is the kind of role that happens only once in any actor's life." The film *Home of the Brave* transformed Edwards into a symbol of a new era for African Americans in movies. "He was at the time the only really famous black actor," actress Diahann Carroll recalled, "who had done the undoable by creating an image of the black man as a sensitive, intelligent, articulate human being who had to be reckoned with."

Edwards knew fortune had smiled on him. He was now thirty-three years old. At that age, most actors who hadn't made it knew that time was running out. Maybe that fear of not having much time propelled and also unnerved him. Considered "artistic," smart, moody, edgy, and a little crazy in the way that talented offbeat actors were supposed to be during the postwar era of Brando, Clift, and James Dean, he was rumored to be a heavy drinker, a womanizer, and at times, his own worst enemy. What happens to a man who is regarded by his own community as a star and who enjoys playing the part, who looks like a star, dresses like a star, lives like a star—yet knows, in essence, that no one is beating down a door to give him work, that each time he goes to the office of a producer or director for an interview, it is like starting out all over again? What was Edwards to do when, not long after his rise, his career stalled?

Eventually, two damning stories about Edwards made the rounds and surely affected his career. Each story also had an impact because of the times—and the atmosphere in Hollywood, about which Edwards apparently didn't give a damn. The first concerned Edwards's politics.

During these years of the Cold War, Edwards found an industry, much like himself, locked in a frenzy of doubt and paranoia. But Hollywood's concerns were about communist infiltration. Accused of dramatizing pro-communist doctrines as well as harboring creative artists who were "Red," the motion-picture industry had come under the scrutiny of the government. What kind of screen messages were Hollywood movies promulgating? What were the political affiliations, past and present, of stars, writers, directors, producers? Publications such as *Attack, Counter Attack,* and especially *Red Channels* listed artists thought to be communist or communist sympathizers. The House Committee on Un-American Activities called Hollywood personalities to testify about their own political activities or to name names of others in the business with "Red" connections.

Stars such as Robert Taylor and Adolphe Menjou testified before the committee, eager to profess their pro-American attitudes and convictions. Studio executives such as Jack Warner and Louis B. Mayer cooperated with the committee, promising to weed out subversive writers and directors. Director Elia Kazan and writer Clifford Odets were among those who named friends and associates who had been members of the party. A group of creative artists that became known as the Hollywood Ten, which included writer Dalton Trumbo and producer/director Herbert Biberman, refused to divulge their political affiliation, were tried in the U.S. Federal Court in Washington, D.C., convicted of contempt of Congress, and sentenced to a year in prison. Studio blacklists were created of those actors, actresses, writers, directors, and producers whose politics were questionable. Many careers were wrecked.

For Black Hollywood, the focus during this era of witch hunts was on a star who was only an occasional West Coast sojourner: Paul Robeson. Always outspoken about racial, social, and political issues, Robeson supported the Soviet Union before and during the war, when it had been an

American ally, and then afterward, when the Soviet Union was not. Refusing to change his politics, Robeson found himself hounded and haunted, his career left in shambles.

The activities and affiliations of other African American stars were also scrutinized. Lists were drawn up of rallies and benefits they had attended as well as their relationships with other supposedly "Red" associates. Lena Horne said that her friendship with Robeson made her suspect. So did her activities in HICCASP, the Hollywood Independent Citizens Committee of Arts, Sciences, and Professions. Along with Hazel Scott and Fredi Washington, Horne was listed in *Red Channels.* "I was unable, during the early fifties, to get on any television programs," she said. When Sidney Poitier's "loyalty" was questioned—just before he was to play an important role in a New York production—he was asked to repudiate Robeson and actor Canada Lee. In the end, he repudiated neither. Dandridge's association with HICCASP as well as her attendance at political rallies were questioned. When she had given a fundraiser for *The California Eagle* at her home, Robeson had been a guest. Asked to sign a loyalty oath, Dandridge, said Geri Branton, flatly refused. But before MGM signed her for the lead in *Bright Road,* Dandridge had to write a letter to Nicholas Schenck, the president of MGM's parent company, Loew's, explaining her political activities and even her decision to study at the Actors Lab, which was considered a "Red" hangout. For Dandridge, as for other black actors and actresses who studied there, the Actors Lab was not only an institution where they could hone their craft but also an integrated, open, progressive environment. In a very touching manner, Dandridge wrote only in glowing terms of her Actors Lab experience. "It was a terrible time for so many people," said Branton.

In the midst of these fears, James Edwards announced at a meeting of HICCASP that he had been visited by three FBI agents who asked him to denounce Robeson. He refused. Yet by going on the public record about the visit, Edwards may have hurt his career.

Another story, true or not, linked Edwards with a glamorous blonde star under contract to MGM. At a party, the two were said to have argued. In a fit of anger, Edwards allegedly slapped her. In Hollywood, a fast-moving rumor that had a shelf life and refused to die could be more detrimental to a career than the truth.

By 1954, Edwards appeared opposite Dorothy Dandridge in *her* screen test for Otto Preminger's *Carmen Jones.* But when Preminger shot the film, Harry Belafonte was cast as Dandridge's love interest. Ultimately, the other big roles of the decade went to Poitier. Most in Black Hollywood sadly watched Edwards's decline. When she first arrived in Los Angeles— at age nineteen—to play a supporting role in *Carmen Jones,* Diahann Carroll was transfixed by the handsome Edwards, who she thought was "one of the most seductive men" she had ever met, with "a kind of animalistic awareness of himself that made me feel feminine yet somewhat on edge."

When he asked her out, she was thrilled, though she knew he was married. "I saw the nice house, the expensive clothes, the big convertible, and all the other accoutrements of success," said Carroll. But up close, she witnessed his frustrations and torment. "I listened to him carry on about how he was meeting producers and developing projects and negotiating for the lead in this or that movie, and I bought every word of it, even though for one reason or another none of these prospects ever materialized. I thought he was wonderful." Still, Edwards "always smelled of alcohol. He drank constantly from morning until night. He was always full of anger, vengeance and pain. 'You know what I did yesterday?' he would ask, then tell me about how he screwed some producer's wife and, small world, would be seeing her husband tomorrow about a job. Then he'd go on to regale me with stories about the scandalous personal lives of all the powers in the business and how this s.o.b. owed him and this so-and-so better do what he wanted."

Though he frequented restaurants in Beverly Hills and Hollywood, he was rarely welcomed. It was known in town that he might explode at any given moment. "He'd create a nasty scene, start a fight with the waiter or threaten the people at the next table." Yet she saw a different Edwards when they dined in the dying black part of town. "Everyone realized he drank too much and misbehaved," said Carroll, "but they loved him and treated him like a king, allowing him to salvage some small shred of his tattered pride."

No matter what, Carroll was drawn to him, always fascinated. "I was skinny, devoid of sexuality, not really attractive," she said. "So when someone found me attractive, I didn't choose—I jumped." She waited in anticipation for the moment when their relationship would be consummated. One evening after she sat in a bar with him, he took her upstairs to a bedroom and asked her to remove her clothes, which she did. "I knew it didn't have anything to do with sex," said Carroll. "For all his stories about his sexual conquests, there was no sex between us, no displays of affection— no hugging or kissing or tenderness. Maybe he was turned off by my naivete and inexperience. Maybe the booze and the sense of failure and the years of using and abusing everyone including himself had finally taken their toll and burned him out. He just sat there staring at me for the next hour, and then he got up to leave."

Edwards kept working in films such as *Battle Hymn, The Manchurian Candidate,* and *The Sandpiper* and in television. For a time, he was signed—as a writer—at Universal-International Studios. He also worked closely with Nick Stewart's Ebony Showcase productions. He also wrote and appeared in West Coast stage productions. In any place other than Hollywood, he would have been considered at least *reasonably* successful. But by industry standards—and in all likelihood, by his own—he had failed to fulfill his early promise. The big roles hadn't come. "Jim Edwards was not prepared to compromise or duck," said Ossie Davis, "to make that adjustment which would make white folks comfortable. Not at all." Most painful for him must have been seeing Poitier's success—and perhaps even Carroll's first flush of acclaim. It was rumored that the drinking continued, along with some reckless behavior.

Years later, Diahann Caroll saw Edwards on Sunset Boulevard. "I suppose he was afraid I'd flaunt my success in his face. But I planted myself in his path, gave him a big hug, and insisted he stop to talk. I was devastated by his looks. The alcohol had ravaged him, and he seemed very sad and defeated. Yet he was still quite beautiful, and much more soft and gentle than the James I had known. I told him that I'd heard he had married a beautiful young girl who adored him. He said, yes, that was true." The two parted. "We were both late for our appointments, so we wished each other luck and went our separate ways. A few months later I read in the paper that he had died."

INTERRACIAL ROMANCE: THE ENDURING TABOO

As much as Hollywood adjusted to the new attitudes about African American roles in movies and, in some cases, to more open socializing between the races, the taboo of interracial romance and marriages was not so easily broken. There had been well-known interracial marriages in New York and abroad. Katherine Dunham married her company's set designer, John Pratt. Josephine Baker had audaciously acquired a string of European lovers and husbands. But these were not Hollywood stars. Though the industry had many open secrets (such as a performer's sexuality—notably, that of an actor such as Rock Hudson in the 1950s), interracial relationships were an entirely different matter and were usually *secret* secrets. Otherwise, as silent-screen actress Helen Lee Worthing had learned decades earlier, a career could be destroyed.

Industry insiders were aware of Lena Horne's relationship with Lennie Hayton, the white arranger/composer at MGM. Yet so concerned was Lena Horne about public reactions, black and white, to an interracial marriage that, in 1947, she slipped into a black Balenciaga dress and quietly married Lennie Hayton in Paris. "It wasn't easy to make the decision to marry," said Horne. "But we did marry, and they didn't kill us." Interracial marriages were also still illegal in California. When Horne told family members of the marriage, they stopped speaking to her, she said. There was a rift with her father. Otherwise, the couple kept the union a secret for three years. Even Horne's daughter Gail was sworn to secrecy. The couple moved into a home in Nichols Canyon in Beverly Hills. Some neighbors protested, but gradually, the two were accepted. Still, because Horne was often on tour, the two were rarely together in public. Finally, columnist Louella Parsons got Lena to admit to the marriage. Horne also feared criticism from the Negro press.

Just the mere sight of an interracial Hollywood couple was enough to set tongues indignantly wagging. In the late 1940s, at a benefit for the Actors Lab, Anthony Quinn had asked Dorothy Dandridge to dance. As Quinn held the ravishing Dandridge in his arms, none of the Actors Lab students or faculty—already considered bohemian and politically radical—thought anything about it. But word leaked out—and Jim Henaghan, a columnist for *The Hollywood Reporter*, was up in arms: "We've been swamped with protests from the Sunset Strip area the last couple of days objecting to the 'impromptu' show put on by Actors Lab Players. . . . The report has it that mixed dancing, Colored and Whites, and the overall tenor of the program was pretty party-linish. There is also a report that the studios which subsidized the so-called school for actors by sending them youngsters for training are mulling dumping the group."

Joining the outraged chorus was Hedda Hopper, who commented on the event in her *Los Angeles Times* column. "The Actors Lab made no friends when they gave an open-air barbecue, which included dancing between Whites and Negroes," wrote Hopper. "The situation has nothing whatever to do with racial prejudice or discrimination; every man in the world is as good as he is in his heart, regardless of race, creed or color. But that doesn't mean they have to intermix. Right or wrong, the great balance

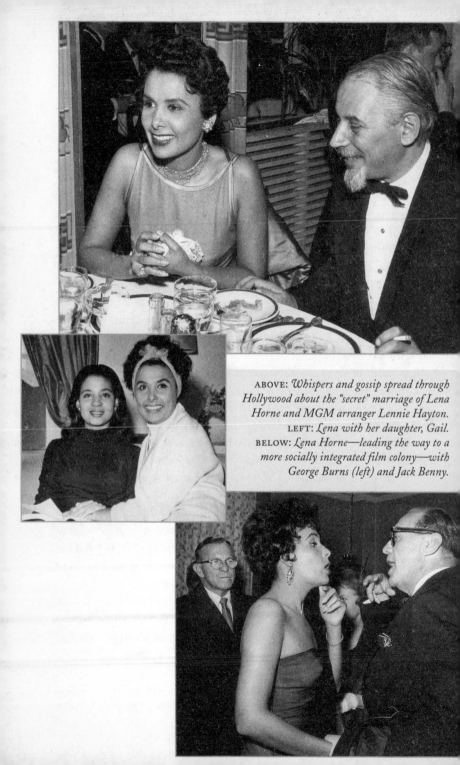

ABOVE: *Whispers and gossip spread through Hollywood about the "secret" marriage of Lena Horne and MGM arranger Lennie Hayton.*
LEFT: *Lena with her daughter, Gail.*
BELOW: *Lena Horne—leading the way to a more socially integrated film colony—with George Burns (left) and Jack Benny.*

of the community has the deep-rooted conviction, and they were shocked at this display by the Actors Lab." Hopper also believed that such race mixing could lead to race riots!

Yet in the Eisenhower era, a few stars were more open. When Marlon Brando arrived on the West Coast in the late 1940s to film *The Men,* he was already an established Broadway star, following his legendary appearance in *A Streetcar Named Desire.* Considered a maverick, ever ready to shake up the status quo, refusing to live by the old star rules and fears, refusing also to court the gossip columnists Hedda Hopper and Louella Parsons, he shocked the town by showing up at events in a T-shirt and jeans. Stories spread about his preference for "exotic" darker women. Seemingly unfazed by what anyone might think, Brando was seen with the young black actress Lena Torrence. Dark-skinned, shapely, and ambitious, Torrence had studied for a while at the Actors Lab and was considered within Black Hollywood one of its promising starlets when she made the cover of the Negro publication *Our World* in a pose every bit as seductive as Monroe's during the era. But Torrence got nowhere with her career. Her relationship with Brando made the news in the black press. But mainstream periodicals either didn't know about the couple or chose to politely ignore them. Brando also took a special interest in newcomer Diahann Carroll.

Another rebel, new in town, was Eartha Kitt. Stardom was still new to her. Born in South Carolina, she had gone to New York, at age eight, to live with her aunt. Fascinated by the city, she studied dance and toured with Katherine Dunham's troupe. In 1946, she had come to Hollywood when Dunham with her company appeared in the film *Casbah.* Though Dunham stayed in a home in Beverly Hills, the rest of the company "was assigned places to live: the Black area only." Later, while touring in Europe with Dunham, Kitt struck out on her own. Openly captivated by her when they met in Paris, Orson Welles cast Kitt as Helen of Troy in his production of *Faust.* He also proclaimed her the most exciting woman in the world.

Once back in the United States, Kitt struggled to make a name for herself, then finally succeeded on Broadway in *New Faces of 1952.* Touring with the show, she arrived in Los Angeles in 1953 and stayed at the Garden of Allah—far from Central Avenue. Located on Sunset Boulevard, the Garden of Allah, like its nearby neighbor, the Chateau Marmont, was not one of Hollywood's lush, grand hotels such as The Beverly Hills Hotel or the Beverly Wilshire. Established by the legendary stage and silent-screen star Alla Nazimova, the Garden of Allah was a series of cottages where legendary literary and artistic figures had stayed. Kitt felt she could live wherever she chose. Forget those old social or residential restrictions. But later, when Kitt tried to buy a home in Bel Air, she was turned down. The real estate agents were quite open about what had happened, explaining "over lunch that the neighbors in Bel Air were nervous about a colored person moving into the area." Eventually, she purchased a beautiful home sitting on two acres of land in Beverly Hills.

During her initial stay in Los Angeles, Kitt maintained an often-grueling schedule. In the mornings, she worked on a movie version of *New Faces of 1954,* then performed in the stage version in the evening, and afterward appeared at the Mocambo, where business was brisk. As with Horne and Dandridge, the club brought her to the attention of the big names in the industry, including Arthur Loew Jr., the heir to Loew's, Inc., then an executive at MGM. Well bred and sensitive, Loew had a reputation as a dashing young man-about-town. Before long, he was dashing about town with Kitt. For a brief time, the two settled into Loew's house on Miller Drive, with Kitt moving her things into the second bedroom. "Hollywood gossip columnists such as Hedda Hopper and Sheila [*sic*] Graham were all for the relationship between Loew and me," said Kitt. "They said they had never seen Loew so happy." Graham was liberal. But given Hopper's conservatism—and her reaction to interracial dancing at the Actors Lab—one questions Hopper's enthusiasm for this match.

Their relationship certainly was whispered about within the movie colony. Then it was publicly exposed in the pages of a new scandal magazine called *Confidential.* The precursor to such later tabloid publications as *The National Enquirer* and *Star, Confidential* was the first full-scale publication to specialize in uncovering Hollywood's lurid underbelly, all those clandestine meetings and pairings, all those drunken brawls, all those marital infidelities, all those previously unprintable peccadilloes. In the past, the studios had wielded enough power to cover up details of what could have been big scandals. But now, with their decline and with the end of those long-term contracts that meant stars were significant studio investments, the stars were left on their own. Rather than settling for glossies, *Confidential* sought photos of stars caught off guard, looking disheveled or distressed. Those Hollywood icons of physical perfection now appeared tawdry and trashy. *Confidential* also dared to speak of the two big movieland kinds of stories of which Hedda and Louella knew but didn't touch: gay life and interracial love in Hollywood.

The magazine appeared to delight in exposing or suggesting interracial relationships. One issue reported on Sammy Davis Jr.'s "friendship" with Ava Gardner. "What Makes AVA GARDNER Run for SAMMY DAVIS JR.? Some girls go for gold, but it's bronze that 'sends' sultry Ava." Another ran a cover photo of Davis and a young white woman with a banner that read, "Heard the Latest about Sammy Davis Jr.?" Another ran a picture of Kitt on its cover with the words "Eartha Kitt and the Man Who Sat There—All Night." "If you're wondering how a fellow can find himself stranded in the heart of New York with a desirable damsel, it can happen," read the article. "The elevator that went to [Eartha's] penthouse stopped at 4 A.M. . . . There were no stairs and if you wanted to get out in a hurry . . . you'd have to jump out the window, but no one ever did. One guy almost did—but not because he wanted to. He was free, white and over 21, but there he was, caged up in the clouds with Eartha." Of Kitt and Loew, *Confidential* declared, "When Eartha comes to Hollywood, she and Arthur Loew Junior set up white and tan housekeeping."

Yet another issue ran a story about Dorothy Dandridge's reported romantic romp in the woods with a white musician. Outraged by what she called a lie, Dandridge was one of the few stars, black or white, to sue the publication—and to win a settlement. Other scandal magazines such as *Uncensored, Whisper, Hush-Hush,* and *Inside News* hit the newsstands. Black stars had never had this kind of coverage. Though the lively publication *Jet* reported in some detail on very public black star scandals and though Negro newspapers could sometimes be critical, the black publications such as *Ebony, Our World,* and *Hue* promoted black stars as beacons of success for race emulation. *Ebony* commented on Kitt's supposed attraction to white males, but its article was hardly sensationalized. But now, the black stars had become such mainstream celebrities that they were as open as any other Hollywood stars to such tabloid exposure.

Studio heads and executives took note of *Confidential*'s tales of interracial hanky-panky. But the industry maintained a double standard. Relationships between white men and beautiful black female stars might be tolerated as long as those relationships were not discussed in the press and certainly not publicly exposed. In the case of Eartha Kitt and Arthur Loew Jr., the studio executives seemed blasé. Her platonic friendship with James Dean, whom she knew from New York, went unnoticed. Though Kitt would appear in such movies as *Mark of the Hawk, Anna Lucasta,* and *St. Louis Blues,* she was never considered a Hollywood star. And, frankly, the town didn't seem to care much about anything she did. The Loew/Kitt relationship ended anyway.

The new scandal magazines that titillated readers with stories about the great Hollywood taboo, interracial love.

NOW—SURGERY CURES FRIGID

Confidentia

...S AND NAMES THE NAMES July

WHEN NANCY KELLY LEARNED HER LOVE SCENES IN A CAR...

ANTHONY QUINN CAUGHT WITH A GA... IN A POWDER ROOM

...BEHIND ...OTTA'S ...TION

EARTHA KITT AND THE MAN WHO SA... THERE — ALL NIGHT

What the U.N. Is Hiding... **THE TRUTH ABOUT WHITE SLAVERY!**

UNCENSORED

DEC. 25¢

WHAT AVA FOUND IN FRANKIE'S BOUDOIR!

PHIL SILVERS: Why Babes are Bad for Sgt. BILKO

THE UNTOLD STORY OF MALE NURSES

Why Stewart Granger needs Dale Carnegie!

THE WHISPERS ADLAI STEVENSON COULDN'T STOP!

ANITA EKBERG'S 'FORGOTTEN MAN'

ELVIS PRESLEY: Is He Marvel or Menace?

HOW THAT MAE WEST SCANDAL STARTED!

THE LOVE HIDEOUT OF DOROTHY DANDRIDGE

Horne, however, was now considered part of Hollywood. The fact that she married Hayton—and perhaps the fact that she was often out of town on tour and still a favorite of the New York critics—eventually made their union acceptable and even palatable. Secretly, those powerful executives, much like Joe Schenck, no doubt harbored fantasies of holding Horne in their arms. The same held true for Dandridge. In time, her public appearances with white escorts became accepted. Dandridge, however, felt compelled to keep her two most serious interracial romances secret for years. During the era, the marriage of Pearl Bailey and white drummer Louis Bellson made headlines. For a time, the two had a home in Hollywood. Yet like Kitt, Bailey was never really a Hollywood personality, and in time, the marriage was accepted.

But the industry had a different attitude about black male stars who became involved with white female stars. Black actors such as Sidney Poitier and Harry Belafonte would eventually marry white women. But their wives were not big stars. The same was true of Herb Jeffries, who raised some eyebrows when he first married Elizabeth Alinsworth, a Rose Bowl Queen, and later the white stripper—or rather, *exotique* dancer—Tempest Storm. But again, neither was considered a part of the industry. So no pressures were exerted on Jeffries to end the romances before they led to marriage. Jeffries and the East Coast–based Belafonte also didn't depend on Hollywood for their livelihoods. So neither seemed to care what anyone thought of his marriages.

But anger and animosities could flare up if a black man became involved with a white female star. No doubt James Edwards came to understand the effect of even such a rumor on a career. At the same time, Sammy Davis Jr.'s courtship of white women made him—for a time—controversial, contemptible, and even something of a joke. He was considered too puny and ugly to be a dashing dark Lothario. Yet a joke that had to be taken seriously. At Columbia Pictures, where blonde Kim Novak was the studio's new box-office sensation, studio chief Harry Cohn reportedly was enraged by the stories of a Davis/Novak dalliance, which first surfaced after Chicago newspaper columnist Irv Kupcinet reported that Davis had spent time with Novak's family in Chicago. Cohn was also puzzled. "I could understand Belafonte," Cohn reportedly said, "but him!" For years, even decades afterward, the rumors ran rampant that the Mafia, at Cohn's behest, put a hit on Davis and caused the car accident in which he lost an eye. Never mind that the accident occurred in 1954, before Davis had even met Novak! Such was the power of the taboo.

Kim Novak later acknowledged that the studio told her not to see Davis and "put guards in my house and all that." She heard the stories that Cohn threatened to take out Davis's *other* eye. Novak believed that Davis "did get frightened by the threat of the studio." But the rumors were only rumors. "He was like a friend. But it was not romantic," said Novak. "But even if it were, I saw nothing wrong with that." The studio's attitude, however, made her defiant. "I felt like who's going to say because he's black that you shouldn't see each other. He was a great friend." Yet when Novak was asked whether Davis was in love with her, she said, "I think he was."

Ironically, the public coverage of the interracial relationships, romances, and marriages brought the black stars more into the mainstream.

NEW-STYLE STAR POWER: REDEFINING THE TOWN, RECONFIGURING ITS BORDERS

During the Eisenhower era, Hollywood, black and white, was ultimately redefined by three major black stars. Essential to the new way Black Hollywood lived—and the way it viewed itself—were the careers and social lives of Nat "King" Cole, the suave sophisticate who rarely made a false move; Sammy Davis Jr., the young extroverted dynamo who crossed social/racial/class boundaries in a daring way; and Dorothy Dandridge, the greatest movie star symbol of all, who exuded a glamour and an audacity, and ultimately a tragic grandeur that was unprecedented in Black Hollywood's history. As former child stars of the prewar era, Dandridge and Davis also represented a bridge between the old and the new Black Hollywood.

NAT "KING" COLE

By the early 1950s, Nat Cole had already been in the film capital for well over ten years. Born Nathaniel Adams Coles on St. Patrick's Day, 1919, in Montgomery, Alabama, one of six children of a minister, Edward James Coles, and his homemaker wife, Perlina Adams Coles (later, Nat would drop the *s* from his surname), he grew up mostly in Chicago. Precocious, he was playing the piano by age eight, performed with amateur groups, and at sixteen, opened at Chicago's Savoy Ballroom. In January 1937, he married a young dancer named Nadine Robinson, whom he met in Chicago. Together, the couple went to Los Angeles. Without much money, they lived simply in a home apparently owned by one of Nadine's relatives in the Forties near Avalon. Later, they moved to South St. Andrew Place off Adams Boulevard. On the West Coast, he took work wherever he could, sometimes playing at clubs for five dollars a night, and for a time, wrote arrangements for The Dandridge Sisters. He also rehearsed at the home of future singing star Nellie Lutcher.

Recognized by musicians as a gifted pianist, he had an appealing laid-back urbane sophistication. The essence of his very cool persona was that nothing seemed to faze him. No one could have predicted where he was headed, but he seemed headed *somewhere*. Yet stardom didn't come easily. In 1938, he formed the first King Cole Trio, with guitarist Oscar Moore and bassist Wesley Prince, two men familiar with the California music scene. When Mickey Rooney pretended to strum the guitar in *Girl Crazy*, it was actually Moore who performed. By 1943, Prince had left the trio, replaced by Johnny Miller. During these years, Cole, hardly known for his singing, developed into a fine and underrated jazz pianist. Then the trio signed with Capitol Records and, with Nat doing the vocals, recorded the song "Straighten Up and Fly Right," which, by May 1944, climbed the pop charts from number eight to number three and sold half a million copies. "I'll never forget it," Cole said. "One night we closed at the 331 Club in Los Angeles at about $400 a week, and the next day we were making $1000 at the Orpheum." Other hits, such as "Sweet Lorraine" and "The Christmas Song," followed. The group performed on its own NBC radio show, *King Cole Trio Time*.

The Cole career and life underwent their greatest change in 1946, when Cole was booked for a month at the Club Zanzibar in New York. Also appearing was a young singer named Marie Ellington. "She was a good-looking woman," said Bobby Short. "Very good-looking and had gone to some sort of black finishing school on the East Coast, and she had high ideas about this and about that and about the other."

Born Marie Hawkins in Massachusetts, she was the second of three daughters of a black postal worker named Mingo Hawkins and his wife, Carol, who died giving birth to her third child. Mingo's sister, the educator Dr. Charlotte Hawkins Brown, took the children south to live with her in Sedalia, North Carolina. There, she headed the Negro school the Palmer Memorial Institute. In many respects, despite the rigid racial lines drawn in the South, the three Hawkins sisters had a rather privileged childhood. Taught the importance of grooming, manners, carriage, and proper speech, they were exposed to a host of luminaries who visited their aunt's school: Eleanor Roosevelt, Mary McLeod Bethune, and W.E.B.

Du Bois. The educated, polished, and ambitious Marie Hawkins Ellington's background impressed Nat *and* later Hollywood.

After high school, Marie studied at Boston Clerical College. But she had far different aspirations than sitting at a typewriter all day. She wanted a career as a singer. She had a good voice. And she had a good look. She understood the appeal of simplicity and understatement. Slender and stylish, she wore clothes well, with her hair often pulled back from her face and sometimes tied at the nape of her neck. Following an early short-lived marriage to a young serviceman named Ellington, who died in an accident in 1945, her career became her priority. Known for a time as Marie Hawkins, then Marie Ellington, and later Maria, she was an ever-climbing girl singer who performed with the big bands of Benny Carter, Fletcher Henderson, and Duke Ellington. Contrary to what some assumed, she and Duke Ellington were not related. Then, she struck out on her own. Though some critics thought she showed potential—and Duke appeared to genuinely like her—others believed that her voice was not distinct enough to carry her to the top ranks of stardom. Regardless, upon meeting Nat Cole at the Zanzibar, everything changed for Maria—and for Nat.

Seeing a potential in Nat that Nat himself apparently had not realized, she helped him to redefine himself, to develop a more sophisticated style of dress, demeanor, and speech. She persuaded him to sing more in his act—and to stand up with a mike in his hand rather than sit at the piano. Eventually, Nat left the trio.

The romance with Maria was serious enough for Cole to decide to divorce Nadine, who was well liked in entertainment circles. Yet, said Bobby Short, "I don't think anybody was particularly taken aback when Nat divorced Nadine." In Hollywood, it was no doubt assumed that at some point, as Nat became more successful, he would move on to a new wife. That kind of thing happened all the time. But the fact that the new wife would be Maria was another matter altogether. "I just think people were generally sort of surprised and curious, of course," recalled Short. "They were very curious about Maria because Maria was from the East. *The East* was a very popular phrase out there. *Back east.* She came from *back east.* And so, when she arrived, several of Nat's old friends had parties for her." Her style and attitude made her the subject of many a conversation in Black Hollywood. Nat and Maria married in 1948. That same year, Cole had a huge hit, "Nature Boy," which sold 1,500,000 copies. It "removed his singing from the 'race artist' category," wrote *Ebony,* and thrust him into the national spotlight, where he would remain for the rest of his life. And the Nat/Maria marriage and luxurious lifestyle would long arouse the curiosity of Black Hollywood.

Their honeymoon in Mexico put the couple on the cover of *Ebony*. A photographer from the magazine had accompanied them to document their every move. The cover photo oozed a newfound star power: There was Nat, in swim trunks with a towel over his shoulder, gazing with joy and admiration at Maria, standing and showing off her terrific figure and legs, in a one-piece bathing suit with a swim cap and a towel slung over her shoulder.

For postwar black America, few magazine covers could match it in sheer glamour and sexy sophistication. *Ebony*, however, would raise the bar and continue to have a steady array of dazzlers: Herb Jeffries, spiffy and bad-dude sexy with his former Rose Bowl Queen of a wife by his side; Dorothy Dandridge, unbelievably beautiful and composed as she sat in her ultramodern Hollywood Hills home. White stars had long been presented to the public in this way. Now, *Ebony* established an iconography for black stars. Founded in 1945, *Ebony*—along with such other black glossies as *Our World, Sepia,* and the pocket-size *Jet* and *Hue*—continued the tradition begun in the entertainment pages of *The California Eagle, The Pittsburgh Courier,* and *The Los Angeles Sentinel* of adding even more structure to the concept of a glamorous Black Hollywood, making it even more cohesive. At this point, of course, the mainstream media would start to cover such black stars but certainly still wouldn't provide the reader with a sense of a black entertainment community; *that* was the aim of the Negro press.

In the years to come, Nat and Maria would regularly turn up on other *Ebony* covers as the magazine chronicled their comings and goings. In the 1940s, Adam Clayton Powell Jr. and his second wife, Hazel Scott, had represented the modern black couple: educated, articulate, attractive, and highly motivated with a strong social/political consciousness. Now, in the 1950s, Nat and Maria were depicted as the ideal Hollywood Negro couple: bright, sophisticated, and working together for a common goal. That goal was Nat's career, yet Maria never really discarded her own ambitions.

One year after the marriage, Nat and Maria were in the headlines. Like those black residents of Sugar Hill, the couple branched out from the Negro dwelling areas created by the restrictive covenants. They purchased—for the then-hefty sum of sixty-five thousand dollars—a twelve-room, redbrick English Tudor–style home on Muirfield Road in Los Angeles's Hancock Park. A wealthy and exclusive area where lawyers, physicians, oilmen, and even the governor resided, Hancock Park was

Nat "King" Cole's famous home—on the front of a postcard.

lined with large, splendidly designed homes with an infinite variety of stunning trees, shrubs, and flowers in beautifully landscaped lawns and gardens. Driveways—sometimes sweeping, sometimes sedate—led to two-car garages. In the back of the homes were patios, swimming pools, and guest houses. At one time, Maria hoped to buy a home in Connecticut. "Are you kidding?" Nat said. "I love Los Angeles." When the Realtor first took the couple inside the home, Nat exclaimed, "This is it." Hancock Park appeared to be an ideal community. It was also all-white.

Once the news broke of the Coles' purchase of the home, some members of the seemingly ideal community turned vicious and ugly. Both the previous owner and the Realtor who had negotiated the sale received anonymous threatening phone calls. The Hancock Park Property Owners Association was formed, at one point offering to buy the house back from Cole at a profit. Nat refused. The Coles were threatened with a lawsuit. The family, it was argued, had no legal right to live there. This was August 1948, only a few months after a Supreme Court decision had struck down the restrictive covenants. Once Nat and Maria moved in, a sign appeared on their lawn that read "Nigger Heaven." One night, gunshots went off, shattering windows in the home.

Cole appeared to take it in stride. Beneath his calm, smooth demeanor—which continued to enhance his star appeal—Nat hid his emotions and inner conflicts, and no one was ever quite sure of his true feelings. During the years of touring, no matter the hotels and other accommodations, no matter the lousy food on the road, no matter the hassles of traveling, Nat was known never to complain about anything. Though he held his ground about the home, he was never considered a real fighter, especially during the rise of the civil rights movement. Not so Maria. With the kind of extroverted determination and single-mindedness that had carried her to Hollywood and now this celebrated marriage, Maria kept everything front and center—and never backed off from a fight. The Coles had no intention of leaving. Certainly, Maria didn't. To hell with the neighbors. By God, it was her property, and she was going to make the Muirfield Road residence a showplace, the most beautiful of all the homes in Hancock Park.

"When Nat and Maria bought that house in Hancock Park," said Bobby Short, "they called up the most expensive decorator in Beverly Hills to do the house. And I know because a friend of mine worked for him. And he came out to me one day and said, 'Oh, I've got a new job for this couple.' He said, 'I think she's Duke Ellington's daughter. And I met him. And he's just nothing at all.' And I thought to myself, 'Who can they be?' And then it turns out it was Nat Cole and Maria."

Beverly Hills designer Tom Douglas worked with Maria Cole to create a California-modern setting with "accents in bold colors." The April 1949 issue of *Ebony* rhapsodized over the house, describing it in vivid detail. Entering the house, one stepped through a massive oak-paneled door. The living room was appointed with striking, expensive black lacquer pieces: "black lacquer modern Regency chairs with tight button-tufted seats in butterfly yellow satin"; black lacquer coffee tables with a gunmetal glass top "and marbleized black lacquer pedestals." Guests could sink into an eight-foot custom-built sofa or the four armchairs done in white quilted silk and chartreuse. Illuminating the room were six thirty-inch column lamps with white and salmon-colored silk shades. Painted onto a four-foot by four-foot mirror was a scene by a Chinese artist, its patterns given radiance by neon tubing. Another thirteen-foot-wide mirror went from floor to ceiling.

From the living room, guests could step into the large sixteen-foot by thirty-foot dining room—its centerpiece, a silver-leaf table surrounded by twelve chairs upholstered in butter yellow antique, all sitting on a green-

Nat, the family man, with the best-known of Black Hollywood's wives, Maria Cole, and the Cole daughters, Carol and Natalie.

stained floor. There was also a rumpus room with a pool table, a poker table, a built-in bar, a piano, a small bandstand, and windows that looked out onto a garden. Upstairs, the master bedroom was swankily done in baby blue and pink with a king-size bed and a five-foot by eight-foot headboard done in antique pink satin with white trim. A two-foot cornice stood over the bed. On the floor was a white string carpet. The walls and ceiling were done in blue. There were white satin armchairs with pink trim, a leather-topped desk, and a white fireplace, above which was a painting of—who else but—Maria. Shortly after the couple's first anniversary, when the interior decoration was completed, plans were made for a music room, a nursery, and a guest room. Maria Cole had her showplace.

The couple entertained lavishly. Like other Hollywood wives, Maria had her charities—and her charity events. What better suited one's image as a grand, socially conscious hostess? One such affair was a summer garden party for the benefit of Maria's group the Hill Toppers Charity Guild to raise money for the Damon Runyon Cancer Fund. Some 350 guests were seated on the back lawn of the home by the flower-strewn swimming pool, where they were treated to a fashion show titled "The Glamour of

Summer Travel." In attendance were stars, including singer Billy Eckstine, boxer Sugar Ray Robinson, and Harry Belafonte. Modeling the clothes were the wives of such stars as Eckstine and TV cowboy hero Guy Madison—as well as a few professional models such as the young Barbara January, who later became the third Mrs. Fayard Nicholas. Recording the proceedings with his home movie camera was a cool and debonair Nat, so caught up in his role as movie director that he accidentally walked backward into the swimming pool! Of course, that mishap only made the proceedings all the more memorable. All the guests marveled that it was a wonderful, wonderful afternoon. How did Maria do it all?

But Maria did. She knew which silver, china, and crystal added the right touch for a particular occasion. Both she and Nat were fashion plates. Not only was she known for having an impeccable eye for her own wardrobe, but she understood which clothes—and no doubt, which tailor—suited Nat best. Maria always shopped for the best clothes, by the best designers, at the best stores. Always slender with great legs and with hair always appropriately coiffed and makeup always subtly but expertly applied, she was never seen in public not looking like a star. Likewise, she and Nat had a model family life. They adopted two children: little Carol, whom they called Cookie, the daughter of Maria's deceased sister; and later a son named Kelly. Maria also bore Nat three children: a daughter Natalie and twins, Timolin and Casey (named after the Yankee's Casey Stengel). Maria's sister Charlotte Hawkins Sullivan lived with the family, the perfect trusted aunt who could look out for the children when Maria was away with Nat.

Able to socialize with black *and* white, Maria could hold her own with almost anyone, be it Sinatra, Lena, Harry, Ava, Sammy, or Jack Benny. She struck up friendships with Geri Nicholas and Dorothy Dandridge, two other women of style and presence with whom it seemed appropriate to be seen. Dandridge was even asked to be godmother to Maria's twins. Could anything have been more perfectly Hollywood?

EISENHOWER-AGE HOLLYWOOD WIVES

In short, Maria Cole became the prototypical Hollywood wife of the 1950s. Before her, Fannie Robinson had been outgoing and apparently sweet-tempered, there to please Bojangles and certainly not one to call the shots. During her years in Hollywood and afterward, Gladys Hampton still possessed perhaps the greatest managerial skills, cognizant of the fine print in her husband's contracts and socially skillful enough to make important professional contacts without alienating anyone. In the 1940s, Dandridge and Geri had been modern and forward-looking. Dottie brought her glamour to her marriage with Harold Nicholas as well as the ability to keep the guests in her home entertained. Because she had been Hollywood-bred, socializing in the movie capital was second nature to her—and she had not thought seriously of her role as Harold's wife. Geri clearly had the right look—a well-dressed knockout. And she enjoyed the social interplay. But she kept everything in perspective. Brainy, political, and known for her intelligence and outspokenness, she didn't put much stock in the unending stream of material acquisitions that was so important in Hollywood life. Nor was she—or Dandridge, for that matter—bent on social climbing. Her identity went beyond being Mrs. Fayard Nicholas. Over the years, she took courses at colleges and universities at home and abroad, learning more about the world and herself: classes in history, sociology, psychology.

n the 1950s, she divorced Fayard, became a successful real estate agent, and with her 1956 marriage to the prominent Los Angeles lawyer Leo Branton, she entered a new phase of her life. The couple had a son, Chip. Her husband, Branton—born in Pine Bluff, Arkansas, in 1922, a graduate of Northwestern University's law school and a World War II veteran—had set up a private law practice in Los Angeles in the late 1940s. In a city in which there were no integrated law firms, he quickly made a name for himself. Working with the NAACP on the 1950 trial of an African American veteran accused of having murdered a white couple in Riverside County, Branton audaciously challenged Riverside's jury system, which led to the selection of the county's first black juror. Sometimes considered arrogant and short-tempered, even ruthless, Branton was also a charismatic political firebrand, who had a brilliant comprehension of the law and who shrewdly knew when to turn on the charm. He soon had a varied and impressive roster of clients through the 1950s into the late 1960s and 1970s: show-business stars such as Dandridge, Nat Cole, Diahann Carroll, and white actress Inger Stevens and politically motivated clients such as Angela Davis and the Black Panthers. It was Leo Branton who successfully represented Dandridge in her suit against *Confidential* magazine.

With her past connections and contacts—as well as Leo's client list—Geri Branton remained an important figure in Black Hollywood. In many

Clubbing 1950s-style: Geri Branton (left), Maria Cole, and Dorothy Dandridge (right).

respects, she was the ideal link between the worlds of show business and politics. She also balanced her husband's quick temper. Together, Leo and Geri Branton were a formidable couple: highly intelligent, exceptionally well informed about national and international issues—as well as local politics and social matters—and knowledgeable about any number of other aspects of African American life, be it the cultural history or the work of prominent black Angelenos such as Paul Williams. They attended the town's important events and gatherings. It might be the annual affairs of the Urban League. Or an opening night for Nat Cole. Or an opening for Dottie in Vegas. Of all the Black Hollywood wives, Geri was the best read and perhaps the most brilliant. No one in town ever doubted that.

Maria Cole would never be what Geri Branton was. Nor would she necessarily have wanted to be that. But Maria was as dynamic, stylish, and well tutored a wife as those of famous stars in the larger Hollywood community: Kirk Douglas's wife, Anne; Jimmy Stewart's wife, Gloria; and Gary Cooper's wife, Rocky. No African American woman in her position in Hollywood ever became as well known or was considered as socially important. Some, such as Millie Robinson, the wife of boxer Sugar Ray, would attain a certain prominence. In the 1960s, Millie struck up a publicized friendship with the Burtons—Richard Burton and Elizabeth Taylor. A tremendous coup. But Millie's role as Robinson's wife never had the resonance of Maria's.

Yet like other Hollywood wives, Maria Cole most likely lived with a cloud over her head. The identity of such women was always tied to their husbands' accomplishments, endeavors, goals, triumphs, and failures. Their identities were always tied to being *Mrs.* somebody. And Hollywood, being the place it was, where affairs and divorces were commonplace, where the big stars were always pursued or in pursuit, the wives knew the day might come—it could be any day—when the husband wanted out of the marriage, often to marry some sweet young thing. If that happened, the Hollywood ex-wife would discover that the invitations to the important dinners and parties would no longer come. Nor would those darling friends—who had adored her—be around. Though alimony would secure her financial stability, she wouldn't have those unlimited spending sprees on Rodeo Drive. Loneliness and bitterness could creep in, even before the husband had decided to leave. The Hollywood wife was always aware that it could end at any time. Her very identity could be snapped away from her in an instant.

Living this precarious position, Maria Cole was said to have kept Nat on a very short, very tight leash. For years, she traveled with him on his tours, which may well have alienated her children. Legendary and publicized battles with her children would emerge in the years to come. Some catty observers whispered that Maria traveled with Nat in order that Nat's eyes might not fall on another woman—just as they had fallen on Maria a few years earlier when he was still married to Nadine. Eartha Kitt once commented on Maria's possessiveness and jealous fears. When Kitt and Cole had worked together, playing the characters of Go-Go and composer W. C. Handy in the film *St. Louis Blues,* they struck up a platonic friendship. On one occasion, Nat had sent Eartha a thank-you note and roses. Signing the note, Cole wrote "Handy misses Go-Go." In response, Kitt wrote to thank him for the roses with the words "Go-Go also misses Handy." "The note got into the hands of Maria," recalled Kitt, "who sent me a beaded cashmere sweater as a thank-you gift with a note pinned to it that must have poisoned the pen that wrote it." According to Kitt, Maria's note read, "I don't know if you think of yourself as some kind of temptress siren, but the film is over and Go-Go is gone, let's leave it that way." Never was Maria Cole considered the warmest of Hollywood wives.

In 1955, Maria Cole set out to fulfill herself professionally—and perhaps at the same time make a bid to secure herself against the possible fate that might await her. She announced that she, a onetime vocalist with Duke Ellington, was returning to her career. She landed a deal to appear

Co-stars Nat "King" Cole and Eartha Kitt with visitor Bing Crosby on the set of St. Louis Blues.

at Ciro's, no less, a real coup. Her opening garnered press attention and a celebrity turnout: Dorothy Dandridge; singer Billy Daniels; Milton Berle; baseball star Leo Durocher and his wife, actress Laraine Day; actor Richard Egan; and bandleader Spike Jones. So that he could attend the opening—the perfect picture of a doting, adoring Hollywood husband—Nat gave up a week's engagement at Philadelphia's Latin Casino. Following the opening-night performance, songwriter Jimmy Van Heusen hosted a party for Maria at his home in the Hollywood Hills.

Briefly, Maria was the talk of the town. But not so much because of her performance as because of her determination to perform. Other engagements followed at some pretty tony clubs: the Fairmont Hotel's Venetian Room in San Francisco, Chicago's Chez Paree, New York's La Vie en Rose, as well as an appearance on Ed Sullivan's television show. But the comeback never took. Perhaps unfairly, she was compared by audiences and critics with her husband, and who could compare with the incomparable Nat? Soon, Maria Cole was back to being a Hollywood wife, a role to which she seemed resigned but now with even more of a vengeance.

Nat's career continued on a high roll through most of the decade. From

1956 to 1957, he hosted the groundbreaking television program *The Nat "King" Cole Show*. Though Hazel Scott and Billy Daniels also had hosted their own TV programs, neither drew the attention of Nat's program nor the support of Hollywood, black and white. Everyone wanted to see *The Nat "King" Cole Show* succeed. To boost ratings, guests such as Sammy Davis Jr., Ella Fitzgerald, Mel Torme, and Peggy Lee appeared. Though the show lasted only a little over a year, no one considered it a total failure.

Like other black stars who headlined in Las Vegas, Nat had to use back entrances and elevators at the casino/hotels where he appeared, but he drew huge crowds. He also performed in movies such as *The Blue Gardenia, China Gate,* and as W. C. Handy in the 1958 biopic *St. Louis Blues,* heading a cast that included Eartha Kitt, Pearl Bailey, Ruby Dee, Cab Calloway, and Mahalia Jackson. Nat remained as famous as ever. Most important, he also had become an integral part of the larger Hollywood community in a way previous Black Hollywood stars such as Bill "Bojangles" Robinson and Eddie "Rochester" Anderson had not.

Like everyone else, Nat realized that socially his marriage was important, that, indeed, part of his social acceptability had been the fact that the Hollywood community thought of Nat *and* Maria, who lived in the perfect home with the perfect family and had the perfect manners. But it was long whispered that he was growing weary of the marriage. "All Nat really cared about was his music. His mind was always on music. He *thought* music," said Geri Branton. So much of his time was spent on the road, earning a living to maintain his high-flying lifestyle, that he also looked as if he didn't have time enough to pause and enjoy it all. In all likelihood, he felt imprisoned by it all and especially entrapped by Maria. In the late 1950s and 1960s, his career began to slip into a slight decline as popular tastes clearly changed, especially among the young who danced to the beat of rock 'n' roll stars such as Little Richard and Chuck Berry or grooved to the mellow sounds of Johnny Mathis. Nat drifted away from Maria and later had an affair with a nineteen-year-old Swedish actress. When Maria learned of the affair, most likely her worst fears had nearly come true. But she tenaciously held on and would be devoted to Nat during the painful lung cancer that later took his life. Maria would be remembered as the widow of Nat "King" Cole.

Still, in the 1950s, Maria and Nat had put the Black Hollywood couple on the map socially—and, ironically, had moved themselves out of Black Hollywood into the larger Hollywood culture.

SOCIALIZING SAMMY

Also altering the town socially was Sammy Davis Jr. From the time his career shifted into high gear after the war, Davis lived a lifestyle wholly different from that of previous Negro stars.

Davis would always admire great black artists such as Ellington, Armstrong, and Ethel Waters along with the up-and-coming stars of his era: Poitier, Belafonte, Pearl Bailey, Eartha Kitt. And he was as dazzled by the glamour and beauty of Horne and Dandridge as everyone else. But great black stars aside, Davis appeared absolutely enthralled by white Hollywood. He struck up an early friendship with Mickey Rooney and even cowrote a song with him. In the 1950s, he seized every possible opportunity to socialize with the young Hollywood stars who came to see him perform. He hung out with Tony Curtis and his wife, actress Janet Leigh; with actor Jeff Chandler; and with comedian Jerry Lewis. He was a guest at their homes, swam in their pools, played with their children, ate at their tables. That he might be the only Negro guest didn't seem to faze him. If anything, he might have seen that as a sign of his status as a one-of-a-kind Negro entertainer not bound in by the old rules. Taking his camera with him to various openings and gatherings, he snapped pictures of the big-name celebrities of the era: Humphrey Bogart, Betty Grable, Curtis, Leigh, Dinah Shore, Eddie Fisher, Marilyn Monroe. In turn, he would be photographed by some of the top photographers of the age, such as *Life*'s Philippe Halsman.

Though some Negro performers had always mixed and mingled with the larger Hollywood community, none had done it so openly. Nor had any black star so aggressively appeared to have that type of social life as such a high goal—or need. Black America would long have conflicted feelings about Davis, in part because he seemed too eager to become a part of the white entertainment establishment. Then, too, not since the days of Fetchit had a black star lived so ostentatiously extravagant a life as Davis.

By 1957, he would be earning $25,000 a week in Vegas and living high on the hog with his flashy cars and his fancy high-priced clothes. He moved into a $75,000 fourteen-room split-level, Spanish-style home, once owned by Judy Garland, on Evanview Drive. The house was a showcase with five bedrooms, one of which had French doors that opened onto a magnificent patio where one could sit sipping martinis and enjoying the rarefied air of the Hollywood Hills. Throughout, large picture windows provided spectacular views of the canyon roads. Here, Davis resided in grand style. He prided himself on his state-of-the-art electronic toys: the very latest in high-fidelity radio-phonograph sets; a TV remote control—in the days before remote controls were commonplace—that was built into a coffee table. Davis also had a vast collection of photographs, along with a collection of pipes and more than three hundred cuff-link sets—as well as twenty thousand records. He liked to boast that he had every recording Frank Sinatra had ever made.

Of all the Davis celebrity friends, none was more important to him than Sinatra, of whom he was clearly in awe. Known as a liberal, who felt comfortable with African American entertainers—whose talents he valued—Sinatra, throughout his career, performed with such black stars as Lena Horne, Ella Fitzgerald, and Count Basie. Davis had first gotten to know Sinatra in New York when the entertainer had appeared at the Capitol Theatre and insisted that management have the Will Mastin Trio—mainly, Sammy—open for him for the hefty sum of $1,250. Then, Sammy had watched Frankie from afar, impressed by his talent, awed by his hip, sophisticated lifestyle. He emulated Sinatra in a way he emulated no one else. Psychologists could have had a field day with the relationship. At times, Davis almost looked as if he were in love with Frankie. In turn, Sinatra appeared to genuinely like Davis, whom he took under his wing. The men partied together, drank together, caroused together. Davis knew the Sinatra family. Sinatra knew the Davis family. Eventually, Davis became a part of Sinatra's group of freewheeling, heavy-drinking, hard-partying buddies, which included Dean Martin, Peter Lawford, Joey Bishop, and at times, Shirley MacLaine, all of whom played and worked together in Las Vegas. Few stars drew as much excitement on the Strip. One can only wonder how Davis could so eagerly accept being part of a group originally know as the Clan—but dubbed the Rat Pack by the press.

During the rise of the civil rights movement in the 1950s and 1960s, the Clan was a sign—for mainstream America—of a new integrated Hollywood. Audiences seeing the group in live performances or in movies such as *Ocean's 11, Robin and the 7 Hoods,* and *Sergeants Three* liked telling themselves that there was equality among the entertainers. Yet black America had mixed reactions. Sammy Davis Jr. was undeniably talented. But too often, he looked like a token figure. And why did he let himself be the butt of racial jokes onstage and on-screen? Once during a performance, Dean Martin came on carrying little Sammy. "I'd like to thank the NAACP for this wonderful trophy," quipped Martin. "Put me down," said

Sammy Davis Jr.: multitalented and multifaceted.

Sammy, who seemed annoyed. Yet soon, he was back to clowning and laughing. And why did Davis sometimes kiddingly speak in an Amos 'n' Andy kind of dialect, which drew laughs from audiences but seemed out of place in this new age? Too often, there was something exaggerated and overblown about Davis—on-screen and off. Even when he spoke in interviews in those very clear, very clipped, seemingly very sophisticated tones, it seemed something of a put-on, one more shtick. Too often, Sammy seemed to have a minstrel-man quality. Was this the price for black entertainers of being in an integrated Hollywood? Other new stars, such as Belafonte and Poitier, worked in the new social atmosphere in Hollywood, without jokes at their expense, without black America's believing they had sold out.

Davis also made headlines when he converted to Judaism. He liked to refer to himself as a "one-eyed black Jew." For much of black America, Davis looked like a man running away from his roots, trying very hard not to be black. Perhaps a harsh judgment—but a judgment that many had of him at that time and in the years to come. And a segment of the industry was also repelled by Davis. When Samuel Goldwyn was said to be considering Davis for the role of Sportin' Life in his film version of George

Gershwin's *Porgy and Bess*, Ira Gershwin's wife, Lee, reportedly pleaded with Goldwyn not to cast Davis. "Swear on your life," she said. "You'll never use him." Goldwyn assured her. "That monkey!" he reportedly said.

Seeing himself as part of Hollywood's new social order, Davis also, perhaps daringly, challenged that long-standing taboo on interracial romance and marriage.

In the beginning, Davis was seen with beautiful black women, models or aspiring actresses. In 1953, he had a well-publicized romance with Eartha Kitt. Here were two vibrant, successful postwar-era Negro stars who appeared—at least, in the newspapers and magazines—to be a perfect couple. But both Davis and Kitt seemed to have their sights on bigger fish. Both seemed to be relentless social climbers who were too much on a quest to be a part of the larger community to settle for each other. For a time, Davis also had a crush on the young Diahann Carroll.

Then, in 1957, after the reports of Davis's friendship with actress Kim Novak surfaced, Davis was briefly married to black singer Loray White. Even he admitted it was something of an arrangement to keep the heat off him during all the talk about his "affair" with Novak. Terrified of a possible Harry Cohn–initiated mob attack, Davis went through his address book one day. When his agent Arthur Silber asked him what he was doing, Davis replied, "I got the call this morning. I have to marry a Black chick." Silber also recalled that Davis later sat Loray White down "and made her a proposition, to marry him for a certain sum of money. She would have all the rights that Mrs. Sammy Davis Jr. would have, but at the end of the year they would dissolve the marriage. She agreed to that, and that's what took the heat off." Davis showered her with gifts: a mink stole, a rose-cut diamond ring, and emerald baguettes. After six months, he paid White twenty-five thousand dollars to get out of the marriage.

Then, Davis began seeing Swedish actress May Britt, whom he met at the Mocambo. Having just made a splash in the films *The Blue Angel* and *The Young Lions*, Britt was a slender, blue-eyed blonde who seemed on the way to stardom. Word that the two would marry further fueled outrage in the industry—and in the country. During Davis's trip to appear at the Lotus Club in Washington, D.C., neo-Nazi protesters carried signs with shocking slogans. "Go Back to the Congo, You Kosher Coon," read one of them. While he was campaigning for John F. Kennedy for president, Davis's appearance at the Democratic convention in Los Angeles led the Mississippi delegation to boo him. Davis even delayed his marriage to Britt until after the election, hoping not to cost Kennedy any votes. After-

The marriage that rocked the industry: Sammy Davis Jr. with wife May Britt and their children.

ward, just three days before the inauguration, the new president's secretary, Evelyn Lincoln, phoned Davis to ask him not to attend the big inaugural party. It was feared that southern congressmen would be offended by his appearance.

Davis and Britt married—with Sinatra as best man. Afterward, Britt gave up her career. But by then, the industry in all likelihood considered her unhirable, a blonde goddess who had been defiled by her union with a runty black man. Twentieth Century Fox reportedly did not renew her contract option. Many wondered what effect the marriage would have on Davis's career. But to his credit, he was too great a talent with too much energy and drive to leave show business behind or to be forgotten. During the 1950s and 1960s, Davis did Broadway and Vegas, made records and movies, and continued to appear on television, becoming one of the first black performers to play a dramatic role on the tube when he appeared in "Auf Wiedersehen" on *General Electric Theater*. Becoming all the more famous and no less controversial, he ultimately was known as the "world's greatest entertainer." He endured. And in doing so, he, too, went beyond the boundaries of Black Hollywood.

DANDRIDGE AND *CARMEN JONES*:
THE NEW BLACK HOLLYWOOD

Whereas the feelings about Davis were always mixed, Dorothy Dandridge emerged during the era as Black Hollywood's—and black America's—great movie icon. She was the local girl in whom the town took pride. After all, the black colony had watched her grow up, weathering the adversities of an unhappy marriage, a disabled child, and the vagaries of the entertainment industry itself. Black Hollywood's older generation also knew and worked with her mother, Ruby.

Through focus, drive, and a surprising ambition, she had made it to the top in nightclubs, drawing more attention in the early 1950s than any other African American woman appearing in niteries. Patrons went wild for her. Nightclub managers and owners pursued her, along with hordes of male admirers, white and black, young and old. And the media paid attention, with coverage in *Life, Ebony, Jet,* and *Time*. With the leading role in MGM's *Bright Road,* the drama about a young teacher struggling to reach a wayward student, Dandridge projected a vision of a modern postwar African American woman: smart, articulate, sensitive, and strikingly beautiful without the old dialect and gingham or the giggling maid antics. Much the same modern image was projected in her television appearances on such variety shows as *The Colgate Comedy Hour* and *The Ed Sullivan Show*.

Yet a nagging question still plagued her: How was a young woman such as Dandridge, who yearned to be a film actress, to survive in an industry that seemed to have no place for her? Her predecessor Lena never got to play big dramatic roles. It was a question similar to that posed after Dandridge's triumph at the Gala. What's the next stop?

The story of how Dandridge would ultimately play Carmen Jones would be told time and again and would become part of Black Hollywood's legend and lore, similar to the story of how David O. Selznick finally found his Scarlett O'Hara—when his agent brother Myron brought young British actress Vivien Leigh to the location where Selznick was then filming the burning of Atlanta and the producer saw her amid flames in the background. When word swept through town that director Otto Preminger planned a movie version of Oscar Hammerstein II's dramatic stage musical *Carmen Jones,* the black movie colony knew it offered the role of a lifetime for an African American actress. Preminger interviewed any number of women, including a young New Yorker, Diahann Carroll, who knew she lacked the lush sensuality to play Carmen. But Dandridge was angered that she had not been considered, not even called in for a meeting. After prodding her manager to do something about the situation, she was relieved that an appointment was finally set up for her in the director's L.A. office. A cordial Preminger was frank with her. Having seen her perform in nightclubs and having once glimpsed her walking in Manhattan, he thought of her as Saks Fifth Avenue, far too sophisticated and sleek for his earthy Carmen. Handing her a copy of the script, he suggested she study the role of the good girl Cindy Lou, then come back to see him.

Leaving the meeting, an even angrier Dandridge was determined to prove the part should be hers. For her next appointment, she walked in seductively, working her hips overtime, with a sexy new wardrobe (tight skirt and low-cut blouse), a tousled hairdo, and a more sensual makeup devised at the salon of the legendary Max Factor. Taking one look at the vixen who stood before him, Preminger exclaimed, "It's Carmen." "He couldn't reach for the phone fast enough. He arranged a screen test," said Dandridge's manager, Earl Mills. The story read like a press agent's dream. But all concerned parties attested to its truth. And it became a key incident in the Dandridge star legend.

Preminger's film signaled the full emergence of the new Black Hollywood with a cast that included not only Dandridge but Harry Belafonte, Pearl Bailey, Olga James, Diahann Carroll, Brock Peters, and Joe Adams. Most had made their names in New York. "Pearl was the biggest star," recalled Olga James. "Harry was just about to happen." Included in the club sequence were Katherine Dunham's onetime lead dancer Archie Savage and a new generation of dancers from the Lester Horton dance troupe: Alvin Ailey, Jim Truitt, and Horton's golden girl Carmen de Lavallade. With her hair pulled back in a ponytail, de Lavallade would be the dancer whom moviegoers would never forget. Also in the cast: Roy Glenn, Nick Stewart, June Eckstine, Bernie Hamilton, and that tough relic from the past Madame Sul-Te-Wan.

For the newcomers, the experience of working on the film and seeing the town seemed glorious. "It was a big, big deal," recalled singer Olga James. "It seemed like an enormous piece of luck that had just fallen into my lap because I didn't audition more than once. I did a screen test [in New York]. I didn't have to go through a committee that made a decision about me. It was a big, big deal to come out here to do a movie." James and Diahann Carroll were booked into a small motel on Sunset Boulevard, near

Sweet and endearing Olga James, in her first Hollywood movie, with Harry Belafonte.

Ciro's. Staying at the motel, down the hall from them, was folk singer Josh White, who could be heard quietly strumming on his guitar. Sammy Davis Jr. was also a guest, who was often partying and surrounded by friends.

As Eastern cuties—the new girls in town—James and Carroll had their share of suitors. James struck up a friendship with handsome Ike Jones, who played a small role in the movie and later became involved in an interracial love affair with actress Inger Stevens. Pursued for a time by Davis, Carroll had a friendship with the town's new rebel. Olga James never forgot the evening her date brought her back to the motel "and there was Diahann parked in the front of the motel with Marlon Brando. Talking." Brando and Carroll went out on various dates, including one to a party at Betty Comden's. There Carroll met Humphrey Bogart, who she found tedious and apparently so threatened by new star Brando that he chose to be rude to Brando's date. On another occasion, in a restaurant, when Brando patted her backside, Carroll turned around and slapped him. Though flattered by Brando's attention, Carroll was then still too fascinated with James Edwards to think about anyone else.

Hollywood was clearly not as closed as in the past, yet it still was not a completely open town. "There weren't many places that black people could go at that time," recalled Olga James. "I remember that Preminger took Harry Belafonte somewhere, and I remember overhearing him call ahead to make sure they knew that Harry was a star and that he was bringing the star." At the studio, James also recalled that other than a black hairdresser, "I can't remember anybody else of color on that film." There weren't any African Americans in the makeup or wardrobe departments and certainly not on the crew.

Aware of what a major undertaking this black film was, most of the cast watched Preminger closely. By now, he had a reputation as a demanding, difficult director. Sometimes he exploded on the set. Other times he took members of the cast to the commissary for lunch. "I thought his attitude toward race had to be okay," said James. "Otherwise he would not have made this film. And wouldn't have used such a variety of beautiful looking black people. I don't think he was prejudiced. I do think that he could be mean but it didn't have anything to do with color. He would be mean in a kind of sadistic way to test the meekness in you. Or to test the fear of him in you. Or he could just be mean because he chose a target. And I have to say that he was probably harder on the men than he was on the women because he used to ride Brock Peters." Though he lost his temper with James, she felt that "basically he was kind to me."

But the making of *Carmen Jones* revealed signs of the on-going death of the old Black Hollywood. "I didn't know about Central Avenue," said James. "I didn't know about the Dunbar Hotel." Now it was beginning to look as if that old centralized community had never existed. Years later James regretted that in 1954 she had not known about Madame Sul-Te-Wan, who appeared as the grandmother of Carmen. It also made her sad that here was "a part of history, and she's doing a bit role." But James soon learned something else about Hollywood attitudes, white and black, that explained why some of the oldtimers were now forgotten. "It's such a company town," said James. "You were totally invisible in this town if you weren't doing something. [It determined] the way that people respond to you. And this goes all the way up the line, from the people that you encounter in shops to the people that you encounter in social situations, who kind of glaze over if you're not doing something. If I came out and I was doing something, then I was visible. That was my impression of Hollywood."

The filming of *Carmen Jones* on the RKO lot moved swiftly and smoothly with the attention of cast and crew focused on Dandridge, which did not make Pearl Bailey very happy. "Pearl wasn't all that secure," said James, "and she really was not that gracious to me or Diahann. She was also very envious of Dorothy." Choreographer Herb Ross, who later directed such films as *The Turning Point* and *Steel Magnolias,* also detected Bailey's jealousy of Dandridge. Like everyone else though, Ross found Dandridge compelling. "She was quite solitary," he said. "My impression of her was that she was always alone. She didn't go out to socialize with the others. I remember Diahann was always going out to a jazz club on the Strip. But Dorothy was always somber and more serious." Usually, she ate in her dressing room rather than in the commissary with the rest of the cast.

Once the film was completed, James felt a sadness. "I realized that there probably would not be any more black films for a while. I never expected to be in any more films." Diahann Carroll recalled that most of the cast also felt they wouldn't be back in a Hollywood studio. Yet she believed Dandridge was the exception—with too great a beauty and talent not to become a star.

The year 1954 saw the decision in *Brown v. Board of Education,* which stated that segregation in public schools was unconstitutional, followed a year later by the Montgomery bus boycott, when Rosa Parks was arrested for refusing to sit in the back of the bus and when a young Martin Luther King Jr., a leader of the boycott, came to national fame—signal events that propelled the civil rights movement. *Carmen Jones* seemed one more sign of an emerging new era in American life. It was a hit with critics and audiences, especially black moviegoers, who loved its fiery leading lady and the film's modern romance. *Life* ran Dandridge on its cover. Come Oscar time, she became the first African American woman ever nominated for an Academy Award in the leading actress category.

DANDRIDGE: BLACK HOLLYWOOD'S QUEEN

On Oscar night, Dandridge was a resplendent goddess dressed elegantly in a light-colored, form-fitting gown with a mink stole wrapped around her shoulders. In Manhattan, her sister Vivian accompanied her to the ceremony, which was then held in both New York and Los Angeles. Only a few years earlier, Dr. Ralph Bunche, winner of the Nobel Peace Prize in 1950, had presented the Oscar for best picture of 1950. But Bunche was, in the industry's eyes, a guest star. Dandridge, however, became the first African American actress to present an award at the cere-

Making movies and having fun: Dorothy Dandridge and Brock Peters on the set of Carmen Jones.

mony—for best editor. As millions of viewers watched her in their living rooms, she was about to reach the pinnacle of her fame. Grace Kelly took home the award that night for her performance in *The Country Girl*. But for Black Hollywood—and the rest of America—Dandridge had arrived.

Once Dandridge signed a major contract with Twentieth Century Fox, in the eyes of many, Hollywood had its first authentic black leading lady, its first authentic movie star, as sexy and alluring as Monroe, Kelly, and Taylor. Offscreen she personified the high-voltage glamour that all of Hollywood valued. "Dottie was the kind of woman," said Geri Branton, "who, if you wanted a glass of water, she'd bring it to you in crystal. If you had a sandwich, it was served on Wedgwood. I don't know where she got that. But that's who she was." Director Gerald Mayer, the nephew of MGM chief Louis B. Mayer, recalled that during the time of his brief romance with Dandridge after the completion of their film *Bright Road,* he loved those evenings when he walked into her bachelor girl's pad on Hilldale, which was simply but beautifully decorated. "It was impeccable," said Mayer. "Not show businessy in any way. Because she was not what you would consider show business."

Dandridge, being fitted for a gown.

During trips to Europe, she attended the designers' previews of their new collections and dazzled the international set. *Jet* reported on the evening when Greek tycoon Aristotle Onassis couldn't take his eyes off her. Back in the States, she could be spotted driving a snazzy Thunderbird. As she pulled up to the town's top department stores—I Magnin, The Broadway, the May Company—the parking valets snapped to attention, eager not simply to park the car but to get a glimpse of the star. Elegantly dressed, perfectly made up, and articulate and intelligent, she moved within the town's top social circles even before and clearly after the release of *Carmen Jones.*

Some evenings sparkled more than others. At the National Urban League's annual winter ball, held at the Deauville Club in Santa Monica, she was the glittering center of attention of the powerful and influential in both the black and white communities: former L.A. Mayor Fletcher Bowron; Mrs. Fleur Cowles, associate editor of *Look* magazine; MGM chief Dore Schary; and Samuel and Frances Goldwyn. "She took real pride in her work for the Urban League," said Branton. Dandridge was aware of the way her fame could be used for the benefit of the civil rights organiza-

A historic night—the 1954 Oscar ceremony—with the spotlight on nominee Dorothy Dandridge (left), seen here with her sister, Vivian.

tion—to raise money and to bring attention to its battles. But in Hollywood, you couldn't raise a dime without pouring on the glamour.

When the powerful agent Charles Feldman and his wife, Jean Howard, threw one of their big parties—this time, for Cole Porter—Dandridge joined the festivities along with such brights of the entertainment world as Judy Garland and husband Sid Luft; Norma Shearer; director Billy Wilder and wife Audrey; Moss Hart and wife Kitty Carlisle; Ray Milland; Merle Oberon; Clifton Webb; Roger Edens; Rocky Cooper (wife of Gary); and director Charles Vidor. That evening, Peter Lawford was Dorothy's date. But concerned about gossip, Lawford asked his friend agent Peter Sabiston to escort her, which Sabiston did with pleasure. "Peter didn't have the courage to take Dorothy Dandridge to parties," said Sabiston. "When we walked in every man in the room started paying attention to her. Richard Burton, William Holden, all of them. She was a gorgeous woman and a very nice person."

A dashing young man-about-town, British-born Peter Lawford found her irresistible. In turn, she was drawn to his good looks, his breeding, and perhaps that English accent. Neither publicly acknowledged their affair.

"She was a bigger star then than he was," said Geri Branton. And Lawford was far more taken with her than she was with him. Yet he told her that they could never marry. "Look, I love you. I would like to marry you. But let's face it," he said, "I wouldn't work another day if we married. And neither would you."

Director Preminger was also dazzled. Their romance began during the filming of *Carmen Jones*. "There were rumors," said Diahann Carroll, "that Preminger was involved with her and had made her success his personal goal." When they attended the screening of *Carmen Jones* at the Cannes Film Festival, Preminger was openly seen by Dandridge's side. In the States, said Vivian Dandridge, they felt they had to keep things low-key. He enjoyed having small dinner parties with her as his hostess. And he preferred that she wear one of two colors: white or beige, which he believed highlighted the beauty of her skin tones. In Hollywood, the "secret" romances, especially with Preminger, only added to Dandridge's allure. What could heighten her glamour and appeal more than word that one of the most powerful directors/producers in the film capital was in love with her?

Great movie goddesses often had powerful men—their consorts—at their sides. The devotion of such talented, complicated men became testaments to the goddesses' supreme power. Garbo had mesmerized silent-screen romantic hero John Gilbert. Monroe had baseball star Joe DiMaggio and later playwright Arthur Miller. Taylor had hotel heir Nicky Hilton, then legendary producer Mike Todd, and later actor Richard Burton. For Black Hollywood, Dandridge had conquered its young prince Harold Nicholas. Now, one of Hollywood's most famous and successful directors had succumbed to her charms. When Dandridge moved from her apartment on Hilldale to her first home in the Hollywood Hills on Evanview Drive, Geri Branton said, "Preminger *bought* her that house."

Of course, the move to Evanview—*before* Sammy—was yet another sign that the queen of the new Black Hollywood could live wherever she chose. Dorothy transformed the house into the type of star residence about which the town loved talking. "It was a gorgeous house," said Geri Branton. "It had only one bedroom. And it was just furnished to perfection. Beautiful drapes and carpeting. She loved thick carpeting. And large couches. It didn't have an entrance hall. You just go in. And to your right was the huge living room and then across from that was a lovely library, and it was beautifully done." An ebony Steinway grand piano sat in the living room, not far from a brick fireplace framed in gold and a large bay window that offered a panoramic view of Hollywood and Beverly Hills, both of which lay almost literally at her feet. "Her bedroom—*gorgeous*," said Branton. "Like a movie star's. All in white. And these heavy, heavy, thick blackout drapes. A lovely kitchen. A dining room. A den." Outside was a covered patio, where she could entertain.

With Sammy as her neighbor in the Garland house, said Geri Branton, Dottie felt she had to be higher up on the hill. Once she married Jack Denison—the onetime maître d'hôtel at the Riviera in Las Vegas, a man no one felt was right for her—she lived even more lavishly, moving literally around the block but *up* to a larger home on Viewsite. In this three-level residence, visitors walked on marbleized floors, as they entered the foyer. "It was like tile," said Branton. "But it was marble that was installed like tile. In panels." Upstairs were four bedrooms and a huge dressing room for Dorothy. In the master bedroom at the back of the house, Dorothy again had a magnificent view of the city. "Her bedroom was always in white with heavy blackout drapes," said Geri. "Always the blackout drapes. So when you pulled them, it would be absolutely pitch black inside." When depressed, she stayed in bed with the drapes drawn, shutting out the rest of the world. In the evening, floodlights illuminated the house, giving it a warm glow. *Ebony* celebrated both Dandridge's stardom *and* her home with a cover story. For Black Hollywood, here was a striking visual symbol of unparalleled success for an African American movie actress. None had ever lived so glamorously.

Dandridge enjoyed entertaining. At her smaller, more intimate gatherings, everything was very casual. She liked to prepare dinner herself, often a soul-food menu. "She was an excellent cook," said Branton, "and loved the staples of black cuisine: collard greens, mashed potatoes, and chitlins." Dandridge was known for serving chitlins as hors d'oeuvres—in long-stemmed glasses with paprika sprinkled on them. Of course, she couldn't eat that way every day, just once a week or when she had guests. Her more formal dinner parties might include Gary and Rocky Cooper or James and Pamela Mason or Peter Lawford or Fredric March or agent Harold Jovien and his wife, Mildred, as well as Geri and Leo Branton and her former sister-in-law Dorothy Nicholas and her husband, Byron Morrow. Sometimes, Joel Fluellen was a guest. Other times—for the really big to-dos—Joel might cater and serve the guests. If some guest who knew him spoke to him, he'd snap, "Don't say anything to me. Can't you see I'm working tonight!"

Dandridge herself would appear only *after* the guests arrived. Hours were spent on makeup and hair and making the final decision as to which dress or gown looked best. Guests could grow restless. So would Fluellen, if he was working that night. He'd let her know a houseful of people awaited her appearance. And an appearance it was, as Dandridge, at long last, would descend her staircase to greet her admirers.

Dandridge was Hollywood's idea of a star. Unlike Sammy, who seemed too eager to impress and climb, Dandridge had the aura of a goddess who was simply assuming her divine right. Yet beneath the haughty appearance—she usually made her entrances with her head held high and her back ramrod-straight—there lay a troubled, insecure, jittery woman, never sure of herself, ill at ease with being a sex goddess, and also keenly aware of another reality: Even in this new age, Dandridge knew that Hollywood had changed, but not enough. After her Oscar nomination, she went three years before appearing in another movie, *Island in the Sun.* Though she made such films as *Tamango, The Decks Ran Red,* and *Malaga,* none was a worthy follow-up to her *Carmen Jones* triumph. Yet, ironically, even her desperate efforts to find roles ultimately became part of her legend.

FADED GLORY ON THE OLD THOROUGHFARE, NEW VENUES

In the wake of stars such as Dandridge, Davis, Kitt, and Bailey at the Sunset Strip clubs, black club patrons journeyed even less frequently to Central Avenue. The great clubs of the avenue—Club Alabam, The Last Word, Memo, even a great after-hours hangout such as Brother's—were either gone or on their way out. The old playing grounds of Black Hollywood started to fade, their glamorous days dimming and diminished. New-style jazz joints featuring the new stars such as Miles Davis, John Coltrane, and Max Roach drew in black patrons and the movie stars, but in other parts of town.

Off-limits restaurants opened their doors. Lena Horne once commented that she married Lennie Hayton knowing that he could take her places where a Negro man could not. It could still be tough for black men to make their way around town. But stars such as Horne, Dandridge, and in all likelihood, a Belafonte or Poitier knew they would never be turned away from the restaurant Romanoff's. It would be at Romanoff's that director Rouben Mamoulian informed Dorothy of his desire to cast her in Twentieth Century Fox's new version of *Cleopatra.* Now other restaurants, diners, and small clubs were hospitable. Of course, the greatest change for city residents came in the 1960s. But for the stars, it began in the Fabulous Fifties.

The trend that started in the 1940s of moving farther west of Central Avenue continued. "You could move other places away from the old East-side," said Johnetta Jones. "Everybody just kept going farther and farther west," said Willard Brown. "What was happening was that whites were moving farther and farther to the west," Barbara Molette recalled. "As soon as they would get a spot developed, some black people would move in and some Asians, and the white people would move farther out. Finally, the whites went out to the counties like Orange County. Or a place like Simi Valley." But gradually, black residents had moved west of Western Avenue, then west of Washington Boulevard, then onto Crenshaw.

New residential areas sprouted up. One was an enclave for the black elite, some in show business, some not, centered in Lafayette Square, off Crenshaw Boulevard. Leading the way was Paul Williams, who designed his first home for himself in the area in 1951: a two-story California-style residence with a living room; a dining room furnished in eight shades of green, including a stained green oak tabletop; a kitchen with appliances built into cabinets and controlled by push buttons; two bedrooms that opened onto sundecks; two baths; dressing rooms; and a special den for watching television. Perhaps most impressive was the lanai room on the first level, done in coral and green, with a slate floor and large folding doors that opened onto a flower garden. At the front of the house were palm trees and tropical shrubs. "Designed for the utmost in informal living," wrote *Ebony*, "the neo-modern home has rooms so arranged that there is a flow of movement throughout the house and even from house to gardens through a lanai—an indoor-outdoor living room patterned after the Hawaiian tropical terrace."

Hollywood interior decorator Helen Franklin designed the interiors. The fabrics for the draperies and furniture were handwoven by Maria Kipp of Beverly Hills. Lamps in the home were custom-built by Dorothy Thorpe of Hollywood. Williams appeared to delight in this latest type of modern living. On the dashboard of his car, he had a control panel that opened his garage door from two blocks away, a device then still new to the California scene. "I wanted it to be a place to live in first and foremost," said Williams, "not just something to show off." But it was a showplace. When Paul and Della Williams arrived, the area was predominantly white. But other African Americans moved into beautiful homes on the tree-lined streets. Joe Louis bought a house there. So did Ruby Dandridge. Later, Paul Williams's daughters Marilyn and Norma followed—with their families. Geri and Leo Branton also moved into a home there. For decades to come, Lafayette Square remained an oasis, as did areas such as Leimert Park and Baldwin Hills.

By the start of the next decade, Black Hollywood was stunned as Sugar Hill was just about sliced in half to make way for the construction of the Santa Monica Freeway in 1961. As much as they might protest, nothing could stop the city's plans. By now, Los Angeles had become a car-mad town as it relegated its trolley lines and Red Cars to the trash heap. With the fumes emitted by the lanes upon lanes of cars, there also came the smog. The Sugar Hill homes of Hattie McDaniel and Louise Beavers remained intact. But gone were the residences of others. Gone, too, was that glamorous fantasy that fans might have of Ethel Waters sending her maid over to Hattie's to borrow a cup of sugar. Gone was that sense of a grand neighborhood for Black Hollywood's high and mighty.

PORGY AND BESS: FAREWELL TO THE OLD ERA

Porgy and Bess—Dorothy Dandridge's last major film—proved to be the decade's last black-cast spectacle and symbolically also marked the close of the old Black Hollywood. Within the corridors of mainstream Hollywood, Porgy and Bess at first generated great excitement. Under the aegis of producer Samuel L. Goldwyn, a Hollywood pioneer known for his well-made, dramatically coherent, and sometimes serious-minded dramas, Porgy and Bess would be the most sumptuously mounted black film in Hollywood history—a truly big-budget, first-class extravaganza with dazzling black talents and top-of-the-line production values. Yet within the African American community, protests sprang up: Although the George Gershwin musical had a magnificent score, it was otherwise replete with stereotyped characters and situations. In this era of civil rights, who wanted to hear the old dialects in a film in which the two leading characters were a beggar and a whore? Already such films as No Way Out, Edge of the City, and Island in the Sun had depicted intense black characters living in an integrated world, confronting problems of race and racism.

Harry Belafonte flatly turned down the role of Porgy. Diahann Carroll did not want to play a supporting role because she too felt the characters were stereotypes and the story was offensive. Eventually, she reconsidered. Dandridge and Sidney Poitier vacillated but finally agreed to play the leads. "I decided that if Goldwyn was that bent on doing the picture," said Dandridge, "he might as well do it with me." A determined Goldwyn finally gathered an all-star cast to back his leads: Sammy Davis Jr. as

Sportin' Life, Pearl Bailey as Maria, Brock Peters as Crown. Also cast in small roles: Ivan Dixon, Nichelle Nichols (later to be known for playing Uhura on television's *Star Trek* series), and a budding writer/actress, Maya Angelou. Alongside these performers of the postwar Black Hollywood were the prewar performers: Clarence Muse in a small role as Peter; the stage actress Ruth Attaway; and Eugene Jackson, the onetime Pineapple of Our Gang. In this respect, *Porgy and Bess* represented—as had *Carmen Jones*—a mix of the old and the new.

Filming was long and arduous. A fire destroyed the sets and delayed the production. Original director Rouben Mamoulian, who had directed both the original play *Porgy* in 1927 and the first production of the opera *Porgy and Bess* in 1935, clashed with Goldwyn and was replaced by Otto Preminger. Goldwyn and Preminger disagreed on the look of the film. Preminger wanted to open it up, shoot scenes on locations rather than on the classy but claustrophobic stagy sets of Oliver Smith. By now, Preminger's romance with Dandridge had ended—bitterly. On the set, the director berated her to such a point that most of the cast felt he humiliated her. Poitier couldn't quite believe Preminger's behavior or the vulnerable Dandridge's reactions. "He treated her like a dog," said Ivan Dixon. "She would cry. It was terrible to see." Throughout, Dandridge seemed lost and isolated, emotionally frayed, fragile, and adrift, distant from many in the cast. "Dorothy now barely spoke to anyone," said Eugene Jackson, who remembered the days when as children they had performed in Ben Carter's choir. Yet the eyes of everyone working on *Porgy and Bess* were always on her. Poitier might then have been a bigger name. But, said Ivan Dixon, Dandridge was the one everyone considered the Hollywood star. "She was our queen," said Nichelle Nichols.

Away from the studio, Dandridge was sometimes social, entertaining Diahann Carroll, Dixon, and Poitier at her home on Evanview Drive. During such evenings, Dixon noted that even in private, "She was always Dorothy Dandridge, the star." Once the film was completed, Dandridge retreated to her home in the hills, exhausted and depressed.

The film opened to mixed reviews—and mixed reactions from moviegoers. Striding through it was a haunting Dandridge who surprisingly invested her Bess with a modern sensibility: a high-strung beauty, sad and lonely, struggling to pull together the pieces of a life gone astray—and to find refuge in a world that neither understood nor had a place for her. Her performance reflected her personal feelings about her place in the movie industry—and the disastrous, tragic course her life would soon take. But

The last of the old-style black movie musicals which also marked the end of an era: Porgy and Bess, *with Davis, Dandridge, and Peters.*

otherwise, though at times elegant and moving, the film seemed airless and anemic, with images indeed from an earlier era.

Porgy and Bess was the last of the grand old-style, all-star musicals as well as the last black production about which the entire town would talk. Nothing better symbolized the close of one era and also the opening of another.

THE PASSING OF THE OLD GUARD

Other signs in the 1950s indicated the passing of the old order. In 1951, Charlotta Bass, after struggling to keep her paper alive, sold *The California Eagle* to attorney Loren Miller. Despite being labeled a communist and receiving death threats, Bass remained politically active. For years, she had been a Republican but had increasingly moved toward the left. In 1952, she made history as the first African American woman to run as a vice presidential candidate on the Progressive Party ticket. In 1960, she wrote a book on her experiences: *Forty Years: Memoirs from the Pages of a Newspaper.* With Bass no longer at the helm of the paper that had fought against *The Birth of a Nation* and had called for better roles for black performers, Black Hollywood knew an era had passed. Without Bass, *The California Eagle* was never the same. The paper folded in 1965. Bass died in 1969.

In 1952, the town was shocked to learn that Hattie McDaniel had died. With her home in Sugar Hill, McDaniel had lived on a grand scale for Los Angeles's black community. With her cherished Oscar win, she had attained the kind of recognition the industry still appeared unwilling to bestow on other African American performers. The Oscar nominations of Ethel Waters and especially Dandridge had been milestones for the black movie colony. And in 1959, Juanita Moore would win a Best Supporting Actress nomination for her performance in the remake of *Imitation of Life*. But not until twenty-four years after McDaniel's win would an African American performer—Sidney Poitier, for his performance in 1963's *Lilies of the Field*—stand at the Academy Awards ceremony with an Oscar in his hands. McDaniel's funeral drew an estimated five thousand mourners— some lining up twelve hours in advance—to the People's Independent Church of God in Christ, which could seat only a thousand. One hundred and twenty-five limousines crawled toward the church, causing the police to cordon off four blocks. Flowers came from Clark Gable, Eddie Anderson, Claudette Colbert, Walt Disney, and scores of others. Louise Beavers introduced actor Edward Arnold to deliver the eulogy. Lillian Randolph sang "I've Done My Work."

McDaniel had been fortunate, because Hollywood by now was known for eating its young—and for forgetting its old. If the new Black Hollywood—no longer that circumscribed world with clear borders and clear ties—thought at all of pioneers like Madame Sul-Te-Wan and Noble Johnson, it thought of them as those old bit players. In the late 1940s, Noble Johnson still worked—often playing Native Americans and sometimes unbilled in such films as *Along the Oregon Trail, Unconquered,* and as Red Shirt in John Ford's *She Wore a Yellow Ribbon.* He had also married a young white woman named Gladys Blackwell. Financially secure, he had invested in real estate in Los Angeles and other parts of California. In 1950, at age sixty-nine, he made his last film—as Naqua, Oseka chief—in *North of the Great Divide.*

Finally, Johnson, the loner, still handsome and looking years younger than he was, but disgruntled—and perhaps tired of having toiled for years in the Hollywood factory—packed his bags and left Los Angeles. As restless as ever, Johnson moved with his wife, Gladys, to Northern California,

Oregon, and Washington. In all these places, he bought and sold real estate. Stories circulated that he now used the name Mark Johnson and eventually passed as white. When Johnson took ill, the couple settled in Yucaipa, near San Bernardino. There, he died—as Mark Johnson—at age ninety-seven in 1978.

Madame Sul-Te-Wan, however, remained a grizzled, tough Hollywood fighter to the bitter end. Colorful as ever, dressing exotically with her scarves and bold costume jewelry, her fanciful hats, and her stylish dresses, she refused to let the town forget her. At age sixty-three, she mortgaged her home in Beverly Hills to finance a stage comeback as a chorus girl! It failed. No matter. At age seventy-seven, she married a fifty-five-year-old French interior designer, Anton Ebenthur. The marriage lasted three years. No matter! When she was cast as the grandmother of Carmen in *Carmen Jones,* she had said to Preminger, "I guess you want me to play her like an old woman." She had not one gray hair on her head. But she liked the idea of being grandmother to the woman she believed in all likelihood Hollywood's greatest black star. Thereafter, she liked telling everyone that Dandridge was her adopted granddaughter.

In 1956, old Black Hollywood, aware that Madame could not live forever, threw a testimonial banquet in her honor with more than two hundred performers and civic leaders, which included Louise Beavers; Mantan Moreland and his wife, Hazel; Ruby Dandridge; Rex Ingram; Cleo Desmond; as well as white character actor Eugene Pallette and D. W. Griffith's onetime star Mae Marsh—and as a sign of continued change within the industry, African American actor William Walker, who served on the board of the Screen Actors Guild. The next year, Madame suffered a stroke but recovered and did small parts in the 1958 DeMille-"supervised" *The Buccaneer, Something of Value,* and *Porgy and Bess.* But two years later, she suffered a second stroke and died. The news received front-page coverage in the February 5, 1959, issue of the *Los Angeles Sentinel.* The old days had ended.

Epilogue

lowly, Black Hollywood's old guard disappeared from the local scene. No longer MGM's golden black goddess, Lena Horne sold her house on Nichols Canyon in the late 1950s, then lived mostly in hotel suites with her husband, Lennie Hayton, as she performed in the States and abroad. Later, she settled back in New York. In 1962, Louise Beavers, sixty years old and suffering from diabetes, suddenly died at Cedars of Lebanon Hospital. More than four hundred fans and friends turned out for Beavers's funeral at the People's Independent Church of God in Christ. Four months later, Beavers's husband, Leroy Moore, died. That same year, Sam McDaniel also died.

Three years later, the film capital was rocked by the premature deaths of two icons of the postwar Black Hollywood. In December 1964, word leaked out that a frail and fatigued Nat "King" Cole had entered St. John's Hospital in Santa Monica, suffering from lung cancer. On February 15, 1965, he died at the age of forty-five. His was one of the last of the grand-style Hollywood funerals as more than three thousand people, including some of the entertainment industry's top stars and executives, paid their respects at St. James Episcopal Church on Wilshire Boulevard. Jack Benny delivered the eulogy. Among the pallbearers were Benny Carter and Frank Sinatra. Those in attendance included Duke Ellington, Count Basie, Senator Robert Kennedy, California governor Edmund Brown, George Burns, Edward G. Robinson, Peter Lawford, Jimmy Durante, Rosemary Clooney, Frankie Laine, Billy Daniels, Ricardo Montalban, Danny

Thomas, and Jerry Lewis. Afterward, Maria Cole remained in Los Angeles, resumed her singing career in the late 1960s, and cohosted a local television show. In 1971, she remarried and moved back to the East Coast. The showplace home in Hancock Park was sold.

Almost seven months after Cole's death, the town was caught off guard by the news that Dorothy Dandridge had been found dead in her Hollywood apartment on September 8, 1965. For Dandridge, the late 1950s and early 1960s had been a troubled and heartbreaking time. Following *Porgy and Bess,* she worked abroad in the film *Malaga,* then married a Las Vegas maître d'hôtel named Jack Denison. Hollywood gossiped that the smooth and slick Denison had persuaded Dandridge to pour much of her life's savings into a restaurant/club he opened on the Sunset Strip—just at the time when the Strip was in decline. He also persuaded her to sing at the club. It all proved disastrous. The restaurant failed. So did the marriage, amid charges that Denison had physically abused her. Then, an investment that Dandridge had made in oil wells—along with such other top Hollywood personalities as Doris Day, Billy Eckstine, director Stanley Kubrick, and Gordon MacRae—left her broke, the victim of a fraudulent deal. After filing for bankruptcy, Dandridge tried to pick up the pieces of her life and her career. But most felt that she was never again the same person.

Her last days were long and lonely, with late-night calls to friends and a deep depression. The coroner's report attributed Dandridge's death to an overdose of an antidepressant, Tofranil, and for years, it would be debated whether her death was a suicide or an accident. Dandridge's funeral was a subdued and unbearably sad affair without hordes of fans, without a wave of celebrities in attendance. Arriving solemnly were Geri Branton and her husband, Leo; Harold and Fayard Nicholas; Ruby Dandridge; Etta Jones; Joel Fluellen; and Peter Lawford, who was set to deliver the eulogy but was emotionally too overcome to speak.

For some, she represented unfulfilled promise. For others, she was a sign of the power of drive and ambition to break down barriers. For others, she was a doomed beauty, struggling heroically against personal demons and the fundamental racism of the industry. "Her own personal demons," said actor Brock Peters, "came out of everything the industry was at that time. I mean there's no putting those things aside. Her personal life and her personal demons in terms of the negative things that occurred in her personal life are not really that separate from who she was." Mainstream media and Hollywood would forget Dandridge within a relatively short period of time, wiping her from its historical record. Later, part of her compelling legend was the very fact that she had been forgotten—except by black America, which would pass her story on, one generation after another. For African Americans in Hollywood, especially actresses at the close of one century and the opening of another—Janet Jackson, Angela Bassett, Lela Rochon, Vanessa Williams, Whitney Houston, Jasmine Guy, and Halle Berry—Dorothy Dandridge's story would resonate. As the great tragic African American actress of twentieth-century cinema, she became a potent mythic goddess, every bit as haunting and significant a symbol as Monroe would be for the mainstream community.

Other deaths came later. Eddie "Rochester" Anderson and Mantan Moreland lived into the 1970s. So did that crafty survivor Clarence Muse, who tenaciously held on, appearing in such movies of the 1970s as *Car Wash* and *The Black Stallion.* Stepin Fetchit, the sisters Amanda and Lillian Randolph, and Phil Moore lived into the 1980s. So did Paul Williams. Sammy Davis Jr. died in 1990; Fredi Washington, in 1994; Harold Nicholas, in 2000.

Like the rest of America, the movie colony was jolted when Watts went up in flames in 1965. Afterward, long-festering racial/social tensions were indelibly stamped on the national consciousness as the country was forced to examine itself: its history, its values, its evasions. In time, the social and political shifts brought on by a wave of movements among the young—the Black Power movement, the antiwar movement, the youth movement, the feminist movement, and the counterculture generation—all affected the movies and the way Hollywood, black and white, viewed itself.

A new generation of performers worked and lived in the film captial in the 1960s and the 1970s. Comedian Bill Cosby found success on the television series *I Spy.* Diahann Carroll returned to town to star in television's *Julia* and ended up a resident. Black director Luther James and actor-turned-director Ivan Dixon began to work in television, too. So did others: Denise Nicholas, Greg Morris, Nichelle Nichols, Lloyd Haynes, Clarence Williams III, and Hari Rhodes. In the 1970s, a new black movie and television boom—movies such as *Lady Sings the Blues* and *Sounder,* along with such blaxploitation hits as *Coffy, The Mack, Foxy Brown, Slaughter,* and any number of other titles, some shot on L.A.'s streets, corners, and alleyways, as well as such television series as *Sanford and Son, Good Times,* and *The Jeffersons,* and the groundbreaking *Roots*—offered employment to an unprecedented number of African Americans: Richard Pryor, Cicely Tyson, Paul Winfield, Pam Grier, Vonetta McGee, Jim Brown, Ivan Dixon, Fred Williamson, Billy Dee Williams, Louis Gossett Jr., Sherman Hemsley, Isabel Sanford, Marla Gibbs, Madge Sinclair, Rosalind Cash, Robert Hooks, writer Lonne Elder III, and directors Stan Lathan, Michael Schultz, and Hugh Robertson. The pioneering Detroit-based record company Motown relocated to L.A., bringing its stable of stars west.

The new personalities as well as the new post-1960s attitudes led to the birth of a new Black Hollywood. Actors hung out together, auditioned together, griped and gossiped together, and pursued the almighty entertainment dream together. Many also fought against industry attitudes and struggled to find better roles—sometimes just more work, period. In that respect, they were no different from those earlier generations of the 1920s through the 1950s.

But by then, the great venues of Central Avenue had either closed up shop or were forever altered. The Lincoln Theatre was bought in the 1960s by the Reverend Samuel Crouch and became the Church of God in Christ Assemblies. Having lost its luster, the Dunbar Hotel was almost torn down but was saved and later became a residence for senior citizens. It was also given status as a city landmark. Nightclubs such as Club Alabam and The Last Word had shut their doors. Mocambo's and Ciro's, too, had folded up as the age of the great nightclubs in America ended.

Black Angelenos understood that the old centrality that had united Black Hollywood and a signficant part of black Los Angeles was now dead. "One of the things I used to hear my parents remark," said Marilyn Williams Hudson, "was that integration was great. But we didn't have our own hotels anymore. We didn't have our own nightclubs." "Central Avenue disintegrated," said L.A. resident Johnetta Jones. "It was like a ghost town. Because we could go anywhere. We could go to the hotels. We could go into the different restaurants." Now, Black Hollywood would be as scattered and sprawling as the rest of the film community. Beverly Hills, Santa Monica, and Toluca Park beckoned.

By the beginning of a new millennium, African American stars such as Denzel Washington, Will Smith, Martin Lawrence, Wesley Snipes, Samuel L. Jackson, and Morgan Freeman would command multimillion-dollar salaries and star in films that opened big and raked in huge profits. The list, however, did not include African American actresses, except perhaps Halle Berry. A few—though not nearly enough—African American writers, directors, and producers would now take meetings in executive offices, where they would pitch their projects eagerly and enthusiastically.

Around town, there would remain a few places, mainly restaurants, where young African American artists might hang out, such as Roscoe's

for chicken and waffles—and lots of shop talk. Ceremonies such as the
black Oscars—to honor those artists the Academy of Motion Picture Arts
and Sciences had not recognized—as well as the music award shows and
the NAACP's Image Awards would draw together the new Black Hollywood. The West Angeles Church of God in Christ would be a place of
worship for African American stars such as Angela Bassett and Denzel
Washington. Some members of the new Black Hollywood would also purchase homes in Lafayette Square. But these were special "occurrences," not
the stuff of everyday life.

By the 1960s and 1970s, when Ossie Davis came west, he saw that all
that activity on Central Avenue was gone. "The town had changed radi-
cally," recalled Davis, "and the sense of community that was palpable when
Ruby and I were there before had, in a sense, completely disappeared. I
don't know what had happened. But Central Avenue was out of the picture. It wasn't necessary for us to go into the black community to live, and
therefore I could live at the Roosevelt Hotel or the Beverly Wilshire.
Whatever. But I never went back, in a sense, to the old Los Angeles. It was
like a different place. The heart and gut of it was gone." For Davis, Los
Angeles became a place where he went to the studio, did his job, and came
back to his hotel without much thought of socializing—and afterward returned east.

The old walls and barriers had been—at least partially—knocked down.
No one would ever regret that. But something had vanished: that sense of
a vibrant cohesive community where black entertainers worked, played,
and had fun together. Those nights when Herb Jeffries or Bobby Short or
Lena Horne with Billy Strayhorn might step into the after-hours hangout
Brother's. Those times when Stepin Fetchit or Ben Carter or the Nicholas
Brothers would suddenly appear on Central Avenue and be the talk of the
whole block. Those late nights when Louise Beavers and friends would
play cards and laugh and talk and have a heck of a time into the early hours
of the morning. Those Sunday afternoons when Geri Branton and
Dorothy Dandridge might go to Billy Berg's to hear some jazz or stop by
one of those outdoor restaurants where a waiter or waitress would come to
take the order from their car. Those other afternoons when a neighborhood kid like Barbara Molette could swim in Rochester's pool or bicycle
over to Hattie McDaniel's house for milk and cookies. Those days now
were long gone and long forgotten.

NOTES

U nless otherwise noted below, all quotations are from interviews (or in rare cases, conversations) conducted by the author. Also consulted was material from the author's personal collection on Black Hollywood, which is composed of the author's past taped interviews of such figures as Fredi Washington, Geri Branton, Fayard Nicholas, Harold Nicholas, Vivian Dandridge, Bobby Short, Clarence Muse, King Vidor, Mantan Moreland, Dorothy Nicholas Morrow, Byron Morrow, Brock Peters, Lennie Bluett, Avanelle Harris, Clora Bryant, Mel Bryant, Jeanne Moore Pisano, Harold Jovien, Gerald Wilson, Leonard Feather, and many others. New interviews were also conducted with a number of figures who had previously been interviewed, such as Geri Branton, Fayard Nicholas, Bobby Short, Herb Jeffries, Isabel Washington Powell, Olga James, Dorothy Nicholas Morrow, Byron Morrow, and others. Some background material on Hollywood in general was drawn from Ephraim Katz's *Film Encyclopedia* as well as numerous Hollywood autobiographies, biographies, and histories. Some background material on the African American community in Los Angeles—as well as the early black entertainment scene in Los Angeles—has been drawn from such books as Delilah Beasley's *The Negro Trail Blazers of California*, William Loren Katz's *The Black West*, Betty Cox's *Central Avenue: Its Rise and Fall*, Tom Reed's *The Black Music History of Los Angeles—Its Roots*, parts of J. Max Bond's *The Negro in Los Angeles: A Dissertation*, and the collection of individual reminiscences *Central Avenue Sounds*. Also helpful were Eugene Jackson and Gwendolyn Sides St. Julian's *Eugene "Pineapple" Jackson: His Own Story*, Lena Horne's *Lena*, Carlton Jackson's *Hattie: The Life of Hattie McDaniel*, Diahann Carroll and Ross Firestone's *Diahann!*, Gail Lumet Buckley's *The Hornes: An American Family*, Ossie Davis and Ruby Dee's *With Ossie & Ruby: In This Life Together*, Sidney Poitier's *This Life*, and Marshal Royal's *Marshal Royal: Jazz Survivor* as well as numerous other titles listed in the bibliography. Material in the George P. Johnson Negro Film Collection at UCLA was helpful in reconstructing the early life of Noble Johnson; so, too, was a two-part article—titled "Noble Johnson"—by Bill Cappello in the January/February 1992 issues of *Classic Images* as well as part of Henry T. Sampson's *Blacks in Black and White: A Source Book on Black Films*. Material was also drawn from various periodicals, as cited in the individual chapter notes. Also consulted were the author's earlier books: *Dorothy Dandridge: A Biography; Toms, Coons, Mulattoes, Mammies, & Bucks: An Interpretive History of Blacks in American Films; Primetime Blues: African Americans on Network Television; Blacks in American Films and Television: An Illustrated Encyclopedia;* and *Brown Sugar: Eighty Years of America's Black Female Superstars.*

7 "My father didn't mount": Madame Sul-Te-Wan, interviewed by Raymond Lee, 1948, Los Angeles, "Madame Sul-Te-Wan and D. W. Griffith," edited by Gloria J. Gibson-Hudson, *Black Camera: The Newsletter of the Black Film Center/Archive*, Indiana University, 10, no. 1 (Spring 1995).

8 "We never did discover": Lillian Gish and Ann Pinchot, *The Movies, Mr. Griffith and Me* (Englewood Cliffs, N.J.: Prentice Hall, 1969).

8 "Mother, you are not": Delilah Beasley, *The Negro Trail Blazers of California* (1919; reprint, Westport, Conn.: Greenwood Press, 1969).

8 "Madame, if you ever": Sul-Te-Wan, interviewed by Lee.

9 "California left much to": G. W. Bitzer, *Billy Bitzer: His Story* (New York: Farrar, Straus and Giroux, 1973).

9 "*The Birth of a Nation*": Ibid.

9 "So one day I": Sul-Te-Wan, interviewed by Lee.

9 "Pardon me, gentleman, but": Ibid.

9 "Well," he said, "I don't": Ibid.

9 "and his coat was hitting": Ibid.

10 "I moved on up": Ibid.

10 "Pardon me, gentlemen," Madame: Ibid.

10 "I'm out here on": Ibid.

10 "I don't care how much": Ibid.

11 "There were practically no": Gish and Pinchot, *The Movies, Mr. Griffith and Me*.

11 "To economize, Mr. Griffith": Ibid.

11 "Go on. I will": Beasley, *Negro Trail Blazers of California*.

11 "the first colored woman": Sul-Te-Wan, interviewed by Lee.

11 "You have to be": Ibid.

12 "After the picture was": Beasley, *Negro Trail Blazers of California*.

12 "Mr. Griffith gave her": Ibid.

12 "Later, when Madame was": Gish and Pinchot, *The Movies, Mr. Griffith and Me*.

12 "It is like writing": Richard Schickel, *D. W. Griffith: An American Life* (New York: Simon & Schuster, 1984).

13 "our civic organizations and": "The Civic Walk," *California Eagle*, Feb. 6, 1915.

13 "misquotes the history of": "Fight against 'The Clansman' Lost by City Council and Many Citizens of Different Races," *California Eagle*, Feb. 13, 1915.

13 "You are no longer": Beasley, *Negro Trail Blazers of California*.

13 "Madame Sul-Te-Wan was very angry": Ibid.

14 "She was devoted to": Gish and Pinchot, *The Movies, Mr. Griffith and Me*.

14 "Why you know I": Sul-Te-Wan, interviewed by Lee.

14 "offered to take their": Gish and Pinchot, *The Movies, Mr. Griffith and Me*.

14 "waiting outside the hospital": Ibid.

14 "Yeah, he left me": Sul-Te-Wan, interviewed by Lee.

15 "To Whom It May": Beasley, *Negro Trail Blazers of California*.

15 "to some of the": Ibid.

16 "on the South by": J. Max Bond, *The Negro in Los Angeles* (Ph.D. dissertation, University of Southern California, 1936).

17 "stately homes representing the": Lonnie G. Bunche, "Vernon Central Revisited," lobby display, Dunbar Hotel, Los Angeles.

17 "the largest Negro hotel": "The Golden West Hotel," *California Eagle*, Feb. 21, 1914.

20 "the race's daredevil movie": Bill Cappello, *Classic Images*, no. 199, Jan. 1992.

20 "America's premier Afro-American": "The Trooper of Company K," *California Eagle*, Mar. 14, 1916.

22 "The Lincoln Motion Picture": Ibid.

23 "an exceptional picture if": Ibid.

25 "led me to the": Gloria Swanson, *Swanson on Swanson* (New York: Random House, 1980).

25 "While she worked": Ibid.

25 "Many of our women": Beasley, *Negro Trail Blazers of California*.

25 "Ever since my early": Lillian Moseley, "The Secrets of a Movie Maid," *Ebony*, Nov. 1949.

25 "Then in 1918": Ibid.

CHAPTER 2: THE TWENTIES

Parts of this chapter, including quoted comments, are drawn from the author's interviews and conversations with Fayard Nicholas, Melanie Lomax, Avanelle Harris, Etta Jones, Willard Brown, Johnetta Jones, Marian Patterson, and others. Also consulted for information on early Los Angeles: *Eugene "Pineapple" Jackson: His Own Story;* parts of *The Negro in Los Angeles: A Dissertation*, by J. Max Bond; Bette Yarbrough Cox's *Central Avenue: Its Rise and Fall, 1890–1955; Central Avenue Sounds*, by Clora Bryant et al.; and Budd Schulberg's *Moving Pictures: Memories of a Hollywood Prince;* as well as articles in *The California Eagle, Opportunity, Ebony,* and other cited publications. Also consulted for information on the murder mystery surrounding William Desmond Taylor was Sidney D. Kirkpatrick's *A Cast of Killers*.

33 "About 40,000 children were": Eugene Jackson with Gwendolyn Sides St. Julian, *Eugene "Pineapple" Jackson: His Own Story* (Jefferson, N.C.: McFarland & Company, 1999). Jackson may have meant 4,000 children.

33 "just signed a 5": " 'Sunshine Sammy' to Receive $10,000 a Year," *California Eagle*, Feb. 25, 1922.

34 "Sammy was such a": Jackson with St. Julian, *Eugene "Pineapple" Jackson*.

35 "completed his contract with": "Studio Gossip," *California Eagle*, June 20, 1924.

35 "The kid situation seems": "Studio Gossip," *California Eagle*, July 4, 1924.

35 "the largest ever granted": " 'Sunshine Sammy's' Granted Divorce-Alimony," *California Eagle*, Dec. 7, 1928.

36 "the chocolate-coated fun": Leonard Maltin, *Our Gang: The Life and Times of the Little Rascals* (New York: Crown, 1977).

36 "a home of his own": " 'Farina' and Flying Fish, and the Studios of Great 'Movie' Producers," *California Eagle*, May 28, 1926.

38 "YMCA, Second Baptist Church": Jackson with St. Julian, *Eugene "Pineapple" Jackson*.

38 "It was a Broadway": Ibid.

39 "Saturday matinees would star": Ibid.

39 "Shimmy King": Ibid.

40 "I met with Mr.": Ibid.

41 "I was hot as": Ibid.

42 "In the old days": Rosalind Russell and Chris Chase, *Life Is a Banquet* (New York: Random House, 1977).

44 "clean off the seat": Ibid.

44 "Because I was willing": Russell and Chase, *Life Is a Banquet*.

45 "Even if you tell": Budd Schulberg, *Moving Pictures: Memories of a Hollywood Prince* (New York: Stein and Day, 1981).

45 "nodding at me with": Ibid.

46 "watchdog, dresser, personal maid": John Moffitt, *New York Times,* June 9, 1935; also found in *Becoming Mae West,* by Emily Worth Leider (New York: Farrar, Straus and Giroux, 1997).

47 "Oscar the Bootblack, as": Schulberg, *Moving Pictures.*

47 "has made a huge": Lawrence F. LaMar, "Camera!!!" *California Eagle,* Aug. 26, 1927.

47 "The closest I had": Schulberg, *Moving Pictures.*

48 "We even compared bootblacks": Ibid.

49 "didn't want a brown-skinned": "Foot Doctor to Film Stars," *Ebony,* Sept. 1948.

50 "fight right to the": Ibid.

50 "a lot of race talk": Ibid.

50 "In my work with": Lillian Moseley, "The Secrets of a Movie Maid," *Ebony,* Nov. 1949.

51 "I wasn't a servant": Ibid.

51 "This must be our": Ibid.

51 "One never could get": Ibid.

52 "three bottles of champagne": Ibid.

52 "people who never get": David Stenn, *Bombshell: The Life and Death of Jean Harlow* (Garden City, N.Y.: Doubleday, 1993).

54 "Henry Peavey, the soprano": Kenneth Anger, *Hollywood Babylon* (San Francisco: Straight Arrow Books, 1975).

54 "During all of this": Sidney D. Kirkpatrick, *A Cast of Killers* (New York: Dutton, 1986).

55 "queer meeting places": Anger, *Hollywood Babylon.*

55 "Taylor had been killed": Kirkpatrick, *Cast of Killers.*

56 "Miss Worthing is capital": Mordaunt Hall, "The Screen," *New York Times,* Mar. 2, 1925.

56 "That I do, Miss": Worthing, "Hollywood's Most Tragic Marriage." *Ebony,* February 1952.

56 "I don't care if": Ibid.

56 "something happened to my": Ibid.

57 "To the loveliest lady": Ibid.

57 "Well, that night": Ibid.

57 "high up in the": Ibid.

57 "the jewel of the": Ibid.

57 "What I saw stopped": Ibid.

58 "I took Sally with": Ibid.

58 "turned and looked at": Ibid.

58 "aware of all the": Ibid.

60 "she is the only": Helen Kenlin, "Leave It to Madame Sul-Te-Wan," *California Eagle*, June 24, 1927.

60 "Madame is a real": Ibid.

60 "Sul-Te-Wan had the misfortune": "Mme. Sul-Te-Wan Scores Again," *California Eagle*, May 27, 1928.

61 "There were dozens": Christopher Finch and Linda Rosenkrantz, *Gone Hollywood: The Movie Colony in the Golden Age* (Garden City, N.Y.: Doubleday, 1979).

62 "The casting people came": Buck Clayton with Nancy Miller-Elliot, *Buck Clayton's Jazz World* (New York: Oxford University Press, 1987).

62 "The casting people asked": Ibid.

62 "with a dark complexion": Jackson with St. Julian, *Eugene "Pineapple" Jackson*.

62 "A casting office for": Ibid.

62 "Mr. Butler is responsible": Floyd Covington, "The Negro Invades Hollywood," *Opportunity*, Apr. 1929.

63 "the revered Lon Chaney": Harry Levette, "Behind the Scenes," *California Eagle*, Mar. 2, 1934.

63 "Negroes are natural actors": Covington, "Negro Invades Hollywood."

63 "did more to encourage": Langston Hughes, *The Big Sea* (New York: Hill and Wang, 1963).

64 "He stared at me": Karen E. Hudson, *The Will and the Way: Paul R. Williams, Architect* (New York: Rizzoli International Publications, 1994).

64 "Williams had his first": Karen E. Hudson, *Paul R. Williams, Architect: A Legacy of Style* (New York: Rizzoli International Publications, 1993).

65 "I looked forward to": Hudson, *The Will and the Way*.

65 "the same Senator Frank": Ibid.

65 "memories of his childhood": Ibid.

66 "I had grown up": Ibid.

66 "Los Angeles grew as": Ibid.

67 "the finest and most": "Lincoln Theater to Open Soon," *California Eagle*, Sept. 23, 1927.

67 "On top of that": Clora Bryant, Buddy Collette, William Green, Steven Isoardi, Jack Kelson, Horace Tapscott, Gerald Wilson, and Marl Young, eds., *Central Avenue Sounds* (Berkeley and Los Angeles: University of California Press, 1999).

68 "at the annual ball": Lionel Hampton and James Haskins, *Hamp: An Autobiography* (New York: Warner Books, 1989).

69 "came to go slumming": Bryant et al., *Central Avenue Sounds*.

69 "I'd rather work than": "Carolyn Snowden Starring in Pictures," *California Eagle*, Sept. 23, 1927. Snowden's first name is sometimes spelled "Carolyn."

70 "I never had a": Joseph Polonsky, "Carolynne Snowden Is Boosted by M-G-M Folks," *Pittsburgh Courier*, Sept. 29, 1927.

70 "Creole Carolynne Snowden with": Clipping file, George P. Johnson Negro Film Collection, UCLA.

72 "Carolynne Snowden, Hollywood Movie": Floyd J. Calvin, "Carolynne Snowden, Hollywood Movie Star Dazzles New York When She Steps Out," *Pittsburgh Courier*, Oct. 27. Year not given. Clipping file: George P. Johnson Negro Film Collection, UCLA.

73 "Let us hope it": "Police on with Their Program of Prejudice and Hate," *California Eagle*, Nov. 8, 1929.

74 "was in somebody's way": "Apex Wins Court Fight," *California Eagle*, Nov. 29, 1929.

74 "fair-minded and just": Ibid.

77 "It was a hotel": W.E.B. Du Bois comments, on lobby display at the Dunbar Hotel lobby, Los Angeles.

77 "climbed into his Stutz-Bearcat": Lucius Lomax, "Dreaming in Black and White," *Texas Observer*, Sept. 26, 1997.

78 "He was a thief": Ibid.

78 "He was the boss": Phil Moore, "Things I Forgot to Tell You" (unpublished, 1986).

78 "rather tall and bronze": Ibid.

78 "He did not marry": Lomax, "Dreaming in Black and White."

78 "always parked, forever immobile": Ibid.

78 "He now was a": Moore, "Things I Forgot to Tell You."

79 "The Old Man laid": Lomax, "Dreaming in Black and White."

80 "To a race that": Polonsky, "Carolynne Snowden Is Boosted by M-G-M Folks."

81 "I am a race man": Louis Sheaffer, *O'Neill: Son and Artist* (Boston: Little, Brown, 1973).

82 "The question has been": Covington, "Negro Invades Hollywood."

84 "Only those who are": C. Gerald Fraser, "Ethel Waters Is Dead at 80," *New York Times*, Sept. 2, 1977.

84 "Mr. Zanuck listened to": Ethel Waters with Charles Samuels, *His Eye Is on the Sparrow* (New York: Doubleday, 1950).

84 "Well, Mr. Zanuck": Ibid.

84 "How much do you": Ibid.

84 "I will probably lose": Ibid.

85 "You drive a pretty": Ibid.

86 "Lorainne was out of": Levette, "Behind the Scenes."

87 "I didn't make any": CBS studio biography.

88 "drank himself out of": Jackson with St. Julian, *Eugene "Pineapple" Jackson*.

88 "a timeless resignation": Sheaffer, *O'Neill: Son and Artist*.

89 "Family and friends could": Jackson with St. Julian, *Eugene "Pineapple" Jackson*.

90 "Bring that nigger over": Ibid.

90 "For several years": King Vidor, *A Tree Is a Tree* (New York: Harcourt, Brace, 1952).

92 "the third from the": Vidor, *Tree Is a Tree*.

92 "self-inflicted penance for": Louise Brooks, *Lulu in Hollywood* (New York: Knopf, 1982).

93 "She was beautiful and": Vidor, *Tree Is a Tree*.

95 "I can't see how": William Rollins, "Stepin Fetchit Looks Back," *Los Angeles Times West Magazine*, Nov. 16, 1969.

96 "In place of putting": Joseph McBride, "Stepin Fetchit Talks Back," *Film Quarterly*, Summer 1971.

97 "Go and see what's": Rollins, "Stepin Fetchit Looks Back."

97 "Much mush stuff, but": "*In Old Kentucky*," *Variety*, Dec. 14, 1927.

97 "truly one of the": *California Eagle*, Dec. 21, 1928.

97 "He had me stay": McBride, "Stepin Fetchit Talks Back."

97 "I was an artist": Ibid.

98 "the fastest comical dancer": Lindsay Patterson, "Focus on Clarence Muse," *Essence*, Apr. 1976.

98 "I always said": Rollins, "Stepin Fetchit Looks Back."

98 "I had a couple": Ibid.

98–99 "Hollywood was more segregated": McBride, "Stepin Fetchit Talks Back."

100 "Negro 'extra' receives more": Covington, "Negro Invades Hollywood."

100 "that when colored drama": Ibid.

100 "One of the chief": Robert Benchley, "*Hearts in Dixie* (the First Real Talking Picture)," *Opportunity,* Apr. 1929.

100 "In the wake of this": Covington, "Negro Invades Hollywood."

CHAPTER 3: THE THIRTIES

Parts of this chapter, including quoted comments, were drawn from the author's interviews and conversations with Mel Bryant, Vivian Dandridge, Fayard Nicholas, Joe Adams, Carmen de Lavallade, Johnetta Jones, Marian Patterson, Willard Brown, Geri Branton, Lennie Bluett, Fredi Washington, Jean Bach, Isabel Washington Powell, Ruby Dee, Clarence Muse, Alberta Hunter, and others. Also helpful were the autobiographies "Things I Forgot to Tell You" and *Lena* as well as *Dorothy Dandridge: A Biography, Hattie: The Life of Hattie McDaniel,* and articles in such periodicals as *The California Eagle, The Pittsburgh Courier, Variety,* and *The New York Times,* as cited below.

103 "Yes. It was called": William Manchester, *The Glory and the Dream: A Narrative History of America, 1932–1972* (Boston: Little, Brown, 1973).

104 "months with Nite Clubs": Harry Levette, "Behind the Scenes," *California Eagle,* Aug. 28, 1931.

106 "a colored jazz orchestra": "*Ex-Flame,*" *Variety,* Jan. 28, 1931.

106 "They Must Black Up": A. H. Lawrence, *Duke Ellington and His World: A Biography* (New York: Routledge, 2001).

106 "It was a real": Clora Bryant, Buddy Collette, William Green, Steven Isoardi, Jack Kelson, Horace Tapscott, Gerald Wilson, and Marl Young, eds., *Central Avenue Sounds: Jazz in Los Angeles* (Berkeley and Los Angeles: University of California Press, 1999).

107 "giving the loud hee-haw": Harry Levette, "Behind the Scenes," *California Eagle,* Aug. 28, 1931.

109 "I used to get": Dorothy O'Leary, no title, *New York Times,* Mar. 7, 1948 (clippings file, Library for the Performing Arts at Lincoln Center).

111 "Having that organization as": Dorothy Dandridge and Earl Conrad, *Everything and Nothing: The Dorothy Dandridge Tragedy* (New York: Abelard-Schuman, 1970).

111 "Go back east, Mrs.": Author's interview with Vivian Dandridge.

115 "was a pretty town": Lionel Hampton and James Hoskins, *Hamp: An Autobiography* (New York: Warner Books, 1989).

117 "In the Central Avenue": Etta James and David Ritz, *Rage to Survive* (New York: Villard Books, 1995).

118 "Stepin Fetchit came by": Bryant et al., eds., *Central Avenue Sounds.*

118 "Willie dressed superclean and": James and Ritz, *Rage to Survive.*

119 "Not the slightest bit": Harry Levette, "Behind the Scenes," *California Eagle,* Mar. 4, 1934.

121 "Everyone in Hollywood absolutely": Sam Robins, "Green Pastures, Indeed!" *New York Times,* Dec. 15, 1940.

122 "I'm certainly glad I": Ben Carter studio biography.

122 "I haven't lost a": Robins, "Green Pastures, Indeed!"

123 "I've got to put": Ibid.

124 "You play it." "But I'm": Carter studio biography.

125 "Some one was smart": Bosley Crowther, review of *Maryland, New York Times,* July 13, 1940.

126 "I never felt the": Fay M. Jackson, "Actress Compares Race Company to Hollywood Films," *California Eagle,* Aug. 26, 1937.

127 "Universal to Film Story": "Universal to Film Story on 'Passing for White," *California Eagle,* Dec. 1, 1933.

128 "Universal Sends East For": "Universal Sends East for Colored Girl in Big Part," *California Eagle,* Jan. 5, 1934.

128 "Universal Still Looks for": "Universal Still Looks for White-Negro Girl," *California Eagle,* Jan. 26, 1934.

129 "This girl is the": Ibid.

129 "She looked like *white*": *Brown Sugar,* episode 2, PBS documentary series, 1987.

129 "I expected to see": Arthur Pollock, "Theater Time," *Daily Compass,* no date (clippings file, Library for the Performing Arts at Lincoln Center).

131 "It was no secret": Lawrence, *Duke Ellington and His World.*

133 "There were five musicians": Ibid.

136 "Mr. Stahl has made": "Claudette Pleased with Freddi [*sic*] Co-star in 'Imitation' Film," *California Eagle,* June 8, 1934.

137 "How would you read": Author's interview with Fredi Washington.

137 "Daily on the set": Bernice Patton, "Critics Weep at the Preview of 'Imitation of Life,'" *Pittsburgh Courier,* Dec. 8, 1934.

138 "I've got to stay": Eileen Creelman, "Picture Plays and Players," *New York Sun,* Feb. 14, 1935.

139 "*The Avenue*": Phil Moore, "Things I Forgot to Tell You" (unpublished, 1986).

139 "Father Divine was a": Ibid.

140 "I didn't know the": Hampton and Haskins, *Hamp.*

140 "she was a beautiful": Ibid.

141 "She bought a building": Ibid.

141 "a big Italian community": Woody Strode and Sam Young, *Goal Dust* (Lanham, Md.: Madison Books, 1990).

142 "Coming out of the": Ibid.

142 "He liked the girls": Ibid.

142 "He was the only": Ibid.

143 "Every morning the studio": Ibid.

143 "They dressed us up": Ibid.

143 "when I was told": Ibid.

145 "He's as sweet as": Martin Duberman, *Paul Robeson* (New York: Knopf, 1988).

146 "We are proudest of": Ibid.

146 "What we all three": Ibid.

146 "Impossible let him okay": Ibid.

148 "I'm getting a lot": "Louise Beavers 'On Spot,'" *Pittsburgh Courier,* Dec. 15, 1934.

148 "Picture is stolen by": "*Imitation of Life,*" *Variety,* Nov. 27, 1934.

148 "the best picture of": C.A.B. (Charlotta Bass), " 'Imitation of Life' a Better Picture," *California Eagle*, Dec. 7, 1934.

149 "who cried openly as": Bernice Patton, "Critics Weep at the Preview of 'Imitation of Life,' " *Pittsburgh Courier*, Dec. 8, 1934.

149 "Fredi Washington expresses the": Fay M. Jackson, "Fredi Washington Strikes New Note in Hollywood Film," *Pittsburgh Courier*, Dec. 15, 1934.

150 "no searching analysis to": Sterling A. Brown, "*Imitation of Life:* Once a Pancake," *Opportunity*, Mar. 1935.

150 "a brave white man": Chappy Gardner, "Beavers Has Lost Screen Award," *Pittsburgh Courier*, Mar. 9, 1935.

151 "Louise Beavers, Hollywood's most": "Louise Beavers Comes for Week at the Granada," *Pittsburgh Courier*, Mar. 16, 1935.

152 "I've worked with most": Eileen Creelman, "Picture Plays and Players," *New York Sun*, Feb. 14, 1935.

152 "I am the worst": Ibid.

152 "Film marks reappearance of": "*One Mile from Heaven*," *Variety*, July 21, 1937.

153 "The Negro comedian, recently": "Stepin Fetchit Resumes Screen Career with Fox," *New York Evening Post*, Mar. 3, 1934.

154 "He was a fabulous": Ralph Cooper and Steve Dougherty, *Amateur Night at the Apollo: Ralph Cooper Presents Five Decades of Entertainment* (New York: HarperCollins, 1990).

154 "Step hit the floor": Ibid.

155 "I don't have time": Ibid.

155 "There is nothing, absolutely": Shirley Temple Black, *Child Star: An Autobiography* (New York: McGraw-Hill, 1988).

156 "Organically, Bill Robinson is": "Profiles: Bojangles-1," *New Yorker*, Oct. 6, 1934.

156 "I didn't pay too": Fannie Robinson, "After 20 Years of Marriage, Separation and Death, Fannie Robinson Still Loves Bill Robinson," date and publication information unknown (clippings file, George P. Johnson Negro Film Collection, UCLA).

157 "The first thing I": Temple, *Child Star*.

158 "Most relationships spawned on": Ibid.

159 "quit cold last Thursday": Harry Levette, "Behind the Scenes," *California Eagle*, Sept. 27, 1935.

159 "was caught at home": Ibid.

162 "A staff of two": Temple, *Child Star*.

162 "But that's where the": Ibid.

162 "Now, darlin', don't you": Ibid.

162 "We were performing in": Ibid.

162 "I like white folks": "Profiles: Bojangles-1," *New Yorker*.

162 "was the biggest Uncle": Gail Lumet Buckley, *The Hornes: An American Family* (New York: Knopf, 1986).

162 "to wedge his roadster": "Bojangles Wins a Fight, Spends an Hour in Jail," *New York Post*, Sept. 21, 1938.

163 "suspicion of assault with": Ibid.

163 "It seemed to me": Ibid.

163 "slashed by knives and razors": "Profiles: Bojangles-1," *New Yorker*.

164 "Who the hell ever": Henry Wiencek, *The Hairstons: An American Family in Black and White* (New York: St. Martin's Press, 1999).

165 "directing, script writing, lighting": Cooper and Dougherty, *Amateur Night at the Apollo.*

166 "the breaks in Hollywood": Ibid.

166 "reputation in joining pioneer": Ibid.

166 "Only after hours of": Cooper and Dougherty, *Amateur Night at the Apollo.*

167 "There is an awful": Lena Horne and Richard Schickel, *Lena* (Garden City, N.Y.: Doubleday, 1965).

167 "Gail could not have": Ibid.

167 "Louis immediately insisted that": Ibid.

168 "He knew nothing about": Ibid.

171 "much box office promise": *"Harlem on the Prairie," Variety,* Feb. 9, 1938.

171 "the first Negro musical": Ibid.

172 "In those days": Robert Epstein, "A West That Wasn't," *Los Angeles Times,* May 12, 1992.

172 "Our wages are satisfactory": Jackson, "Actress Compares Race Company to Hollywood Films."

172 "I never did hit": Cooper and Dougherty, *Amateur Night at the Apollo.*

174 "under the broiling California": Arnold Rampersad, *The Life of Langston Hughes,* 2nd ed., vol. 1, *1902–1941: I, Too, Sing America* (New York: Oxford University Press, 2001).

175 "had dared make one": Review of *Way Down South, Daily Worker,* June 5, 1939.

175 "picture-perfect": Review of *Way Down South, Los Angeles Times,* July 19, 1939.

175 "slow-going": *"Way Down South," Variety,* Aug. 23, 1939.

175 "Everybody says they cannot": Rampersad, *Life of Langston Hughes,* vol. 1.

176 "There has been more": Earl Dancer, "Negro Public and Press Demand Recognition from Hollywood Motion Picture Moguls Who Ignore Race," *California Eagle,* June 30, 1938.

178 "She had the most": *Brown Sugar,* episode 2, PBS documentary series.

178 "rates number one box": "Georgette Harvey Tests for 'Gone with the Wind' Picture Role," *California Eagle,* Feb. 17, 1938.

178 "report that Hattie McDaniel's": "Home of Famous Movie Star Furnished by Popular Neighborhood Store," *California Eagle,* Mar. 10, 1938.

180 "treating these actors as": Marcella Rabwin to John Hay Whitney, Feb. 11, 1939, Selznick Papers. The University of Texas. Austin, Texas.

180 "left no stone unturned": Carlton Jackson, *Hattie: The Life of Hattie McDaniel* (Lanham, Md.: Madison Books, 1990).

180 "I feel so keenly": David O. Selznick to John Hay Whitney, Feb. 10, 1939, Selznick Papers.

181 "Mammy, may I go": Jackson, *Hattie.*

181 "If for nothing else": Carlton Moss, "An Open Letter to Mr. Selznick," *Daily Worker,* Jan. 9, 1940.

182 "will go down in": Louella Parsons, "Mammy's Gold Oscar Most Popular Award," International News Service, Mar. 9, 1940.

182 "Fellow members of the": *Brown Sugar,* episode 2, PBS documentary series.

183 "I found I couldn't": Jackson, *Hattie.*

CHAPTER 4: THE FORTIES

arts of this chapter, including quoted comments, have been drawn from the author's interviews and conversations with Geri Branton, Fayard Nicholas, Dorothy Nicholas Morrow, Byron Morrow, Rigmor Newman, Etta Jones, Phil Moore, Bobby Short, Jean Bach, Marilyn Williams Hudson, Herb Jeffries, Ossie Davis, Ruby Dee, Johnetta Jones, Marian Patterson, Willard Brown, Sydney Guilaroff, Barbara Roseburr Molette, Avanelle Harris, and others. Some comments by Phil Moore, as indicated below, are from his unpublished memoir "Things I Forgot to Tell You." Also helpful have been *Lena; Music Is My Mistress; The Will and the Way: Paul R. Williams, Architect; Paul R. Williams, Architect: A Legacy of Style; The Hornes: An American Family; Hattie: The Life of Hattie McDaniel; Dorothy Dandridge: A Biography; Blacks in American Films and Television: An Illustrated Encyclopedia;* as well as articles in such periodicals as *The California Eagle, The Los Angeles Sentinel, The Pittsburgh Courier, Ebony, Variety,* the *Los Angeles Times,* the *Los Angeles Examiner,* and others as cited below.

193 "You're very pretty": Interview with Fayard Nicholas.

194 "Jumping for Joy!": David Hajdu, *Lush Life: A Biography of Billy Strayhorn* (New York: Farrar, Straus and Giroux, 1996).

194 "a team of scholarly Hollywood": Duke Ellington, *Music Is My Mistress* (Garden City, N.Y.: Doubleday, 1973).

194 "black humor performed by": A. H. Lawrence, *Duke Ellington and His World: A Biography* (New York: Routledge, 2001).

196 "The audience itself was": Ellington, *Music Is My Mistress.*

196 "not only a hit": John Kinloch, " 'Jump for Joy' Is Sensational Eve in Theater—Kinloch," *California Eagle,* July 17, 1941.

196 "The performance of two acts": Florence Lawrence, "Ellington Hit Opens at Mayan," *Los Angeles Examiner,* July 11, 1941.

197 "We were always on": Ellington, *Music Is My Mistress.*

197 "most of our young": Ibid.

202 "The myth of enormous": Hortense Powdermaker, *Hollywood, the Dream Factory* (Boston: Little, Brown, 1950).

208 "When are we going": Cynthia Gorney, "The Fragile Flame of Dorothy Dandridge," *Washington Post,* Feb. 9, 1988.

210 "Dorothy was the loveliest": Ibid.

212 "pointed out the incalculable": Walter White, *How Far the Promised Land* (New York: Viking Press, 1955).

213 "I'd never seen anything": Clora Bryant, Buddy Collette, William Green, Steven Isoardi, Jack Kelson, Horace Tapscott, Gerald Wilson, and Marl Young, eds., *Central Avenue Sounds: Jazz in Los Angeles* (Berkeley and Los Angeles: University of California Press, 1999).

213 "lived in this fine": Interview with Clora Bryant.

213 "It was a point": Bryant et al, eds. *Central Avenue Sounds.*

214 "were living in a": Lena Horne and Richard Schickel, *Lena* (Garden City, N.Y. Doubleday, 1965).

215 "Damn, she was a": Phil Moore, "Things I Forgot to Tell You" (unpublished, 1986).

215 "Aren't you the guy": Ibid.

215 "asked me if I": Ibid.

215 "It's kinda hard": Ibid.

215 "Often when I start": Ibid.

216 "joint was packed every": Ibid.

216 "At first the audience": Ibid.

216 "And the owner was": Author's interview with Phil Moore.

217 "I heard you sing": Horne and Schickel, *Lena*.

217 "L-l-lovely, my dear": Gail Lumet Buckley, *The Hornes: An American Family* (New York: Knopf, 1986).

221 "Walter White and Paul": Buckley, *The Hornes*.

221 "sent me a note": *Brown Sugar*, episode 2, PBS documentary series, 1987.

221 "Basie told me": *Brown Sugar*, episode 3, PBS documentary series, 1987.

221 "I'm Billy Strayhorn": Buckley, *The Hornes*.

221 "the Negro section": Horne and Schickel, *Lena*.

222 "In Hollywood my first": Ibid.

222 "the girl with the": Frank Nugent, ". . . She's Nobody's Mammy," *Liberty*, Apr. 7, 1945.

223 "After an extremely formal": Buckley, *The Hornes*.

223 "Our house, which rested": Ibid.

223 "Below our hill was": Ibid.

223 "Fortunately, our allies were": Ibid.

223 "My California was pre-freeway": Ibid.

224 "was so carried away": Joe Louis with Edna Rust and Art Rust Jr., *Joe Louis: My Life* (New York: Harcourt Brace Jovanovich, 1978).

224 "I have a temper": "*Ebony* interview: Lena Horne," *Ebony*, May 1980.

225 "because I was the": Moore, "Things I Forgot to Tell You."

225 "How old are you": Ibid.

225 "we drove all over": Ibid.

226 "At about five minutes": Ibid.

227 "What else can you": Ibid.

227 "Yes, sir": Ibid.

227 "Can you play for": Ibid.

227 "Yes, sir": Ibid.

227 "Can you read well": Ibid.

227 "Yes, sir, practically": Ibid.

227 "I can't put you": Ibid.

227 "I didn't get the": Ibid.

227 "were mammoth factories developing": Ibid.

228 "They'd always send a": Leonard Feather, *The Pleasures of Jazz* (New York: Horizon Press, 1976).

228 "Kinda gave you a": Moore, "Things I Forgot to Tell You."

228 "Upon becoming a full-fledged": Ibid.

228 "After I graduated to": Feather, *Pleasures of Jazz*.

230 "The title song, though": Moore, "Things I Forgot to Tell You."

230 "a self-made man of": Ibid.

230 "didn't seem to catch": Ibid.

231 "I made many recordings": Clora Bryant et al., eds., *Central Avenue Sounds*.

231 "I was up in the": Moore, "Things I Forgot to Tell You."

231 "He gave me": "The Star Maker," *Ebony,* Nov. 1960.

233 "was always a difficult": Bette Davis, *The Lonely Life* (New York: Putnam, 1962).

233 "Are you sure the": Nugent, ". . . She's Nobody's Mammy."

234 "A rough estimate of": John Hope Franklin and Alfred A. Moss Jr., *From Slavery to Freedom* (New York: McGraw-Hill, 1994).

235 "I know I'm in": Nugent, ". . . She's Nobody's Mammy."

236 "the charm and beauty": Ibid.

236 "Take me to the": Buckley, *The Hornes.*

239 "No bandana on her": *Brown Sugar,* episode 3, PBS documentary series, 1987.

240 "She would bring out": "Movie Dance Director," *Ebony,* Apr. 1950.

241 "one of the world's": Ibid.

241 "They're pretty shocked when": Ibid.

241 "This consists in finding": Ibid.

243 "She always refers to": Ibid.

244 "That two-week engagement stretched": "Hep Cat," *Los Angeles,* Aug. 1994.

244 "Benny opened up the": Ibid.

244 "then he was as": *Brown Sugar,* episode 3, PBS documentary series, 1987.

245 "Be real small": Buckley, *The Hornes.*

245 "She flew into a": Ibid.

246 "been conflict between the": Ethel Waters with Charles Samuels, *His Eye Is on the Sparrow* (Garden City, N.Y.: Doubleday, 1950).

247 "It was people going": Clora Bryant et al., eds., *Central Avenue Sounds.*

250 "It would be crowded": Horne and Schickel, *Lena.*

253 "cross between a somewhat": Jim Heimann, *Out with the Stars: Hollywood Nightlife in the Golden Era* (New York: Abbeville Press, 1985).

255 "notoriously segregated": Buckley, *The Hornes.*

256 "The glamour was back": Karen E. Hudson, *The Will and the Way: Paul R. Williams, Architect* (New York: Rizzoli International Publications, 1994).

257 "It was a very": Bernard Weinraub, "A Grand Hotel, Still Pink, Still Posh," *New York Times,* June 1, 1995.

258 "Once again I found": Hudson, *Will and the Way.*

258 "For too long white-owned": Ibid.

261 "This court is of": Cited in *Los Angeles Examiner,* Dec. 20, 1945.

262 "Twenty-five is a": Waters with Samuels, *His Eye Is on the Sparrow.*

268 "Betty Grable, Lana Turner": Louella O. Parsons, "Actress, Mate Expect Stork," *Los Angeles Examiner,* May 25, 1944.

268 "He thought because he": "Hattie McDaniel Wins Divorce," *Los Angeles Times,* Dec. 20, 1945.

268 "There was a lot": "Divorce Won By 'Beulah,' " *Los Angeles Examiner,* Dec. 6, 1950.

268 "I'm not going to": "Hattie McDaniel's Story Gets Decree," *Los Angeles Times,* Dec. 6, 1950.

271 "Even if it doesn't": Florence Muir, "What's That, Boss?" *Saturday Evening Post,* June 19, 1943.

272 "a drawling, shuffling little": Ibid.

275 "Under Parker—a puritanical": Mike Davis, *City of Quartz: Excavating the Future in Los Angeles* (New York: Vintage Books, 1992).

275 "That was the whole": Interview with Clora Bryant.

277 "WHEREAS, Negro actors have": Cited in Betsy Blair, *The Memory of All That* (New York: Knopf, 2003).

278 "at a board meeting": Ibid.

278 "to show that not": Marsha Hunt, "Letters to the Editor: Joel Fluellen," *Los Angeles Times*, Feb. 18, 1990.

279 "But the details I": Hedda Hopper, "Hattie Hates Nobody." *Los Angeles Times*, Dec. 14, 1947.

279 "the political enemies of": C.A.B. (Charlotta Bass), "On the Sidewalk," *California Eagle*, Dec. 18, 1947.

279 "For twenty-four hours, we": Ossie Davis and Ruby Dee, *With Ossie & Ruby: In This Life Together* (New York: Morrow, 1998).

279 "When the curtain went": Author's interview with Ossie Davis.

280 "Hollywood's lavish opening-night": Davis and Dee, *With Ossie & Ruby*.

280 "The other actors stayed": Author's interview with Ossie Davis

282 "It was a professional": Mel Gussow, *Don't Say Yes until I Finish Talking: A Biography of Darryl F. Zanuck* (Garden City, N.Y.: Doubleday, 1971).

284 "We had a big": Lionel Hampton and James Haskins, *Hamp: An Autobiography* (New York: Warner Books, 1989).

284 "I was assistant campaign": Ibid.

CHAPTER 5: THE FIFTIES

Parts of this chapter, including quoted comments, are drawn from interviews and conversations with Geri Branton, Bobby Short, Ossie Davis, Ruby Dee, Carmen de Lavallade, Carlton Moss, Juliette Ball, Nick Perito, Dorothy Nicholas Morrow, Byron Morrow, Johnetta Jones, Marilyn Williams Hudson, Olga James, Otto Preminger, Vivian Dandridge, Herb Jeffries, Harold Jovien, Phil Moore, Jeanne Moore Pisano, Herb Ross, Gerald Mayer, Barbara Roseburr Molette, Nichelle Nichols, Ivan Dixon, and others. Also helpful were *Dorothy Dandridge: A Biography; Blacks in American Films and Television: An Illustrated Encyclopedia; With Ossie & Ruby: In This Life Together; Yes I Can; Diahann!; Josephine: The Hungry Heart; Primetime Blues: African Americans on Network Television; Confessions of a Sex Kitten;* and articles in such periodicals as *Ebony, Variety, Vanity Fair*, the *Los Angeles Mirror*, the *Los Angeles Examiner, The New York Times*, and others, as cited.

287 "the extent of communist": Ephraim Katz, *The Film Encyclopedia* (New York: Harper-Perennial, 1994).

289 "taking the train, not": Ossie Davis and Ruby Dee, *With Ossie & Ruby: In This Life Together* (New York: Morrow, 1998).

289 "I was transfixed by": Sidney Poitier, *This Life* (New York: Knopf, 1980).

289 "Some were talkies and": Davis and Dee, *With Ossie & Ruby*.

290 "I was beside myself": Poitier, *This Life*.

290 "After I checked in": Ibid.

291 "Early mornings, riding through": Davis and Dee, *With Ossie & Ruby*.

291 "The California sky was": Poitier, *This Life*.

292 "At the studio, we": Davis and Dee, *With Ossie & Ruby*.

292 "an occasional kitchen worker": Poitier, *This Life*.

292 "I made films when": David Ansen, "A Superstar Returns to the Screen," *Newsweek*, Feb. 22, 1988.

292 "I felt the blood": Davis and Dee, *With Ossie & Ruby*.

292 "Every day at work": Ibid.

300 "She leans there on": Dick Williams, "Satiny, Sexy Songstress Has That Starlight Aura," *Los Angeles Mirror*, Feb. 24, 1951.

300 "A new showbiz career": "Dorothy Dandridge," *Variety*, Mar. 28, 1951.

303 "This is the most": Phyllis Rose, *Jazz Cleopatra: Josephine Baker in Her Time* (New York: Doubleday, 1989).

303 "Why don't you go": Jean-Claude Baker and Chris Chase, *Josephine: The Hungry Heart* (New York: Random House, 1993).

304 "It isn't a question": Rose, *Jazz Cleopatra*.

305 "neutralize them [the white bigots]": "The Entertainer," *People*, May 28, 1990.

306 "till the day he died": Sam Kashner, "The Color of Love," *Vanity Fair*, Apr. 1999.

306 "Dear lousy nigger": Sammy Davis Jr. and Jane Boyar and Burt Boyar, *Sammy: An Autobiography* (New York: Farrar, Straus and Giroux, 2000).

306 "Everybody that's anybody will": Jim Heimann, *Out with the Stars: Hollywood Nightlife in the Golden Era* (New York: Abbeville Press, 1985).

307 "pounding on the table": Davis and Boyar and Boyar, *Sammy*.

307 "Everybody was at Ciro's": Kashner, "Color of Love."

307 "We'd taken eight bows": Davis and Boyar and Boyar, *Sammy*.

307 "Once in a long": Ibid.

307 "It was such a big": Kashner, "Color of Love."

313 "No more fights. From now on": Eugene Schroff, "Uncrowned Champion," *Negro Digest*, Dec. 1949.

313 "I hope you feel": Ibid.

313 "I did Romeo to": Ibid.

313 "a purple zoot suit": Ibid.

314 "I told Mr. Kramer": Ibid.

314 "He was at the": Diahann Carroll and Ross Firestone, *Diahann!* (Boston: Little, Brown, 1986).

316 "I was unable, during": Lena Horne and Richard Schickel, *Lena* (Garden City, N.Y.: Doubleday, 1965).

316 "It was a terrible": Author's interview with Geri Branton.

317 "one of the most": Carroll and Firestone, *Diahann!*

317 "I saw the nice": Ibid.

317 "He'd create a nasty": Ibid.

317 "I was skinny, devoid": Ibid.

318 "I suppose he was": Ibid.

319 "It wasn't easy to": Seymour Peck, "Calling on Lena Horne," *The New York Times*, Oct. 27, 1957.

319 "We've been swamped with": Jim Henaghan, "Rambling Reporter," *Hollywood Reporter*, Sept. 9, 1948.

319 "The Actors Lab made": Hedda Hopper column, *Los Angeles Times*, Sept. 13, 1948.

321 "was assigned places to": Eartha Kitt, *Confessions of a Sex Kitten* (London: Sidgwick & Jackson, 1989).

322 "over lunch that the": Ibid.

322 "Hollywood gossip columnists such": Ibid.

323 "What Makes AVA GARDNER": Davis and Boyar and Boyar, *Sammy*.

323 "Heard the Latest about": Neal Gabler, "*Confidential*'s Reign of Terror," *Vanity Fair,* Apr. 2003.

323 "Eartha Kitt and the": Jack Ross, "Eartha Kitt! And the Little Man Who Sat There . . . All Night!" *Confidential,* July 1957.

323 "When Eartha comes to": Kitt, *Confessions of a Sex Kitten.*

325 "I could understand": "Entertainer."

326 "put guards in my": Kim Novak, *Larry King Live,* CNN, Jan. 5, 2004.

327 "I'll never forget it": "$50,000 a Day," *Ebony,* Oct. 1953.

328 "removed his singing from": Ibid.

330 "Are you kidding?": Daniel Mark Epstein, *Nat King Cole* (New York: Farrar, Straus and Giroux, 1999).

331 "accents in bold colors": "King Cole Decorates His New $65,000 Home," *Ebony,* Apr. 1949.

336 "The note got into": Kitt, *Confessions of a Sex Kitten.*

340 "I'd like to thank": *TV Land Presents An Evening with the Rat Pack: Frank, Dean, and Sammy,* TV Land broadcast, 1998.

342 "Swear on your life": Hollis Alpert, *The Life and Times of Porgy and Bess* (New York: Knopf, 1990).

342 "I got the call": Kashner, "Color of Love."

342 "Go Back to the": Ibid.

345 "It's Carmen": Donald Bogle, *Dorothy Dandridge: A Biography* (New York: Amistad Press, 1997).

345 "He couldn't reach for": Ibid.

351 "Peter didn't have the": James Spada, *Peter Lawford: The Man Who Kept the Secrets* (New York: Bantam Books, 1991).

352 "Look, I love you": Author's interview with Geri Branton.

352 "There were rumors": Carroll and Firestone, *Diahann!*

353 "Don't say anything to me": Author's interview with Byron Morrow.

355 "Designed for the utmost": "Paul Williams Builds His Ideal Home," *Ebony,* Apr. 1953.

355 "I wanted it to": Ibid.

356 "I decided that if": Bogle, *Dorothy Dandridge.*

357 "Dorothy now barely spoke": Eugene Jackson with Gwendolyn Sides St. Julian, *Eugene "Pineapple" Jackson: His Own Story* (Jefferson, N.C.: McFarland & Company, 1999).

360 "I guess you want": Bogle, *Dorothy Dandridge.*

EPILOGUE

The quoted comments of Brock Peters, Marilyn Williams Hudson, and Johnetta Jones are from the author's interviews with them.

SELECTED BIBLIOGRAPHY

See the notes for articles and other sources.

Alpert, Hollis. *The Life and Times of Porgy and Bess: The Story of an American Classic.* New York: Knopf, 1990.

American Business Consultants. *Red Channels: The Report of Communist Influence in Radio and Television.* New York: Counterattack, 1950.

Anger, Kenneth. *Hollywood Babylon.* San Francisco: Straight Arrow Books, 1975.

Bailey, Pearl. *The Raw Pearl.* New York: Harcourt, Brace & World, 1968.

Baker, Jean-Claude, and Chris Chase. *Josephine: The Hungry Heart.* New York: Random House, 1993.

Basie, Count, as told to Albert Murray. *Good Morning Blues: The Autobiography of Count Basie.* New York: Random House, 1985.

Bass, Charlotta. *Forty Years: Memoirs from the Pages of a Newspaper.* Los Angeles: self-published, 1960.

Beasley, Delilah. *The Negro Trail Blazers of California.* 1919. Reprint, Westport, Conn.: Greenwood Press, 1969.

Bitzer, G. W. *Billy Bitzer: His Story.* New York: Farrar, Straus and Giroux, 1973.

Black, Shirley Temple. *Child Star: An Autobiography.* New York: McGraw-Hill, 1988.

Blair, Betsy. *The Memory of All That.* New York: Knopf, 2003.

Bogert, Frank. *Palm Springs: First Hundred Years.* Palm Springs, Calif.: Palm Springs Public Library, 1987.

Bogle, Donald. *Blacks in American Films and Television: An Illustrated Encyclopedia.* New York: Fireside Books, 1990.

———. *Brown Sugar: Eighty Years of America's Black Female Superstars.* New York: Da Capo Press, 1990.

———. *Dorothy Dandridge: A Biography.* New York: Amistad Press, 1997.

———. *Primetime Blues: African Americans on Network Television.* New York: Farrar, Straus and Giroux, 2001.

———. *Toms, Coons, Mulattoes, Mammies, & Bucks: An Interpretive History of Blacks in American Films.* Rev. ed. New York: Continuum, 2001.

Bond, J. Max. *The Negro in Los Angeles: A Dissertation.* Los Angeles: University of Southern California, 1936.

Bricktop with James Haskins. *Bricktop.* New York: Atheneum, 1983.

Brooks, Louise. *Lulu in Hollywood.* New York: Knopf, 1982.

Bryant, Clora, Buddy Collette, William Green, Steven Isoardi, Jack Kelson, Horace Tapscott, Gerald Wilson, and Marl Young, eds. *Central Avenue Sounds: Jazz in Los Angeles.* Berkeley and Los Angeles: University of California Press, 1999.

Buckley, Gail Lumet. *The Hornes: An American Family.* New York: Knopf, 1986.

Carroll, Diahann, and Ross Firestone. *Diahann!* Boston: Little, Brown, 1986.

Ceplair, Larry, and Steven Englund. *The Inquisition in Hollywood: Politics in the Film Community, 1930–1960.* Garden City, N.Y.: Anchor Press, Doubleday, 1980.

Clayton, Buck, with Nancy Miller-Elliot. *Buck Clayton's Jazz World.* New York: Oxford University Press, 1987.

Collins, Keith E. *Black Los Angeles: The Maturing of the Ghetto, 1940–1950.* Saratoga, Calif.: Century Twenty One Publishing, 1980.

Cooper, Ralph, and Steve Dougherty. *Amateur Night at the Apollo: Ralph Cooper Presents Five Decades of Great Entertainment.* New York: HaperCollins, 1990.

Cox, Bette Yarbrough. *Central Avenue: Its Rise and Fall, 1890–1955.* Los Angeles: BEEM Publications, 1993.

Davis, Bette. *The Lonely Life.* New York: Putnam, 1962.

Davis, Mike. *City of Quartz: Excavating the Future in Los Angeles.* New York: Vintage Books, 1992.

Davis, Ossie, and Ruby Dee. *With Ossie & Ruby: In This Life Together.* New York: Morrow, 1998.

Davis, Sammy. *Hollywood in a Suitcase.* New York: Morrow, 1980.

Davis, Sammy, and Jane Boyar and Burt Boyar. *Sammy: An Autobiography.* New York: Farrar, Straus and Giroux, 2000.

———. *Why Me?: The Sammy Davis Jr. Story.* New York: Farrar, Straus and Giroux, 1989.

———. *Yes I Can.* New York: Farrar, Straus and Giroux, 1965.

DeGraaf, Lawrence B., Kevin Mulroy, and Quintard Taylor, eds. *Seeking El Dorado: African Americans in California.* Los Angeles/Seattle, London. Autry Museum of Western Heritage in association with University of Washington Press, 2001.

Driggs, Frank, and Harris Lewine. *Black Beauty, White Heat: A Pictorial History of Classic Jazz, 1920–1950.* New York: Morrow, 1982.

Duberman, Martin. *Paul Robeson.* New York: Knopf, 1988

Ellington, Duke. *Music Is My Mistress.* Garden City, N.Y.: Doubleday, 1973.

Epstein, Daniel Mark. *Nat King Cole.* New York: Farrar, Straus and Giroux, 1999.

Finch, Christopher, and Linda Rosenkrantz. *Gone Hollywood: The Movie Colony in the Golden Age.* Garden City, N.Y.: Doubleday, 1979.

Franklin, John Hope, and Alfred A. Moss Jr. *From Slavery to Freedom.* 7th ed. New York: McGraw-Hill, 1994.

Friedrich, Otto. *City of Nets: A Portrait of Hollywood in the 1940s.* New York: Harper & Row, 1987.

Giddins, Gary. *Satchmo.* New York: Dolphin Books, 1988.

Gillespie, Dizzy, with Al Fraser. *To Be or Not to Bop: Memoirs—Dizzy Gillespie.* Garden City, N.Y.: Doubleday, 1979.

Gish, Lillian, and Ann Pinchot. *The Movies, Mr. Griffith and Me.* Englewood Cliffs, N.J.: Prentice Hall, 1969.

Gourse, Leslie. *Unforgettable: The Life and Mystique of Nat King Cole.* New York: St. Martin's Press, 1991.

Gussow, Mel. *Don't Say Yes until I Finish Talking: A Biography of Darryl F. Zanuck.* Garden City, N.Y.: Doubleday, 1971.

Hajdu, David. *Lush Life: A Biography of Billy Strayhorn.* New York: Farrar, Straus and Giroux, 1996.

Hampton, Lionel, and James Haskins. *Hamp: An Autobiography*. New York: Warner Books, 1989.

Heimann, Jim. *Out with the Stars: Hollywood Nightlife in the Golden Era*. New York: Abbeville Press, 1985.

Hine, Darlene Clark, Elsa Barkley Brown, and Rosalyn Terburg-Penn eds. *Black Women in America: An Historical Encyclopedia*. New York: Clarkson Publishing, 1993.

Horne, Lena, and Richard Schickel. *Lena*. Garden City, N.Y.: Doubleday, 1965.

Hudson, Karen E. *Paul R. Williams, Architect: A Legacy of Style*. New York: Rizzoli International Publications, 1993.

———. *The Will and the Way: Paul R. Williams, Architect*. New York: Rizzoli International Publications, 1994.

Hughes, Langston. *The Big Sea*. New York: Hill and Wang, 1963.

Jablonski, Edward. *Harold Arlen: Happy with the Blues*. Garden City, N.Y.: Doubleday, 1961.

Jackson, Carlton. *Hattie: The Life of Hattie McDaniel*. Lanham, Md.: Madison Books, 1990.

Jackson, Eugene, with Gwendolyn Sides St. Julian. *Eugene "Pineapple" Jackson: His Own Story*. Jefferson, N.C.: McFarland & Company, 1999.

James, Etta, and David Ritz. *Rage to Survive*. New York: Villard Books, 1995.

Katz, Ephraim. *The Film Encyclopedia*. New York: HarperPerennial, 1994.

Katz, William Loren. *The Black West*. Garden City, N.Y.: Doubleday, 1971.

Kirkpatrick, Sidney D. *A Cast of Killers*. New York: Dutton, 1986.

Kitt, Eartha. *Confessions of a Sex Kitten*. London: Sidgwick & Jackson, 1989.

Koppes, Clayton R., and Gregory D. Black. *Hollywood Goes to War: How Politics, Profits and Propaganda Shaped World War II Movies*. Berkeley: University of California Press, 1987.

Lambert, Gavin. *GWTW: The Making of "Gone with the Wind."* Boston: Atlantic Monthly Press Book, Little, Brown, 1973.

Lamparski, Richard. *Lamparski's Hidden Hollywood: Where the Stars Lived, Loved and Died*. New York: Fireside Book, 1981.

Lawrence, A. H. *Duke Ellington and His World: A Biography*. New York: Routledge, 2001.

Leider, Emily Worth. *Becoming Mae West*. New York: Farrar, Straus and Giroux, 1997.

Louis, Joe, with Edna Rust and Art Rust Jr. *Joe Louis: My Life*. New York: Harcourt Brace Jovanovich, 1978.

Maltin, Leonard. *Our Gang: The Life and Times of the Little Rascals*. New York: Crown, 1977.

Manchester, William. *The Glory and the Dream: A Narrative History of America, 1932–1972*. Boston: Little, Brown, 1973.

Mapp, Edward. *Directory of Blacks in the Performing Arts*. Metuchen, N.J.: Scarecrow Press, 1978.

Moore, Phil. "Things I Forgot to Tell You." Unpublished, 1986.

Mungo, Ray. *Palm Springs Babylon: Sizzling Stories from the Desert Playground of the Stars*. New York: St. Martin's Press, 1993.

Navasky, Victor S. *Naming Names*. New York: Viking Press, 1980.

Newkirk, Pamela. *A Love No Less: More Than Two Centuries of African American Love Letters*. Garden City, N.Y.: Doubleday, 2003.

Pitt, Leonard, and Dale Pitt. *Los Angeles A to Z: An Encyclopedia of the City and County*. Berkeley, Los Angeles, and London: University of California Press, 1997.

Placksin, Sally. *American Women in Jazz, 1900 to the Present: Their Words, Lives, and Music*. New York: Wideview Books, 1982.

Poitier, Sidney. *The Measure of a Man: A Spiritual Autobiography*. San Francisco: Harper-SanFrancisco, 2000.

————. *This Life*. New York: Knopf, 1980.

Powdermaker, Hortense. *Hollywood, the Dream Factory*. Boston: Little, Brown, 1950.

Rampersad, Arnold. *Jackie Robinson: A Biography*. New York: Knopf, 1997.

————. *The Life of Langston Hughes*. 2nd ed. Vol. 1, *1902–1941: I, Too, Sing America*. New York: Oxford University Press, 2001.

————. *The Life of Langston Hughes*. 2nd ed. Vol. 2, *1941–1967: I Dream a World*. New York: Oxford University Press, 2002.

Reed, Tom. *The Black Music History of Los Angeles, Its Roots*. 4th ed. Los Angeles: Black Accent on LA Press, 1992.

Richards, Larry. *African American Films through 1959: A Comprehensive Illustrated Filmography*. Jefferson, N.C.: McFarland, 1998.

Rose, Phyllis. *Jazz Cleopatra: Josephine Baker in Her Time*. New York: Doubleday, 1989.

Royal, Marshal, with Claire P. Gordon. *Marshal Royal: Jazz Survivor*. New York: Continuum, 2001.

Russell, Rosalind, and Chris Chase. *Life Is a Banquet*. New York: Random House, 1977.

Sampson, Henry T. *Blacks in Black and White: A Source Book on Black Films*. Metuchen, N.J.: Scarecrow Press, 1977.

Schickel, Richard. *D. W. Griffith: An American Life*. New York: Simon & Schuster, 1984.

Schulberg, Budd. *Moving Pictures: Memories of a Hollywood Prince*. New York: Stein and Day, 1981.

Sheaffer, Louis. *O'Neill: Son and Artist*. Boston: Little, Brown, 1973.

Short, Bobby. *Black and White Baby*. New York: Dodd, Mead, 1971.

Short, Bobby, with Robert Mackintosh. *The Life and Times of a Saloon Singer*. New York: Panache Press Book, Clarkson Potter Publishers, 1995.

Stenn, David. *Bombshell: The Life and Death of Jean Harlow*. Garden City, N.Y.: Doubleday, 1993.

Strode, Woody, and Sam Young. *Goal Dust*. Lanham, Md.: Madison Books, 1990.

Swanson, Gloria. *Swanson on Swanson*. New York: Random House, 1980.

Tyler, Bruce M. *From Harlem to Hollywood: The Struggle for Racial and Cultural Democracy, 1920–1943*. New York: Garland Publishing, 1992.

Vidor, King. *A Tree Is a Tree*. New York: Harcourt, Brace, 1952.

Waters, Ethel, with Charles Samuels. *His Eye Is on the Sparrow*. Garden City, N.Y.: Doubleday, 1950.

White, Walter. *How Far the Promised Land?* New York: Viking Press, 1955.

Wiencek, Henry. *The Hairstons: An American Family in Black and White*. New York: St. Martin's Press, 1999.

Wiley, Mason, and Damien Bona. *Inside Oscar: The Unofficial History of the Academy Awards*. New York: Ballantine, 1986.

ACKNOWLEDGMENTS

The generosity, encouragement, and assistance of many people have been important in the writing of this book. Foremost, I'd like to express my gratitude to the people who consented to be interviewed about their experiences in early Black Hollywood. In some cases, I reinterviewed personalities I had previously spoken to for earlier books. In other cases, I used comments from earlier interviews. Of all those interviewed, past and present, Geri Branton provided some of the most perceptive and telling comments that enabled me to reconstruct black life in the Hollywood of the 1940s and 1950s. I cannot thank her enough. Fayard Nicholas, of the Nicholas Brothers, the greatest dance team in motion-picture history, also warmly shared his memories with insight and candor, impressing me time and again with his ability to recall specific names, dates, and places without ever having to think twice. It was also a pleasure to interview again Fayard's sister Dorothy Nicholas Morrow and her husband, Byron Morrow. I found it touching and enlightening to hear Dorothy Morrow as well as Fayard so lovingly recall the life of their mother, Viola Nicholas. Rigmor Newman Nicholas also graciously provided me with recollections of her husband, Harold Nicholas, and graciously granted me permission to look through her extensive collection of photographs of the Nicholas Brothers. Katherine Hopkins Nicholas worked with me to arrange the time and place of my interview with her husband, Fayard, and to insure that it went smoothly.

Once again, it was a pleasure to talk to singer/actress Olga James, who remains warm, insightful, and really delightful and who went out of her way to help me. Through Geri Branton, I was able to meet and interview Marilyn Williams Hudson, the daughter of the extraordinary architect Paul Williams. Her recollections of her parents and of her father's remarkable career were vivid and often quite moving. The Los Angeles attorney Melanie Lomax granted me a fine interview in which she discussed her grandfather Lucius Lomax, the colorful and charismatic owner of the Dunbar Hotel. She made available articles on her grandfather and the Dunbar by her brother Lucius Lomax III and her sister Michele Lomax. In a conference call, she also enabled me to hear the reminisces of her mother, Almena Lomax, who published *The Los Angeles Tribune* with her husband, Lucius Lomax Jr.

Once again, I felt fortunate to interview Bobby Short, who never fails to impress me with his richly detailed memories and his wonderful sense of humor. Having met so many major figures in show business, Bobby remains remarkably knowledgeable about the history of black entertainment in this country. You sit enthralled by the experiences he recounts. The same is true of producer Jean Bach, who regaled me with stories about a number of stars of the 1930s through the 1950s—and who searched through her personal photo archives for photographs. Jeanne Moore Pisano also was of great assistance and graciously granted me permission to quote from her late husband Phil Moore's unpublished autobiography, "Things I Forgot to Tell You."

I had never known that the great ballerina Carmen de Lavallade had grown up in Los Angeles until I had happened to be seated next to her at a dinner one evening. Immediately, I asked for an interview. At her spacious loft in downtown Manhattan, which she shares with her husband, the dancer/choreographer Geoffrey Holder, de Lavallade had splendid stories about Los Angeles in the 1930s to the 1950s—and about studio life in the 1950s.

I was also happy to interview again—over her wonderful lunches and dinners—my dear friend Isabel Washington Powell about her sister Fredi's time in Hollywood. After leaving Isabel, I would often review again my earlier interview and conversations with Fredi, some of which I had used in earlier books. But I had never used the material about her actual experiences at Universal when filming *Imitation of Life*. Nor had I ever used any of the conversation we had one evening at a sumptuous party at Bobby Short's—when Fredi first told me of her love affair with Duke Ellington. I felt fortunate now to be able to write about Fredi again and to do so in a new way.

Still looking every inch the romantic hero, an energetic and high-spirited Herb Jeffries—a born raconteur now in his nineties—was a terrific host, along with his wife, Savannah Jeffries, at their hilltop home not far from Palm Springs. In New Rochelle, New York, Ossie Davis and Ruby Dee were enlightening and engaging as they recounted their early experiences in the movie capital. Having known both for a number of years, it was a great pleasure to finally have a formal interview with them.

I will forever be in the debt of Dorothy Hughes McConnell, my dear friend in Los Angeles, whom I had first interviewed about Dorothy Dandridge and her mother, Ruby Dandridge. She arranged a small gathering at her home, during which I was able to interview three lifetime residents of the city: Willard Brown, Johnetta Jones, and Marian Patterson, each of whom recounted evocative stories of Los Angeles in past decades.

Barbara Roseburr Molette also had fine observations on her childhood years in Los Angeles, during the post–World War II era when the city underwent such major changes. Her memories of her neighbors Hattie McDaniel and Eddie "Rochester" Anderson added much to my awareness of the African American neighborhood's sense of community.

It was also helpful to review my past interviews of a number of perceptive personalities: the great director King Vidor; comedian Mantan Moreland; singer Etta Jones of The Dandridge Sisters; actresses Avanelle Harris and Juliette Ball; former MCA agent Harold Jovien; writer Leonard Feather; actors Ivan Dixon,

Clarence Muse, and Brock Peters; the late directors Gerald Mayer and Herb Ross; performer Maggie Hathaway; and pianist/musical director Nick Perito.

I would also like to express my gratitude to the individuals and institutions that aided me in my research. During the early stages, my former student David Aglow did a fine job of unearthing some real gems: events and personalities I initially had not planned to write about. Morgan Rashida Stiff—another former student—also did a fine job of enthusiastically researching early black performers. Later my friend Kathe Sandler spent hours with me as we went through reels of microfilm. Kim Mason used her terrific online skills to dig up information on early Los Angeles history, as well as on a number of personalities, and then to locate photographs of African Americans at photo archives around the country. I'd also like to thank the staff of the Library of Performing Arts at Lincoln Center; the staff at the Department of Special Collections at the Charles E. Young Research Library at the University of California at Los Angeles, where I spent a number of delirious days going through the remarkable George P. Johnson Negro Film Collection; the staff of the Schomburg Center for Research in Black Culture, especially Sharon Howard and Betty Odabashian, who were helpful and attentive as I searched for information; the staff at the Bancroft Library at the University of California at Berkeley; my colleagues in the Dramatic Writing Department at New York University's Tisch School of the Arts, especially David Ranghelli, Janet Neipris, Richard Wesley, Gary Garrison, and the department chair, Mark Dickerman; my colleagues in the Department of Africana Studies at the University of Pennsylvania, especially Gale Garrison and Carol Davis; and Susan Cohan, who did a fine job of copy-editing this book. I cannot praise highly enough Howard Mandelbaum and his staff at Photofest for helping me wade through countless photographs to find the ideal shots included in this book. Photo archivists Kristine Krueger at the National Information Film Services at the Fairbanks Center for Motion Picture Study at the Academy of Motion Picture Arts and Sciences and Dace Taube at the Hearst Newapaper Collection at the Doheny Library at the University of South California also tirelessly searched for photographs; I am grateful for their fine work as well as their patience and good humor. The same is true of Bobby Short's very astute assistant, Christina Wyeth. My gratitude also goes to Editorial Assistant Signe Pike of Ballantine Books, whose skills, assistance, and good spirits will forever be appreciated. I'd also like to thank Senior Editor Melody Guy and Associate Editor Danielle Durkin for their help.

No book is ever completed without the help of friends and associates, especially those who are willing to respect (and tolerate) your idiosyncrasies. So it is a pleasure to express my gratitude to the following: Fred Charleston of E Entertainment; Alcia Woods Williams; my good friends Sarah Orrick, Carol Leonard, Ronald Mason, Sally Placksin, and Linda "Doll" Tarrant; Robert Katz and Jay Peterson of K2Pictures; Evander Lomke; television veteran Marian Etoile Watson; Dr. Harry Ford and Peg Henehan; Martha Orrick and her husband, Jim Malcolm (who helped me locate material on the history of Palm Springs); Alan Sukoenig and

Hiroko Hatanaka; Daniel Beer; Martin Radburd; Jacqueline Bogle Mosley; Roslynne Bogle; Jeanne Bogle Charleston; Janet Bogle Schenck; Bettina Glasgow Batchleor; Mariskia Bogle; Shaaron Bogle; Ann Marie Cunningham; Joerg Klebe; Susan Peterson; Patricia Ferguson; Clisson Woods; David Crosthwaite; Audrey Smith-Bey; Barbara Reynolds; Herma Ross Shorty; Bob Silverstein; Emery Wimbish; H. Alfred Farrell; Grace and Jim Frankowsky; Josslyn Luckett; Rae Taylor Rossini; Doug and Liza Rossini; Heidi Stack; Leah Hunter; Logan Johnson; John D. Bogle, Jr.; Robert Bogle, publisher of *The Philadelphia Tribune*; Roger Bogle; Gerald Bogle; Jay Bogle; Cheryll Greene; Irene Mecchi; Len Chandler; Carlton Molette; and Dorothy Bell. A very special thank-you goes to Jamie Vega, who always makes sure I can check into my secret hideaway in L.A. while doing research; and my good friend Enrico Pellegrini and his wife, Kelly Brock Pellegrini, who, when I needed a break, entertained me lavishly at their home in Rome.

As in the past, my good friend Jerald Silverhart in Los Angeles was of great help during my extended trips to Los Angeles to do research. The great drama teacher and coach Janet Alhanti was also a source of insight whenever we had the opportunity to discuss film actors, past and present. Also in Los Angeles, there was my dear friend, the producer Debra Martin Chase, with whom I've spent many joyous hours talking about Hollywood, past and present.

In New York, Bruce Goldstein of Film Forum once again astounded me with his vast knowledge of American film history. He very patiently read the manuscript and offered invaluable suggestions and information.

My former researcher Phil Bertelsen, now directing films, also went beyond the call of duty, coming to my rescue at key moments. Because of his knowledge of black movie history and my particular point of view, he was excellent at reminding me of past interviews and events that proved important in writing this book. When we were both in Los Angeles at the same time, he proved helpful in another way: because I still do not drive, he very patiently helped me get to all my appointments and assisted me as I conducted key interviews. He also read the manuscript—in all its drafts—and gave me important comments and insights.

My agent, Marie Dutton Brown, was also wonderfully encouraging, perceptive, and supportive in seeing this book from the early days of its proposal to its publication. I'd also like to thank her excellent assistants, Tynisha Thompson and Khalid Williams, for their help.

Finally, I have to express my deepest gratitude to my editor, the one and only Elisabeth Kallick Dyssegaard, who decided that I should do this book. When she met with my agent, Marie, the two felt strongly that now was the time for a look at Black Hollywood, its evolution and its extraordinary history. Throughout the writing of the book, Elisabeth, in her inimitable, sweet-tempered way, kept reminding me of deadlines and always, as she read various drafts, was encouraging, perceptive, good humored, and patient. This is the third book I've done with her, and she remains an ideal editor.

ILLUSTRATION CREDITS

Photofest: iv (top, right; middle row; bottom, right), viii (second from top; bottom), 15, 22, 38, 43 (top), 45, 48, 53, 92, 94, 99, 116, 149, 154, 157, 158, 161 (both), 171, 174, 182, 218, 220, 229, 235, 245, 248, 252 (top), 271, 274, 295, 305, 308, 310, 312, 320 (top and center), 341, 343, 349, 358

Courtesy of the Academy of Motion Picture Arts and Sciences: iv (bottom row, left), 27, 34, 37, 179, 207, 266, 332, 351

The Collection of Donald Bogle: iv (top row, left), viii (3rd and 4th from the top), 43 (bottom), 85, 96, 112, 124, 127, 131, 132, 151, 170, 195, 201, 204, 206 (bottom), 208, 210, 237, 238, 239, 252 (bottom), 261, 263, 264, 265, 269, 283, 290, 298, 301, 320 (bottom), 324, 330, 335, 337, 346, 350

Courtesy of Rigmor Newman Nicholas: 187, 209, 242

Courtesy of Dorothy Morrow Nicholas: 206 (top)

Courtesy of Bobby Short: 255

Courtesy of Jean Bach: 254

Courtesy of Isabel Washington Powell: 147

Corbis: viii (top), 107

The Hearst Newspaper Collection/The University of Southern California: 76

Los Angeles Public Library: 70, 71, 291

INDEX

ss

ABOUT THE AUTHOR

DONALD BOGLE, one of the foremost authorities on African Americans in film, is the author of several prizewinning books. His book *Toms, Coons, Mulattoes, Mammies, and Bucks: An Interpretive History of Blacks in American Films* is considered a classic study of African-American movie images. His books *Dorothy Dandridge: A Biography* and *Primetime Blues: African Americans on Network Television* have also won wide critical acclaim. Mr. Bogle adapted his book *Brown Sugar: Eighty Years of America's Black Female Superstars* into a highly successful four-episode documentary series for PBS. He is also the author of *Blacks in American Films and Television: An Illustrated Encyclopedia.* Mr. Bogle presently teaches at New York University's Tisch School of the Arts and the University of Pennsylvania. He lives in New York City.